Praise for CAMERA GIRL

"In *Camera Girl*, Carl Anthony slows down the story of Jacqueline Bouvier so that her complexity and wide range of interests can be grasped during the period of her life before marriage, political obligation, and tragedy—when she is forming a distinct sense of what role she hopes to someday play in the larger world. From designing her red 'Bouvier cape,' to her descriptive letters of new cultures and shrewd assessments of individuals, to her cartooning skills, to translating and analyzing French diplomatic and military texts about Indochina, we see Jackie in her fullness. For anyone of any age, the Jackie in *Camera Girl* offers an example of intentional living."

—Secretary Hillary Rodham Clinton, #1 *New York Times* bestselling author of *What Happened*

"Carl Anthony has found a wholly refreshing way to look at one of the most gazed upon women in American history, while also revealing how essential Jackie Bouvier was to Jack Kennedy's intellectual and political development. *Camera Girl* is as delightful as it is insightful."

—David Maraniss, *New York Times* bestselling author of *Barack Obama: The Story*

"In this charming portrait, Carl Anthony traces the genesis of Jacqueline Kennedy's mesmerizing personality. Behind her privileged upbringing, Jackie coped with a dysfunctional family and cultivated an independent spirit as well as a questing intellect. In Anthony's telling, her determination to make her way on her own terms foreshadowed her groundbreaking role as First Lady."

—Sally Bedell Smith, *New York Times* bestselling author of *Grace and Power: The Private World of the Kennedy White House*

"[Jackie's] twenty-month run with [the 'Inquiring Camera Girl' column] is the charming and surprisingly informative heart of Anthony's book. . . . Anthony does nice work, without fetching too far, when he ties the column's subject matter to Jackie's biographical time line."

—*The New Yorker*

"Whether she's avoiding a traffic ticket after speeding in her car named Zelda, or translating books for Kennedy's report on the history of France in Indochina, this portrait of young Jackie Bouvier shines with wit and intelligence."

—*Library Journal* (starred review)

"*Camera Girl* offers one of the most detailed, nuanced portraits of Jackie to date."

—*The Washington Post*

"[Anthony] sheds intriguing light on Jackie's stint as a columnist for the *Washington Times-Herald*, the engagement she called off prior to marrying JFK, and her volatile and occasionally violent relationship with her mother. . . . A convincing and colorful reconsideration of a first lady known more for her style than her substance."

—*Publishers Weekly*

"The Jacqueline Bouvier whom Carl Anthony brings to life in these deeply researched pages is a revelation. She is defiant, curious, independent—and a rule-breaker determined to chart a course that would make history take notice."

—Karen Tumulty, author of *The Triumph of Nancy Reagan*

"Anthony uncovers the root of Jackie's distinctive blend of rebelliousness and vulnerability, independence and insecurity, that would attract and confound supporters and critics alike. By drawing on extensive interviews with Jackie's contemporaries and family, oral histories, and presidential archives, Anthony delivers a well-rounded depiction of this eternally fascinating, covertly complicated, and perennially misunderstood historical and cultural icon."

—*Booklist*

"What shaped Jackie Kennedy Onassis to become one of the most influential women of the 20th century? In this lively, dishy account, author Carl Anthony traces four formative years when she was Jacqueline Bouvier, negotiating her way into adulthood with a determination and an independence that belied the reserved mien she showed to the world. 'Become distinct,' she told herself. And so she did."

—Susan Page, *New York Times* bestselling author of *The Matriarch: Barbara Bush and the Making of an American Dynasty*

"Prior to her marriage to John F. Kennedy, Jacqueline Bouvier was an ambitious journalist and photographer, a remarkable period of her life captured in this engaging coming-of-age biography. . . . Drawing on Bouvier's letters and interviews, Anthony pulls together a compelling portrait of a young woman facing both the problems of her time and timeless issues. Should she focus on her career or getting married? How can she be respectful to her problematic parents while still declaring her own adult independence? . . . A well-crafted biography that could easily spawn both a delightful TV drama or a historical look at female journalists."

—*Kirkus Reviews* (starred review)

Also by
CARL SFERRAZZA ANTHONY

First Ladies: The Saga of the Presidents' Wives and Their Power, 1789–1990 (two volumes)

As We Remember Her: Jacqueline Kennedy Onassis in the Words of Her Family and Friends

Florence Harding: The First Lady, the Jazz Age, and the Death of America's Most Scandalous President

America's First Families: An Inside View of 200 Years of Private Life in the White House

The Kennedy White House: Family Life and Pictures, 1961–1963

This Elevated Position: A Catalog and Guide to the National First Ladies' Library and the Importance of First Lady History

Heads of State: The Presidents as Everyday Useful Household Items in Pewter, Plastic, Porcelain, Copper, Cork, Chalk, China, Wax, Walnut & More

Nellie Taft: The Unconventional First Lady of the Ragtime Era

Ida McKinley: The Turn-of-the-Century First Lady Through War, Assassination, and Secret Disability

Why They Wore It: The Politics and Pop Culture of First Ladies' Fashion

CAMERA GIRL

The Coming of Age of JACKIE BOUVIER KENNEDY

Carl Sferrazza Anthony

G

Gallery Books

New York London Toronto Sydney New Delhi

G

Gallery Books
An Imprint of Simon & Schuster, LLC
1230 Avenue of the Americas
New York, NY 10020

First Gallery Books trade paperback edition May 2024

GALLERY BOOKS and colophon are registered trademarks of Simon & Schuster, LLC

Simon & Schuster: Celebrating 100 Years of Publishing in 2024

For information about special discounts for bulk purchases, please contact Simon & Schuster Special Sales at 1-866-506-1949 or business@simonandschuster.com.

The Simon & Schuster Speakers Bureau can bring authors to your live event. For more information or to book an event, contact the Simon & Schuster Speakers Bureau at 1-866-248-3049 or visit our website at www.simonspeakers.com.

Interior design by Jaime Putorti

Manufactured in the United States of America

10 9 8 7 6 5 4 3 2 1

The Library of Congress has cataloged the hardcover edition as follows:

Names: Anthony, Carl Sferrazza, author.
Title: Camera girl : the coming of age of Jackie Bouvier Kennedy / Carl Sferrazza Anthony.
Description: First Gallery Books hardcover edition. | New York, NY : Gallery Books, An Imprint of Simon & Schuster, Inc., [2023] | Includes bibliographical references and index.
Identifiers: LCCN 2022021736 (print) | LCCN 2022021737 (ebook) | ISBN 9781982141875 (hardcover) | ISBN 9781982141899 (ebook)
Subjects: LCSH: Onassis, Jacqueline Kennedy, 1929–1994. | Women journalists—United States—Biography. | Presidents' spouses—United States—Biography. | Celebrities—United States—Biography. | Times-herald (Washington, D.C.)
Classification: LCC CT275.O552 A74 2023 (print) | LCC CT275.O552 (ebook) | DDC 973.922092 [B]—dc23/eng/20220919
LC record available at https://lccn.loc.gov/2022021736
LC ebook record available at https://lccn.loc.gov/2022021737

ISBN 978-1-9821-4187-5
ISBN 978-1-9821-4188-2 (pbk)
ISBN 978-1-9821-4189-9 (ebook)

DEDICATED TO

My Friends
Peter McManus and John McGuire
For joyous companionship in the "pool of knowledge"
as I wrote this book through the pandemic

My Parents
Whose unrelenting confidence propelled the book
from the start

Author's Note

Unless otherwise indicated, all dollar figures have been translated into today's dollars.

Contents

PART VI: THE CAMPAIGN

PART VII: COURTSHIP

People often forget that I was Jacqueline Bouvier, before being Mrs. Kennedy or Mrs. Onassis. Throughout my life I have tried to remain true to myself.

—JACQUELINE LEE BOUVIER KENNEDY ONASSIS,
IN A 1972 INTERVIEW

Part I

EASTERN SEABOARD

Read, then think. Listen, then think.
Watch, then think. Think—then speak.

—JACKIE'S ADVICE TO HER
FRIEND VIVI CRESPI

1

GETTING HER CAMERA

May–August 1949

As the June 1949 wedding season approached, it seemed like every one of her fellow Social Register debutantes wanted a husband.

All Jacqueline Bouvier wanted was a "terrific camera."

Vassar College had only just begun its final exam period, but the sophomore in slim skirts, who wore her long, tawny hair straightened to drape over one of her luminous hazel eyes, was eager to complete her second year and leave the Hudson River Valley campus behind. Among her innumerable and pronounced contradictions, Jackie was an excellent student who hated school. She credited individual instructors for introducing her to subjects that became lifelong passions, but learned more on her own, outside institutional boundaries.

She lived for socializing every possible weekend. She indulged her expensive tastes until told to stop. She flirted her way into the heart of any beau she wanted, yet she was intellectually ambitious. Her boarding-school headmaster, Ward Johnson, in an unpublished letter to Jackie's mother's friend Molly Thayer (who wrote the first biography of Jackie), noted that her college-board examinations, taken as a high school senior, "really proved the sort of mind she has." Of twenty-six thousand examinations, only twenty-two ranked in the "one-tenth of one percent," and "Jacqueline Bouvier's was one of these." However, she also accepted the era's belief that young women should hide their intellectual gifts. Attesting to her "brilliant work," Johnson noticed that "to avoid doing too well," she would "deliberately leave out one question on a test."

In the weeks before she finished the Vassar semester, she had dashed down to the annual formal Mrs. Shippen's Dancing Class ball in Washington, and the Virginia Gold Cup horse race in Warrenton, Virginia, but, "swamped with work," she then disciplined herself to study "till exams are over." Yet again, she made the honor roll. On the day her sophomore year ended, June 9, she departed the campus immediately, with all she owned.

Her destination was Merrywood, her mother and stepfather's McLean, Virginia, estate. This was a trip she knew well, taking her through New York City, where she'd make her way crosstown from Grand Central Station to Pennsylvania Station to catch the train to Washington. On the way, she would typically stop in at "that camera store by the station," almost certainly Peerless Camera, located at 138 East 44th Street, which was walking distance from Grand Central, and famously offered photographers the full spectrum of new cameras and cutting-edge equipment of seemingly all makes and models, and an array of attachments from lenses to flashes. The object of her desire was the Leica IIc (notable for its fast shutter speeds), which had gone into production the previous year. Inevitably, she asked the exasperated clerks the same question she had the last time she had stopped in: Had the Leica IIc price come down yet? The answer was always the same: No, it had not and would not. She persisted in asking nonetheless, as if by sheer force of will she could reduce the cost of that camera. She wanted the best camera to record her imminent year abroad in Paris.

In the summer of 1948, Jackie had taken her first trip to Europe. With her friend Helen "Bow" Bowdoin, Bow's younger sister Judy, and Julia Bissell, another friend, she'd set sail on the legendary *Queen Mary* for the voyage across the Atlantic to see the European nations that lived vividly in her imagination after years of reading the literature of the Continent. Bow remembered of their crossing that nineteen-year-old Jackie "liked her martini[s and had] a few on [the] boat," and that a "black bug [got] down her dress."

Bow's stepfather, Edward H. Foley, who was a Treasury undersecretary under President Truman, had pulled strings to secure the girls tickets to a garden party at Buckingham Palace. Being greeted by King George VI and Queen Elizabeth in a receiving line beneath a tent in a rainstorm was, Jackie gasped to Bow, "the most exciting moment of my life." They twice shook hands with Winston Churchill. For seven weeks, the foursome toured England, Italy, Switzerland, and France, chaperoned by Jackie and Bow's high school Latin teacher, whom Jackie planned to "lock . . . in a closet at night" so they could go to a nightclub in Paris. Her wish came true when her stepbrother and confidant, Hugh "Yusha" Auchincloss, arrived in town and took her out.

Upon her return to the United States, Jackie began searching for a way to spend her junior year studying in Paris. Vassar didn't offer any such program, but she fatefully spotted a hallway bulletin-board flyer about Smith College's program at the Sorbonne. Non-Smith applicants were rare, and her enrollment was not guaranteed. She applied in January 1949, taking two extra courses in French language and literature in order to improve her French and demonstrate her commitment. Initially, Smith approved her only for study in London, but after agreeing to first take an intensive six-week language course at the University of Grenoble, she was finally granted the Paris option. In her own words, she "finagled into" the program.

Her dilemma was that she had to get that Leica in hand before she left the United States for Europe in August, a month after her twentieth birthday. Getting it as a birthday present seemed like the most realistic way to acquire it in time for her transatlantic crossing. It so happened, though, that one of the very few things John Vernou "Black Jack" Bouvier III and his ex-wife, Janet Auchincloss, could agree on was that this birthday present Jackie was so set on was too great an extravagance. In June 1949, the Leica IIc was retailing for $185 ($2,100 today). She had assured her parents that she'd considered several options, boring them with the technical details regarding the capacity of one camera type versus another. The Leica IIc, she authoritatively explained, would be ideal for both black-and-white outdoor photos and color slides of artwork taken in the museums she would soon be visiting in Paris. Plus, the sturdy Leica would fit into her handbag, or she could wear it around her neck on a leather strap.

They'd both think about it, her parents told her; there was still time. Once school was out, she'd first see her mother at home in McLean, join Daddy for two weeks of vacation with his family in East Hampton, and then visit her mother and stepfather at their Newport, Rhode Island, summer estate, Hammersmith Farm, before leaving for France. Reviewing all this for Yusha, she conceded it would take "a real effort" to get the "little Leica" from either parent. But Jackie Bouvier thrived on challenge.

JACKIE HAD MET YUSHA—TALL, gaunt, and shy—at Merrywood when she was twelve and he was fourteen, just days after the Japanese had bombed Pearl Harbor and the United States entered World War II. Mummy was then dating Hugh D. Auchincloss, Yusha's father, and the two Auchincloss men retrieved Jackie, her sister, Caroline (who was called by her middle name, Lee), and Mummy from Washington's Union Station, already thick with members of the armed forces. Yusha's first impression was of "Jackie's concern for the men in uniform and knowledge of current events. With her French heritage, she was interested in what would become of France now that America was at last in the war." Although Jackie had "dreams of glory at too early an age to be of service," it was clear to him that she wanted a life that left an impact. After dinner, their parents tried to teach them gin rummy. Neither Yusha nor Jackie was interested.

The pair had permanently bonded when, in the course of his showing her the local sights, they had discovered their mutual passion for history. She read aloud the words of Lincoln engraved on the wall of his memorial. In the Smithsonian, she fixated on exhibits about Native American tribes and the First Ladies. Staring at the White House, closed due to wartime restrictions, she "wondered how the Roosevelts must now feel after Pearl Harbor." At Arlington National Cemetery, she wondered how many more graves would be there by the war's end. Six months later, in June 1942, the modest exchange of marital vows between his twice-divorced father and her once-divorced mother made them family.

The intense, enduring connection Jackie and Yusha formed carried over into frequent correspondences when they both attended boarding school and lived away from home. Together, they could endlessly ponder topics from war news to classical literature to existentialism. As she told him in one letter from school: "I'd rather be with you and talk to you than anyone and the things you say about what to do and be like are the things I value more than what anyone else tells me—Mummy, Daddy, everyone. You have some of the most beautiful ideas about—I guess you'd call it life though I feel . . . just to talk to you when things are all mixed up—is so wonderful . . . every minute I realize how lucky I am to have a brother like you."

In another letter from school, she told him: "Anything you write always gives me food for thought & sets me thinking for hours. You always have a lot of ideas that never occurred to me before—or if they did occur to me, I could never express them the way you can."

"If you could just stay the way you are and always be naturally yourself," he wrote her. "Then all people will love you . . . as a friend they love [you] instinctively and can always put their utmost trust in you, and feel when they are broken-hearted or confused that you will always try to help and be part of their grief and happiness."

JACKIE MAY HAVE STILL been a teenager as she prepared to go to Paris that summer of 1949, but she had long been thinking as an adult; she had an impulse to set her own course and rise and fall by her choices. It wasn't that she couldn't enjoy what her friends did or conform when she saw the value in doing so. She wasn't an intentional contrarian. She simply derived the most out of life by taking her own path.

As soon as Jackie returned to Merrywood, she was dashing around. In between a dental appointment and a horse show, she saw Vivi Taylor for lunch. They'd become friends in Newport, when they shared secrets in a code of broken French and Spanish while their mothers and a battalion of formidable matrons played what Jackie wryly called "dragon bridge." A striking, tall divorcée, Vivi led a faster life, educated by tutors in Europe and dating movie star Lawrence Tierney, but that spring she was beset by insecurity about her personal appeal. In love with the Italian count Marco Fabio Crespi and anxious for word that his quickie annulment proceedings in Mexico had begun, she worried that he might decide not to marry her, as they planned. Despite being seven years her junior, the college student calmed her friend with simple advice. "First of all, she questioned why I would even want to marry again," Vivi recalled. Jackie then summarized her operational mantra in two words. "She looked right into me and said firmly, 'Become distinct.' She repeated it: 'Become distinct.'"

Throughout the summer, Jackie eagerly attended wedding after wedding, happy not to be a bride herself. And it wasn't just the peer pressure of fellow debutantes Miss Bouvier had to resist. Two days before Bow's wedding, on the afternoon of Monday, June 27, she was out on the North Shore of Long Island, at the Oyster Bay estate Puddle Duck Farm, for the wedding ceremony and reception of Gladys "Patsy" Pulitzer to David Frost Bartlett. David's best man, his brother, Charlie, was a friend and former beau of Jackie's. Years later, Charlie admitted that his intention that day was to introduce Jackie Bouvier to a man who, despite being a dozen years her senior, he was convinced would make the ideal husband for her. He was equally certain she would make him the ideal wife. He was a rich, handsome playboy congressman, but he was as literate and worldly as she. Charlie Bartlett was certain that he was about to "pull off the introduction," leading and weaving her through the reception, getting her "about halfway across this great crowd" when they ran into the legendary boxer Gene Tunney, a friend of his father's, and "she got involved in a conversation with him. And by the time I got her across, why, he'd [the congressman] left." He shrugged it off. After all, his pal Jack Kennedy was already a man on the move.

At eighteen years old, knowing what postwar marriage meant for women, she had publicly declared her unconventional determination to resist the altar. Even as a high school junior, she made her phobia of domesticity clear to a beau, Bev Corbin, when she asked him: "Can you think of anything worse than living in a small town like this all your life and competing to see which housewife could bake the best cake?" In her 1947 high school graduation yearbook, under the entry of "Ambition," she submitted five stern words: "Not to be a housewife." She calmed one friend whose boyfriend was ambivalent about marriage, advising her that young men "don't want to be tied down before they've had a chance to make a good start in the world in business." She also advised Yusha not to even "think of getting married soon," opining that "it hampers people terribly if they get married when they're still in college."

In fact, Jackie declared that she would rather have even a lowly job than be married. Before the Vassar term had ended, she composed an illustrated poem for her engaged Vassar friend Ellen "Puffin" Gates, in which she contrasted her own likely future: "Jackie skinny and underpaid / Is earning her living as the French maid." While only a jest, it did imply her belief that even if she was performing the same domestic chores as a wife, at least a maid was responsible only for herself.

In the poem, Jackie also warned Puffin of marriage's "thorns," when "wedded bliss turns into wedded strife," and that her husband would begin "moaning about his slovenly wife." The sting of it also likely reflected her feeling about going to Paris alone; Puffin, who she said was as "full of mischief" as herself, had been accepted to the study-abroad program with her, then suddenly abandoned the plan to get married instead. Predicting that Puffin would soon be jealous of "Jackie drinking bourbon at the Sorbonne," she drew a cartoon representing her idea of a woman's married life—feeding a baby at six in the morning and burning toast, adding two sarcastic lines: "Instead of boating on the Seine, alas, Puffin's floating down the drain in Pittsfield, Mass."

Before she began "tearing all over the rest of June for weddings," Jackie had briefly overlapped at Merrywood with her mother, who was about to leave for Newport. Janet appreciated just how much her daughter loved taking pictures with her practical and inexpensive Brownie—a popular camera choice for young people dating back to the turn of the century. When finally relaxed with cigarette and cocktail in hand, Janet could beam a radiant smile as Jackie slinked around family gatherings, sure to take everyone's picture with her Brownie, later pasting them into black album pages. Blending her artistic and journalistic impulses, Jackie annotated her photo albums with drawings referencing the settings, handwritten poetry, and name, date, and place identifications, not just giving the pages a contextual record but capturing the mood each event had provoked. "I love nostalgia," she admitted. Though Janet recognized Jackie's fondness for photography, she didn't realize how much more serious her daughter's interest had become, and certainly didn't believe that buying the expensive Leica was necessary for her to continue snapping away.

Since her daughter would be with Black Jack on her birthday, Janet thrust a card into Jackie's hand with cash folded inside before leaving for Newport. Most of Mummy's money came via "Unk," Jackie's nickname for her stepfather (derived from "Uncle Hughdie"). At times she could withhold the pettiest amount, and then, without warning, become generous. As Jackie once reported to Yusha when Janet bumped her monthly allowance from $25 to $125, "Mummy's being very extravagant all of a sudden, so now I'm wallowing in luxury."

Whether or not Janet expected Jackie to count the cash then and there, she made it clear there wasn't enough to buy the camera, advising, "You can get the rest you need from *him*," meaning Daddy. Once she added up the amount, Jackie was miffed—"it was less than half."

AT POINTS WHEN SHE sensed she'd be particularly vulnerable, Jackie felt she needed the moral support offered by Yusha's presence. At her request, Yusha joined Jackie at Merrywood after Janet left that June. As a bridesmaid to Bow, her third friend to marry that summer, Jackie only felt confident hosting a pool party for those in the wedding with Yusha there.

The estate sat on a high cliff overlooking the turbulent Potomac, and when there together, the stepsiblings shared a ritual that seemed to provide internal stability for Jackie. "I'm glad we walked down to the garden & watched the river," Jackie had written him. "Whenever we do the most peaceful feeling comes over me & I forget the hectic little life of parties & tearing hither & yon." In 1946, as her first round of social events during her first winter break from Miss Porter's School approached, she implored him to join her: "I simply couldn't stand going to a dance without you." At her June 1947 high school graduation, she insisted, "You have to come up . . . [and] see me walk down the aisle. . . . I won't be able to hold my head up if you don't." Anticipating her debutante tea at Hammersmith two months later, she wrote to him that he had "to be there for it and stand in the receiving line with me."

Before Jackie finally left Merrywood to join her father in East Hampton, she had her trunks for Paris sent to Newport. She was already concerned about the long separation from Yusha ahead. "I won't see you for a minute for the next year," she wrote him once their brief reunion in Newport at the end of summer was over, just before she left for Paris.

But if Jackie loved him, Yusha remained *in love* with her. In his March 23, 1943, diary entry, he recorded that while they listened to records in the living room, he'd blurted out to her "that she had a lot of sex appeal, more than anyone because she made people love to be with her and when they see her, they had a tingle run through their veins." Three years later, his ardor had changed: "I don't love her as a brother or as a lover, but as a good friend who can understand and comfort me. I can feel sorry for myself. She makes me feel better."

* * *

ANOTHER MAN IN HER life had an entirely different, though no less intense, love for Jackie. On July 14, she arrived in New York City, met by her father. All year long he looked forward to this annual summer reunion, which also usually included his younger daughter, Lee. They'd seen each other just before Jackie's sophomore exams, but no matter how brief their separation, he was always eager to see her.

He typically welcomed his daughters with an effusion of embraces and kisses, as well as a critique of their appearance combined with flattering praise. Sometimes Black Jack spoke about their physical appeal in a way that might appear inappropriate to anyone other than those who knew them well. "Will you look at her eyes," he once remarked about Lee, "and those sexy lips of hers." After carefully looking over Jackie, dressed for a party, he couldn't resist later writing her, "Pet, I must admit you did look awfully pretty to your old man tonight pink gloves and all."

Then they would typically begin arguing, Bouvier-style—heated and unrelentingly loud. Months earlier, after using his Bloomingdale's charge account with abandon, she failed to call him on Easter Sunday, and he yelled at her for both using the card and ignoring him. His reactions were not entirely predictable. Initially upset when he learned that she applied for the yearlong study-abroad program through Smith College, he then felt such pride at her acceptance that he offered to underwrite it all.

Eighteen months earlier, upon the death of "Grampy Jack," her widowed paternal grandfather, Jackie's twin aunts, Michelle Putnam and Maude Davis, had inherited the family's East Hampton estate, "Lasata," a wood-shingled manor house at 121 Further Lane, a block from the ocean and three blocks from the Maidstone Club. It sat on fourteen acres of manicured lawn and featured groves of graceful trees, a sunken Italian garden, a rose garden, a vegetable garden, fountains, a sundial, and a riding stable and ring. The twins were also left the smaller but still commodious "Wildmoor," a few miles away, with a widow's walk that offered a view of the crashing Atlantic.

By the time of Jackie's visit in July 1949, the Bouvier wealth had so rapidly dissipated that taxes and maintenance costs forced the twins to begin preparing to sell Lasata. Michelle was living in South America with her second husband, Harrington Putnam, but Maude, her husband,

John Davis, and their daughter, Maudie, occupied Wildmoor that summer of 1949 so Maude would be able to manage the sale of Lasata; Wildmoor, which the family had used to generate some income as a summer rental in the three previous years, would next be on the market.

For his summer weeks with his daughters, Black Jack typically rented one of the small East Hampton cottages owned and operated by the Sea Spray Inn. The cottages were about a mile and a half from Wildmoor, where Maude hosted Jackie's twentieth birthday party on July 28. Along with the three Davis-family members, Black Jack, and Jackie, the gathering included her divorced aunt Edith Beale, a permanent East Hampton resident who lived alone in her deteriorating estate, Grey Gardens, and her visiting youngest son, Phelan. In honor of her niece's imminent voyage, Edith warbled "La Marseillaise" instead of "Happy Birthday."

According to the story she told Yusha, Jackie withheld from her father the fact that her mother had given her some money for the camera she wanted. With his trademark drama for making a splash, having noted the make and model of the one she wanted, he didn't give her money toward the purchase of it but rather dispatched a clerk from his office to the camera shop to buy it outright for her. Jacqueline Bouvier got her Leica.

While in East Hampton, Jackie joined a fashion-show fundraiser for the Ladies Village Improvement Society, which maintained the enclave's public appearance. A photo of Jackie was featured in "society" columns, modeling a Mexican *china poblana* folk dress at the outdoor event and afterward posing with her father for photographer Bert Morgan. She was used to this; her name and face had been appearing in newspapers since she was an infant. Whether or not she liked such exposure was moot; fawning publicity was an aspect of privilege that both her parents avidly sought for themselves and insisted on for her as well.

Another instinct Black Jack and Janet shared was to claim that if anything went wrong, it was the other's fault. Before leaving East Hampton on August 5 for Newport, Jackie took a bad fall off her beloved elderly horse, Danseuse. She went briefly unconscious and badly hurt her back. Mummy suggested to her niece Mimi that Jackie's father had been inattentive because "that never happened when she rode with me." Daddy told his sister Maude that Jackie had tumbled because she was upset after a stern call from Mummy before riding.

When Jackie's train arrived at the Kingston, Rhode Island, station, Yusha retrieved her. As they drove into nearby Newport, she crowed about the new possession she wore around her neck as if it were a "diamond necklace"—her Leica—regaling him with the machinations it took for her to get it. (There is no evidence to suggest that Janet, perpetually distracted by running her vast household and tending to her many social obligations, asked about, or indeed even noticed, the camera.)

After years of having her parents use her to attack each other, Jackie remained an ally to both, but had become expert in employing their enmity to her advantage, often with a casual suggestion to one that the other had been more indulgent. She recalled for a friend an incident when her father let her buy three "heavenly dresses" on his charge account; when Jackie told her mother, the news made her "livid," but "she let me keep them!" She also had a tactic for shaking money from both, telling Yusha, "When the allowance Mummy gives me runs out, I ask Daddy for some & vice versa."

Jackie had no need to worry they would compare notes about their gifts to her—the two barely spoke. If Daddy answered the phone when "that bitch" (as his nephew Jack Davis recalled him calling his ex-wife) rang for Jackie, he held the receiver out to her in disgust. If he phoned her at home, Mummy told her it was "the drunk" (also per Jack Davis) calling. Since Janet's remarriage, their only known proximity to each other was at Jackie's 1947 high school graduation. Their one reported phone conversation involved Janet's insisting that Jack pay for Jackie's dental care and his arguing that she should, in that case, go to his New York dentist, a disagreement he lost. Still, very little about money escaped Mummy's attention.

In Jackie's fleeting days at Hammersmith Farm there was a palpable tension, with Mummy fixated on what Jackie might be saying about Black Jack when out and about. Her cousin Jack Davis, then stationed at the naval base in Newport, recalled the tension between Jackie and her mother as Janet sat perched on the arm of a sofa, not even trying to disguise her eavesdropping.

It was no surprise that at one point Jackie animatedly whispered to him, "I'm so excited about France. I can't wait to go!"

Studying at the Sorbonne and learning flawless French was her ostensible objective, but a desire to experience a different life was what truly drove her to cross the Atlantic. As she had written several years earlier to a friend who was relocating abroad, "I envy you in a way because you are going to something new and therefore exciting . . . living with sophisticated people instead of homey little folks like mine!" Now Jackie would be liberated and able to think for herself.

Just before leaving, Jackie won first prize at a Bailey's Beach Club costume party dressed as Rita Hayworth, a fact that made the nation's society columns. The day before departing, she was honored with the thirty-four other students bound for study in Paris at a New York luncheon with Hollywood gossip columnist Hedda Hopper, where the French consul raised a glass to toast them. Jackie was among the handful to pose for a news photo about the event. The next day, August 23, 1949, aboard the *De Grasse*, ready for departure, the group was asked to sing "La Vie en Rose," and an Associated Press photographer snapped images of five students walking the deck, including Jackie. For the third time in a week, "Miss Bouvier" was mentioned in the papers, twice with her picture.

As the ship's horn blew and bells clanged, tubes of colored paper popped, streaming over those on the dock. Waving from the deck to Yusha and Mummy as they grew small in the distance, Jackie left America with not only a "bon voyage bonus"—Mummy's unneeded cash contribution to the cost of the camera—but also her new Leica. As was almost always the case, Jackie Bouvier had gotten exactly what she wanted.

2

DADDY AND MUMMY

1929–1948

Jackie began her transatlantic voyage to France exuberant about what she hoped would be a year ahead of emotional and intellectual independence. Part of her excitement was certainly also relief to be leaving her complex past behind—one that was privileged, but also traumatic.

Even before she was born, Jacqueline Lee Bouvier was generating excitement. She made the newspapers prior to her arrival, social columns elaborating that the "stork is hovering" above the Bouviers, reporting that just a year after "Black Jack Bouvier who was supposed to be as hard hearted a bachelor as ever burned up Broadway" had "succumbed to marriage" and "the other gay bachelors of town are rather amusedly thinking of dark young Bouvier as a staid father." Her mother would later tell Jackie's confidante Nancy "Tucky" Tuckerman that her daughter so wanted to avoid the hard truths of the world that she delayed her own birth by six weeks (she'd been expected in the middle of June). Tucky thought Janet's joke might have contained lingering resentment about the interminable pregnancy that prevented her from competing in horse shows half the summer, although she was back at it before the season ended and won a third-prize ribbon twenty days after giving birth.

As they awaited the baby's birth, at least the family was summering on the East End of Long Island, where it tended to be cooler at that time of year than in the city. Jack's niece "Little Edie" Beale recorded in her Saturday, July 28, 1929, diary entry that her grandmother Bouvier had called to say that "Janet had a little girl . . . Poor Jack was rather disappointed that Janet had a girl. Most men want boys but a girl would be my favorite."

From the start, Jacqueline Bouvier's life was overcast by drama. Forty-two days after her birth, on October 8, her thirty-six-year-old uncle, William "Buddy" Bouvier, died in Los Olivos, California, of acute alcoholism. Less than three weeks after that, on October 24—"Black Tuesday"—the American stock market crashed, which substantially reduced the great wealth of her families. On December 22, she was christened at St. Ignatius Loyola on Park Avenue. Mummy's father, James Lee, was her designated godfather but he got stuck in traffic, so Black Jack substituted his nine-year-old fatherless nephew, Miche Bouvier, to avoid further delaying the ceremony, which enraged his father-in-law. On January 15, 1930, her parents left Jackie behind, although she was only six months old, as they departed on the *Augustus*, traveling for two months through Spain, Italy, France, and England, including an excursion on the legendary Orient Express train, their adventures covered in newspaper social columns.

The first photograph of the infant to appear in the press was published when she was only five months old, posed with her mother in a *Brooklyn Daily Eagle* society column. Her second birthday party—with pony rides, a Jack Horner pie, and nineteen guests—marked the first time she was the sole subject of a news article, in the *East Hampton Star*. At five, the *Star* identified her as "one of the most attractive riders" in a horse show. At eight, the *Daily News* showed her seated on a horse-show fence, and the *East Hampton Star* called her a "little Miss with her lovely curls and well-cut riding habit [who] presented a picture the judges and audience could not resist." Other New York papers featured photos of the toddler at dog shows with beloved Scottish terrier Hoochie, followed by Great Dane King Phar, dachshund Hans, cocker spaniel Bonnet, and Bouvier des Flandres Caprice that, Jackie said, "Daddy got us because of the name."

THE BOUVIER FAMILY'S GREATEST wealth was through the inheritance of Jackie's paternal grandmother, Maude, via both of her own English-immigrant parents. Jackie's great-grandfather, William Roberts Sergeant Jr. of Surrey, was a wood-pulp merchant and paper manufacturer who died a dozen years before she was born. Her great-grandmother Edith Matilda Sergeant was the London-born daughter of furniture merchant Alfred Valentine Leaman, who had developed and owned a full block of residential real estate in New York City, on West 23rd Street between Eighth and Ninth Avenues; he later expanded into commercial real estate. Grandma Maude was born in the Bronx, but when she was a student at Brearley, her family moved to Nutley, New Jersey. After her 1890 marriage to Grampy Jack, they built their home "Woodcroft" there.

Born on May 19, 1891, in New York (where he lived until the age of two), John Vernou Bouvier III was raised in Nutley, attending grammar school in nearby Morristown. After he was expelled from boarding school at Phillips Exeter Academy for gambling, his father pushed him through Columbia Grammar & Preparatory School with the help of tutors until he was accepted at Columbia University. He studied there for two years, then transferred to Yale in 1910. A member of the secret society Book and Snake, he excelled at tennis and was on the rowing team, but Jack—in his white flannel trousers, Bloody Mary in hand, cranking up the phonograph—was mostly renowned for his parties.

An entitled, arrogant rogue, Jack gambled illegally (mainly on prizefights, at the racetrack, and in casinos) for high stakes in the company of his pal New York mayor Jimmy Walker. He sped along the Motor Parkway into Long Island, knowing he'd never be ticketed because the chief of police was a former family gardener. On occasion, he donned goggles for a dangerous flight in a Stinson Reliant monoplane to East Hampton, where he also organized and managed a summertime amateur baseball team, Bouvier's Black Ducks. He never contradicted rumors of his sexual escapades, including that of an affair with fellow Yale Glee Club member Cole Porter. To stand apart from his peers, he devised a distinct appearance, with fashion trademarks such as longer-than-normal shirt cuffs and cuffless trousers, black dancing pumps without socks, and a blue silk straw-hat band that matched his eyes. In 1919, he was thrown out of the Hotel Knickerbocker because he made a "little skip" through the lobby, then in a "rude and unseemly manner stared at the greatly embarrassed ladies . . . made loud noises, used abusive language and by means of threats, force and violence, attempted to enter the ladies dressing room." Jack sued the hotel manager for assault.

Jack also staged grand public entrances. When he exited his shining black Lincoln at the premier of *Showboat*, his diamond cuff links and gold-tipped walking stick were noted in the press. He stood for a moment until he had the attention of the gawking crowds, then swirled off his black cape and gracefully draped it over his arm. (His theatricality even led a talent scout to encourage him to audition for the role of Rhett Butler in the film version of *Gone with the Wind.*) One reliable affectation never failed to get him attention. Night or day, summer or winter, he was never seen without his face glowing with the darkest possible tan, whether obtained from the sun or a lamp.

Borrowing money from his wealthy great-uncle, he bought a seat on the Stock Exchange, proving wildly successful as a broker. He lived a fast, indulgent life—introspection and emotional commitment were not for him. In June 1914, he quickly got engaged to golf champion Lillian B. Hyde, then suddenly broke it off. By April of 1920, his fiancée was Baltimore debutante Eleanor Carroll Daingerfield Carter. The engagement was called off after six months. Pursuing Chicago heiress Emma Stone but failing to commit, he got his comeuppance when she married his brother.

His unwillingness to marry angered his father, and was the subject of a mocking poem his father wrote him for his thirty-third birthday. "The bachelor may e'er contend / He'll thus remain until the end," went one stanza, followed by another about family embarrassment about his single status. "He passes up the very sweetest / The best, the prettiest and the neatest / He jilts. / But when he really needs a wife / who can't be had for mortal life / He wilts. / So, Sonny, marry when you can / Is my advice for everyman / And you."

Jack's July 7, 1928, wedding to his sisters' friend Janet Norton Lee, an eager social climber seventeen years his junior, seemed only to serve the purpose of making his father happy. Jack's views on fidelity were made obvious by his pursuit of heiress Doris Duke on his and Janet's honeymoon voyage to Europe. From the *Aquitania*, the upset bride wired her new sisters-in-law, who then sent their brother a chastising telegram. Certainly Bouvier suffered from what writer Gore Vidal (Unk's stepson by his second marriage) termed a "lack of sexual guilt," even in public, as was shown in a 1933 photograph of him published in the *Daily News*, sitting on a fence and holding hands with socialite Virginia Kernochan as Janet looked away.

* * *

JACKIE BOUVIER'S PRIMARY MEMORY of her parents prior to their 1936 separation was their heading out to a Central Park Casino dance. "I'll never forget the night my mother and father came into my bedroom all dressed up to go out. I can still smell the scent my mother wore and feel the softness of her fur coat as she leaned over to kiss me good night." The "moment stayed with me because it was one of the few times I remember seeing my parents together. It was so romantic. So hopeful."

Later in life, Jackie would idealize this period as a time when she just "thrived on hot dogs and riding smelly old ponies." In this idyllic version: "Both of our parents made us feel they loved us so much. I always saw a great deal of both of them and as their separation was a gradual thing, I was never conscious of it. They were very wise. Children do separate things with their parents anyway. It never occurred to me we should all be doing it together. Every time we were with our parents, we had that one's undivided attention with no other parent to compete with us for their affection."

The truth was quite nearly the opposite. The girls' nurse, Bertha Kimmerle, recalled Janet as "always tired and upset," turning her frustration on Black Jack when he returned from work. She attested to Janet's being largely absent, "doing what she wanted, when she wanted and where she wanted . . . and the children, consistently without their mother."

When twenty-year-old Janet Lee married thirty-seven-year-old Jack Bouvier, she entered a family that lived far more extravagantly than her own. Ironically, the Lees had greater wealth, all earned in one generation by her father, James Thomas Lee.

With an engineering degree from City College and political science and law degrees from Columbia University, Jim Lee made his fortune in luxury residential-real-estate development, and banking. He was elected to the Chase National Bank board in 1928 and became the Central Savings Bank president in 1943.

Born in 1877 to the children of immigrants from Cork, Ireland (his father was a New York public-school superintendent, his mother a Troy, New York, teacher), Jim provided private-school educations and debutante parties for his three daughters. He didn't believe his wealth was to be used to launch them into the highest realms of society. He, his parents, and his grandparents had earned their own income, and as he saw it, Janet and her two sisters could do likewise—or marry someone wealthy. Even though her father eventually left her $12 million from his $94 million estate, Janet perpetually begrudged his refusal to indulge her (an attitude adopted by her daughter Lee, who declared her grandfather "a miser").

In contrast, Jackie valued "Gramps Lee" as the sole example in her life of wealth being entirely earned rather than inherited. She also saw in him a reliable model of happiness, believing that he was driven less by a simple profit motive than by an intrinsic desire to develop architecturally significant buildings. Proud of his granddaughter Mimi for pursuing a law career and encouraging Jackie to excel in math as she did in literature and French, he never considered gender a barrier to professional achievement. While conceding that Jackie could be difficult, he was drawn to her for her intellectual and creative interests.

Gramps looked after Jackie as she was adjusting to the divorce, randomly sending her a "beautiful teddy bear" that she held on to for years, fruit baskets, and boxed chocolates. He generously donated $1,000 for her school's war-bond sale to purchase Jeeps, leaving her feeling that it was "so exciting to floor the teacher" with such an amount. He surprised her with a gold pin that she would wear to get "people to fall in love with me," and she sent him a cartoon of herself as a suitor ogled the piece of jewelry. If, she wrote, she were to pursue an acting career, she promised him "free first row, aisle seats to all my first nights," and told him, "you can hang a big picture of me in the Chase Bank."

She was unintimidated by his reputation for being remote and understood the complexity of his character, because she behaved similarly. After apologizing for being a "stick-in-the-mud" the last time they'd been together, she dared to suggest to him that "everyone is just as scared of you as you are of them—but this summer they are more scared of me than I am of them and I like it like that." She even tried to lure him to Newport, knowing he needed a vacation, and promising fog that would remind him of *Wuthering Heights*.

Jackie's relationship with her grandmother Margaret, though rarely mentioned, was close, according to Mimi Ryan Cecil, one of her five first cousins on the Lee side. Their happiest times were excursions to the Belmont racetrack with their favorite companion, Black Jack, who bought them treats, teased and joked to make them laugh, and took them to the stables to meet the jockeys and horses. Not only did Jack love to "play the ponies" as much as Margaret, but he was more attentive to her than her own daughter was.

Jackie's New York circumference was limited. At three months old, she was brought to her first home, the apartment her parents took after their marriage, at 790 Park Avenue at 73rd Street. The first residence she could remember, from 1932, was a duplex apartment at 740 Park Avenue, a luxurious building owned by her "Gramps" Lee, and where Grandma Margaret lived in a separate apartment (the couple had been estranged for some time). Her father's parents lived within walking distance, at 765 Park Avenue.

"I don't remember any special toys," Jackie claimed of her earliest years, adding, "I hated dolls." Her mother contradicted this, saying she slept with "Sammy, [a] little rag doll [with] red and white checked trousers." Her most cherished furnishings were the bookcases she was given at Christmas in 1936, the repository of the little library she began with ballet books, continuing to collect them through college. She gave credit to Mummy for letting her order as many books as she wanted and Grandmother Bouvier for giving her books as Christmas presents. Her observation that "I loved books . . . most" was an understatement. "I read a lot when I was little, much of which was too old for me. There were Chekhov and Shaw in the room where I had to take naps and I never slept but sat on the windowsill reading, then scrubbed the soles of my feet so the nurse would not see I had been out of bed."

Among her earliest additions to her collection were the Little Colonel and Wizard of Oz series, *Winnie-the-Pooh* and other works by A. A. Milne, *The Jungle Book*, *Black Beauty*, *Little Lord Fauntleroy*, and *Robinson Crusoe*. In the fifth grade, she read both Margaret Mitchell's *Gone with the Wind* and *Life of Byron*, by André Maurois, each three times. After discovering Shakespeare's *Antony and Cleopatra*, she learned "all the great passages by heart." As she matured, her greatest literary passion was Byron, and he, Vaslav Nijinsky, and Noël Coward "were the people I developed passionate interest in." She also loved F. Scott Fitzgerald, "mostly from a nostalgia for the Twenties developed from Daddy."

In a "Book Record" diary from the eighth grade, Jackie offered a glimpse into her literary sensibilities: thumbs-down on *The Daughter of Time*, a biography of writer Katherine Mansfield, whose life Jackie found dull; mixed about *Things to Live For*, an autobiography of the renowned but controversial Irish writer and poet Francis Stuart; enthusiasm for *Nijinsky* by the famous dancer's wife, which she said had "enough excitement and tragedy and everything else for a dozen novels. . . . It shows that fact is stranger than fiction." Also among her favorites were *Rebecca*, by Daphne du Maurier, John Steinbeck's book of short stories *The Long Valley*, and *Macbeth* (she particularly liked the "dagger speech and the ghost speech"). She thought the "uncle thing was wonderful" in *Romeo and Juliet*, whereas after Romeo melodramatically killed himself "you want to tear your hair." Again and again in her capsule reviews Jackie focused on character. She seemed to have an innate sense of structure and pacing, but she was especially excited by the personalities of real and imaginary figures.

Jackie's precociousness made her a novelty, but it created problems in school. Trouble began at Miss Chapin's grammar school on East End Avenue, where she started in September 1935. One teacher, a Miss Platt, considered Jackie to be "very clever, very artistic," but also "full of the devil." Principal Ethel Stringfellow would recall that Miss Bouvier was "the most inquiring mind we've had in school for thirty-five years. So much brighter. She got through everything so much quicker. [This] caused trouble at school because [of] 'idle hands.'" As Stringfellow recorded in one report card, "Jacqueline was given a D in Form because her disturbing conduct in her geography class made it necessary to exclude her from the room."

Jackie admitted to Molly Thayer, "I was always being sent to her [Stringfellow] for breaking rules . . . and though she let me know she was disappointed in one [she] never let you think she gave you up as hopeless. She was my first great moral influence (only one I can think of now!)"

Jackie also recalled that Stringfellow taught through memorization—including historical events, which were to be recited by date; Bible verses; and passages of literature. Tucky remembered that when they were sent home with the assignment of memorizing a single stanza of a lengthy Tennyson poem, Jackie returned knowing *every* stanza by heart.

Despite their being "very strict and classical," she loved the ballet lessons she took at Miss O'Neill's school in the Metropolitan Opera House, and while she was crushed to soon enough learn that she lacked the ideal physicality to pursue ballet further, the process taught her enormous physical discipline, as did her horseback riding lessons.

Mummy considered the exclusive schools which her daughter attended valuable only for the social status they conveyed; while proud of her daughter's high grades, she adhered to the belief that intelligent women were not appealing to men, period. Black Jack, however, believed Jackie's intelligence marked her as destined for prominence, the pathway to such ascent being academic excellence. He would encourage her to be "a standout at school. In fact, I've such high ambitions for you. I know you've got it in you to be a leader." Throughout her education, it was Black Jack who invested himself in her achievements, jubilantly bragging how she'd "taken all the prizes in her class this year." When she dashed in for supper after playing outside, Mummy scolded her in front of relatives: "[Y]our hair looks like a bird's nest." Black Jack exclaimed, "Doesn't Jackie look terrific?"

Jackie's reciprocal appreciation of his unqualified support, faith in her abilities, and devotion was effusive. In a previously unpublished account, she declared that he was "an ideal father . . . a rather childish, imaginative, mischievous side to his nature made him the greatest companion. I was rather a tomboy—he was very proud when I learned to jump on my pony. . . . He let us climb trees and spoiled us by giving us ice cream cones at just the time it would spoil one's supper."

DURING BLACK JACK AND Janet's trial separation, from October 1936 to April 1937, Black Jack moved into a suite at the Westbury Hotel, then moved back home for several months. It was clear there would be no reconciliation, and the final separation came in autumn 1937, when, after briefly staying with his parents, he settled into his permanent apartment at 125 East 74th Street.

As the girls consistently defended Daddy, Mummy's escalating resentment toward her children manifested through her "frequently yell[ing]" and her "very quick and at times violent temper," according to Bertha Kimmerle. "Mrs. Bouvier left the apartment many weekends," Kimmerle continued, speaking about the fall and winter of 1937, "leaving the children alone," including one New Year's Eve and Day, "having gone to Tuxedo with some man." Mummy refused to let the girls see their father, she continued, "jealous of the children's affection for him." Although Janet only threatened to hit Lee, it was different with Jackie. Kimmerle was stunned to witness how "Mrs. Bouvier gave Jacqueline a very severe spanking because the little girl had been too noisy in her play. She would spank Jacqueline quite frequently and became often irritated with the child, but for no reason that I was able to see."

During the summer of 1938, Jack and Janet had rented separate homes, in East Hampton and Bellport, respectively. With Janet "highly nervous and irritable," Jackie "frequently spoke about running away and going to her father's house," one of the household staff, Bernice Anderson, recounted, "when her mother was away. Jacqueline asked me to help her find her father's number in the telephone book as she was so unhappy, she wanted to talk to him without delay." Black Jack ensured that his daughters got exercise and rest, and ate nutritiously; while under Janet's control, said Kimmerle, the children ate canned food at no established mealtime.

That fall brought abrupt displacement from the only true home Jackie knew, in the building owned by her grandfather, to a cheaper and smaller one in his building at One Gracie Square. Here, Janet was "worse," Anderson testified, staying in bed until lunch. She was "highly nervous all during this time . . . and drank even more than at Bellport and almost every night she used to take sleeping pills."

There was increasing conflict. "Jacqueline used to say on many occasions that she hated her mother," Anderson continued. "Jacqueline and her mother frequently had yelling spells; she would yell at Jacqueline and Jacqueline would yell back at her mother. In fact, they both were very high-strung and Mrs. Bouvier seemed to be by far the worse of the two." Her friend Martha Buck thought Jackie suffered "emotional damage" living under Mummy's tyranny and "warped values." Even the cynical Gore Vidal would admit that "her life in the world had been a good deal harder than she ever let on."

By October 1938, the Bouviers had been separated for nearly two years when Janet first filed for divorce. Jack refused, fearing the effect on his daughters, and called on Kimmerle, Anderson, and another household staff member, Bertha Newey, for their testimony defending him. Getting nowhere, Janet hired a detective to find evidence of her husband's adultery, the only grounds on which "absolute divorce" was granted in

New York State. In early 1940, Janet's private eye reported Black Jack's being "overly friendly" with divorced blond St. Louis socialite Marjorie McKittrick Berrien and an "unnamed woman in his summer home in East Hampton."

For all her later declarations about the unseemliness of publicity, Janet was a fixture in the nation's society columns as one of the "smart New Yorkers," and in filing for divorce she took advantage of that to publicly call Black Jack an adulterer, as the January 26, 1940, New York *Daily News* story, "Sues Husband as Love Commuter; 'Other Women' Were Plural," made clear:

"The very social John Vernou Bouvier 3rd, didn't have much time by himself, according to divorce papers filed by his wife. . . . In her plaint she indicated that Bouvier had spent most of his time since the summer of 1936 galloping from one siren to another. Mrs. Janet Lee Bouvier, of the Long Island horsey set, declared the trysting covered a considerable area from East Hampton to Manhattan, with her husband acting as a sort of commuter in love. Mrs. Bouvier said there had been so many women she had been unable to get more than a line on most of them."

Her public declaration about Black Jack's adultery, however, backfired. Not only did she fail to get her divorce based on what were deemed inconclusive claims, but she also humiliated Jackie, who was teased by her cousins and schoolmates. None of this, suffice it to say, further endeared Janet to her daughters.

That summer, Janet took the girls to Reno, Nevada's Lazy-A Ranch for a six-week "vacation" to establish residency in Nevada, which granted no-fault divorce at the end of that length of time. Jackie reveled in her first trip West, befriending the ranch hands and riding Western style. She fondly recalled a mustang pony named Banjo and a larger, wilder horse called Wagstaff, upon whom she "galloped across the Nevada desert."

In the end, Black Jack agreed not to fight the divorce she obtained in Reno on July 22, 1940. Less than a week later, Jackie turned eleven. Perhaps to irritate her now ex-husband (who was enjoying his new single status in East Hampton), Janet returned there with her daughters for the rest of the summer, all of them staying with her father at his home on Lily Pond Lane. When they went to Gracie Square in September, Mummy made it difficult for Jackie to call her father, let alone see him. He retaliated by telling Jackie he would no longer board her beloved horse Danseuse in the city unless she found a way to call him. Such was the predictable trap both set for their daughter out of spite for each other.

For many years after the divorce, Jackie seemed bewildered by her mother's decision to pursue it. When she first met the art critic Bernard Berenson, she asked him rhetorically, "Why did Mummy divorce Daddy?"

It was a question worth closer examination. Money was always a motive for Mummy. In 1926, Jackie's father had earned nearly $11 million in stock market profits and over $1 million as a specialist broker. In 1935, during the Great Depression, however, he earned only around $680,000 in commissions and trading, but his expenses were over $777,000. In 1936, when his income fell below $566,000, he blamed it on the new crackdowns on specialist brokers like himself, initiated by Securities and Exchange Commission chairman Joseph P. Kennedy.

But money was not everything. Janet's reaction to Jack's seductive behavior around other women prompted him to write her in September, just three months after marrying her: "Sweet, all you have to do is to just be your little self, not becoming excited, temperamental, and not shouting angrily at me and we'll get on beautifully." As a newlywed, he had flirted but had had no known love affairs or mistresses. Before becoming pregnant that fall, Janet could have petitioned for an annulment. She didn't. She filed for separation in 1936, the year Jack's income plummeted. Notably, her 1940 divorce claim referenced only affairs during the four years of their separation, when he failed to regain great wealth.

As far as the reason for the divorce, Jackie seemingly accepted Daddy's simplistic rationale that "all men are rats." She adored her father and accepted his overt attempts to seduce other women as inevitable, yet she seemed to consider Mummy's unwillingness to sublimate her resulting humiliation as a weakness that caused the divorce. That conviction—that loyalty to a marriage in which a husband strayed was a sign of strength and proper recognition of duty and priorities—would stay with Jackie.

Janet's mother had angrily opposed her daughter's divorce plans, arguing that Jack's devotion to their children's happiness was the priority. With Jim Lee refusing to provide support beyond housing and emergency needs and Jack's modest alimony denying her a lavish lifestyle, Janet was forced to take a low-paying job modeling clothes at Macy's, which covered the cost of Jackie's dance lessons. Little could she imagine that the humiliating department store work would lead to a permanent and more lucrative position as the wife of a Standard Oil heir. But Janet's fate turned when the flamboyant alcoholic socialite Nina Gore Vidal Auchincloss walked through Macy's revolving door during the holiday rush.

The daughter of a U.S. senator from Oklahoma, Nina had first married aviation engineer Eugene Vidal, with whom she had a son, Gore. In 1935 she divorced Eugene and wed Hugh D. Auchincloss. A graduate of Yale and Columbia Law School and a member of exclusive country clubs, Auchincloss had served in the navy during World War I and in the State and Commerce Departments in the 1920s, and had traced U-boat movements in the Caribbean at naval stations in Jamaica and Washington during World War II. His seven-year marriage to Czarist Russian Maya de Chrapovitsky, who escaped the Bolsheviks, had ended in 1932 after she suffered a brain injury in a helicopter accident; their only child was Yusha. With Hugh, Nina had a daughter, Nini, in 1937, and a son, Tommy, in 1939, but, chatting up Janet in Macy's, she revealed her plan to divorce her husband. Janet knew who that husband was; while living at the Nevada divorce ranch, she had met an heiress, also there to end her marriage. Her maiden name was Esther Auchincloss, and her brother was Hugh.

Nine months after meeting Janet, Nina did divorce Hugh. Eight weeks later, Janet Bouvier suddenly appeared at a Washington party, lengthily quoted in the *Washington Star*'s November 7, 1941, society column, perhaps strategically. Telegraphing a distinct impression that she needed nobody else's money, the article printed her bold lie that "the apartment on Park Avenue which Janet owns" would be leased out, when of course it was owned by her father. She bragged about her own home "with a huge open fireplace in the drawing room and a little entrance hall all its own with stairs leading to the bedrooms upstairs." Mrs. Bouvier further declared that she would be "coming down this winter for a visit" to D.C. The column also included a mention of the appearance, "later on in the evening," of the recently divorced Hugh Auchincloss.

That winter, Janet and Hugh—each traveling with their own group of friends—ended up on the same Caribbean cruise. Coincidental or arranged, it became Janet's version of how they met. Ostensibly for a vacation in the nation's capital, Janet took her daughters to Washington, introducing them to Auchincloss. On her first tour of the White House, Jackie was disappointed by the lack of historical furnishings. On her first tour of Hugh's home, Janet was awed by his obvious wealth. Two months later, she married him. Seven months after that, he inherited nearly $20 million and the family's summer estate, Hammersmith Farm.

Mummy's obsessive fear of living without tremendous wealth affected Jackie. After a school discussion about "labor overthrowing capital," Jackie was anxious about prestigious boarding schools being eliminated and that she would be "begging in the streets & working in coal mines," as she wrote Yusha. That exaggerated scenario reflected Jackie's sheltered privilege; her closest encounter with poverty so far had been laughing at the *Little Rascals* urchins during Saturday movie matinees with Grandma Bouvier. By leaving Jack and marrying Unk, Janet ensured an even more elitist status for Jackie. It came at a cost, however, forever defining a daughter's most primary relationship. Jackie never forgave Mummy for the divorce, and Mummy never forgave Jackie for feeling that way about it.

Throughout the two years of Jack and Janet's separation—1938 to 1940—and then the two years after the 1940 divorce, Jack was able to enjoy the company of his daughters on most weekends during the school year, over part of the Christmas holiday, and for a few summer weeks in East Hampton. However, two months after Janet's June 1942 remarriage to Unk, she and her daughters moved to Unk's Virginia home. From September 1942 until June 1944, Jackie attended the Holton-Arms School in Washington, where she completed grammar school and had her freshman year of high school. During this time, Jackie was unable to see her father much on weekends, and they had just six summer weeks together in East Hampton. Black Jack's brother-in-law John Davis noted how heavily he began drinking and how he raged against Janet and her new husband, whom he dubbed "Take-a-Loss-with-Auchincloss."

Once Jackie left Washington to begin boarding school in September 1944 at Miss Porter's in Farmington, Connecticut, however, she and her father were able to spend more time alone together than ever before, she being close enough for him to visit her and for her to make weekend trips to him. (Mummy's drive to see Jackie could be up to six hours, but it took barely two for Black Jack.) It was also Jackie's first significant escape from Mummy's control. Though life at Miss Porter's came with its own insufferable restrictions, Jackie learned to undermine them, cultivating a bad-girl persona.

"I was playing the Strip Polka," she wrote to Yusha about an encounter with her high school music teacher, who "snatched up the music and said what would Chopin think if he could see me now." As for chapel prayer readings, she asked, "Do you think in your wildest dreams that I would ever get asked to read anything? . . . I shall try to be pious—but what a job!" She implored Yusha to bring her cigarettes so she could be "evil in the woods." After receiving a package of "illegal food" from him, she felt guilty but "not enough to give it up." She liked the nightly challenge of breaking the rules to slip out to the local drugstore to get ice cream. After the headmaster discovered that her phone calls were not from her stepfather, as she had claimed, she "thought of some lovely alibis."

Hearing fire engines, she began "praying that Main House has gone up in smoke," eager to "get out of this place" and "live in luxury and sin." After throwing water over stairs to hit a housemother, she was put "on bounds," prohibited from having visitors for two consecutive weekends. "Damn, damn, damn," she moaned to a friend. When she couldn't stand class, she'd fake illness to get into the infirmary:

"I stuck hot water in my mouth and my temperature went up to 104 degrees after it had been normal for days—and they were furious and took it ten times in a row and told Mr. J and they kicked me out. Now tonight I'm planning to get pneumonia—take a hot bath and stand in front of the open window and go to bed wet—and if they don't let me home then I'll swallow iodine."

When she was able to escape campus and wasn't with her father in New York, Jackie was often at Strawberry Hill, the nearby Farmington, Connecticut, estate owned by Wilmarth Sheldon Lewis—or "Uncle Lefty," as the family nicknamed him—and his wife, Annie, who was Unk's sister. Uncle Lefty was a distinguished literary scholar and author, and his home had a massive library of rare books. Under Uncle Lefty's tutelage, Jackie spent weekends reading through his collection, first grasping how the underpinnings of American democracy as espoused by Franklin and Jefferson were rooted in the philosophies of French Enlightenment writers Voltaire, Rousseau, and Diderot.

Despite her behavior, Jackie would emerge from Miss Porter's with such passion for the world of words that she won an award in literature upon graduating. She especially credited her "hard taskmaster" of a literature teacher for introducing her to "Word Wealth," a process of "drilling and discipline" to expand her vocabulary: "It gave me such an appreciation of good writing and helped me to write."

As he watched her grow up, Black Jack increasingly focused on her looks. He taught her to be "individualistic" like him, encouraging her to wear a single unusual piece of jewelry or a trademark piece of clothing on a regular basis. He also encouraged her to stand out—and stand out she did. At Vassar, for example, she was remembered for striding into the dining hall wearing a full riding costume of black boots and tan jodhpurs. She copied his skin tone. "I've a blazing sunburn and it's killing me," she wrote Yusha, "but I wouldn't give it up for the world." After informing him she was getting a "poodle cut" coiffure, her father was anxious for hours until she appeared, still beautiful to him. When Jackie seemed not to take her father's counsel as seriously as he did, Black Jack would become enraged. On one occasion, while she and his girlfriend Sally Butler were dressing for a formal event, Jackie asked whether she should wear a pearl necklace or a gold chain that Daddy had given her as a symbol of their bond. Butler suggested the pearls, which Jackie put on. In a sudden display of anger, he pulled and broke the necklace on her neck, screaming at her until she put on his chain.

He also began advising her on handling men, writing to her, "I never wanted you to be a prig at any time, but to be able to put guys . . . in their place is always the thing for a girl to do. Therefore, you will definitely have to 'take the offensive' . . . I'd start off as follows, saying . . . while you are still not accustomed to answering letters from boys you don't know or haven't met . . . you always . . . make a point of answering your fan mail. You might add that they must be good boys and grow big and strong for soon they will be GIs. And then, if they look well . . . you'd wave to them or even write to them if they get sent to some awful camp. Insist on them being good and kind to their mothers, and going to church on Sundays, if only to keep up appearances."

While Black Jack had little compunction about describing his sexual conquests with mostly married or divorced women, he lectured his daughter about "not giving in," warning her that "a woman can have wealth and beauty and brains, but without a reputation she has nothing." His advice continued while she was in Europe. He tacitly acknowledged that she might eventually give in if she found one man that she felt especially romantic about but told her to at least play "hard to get." Men like him, he added, "lost respect" for women easily seduced.

Jackie clearly followed his advice, as reflected in Yusha's report on the string of suitors that she lured during the holiday dances but kept at a distance, one boy after another falling hard, the lot of them inevitably disappointed. One described her as "the hardest girl to contact in the U.S.A."

Once divorced, Jack felt free to integrate his lovers into his life. His first and most passionate relationship was with Englishwoman Ann Plugge, from 1942 to 1943. Settled in New York by her wealthy husband, a British military officer, away from the Nazi air raids on London, she had a love for Black Jack that was very much noticed by the young Bouviers. Jack Davis "used to watch them excitedly as they necked on the beach," and once found them "in a wild embrace on the slatted floor of the men's shower room in the Bouvier cabana."

London native Sylvia Hawkes, a model, dancer, and actress, became Lady Ashley after marrying British lord Anthony Ashley-Cooper, the first of her five husbands. After the war, but sometime before her third marriage ended, in 1948, she began a blazing affair with Black Jack. "He carried on something terrible with Lady Ashley," recalled Jackie's friend Martha Buck of those East Hampton summers. "Right in the open. We would look over and they were doing things on the ground."

In 1948, at fifty-seven years old, Black Jack had begun one of his most enduring relationships, with airline stewardess Sally Butler, who, at nineteen, was Jackie's age. She was, he told Jackie, more fun than "those old bags in Newport." Father and daughter both considered it "ignorant and petty" to end a relationship because of an age gap, according to Kathy Bouvier, Jackie's cousin Miche's wife. Her father's example of a romantic life free from conventional judgment also gave Jackie the confidence to pursue those who most fascinated her. When Black Jack voiced disapproval of nineteen-year-old Jackie's going out several times with Russian émigré Serge Obolensky during the summer of 1948, Jackie pointed out that their thirty-nine-year age difference was the same as his and Sally's.

Come college, Jackie's visits would follow a standard routine. She would arrive by train from Poughkeepsie on Friday ("in the day coach, smoking when the conductor wasn't looking"). At Daddy's two-bedroom

Upper East Side rental apartment, where she went to change clothes, every available flat surface, or open wall space, was covered with portraits of her in single or triptych silver photo frames—as if it were the home of an obsessed fan. She would then head out to clubs like Maisonette at the St. Regis Hotel, joining a large table of friends and taking in a cabaret performance, then meet more friends at nightclubs like LaRue, often getting back to Daddy's after three in the morning.

Saturdays were devoted to Black Jack. Sometimes they went to New Haven for a Yale football game. Usually she spent the evening alone with him, but on one occasion she joined friends at two "horrible little dives," the Downbeat and the Three Deuces. In her privileged bubble, she admitted she was "petrified" to find herself one of the "only white people there, but there was this wonderful saxophone player who was really good."

One treat both enjoyed with particular glee was dressing up for a night out at one of New York's café society haunts such as El Morocco, Stork Club, or Latin Quarter, especially when there was an orchestra. Black Jack even critiqued her dancing agility, saying that while she was "just the right height as a partner for me . . . you are a bit stiff in spots, but you will be much better if you just relax."

On Sunday mornings, she liked to sleep in and then see a movie with her father, after which he treated her to "Weekend at the Waldorf" for a champagne lunch and late-afternoon dancing. Dressed up, they would promenade the East Side streets back up to his apartment. On Monday mornings, after her father left for his office, she would call her mother, do some department store shopping, and catch an afternoon train back to Poughkeepsie.

However selfish he could be, Jack Bouvier was strenuously thoughtful about those who lacked his privilege. "Every cab driver or doorman or waiter, Jack spoke to them with warmth, as an equal," Kathy Bouvier recalled. "It wasn't to charm or get something, it was simple respect." He emphasized to Jackie that "empathy, generosity, kindness are the most important values."

On the polished dance floors, observers might mistake the older man and the young woman he was holding during a rhumba or foxtrot for a couple. Jack Davis concluded that his uncle's physical closeness to his cousin was a display "more common in Latin countries . . . in Rome,

Marseilles, and Madrid it is not unusual to see fathers and daughters promenading the boulevards arm-in-arm like lovers . . . the relationship clearly had a special tone to it, a warmth, and even a passion." Her cousin, however, made clear that the relationship never crossed a line into "any overt expression of sexuality." Still, Jackie had some discomfort about how others would perceive their intimacy, later asking that one of his letters to her not be published because "it sounds incestuous."

There was no question that Black Jack came to emotionally depend on his daughter as one might a spouse. "Dearest," he wrote her in July 1945, "a letter from you always has a good effect on me—sort of bolsters my morale, which is a hell of a big compliment to pay a young daughter who is just about sixteen." When he was unable to get her Valentine's Day flowers one year, he even tried to please her with his lame verse: "Yours arrived and were divine, 'Tis a shame I couldn't send mine." (He added, "You Jackie must have laughed because, as it was one of my few attempts at poetry, it must have been rather poor reading.")

As Vassar classmate Harriet de Rossiere recalled, Jackie "absolutely worshipped her father." Just as he did with her photos at home, she did likewise in her dormitory rooms. She displayed a large, silver-framed image of him in his Jazz Age prime, in golf knickers and handsome profile. Her most cherished image was one of him holding her hand at a horse show. She saved every letter he wrote her, "even the most vulnerable ones," when "he was very lonely," and would later create a scrapbook of them demonstrating "how much I loved him."

If her father seemed to love her too much and her mother not enough, the time had come for her to break from the emotional machinations of both of them, even if it meant fleeing the country. Jackie was on the verge of becoming an adult, and yet her parents both still battled to control her, as if she were disputed territory.

It wasn't only to learn French that Jackie Bouvier had to go to France; she had to go to learn about herself.

Part II

EUROPE

The only thing that breaks the monotony is breaking rules.

—JACKIE TO HER STEPBROTHER YUSHA

3

A NEW LANGUAGE

August–October 1949

Considered a proud symbol of postwar France, SS *De Grasse* was dubbed "the only queen of the Atlantic." Built in the 1920s, it had once carried Hitler's bulletproof Mercedes, was sunk by the Germans during World War II, and was then restored. Jackie Bouvier spent her nine days at sea in a cabin-class room she shared with Mary Ann Freedman, who, along with Mary Snyder and Hester Curtis, had posed with her on the *De Grasse* deck. From families in which higher education was valued, her fellow students were never in the running for "Deb of the Year," a society columnist's title bestowed on Miss Bouvier two years earlier, a fact which made the others highly conscious of her status. Yet Jackie stood out more for not having attended Smith, which was considered far more rigorous than Vassar. Beneath these superficial differences, however, she was among her tribe. All the young women had the intellectual wherewithal to defy the societal expectation that they prioritize marriage over education.

Intended to train students for careers as language teachers, Smith's Paris program required a written pledge that the students would write and speak only in French. Studying at the Sorbonne wasn't some idle-rich-girl amusement—it was a serious academic commitment.

The *De Grasse* docked in Le Havre, France, on Saturday, September 3, 1949. As the suitcases and trunks of the students were transported to the bus depot at the Gare de Lyon in Paris, she made her way to the Latin Quarter, heading to the Sorbonne's Reid Hall.

A former eighteenth-century porcelain factory where President James Monroe's eagle-motif White House state china had been made, by 1949 Reid Hall was an academic and social center for Americans studying at the Sorbonne. Walking down Rue de Chevreuse, which she remembered as a "dingy little alley," Jackie found the building both "beautiful" and "shabby." Waiting outside, she first met Claude de Renty, the daughter of her host mother, and started "a friendship that never ended," as Claude put it.

Four months younger than Jackie, Claude had studied at Mount Holyoke College and spoke flawless English. "When she arrived, she spoke fairly good French," Claude remembered. "I took her to have a drink in the Latin Quarter, on the Boulevard Saint-Michel, then we walked around the Sorbonne, just to give her the feeling." As Jackie would later recall of their first brief hours together, "we were full of interest in the world, waiting to discover it and our lives."

Jackie soon dashed over to the depot for the three-hour bus ride to Grenoble. As she was sitting "way in back," with luggage precariously secured above her, a porter stopped the vehicle as it started to pull away and "leapt on the bus and came running down the aisle," having noticed her name on her luggage, calling out "Jacqueline!" Shaking her hand just because she had the same name as his daughter, he told her to come back and see him, wishing her au revoir. The small gesture left her glowing. "To start off in a country with something friendly and gay like that," she wrote, "made me fall in love with it."

Credited with being the cradle of the French Revolution, medieval Grenoble is surrounded on three sides by the French Alps. An eighteenth-century glove-making industry had brought it prosperity. The city was legendary for resisting the Third Reich and its Vichy proxy, with demonstrations against French collaboration with the Nazis and a Resistance network providing protection for French Jews. Even the University of Grenoble, where Jackie would study, had altered documents to prevent young people from being sent to German labor camps.

In Grenoble, Jackie boarded with the Des Francs family. "[T]hey just grow on you so," she reported. "They get nicer every day and open up to us and treat us like members of the family. We all laugh hysterically through meals and the mother is so good-natured." (She pointed out to Mummy, obsessed as she was with distinguished lineage, that "[t]hey are of the old aristocracy and hard up now and have to take in students.")

Jackie's gift for language was evident even in her childhood, when she began learning German by mimicking words and phrases she overheard spoken by her nanny. Following that pattern, she had first learned rudimentary French from the language games of a governess. She wrote from Grenoble that "I have an absolute mania now about learning to speak French perfectly." In a chilly country manor house with primitive plumbing run by the university, she began intensive language lessons with a phonetics instructor who pretentiously trained students with recitations from *Madame Bovary*. She reported her progress to Mummy:

"Last night I went to Mary Ann Freedman's pension . . . and this French girl & her brother were there . . . & this terribly nice boy from Nimes—Marc. They helped us with our comps. I wrote mine first in halting French & Marc did it all over. It really was very hard and they all took it so seriously & searched for words so hard and it was really so nice of them as you know no American boy would be that nice & take all that trouble with some dumb foreigners who couldn't do their homework.

"I am getting fairly good marks but the language isn't coming as fast as I hoped. I think half the reason is that I speak English with [my classmates] Merv & Judith . . . when we've something desperately important to say. . . . Going out with French boys is really the best thing Mummy! I just talk my head off & feel that I've made so much progress when the evenings are over."

In a new world, on her own, Jacqueline Bouvier finally had the distance to think. Even when she'd sat silently or looked away, Mummy had demanded to know "what are you thinking." If she got no satisfactory answer, she snapped about her daughter "escaping into that wild imagination." During her time in France, both parents still sought to dictate her life, even remotely by airmail letters. In none of her responses did she express a longing for home—or them.

With peace to think, she began composing vivid travelogues in her letters home, like one she wrote after exploring a nearby mountain range:

"I just can't tell you what it is like to come down from the mountains of Grenoble to this flat, blazing plain where seven-eighths of all you see is hot blue sky—and there are rows of poplars at the edge of every field to protect the crops from the mistral and spiky short palm trees with blazing red flowers growing at their feet. The people here speak with the lovely twang of the 'accent du Midi.' They are always happy as they live in the sun and love to laugh. It was heartbreaking to only get such a short glimpse of it all—I want to go back and soak it all up."

To Black Jack, she reported on side trips with fellow students to Valence, Nimes, and Arles, along the Rhone River. There was no mention, however, of Pont Saint-Esprit, just over one hundred miles south. It was familiar to her and her father as the Bouvier ancestral village, from which they'd emigrated. Whether or not she already knew that Grampy Bouvier had fabricated the royal genealogy he claimed as their birthright in his self-published book *Our Forebears*, she later confirmed that she never visited the village. Higher on her wish list was an area that she had only heard about, but already so vividly imagined in a letter to her mother:

"The part I want to see is La Camargue—a land in the Rhone delta which is flooded by the sea every year and they have a ceremony where they all wade in on horses and bless it—La Benediction de la Mer—gypsies live there and bands of little Arab horses and they raise wild bulls."

Just outside Grenoble was the village of Sassenage. After walking in its underground rivers (which had carved their channels through the cave), Jackie took tea with unconventional artist Henriette Gröll, a "most wonderful cuckoo woman," who had "children descending on you out of trees." The artist also lived in Paris and invited Jackie to her salons of creative professionals, promising "she would draw me." That night, singing and dancing in a "little restaurant under rustling trees by a brook with a waterfall," she noted the reach of postwar American pop culture, quipping that "the magic [was] broken only by two 'pieces de resistance,' the songs 'Bongo, Bongo, Bongo' and 'Chattanooga Choo Choo.'" Missing the final tram to Grenoble, she and her fellow students had to walk the five miles back.

Putting her camera to use, Jackie took photos of her friends smiling in class and laughing on a balcony, and her window view of a mundane piazza and outbuildings, which she sent to Mummy, providing black-and-white evidence of her steady, earnest routine. But while her letters and photos misleadingly suggested she led a strictly wholesome life filled with many studious hours invested in French translations, as had always been the case with Jackie and school, she bored easily. "The only thing that breaks the monotony is breaking rules," she had written Yusha from boarding school. Yet if she was a secret bad girl, she was careful to always be a *good* bad girl, using pursuit of high culture as a worthy excuse to go have fun. As a ten-day break at the end of September approached, Jackie wrote her father that she wanted to explore Italy alone, arguing that she could uniquely learn some Italian by using her French on Corsica, where an Italian idiomatic French was spoken, and see the birthplace of Napoleon and Joseph Bonaparte, both figures in her grandfather's family mythology. He ignored her lofty intentions to instead warn her that Corsica was "quite a rough place" and not to overtly flirt with Italians, who would act on any encouragement, concluding that "no one knows the low-down on life and the sexes better than I do."

Jackie ended up following her father's advice to visit the Amalfi Coast instead, where she was enchanted by the pastel-colored villas built into the rocky shore with a dramatic overview of the Mediterranean. She next headed twenty-seven miles north, passing Pompei without stopping, to Naples, then caught a ferry to visit the island of Capri, which was "heaven on earth," she wrote Yusha, where "everything is so tiny you feel you're in toyland and a blaze of colors and women and queer men walking the streets with beautiful birds on their shoulders." Swimming in the famous Blue Grotto was "too good to be true." In letters home, she casually mentioned "Florence" as her last stop.

A year after her trip to Italy, she wrote a story for her English composition class at George Washington University that, in the first person, hinted of a more intimate encounter during her visit to Florence. She called the young man "Monty," with the only clue offered to his identity being that he had one American parent and an Italian one. At one point she wrote:

"Teach me something to say in Italian, Monty," I said as we walked toward the river.

He wiped the juice from his face with the back of his hand. "What do you want to say?"

"Something different. Not 'thank you' or 'good morning,' but something really Italian."

"I'll tell you what you can say," he told me. "Como belle fare l'amore en el piazzio." It's a proverb which means "how beautiful it is to make love in the rain."

I said it slowly. "Como belle fare l'amore en el piazzio." And then faster. What a lovely Italian thought! I didn't think it would be very beautiful to make love in the rain, but it was so pretty to say so. (While her intention was to reference rain, "*piazzio*" actually means "place" in Corsican.)

If in fact a romantic interlude had occurred, she offered no hint about it to either parent.

By now, Janet had let her darkest fears take hold, demanding that Jackie send detailed reports about her European activities. "I have to write Mummy a ream each week," Jackie reported in her next letter to Yusha, "or she gets hysterical and thinks I'm dead or married to an Italian." As her sister, Lee, would later note, Mummy was especially suspicious of Mediterranean men. Not without reason did some of Jackie's confessional letters to Yusha warn him: "[D]on't tell Mummy." The only thing remotely scandalous she did, she told her mother, was drinking wine, "because they don't have Coca Cola here." She assured her that she and her school friends never "behaved like bobbysoxers gone wild," further affirming, "I haven't done one thing that I am ashamed of."

JACKIE'S SIX WEEKS OF intensive linguistic study in Grenoble would impact her beyond learning French. As later studies would suggest, adults who master a second language enlarge their capacity to grasp several subjects simultaneously, allowing them to better think, translate, and interpret not only languages but situations, a skill on which her fate would turn.

Trunks packed, Jackie, in her simple traveling uniform of a white blouse and a red cotton dress with a wide hem, joined her fellow students on the regional train to Paris, occupying a third-class car. Student Martha Rusk's presumption that a Deb of the Year expected first-class accommodations was mistaken. As Jackie would write Yusha, "It's so much more fun traveling second and third class and sitting up all night in trains, as you really get to know people and hear their stories." Experience had already taught her that wealth was no barometer of intellect. Writing Mummy about two French students who were "much poorer than anyone at home," she found them "twice as well educated as anyone I have ever met—with beautiful manners."

Which was not to say she was unprepared for the shady characters she'd likely encounter in third class. In Alice Kaplan's account of Bouvier's year in Paris, Rusk recalled how Jackie kept handy a hatpin to use on men who tried to grab her in the dark. Personal space was not the only commodity to be guarded on such trips: passengers knew better than to let any expensive jewelry draw attention, and important items (wallet, keys, passport—or Leica) would be kept on their person or constantly within sight.

As she stepped from the train to enter Paris's Gare de Lyon station, she would have been met by a clamorous din, railroad engines and loudspeaker announcements echoing off the glass-enclosed train shed, while thousands of passengers, not only from southern and eastern France but from Switzerland, Italy, and Germany, too, swarmed one of Europe's busiest rail hubs. If she had stopped at the station's famous brasserie, she would have gazed upon its forty-one frescoes, which romantically depict France's cities and regions. Trailed by a bellman conveying her trunks, Jackie proceeded outdoors to the taxi line, the station's iconic bell tower, faintly reminiscent of London's Big Ben, looming behind her. And Jackie was poised to capture Paris. If she was unlikely to be wearing jewelry when she arrived, around her neck she more certainly would have slung her little Leica.

4

PARIS

October–November 1949

Through a circuitous web of upper-class connections, Jackie had found housing with the widowed countess Germaine de Renty, who had a four-bedroom apartment on the Avenue Mozart. The countess had her own room, renting a second to two American students, while her daughters, Claude and Ghislaine, lived in a third with the latter's young son. Countess de Renty leased the largest one to Jackie.

It was her own piece of Paris, a room of "dark pink walls, green woodwork, a sort of Dubonnet curtains and dark brown wood furniture," she described it to a family friend. "I feel exactly as if I'm in my own home," she wrote Yusha. "I have a deliciously comfortable room with the double bed that makes yours at Newport look like an ironing board."

The sun fell rapidly in the October afternoons when she first took occupancy, and the room was frigid due to a postwar coal shortage. She did her studying under blankets, "swaddled" in "scarf, mittens, sweater and ear muffs," the bedspread strewn with textbooks, graph-paper notebooks, airmail paper for her letters home, and a range of sweets from nearby patisseries. Despite the cold, now and then she couldn't help but dash out of bed, grab her Leica, and snap photographs from her window. When she couldn't capture an image with her camera, she did it with her pen, crafting letters as narrative episodes from her adventures as the American College Girl in Paris.

Into the wee hours, Jackie incessantly wrote. Considering that she did not revise her drafts, her descriptions could be startlingly polished. The sea had "water sparkling like bits of broken glass in the sun" and the view from her room was "always gray with a thick mist that hides the end of the street and the buildings with spiky roofs and steeples of grillwork stand out against the sky about twilight, when it gets clearer and you watch the smoke from the chimneys all blowing in the same direction."

Sometimes upward of six pages long, her letters to Yusha were the most personal. "You just have to get used to 'emotional letters'—I can't stop it," she admitted in one. "I'll just splurge on this first letter and all the others will be very correct and controlled and I'll discuss the weather and Post-War Plans." She expected him to reciprocate: "*Ecrives—or je vous killerai.*" ("Write—or I will kill you" in her own version of French.)

Her increasingly precise writing was likely the result of her ongoing effort to grasp the nuance of written and spoken phrases of a foreign language. Every aspect of life with the de Rentys was French. "We never speak a word of English in this apartment," she reported home. The rooms were furnished with French antiques, and the French cuisine prepared by the widowed countess was served on French porcelain.

Her life was initially limited to the apartment and the Sorbonne, together a "lovely quiet gray rainy world." She told Yusha, "I had every intention of hurling myself into the fray and emerging triumphantly laden with culture and arrived loaded down with pencils & books and two pairs of glasses!" There were so many religious and civic holidays, however, that her class schedule was irregular. Additionally, she found her course load to be "ridiculously vague." It consisted of eighteenth- and nineteenth-century English, French, and German comparative literature, in conjunction with a history class covering the Napoleonic era to World War I, but since it wove together religious, political, and social movements, Jackie admitted she was "terrified" because it was "so complicated." She described her aesthetics professor as a "psychoanalyst theorist of artistic creation," and he likely contributed to her emerging ability to envision and execute a refined sense of personal style.

Surprisingly for someone who had traveled in such elevated circles, a twentieth-century art class was Jackie's first known exposure to modern art. Her lifelong passion for painting was born at the École du Louvre, a class conducted at the museum by its curator of Impressionism. (Joking that "I can almost tell painting from sculpture!" she chose a landscape by Jean-Baptiste-Camille Corot to analyze for one assignment.) Though she worked to coordinate her eye and hand to achieve more realistic proportions in her own drawings (after a three-hour sketching class her sophomore year, she had concluded that drawing "nude women and men in bathing suits . . . couldn't be duller as nothing I ever draw looks like a human being"), she focused primarily on landscapes she encountered on her strolls along the Seine, where she first began painting in watercolors, attempting to copy the Impressionist style of Monet, Degas, and Manet.

In Reid Hall's large "Grande Salle" space, Bouvier was expected to attend symposiums about "our strikes, our political imbroglios, new architectural trends, etc.," overseen by foreign-student program director Jeanne Saleil, who organized social events to encourage students to absorb authentic Parisian life. Saleil told one of Jackie's classmates that she "is so brilliant, she could be a stellar academic, but she hasn't thrown herself into the intellectual life." In truth, the symposium bored her. (She described it as that "dreary thing at Reid Hall we have to go to.") Just as she had at Vassar, she preferred learning outside of school.

Claude recalled that "my mother took her to visit most of the museums in Paris, the Marais district, the Carrousel du Louvre and the Palais-Royal gardens." Doing this, she observed, Jackie "discovered French culture, and acquired knowledge of what makes France attractive and its history and deep-rooted respect for artists and intellectuals."

During their hours together, the countess never told Jackie about her experiences during World War II. Jackie knew the facts, likely through the family that connected them, but never let on. Germaine de Renty and her husband, Guyot, active in the French Resistance following the June 1940 Third Reich invasion of France, were discovered and sent to Nazi labor camps. Guyot did not survive. The countess was sent to Ravensbrück in northern Germany, where she befriended spy Jeannie Rousseau and Communist Marinette Curateau. After they together refused to do work for the Nazis, the trio was sent to the harsher labor camp Königsberg, forced to haul rocks in subzero temperatures until the end of the war. Jackie faintly hinted at it in a letter home, saying the countess "stands for so many things," and how she was awed by her "courage." As Claude recalled, "Jacqueline knew what had happened to my parents, but did not ask any questions. At that time, nobody talked about it."

Long accustomed to sublimating the unpleasant and emphasizing fun activities, Jackie offered Yusha a glimpse of her Paris days of November 1949: going riding with Claude, taking Claude's nephew to the candy store, lunching with Francis de Boury, "a Swiss boy I knew in New York," dining with Newport friend Peter Vought, and attending a performance of Giraudoux's *Ondine*. She was especially excited by the variety of inexpensive live performances, telling him how "all the theaters and operas and ballets . . . you could go out every night all winter and still not have seen everything that's playing."

"We were meeting friends and going around everywhere," recalled Claude. "The attitude was that we should enjoy life. We had gone through troubled times. Go to big parties, go out, have fun. We did that, with Jackie." Claude's diary revealed that they enjoyed an American Thanksgiving, private dinners, René Clair movies, and theatrical productions, and met for lunch between classes at small Latin Quarter restaurants.

Jackie could also slip on a fur coat "being swanky at the Ritz bar" or dine at the exclusive Restaurant Ledoyen with the young aristocratic French society crowd. Jackie wrote Yusha that "all the boys I meet through Claude are very proper and call you Mademoiselle and have squeaking shoes and seem much too stuffy. They are very conscious of how you act if you come from a good family . . . and I go out with them quite a lot and they show me all their little hidden nightclubs and places in Paris you'd never see if you didn't go with a Frenchman."

It was during some of these nocturnal forays that she was exposed to a new type of music, a form of jazz that the French had made their own. Europe's first jazz festival was hosted in Paris the year she arrived, and the club scene was exploding. Claude recalled going with her to Club St. Germain on Rue St. Benoit and the Rose Rouge on Rue de la Harpe, joining her Newport friend George Plimpton, a writer then involved in the planning stage of the literary magazine *The Paris Review* with a group of American friends. She remembered Plimpton, "pale, in a black turtleneck in an airless hole of a night club on the Boulevard Raspail," where "the blue notes of saxophones through smoke-filled haze ushered in the dawns for you, and how you would walk the gray Paris streets in the first light back to a strange bed." Despite depicting herself as virtuous and naïve while in Paris, Jacqueline Bouvier was certainly no nun.

Not every door opened for her. Lacking the necessary degree of wealth to buy the haute couture that had returned to the postwar Paris fashion houses, she began to more often dress in black, which allowed her to give a nod toward chic while being practical at the same time, necessary given her limited wardrobe. It wasn't the little black dress she wore, however, which led to Jacqueline Bouvier's failed attempt to slip into a fashion show. It was her camera.

As she later related to her friend, journalist Gloria Emerson, Jackie showed up in a black dress and simply expected to walk into the seated, invitation-only event. Those in charge knew the reporters assigned to cover it, but even had she been able to talk her way in, Jackie marked herself as an amateur by wearing her Leica around her neck and tucking a large sketch pad under her arm—photographs and drawings were expressly forbidden. Being denied entry, Gloria recalled, "so humiliated" Jackie that she told nobody at the time, paranoid that news of the incident would somehow reach Mummy, and suggest that she was playing too much.

As her first term at the Sorbonne was coming to an end, she reported excitedly to Yusha, "I'm starting to meet lots more people and this term is going to be even better than last." Now settled confidently in Paris, she juggled multiple beaux.

Among these were an up-and-coming writer; an assistant to Prime Minister Georges Bidault; a diplomat's son; and Paul de Ganay, a man from a notable aristocratic family. A significant Paris beau was American writer John Marquand, one of Plimpton's "brilliant and romantic" friends and son of a Pulitzer Prize–winning author.

Gore Vidal would claim that Jackie "lost her virginity" to Marquand "in a lift that he had stalled in a pension on Paris's Left Bank," even though Marquand stated that this was untrue. Vidal's further assertion that they were considering marriage, however, contradicts everything Jackie had said about love at that point in her life "when everything was beginning." Jackie Bouvier's intention wasn't to be a writer's girlfriend; rather, she shared the ambitions of the male writers "that our lives would not be mundane."

"Mostly the boys I knew were beetle-browed intellectual types who'd discuss very serious things with me," she said. "Nothing romantic at all." She was particularly put off by one of them back home, an American who rambled on about the French Nazi collaborationist Marshal Pétain without considering that she'd followed the news story of his commutation and formed an educated opinion. "I tried to look intelligent and nod at the right intervals," she recalled. "I'm no authority on anything, but he sounded like a little boy who's just read a big book and is . . . expounding it all . . . without really knowing what it was all about. I wanted to give him a big maternal kiss . . . and tell him he was really a big boy now!"

IN THE PERIOD PRECEDING her time in Paris, she and Yusha had debated their views on dating and love. He was troubled by her simultaneous beaux: "As far as I can see you're still in the state of mind where you just can't find the right boy yet and you're getting desperate and enjoy them all, but just take it easy." Jackie defended her habitual dating: "Just because I may write to a boy and go out with him doesn't mean I'm in love with him . . . I don't expect to be desperately in love now and it's alright to like a lot of people—so don't think that any boy I mention in a letter to you is my grand passion."

"I did love going to all the dances," Jackie said of the Newport social scene, where the frothy music of the Lester Lanin Band and the Meyer Davis Band set the mood for her 1940s summers there, as she did the rhumba or led a conga line. There, too, however, were hints of her boredom with the young men interested in her. "I had a feeling she was looking over my shoulder to see who her next dance partner would be," recalled one among many potential beaux on the parquet.

She admitted as much: "When I was about nineteen, I knew I didn't want the rest of my life to be there. I didn't want to marry any of the young men I grew up with—not because of them but because of their life."

For her debutante tea, she bought her plain white dress off the rack at a department store. After being dubbed "Deb of the Year" four months later, she became a familiar presence at Social Register dances, dinners, luncheons, and teas. She demonstrated noblesse oblige by joining the effort supporting the Free Milk for Babies Fund charity, selling tickets to benefit performances of *Lucia di Lammermoor* and a Verdi Festival at the

Metropolitan Opera, fundraising for the Madison Square Boys' Club, and posing for a November 1947 *New York Times* publicity photo. Inwardly, she found it stultifying. "I wanted terribly to do the Virginia reel in the middle of the Plaza ballroom," she quipped after a winter dance.

Still, with her Deb of the Year status and education at Miss Porter's, Vassar, and the Sorbonne, Jacqueline Bouvier already had a public profile that marked her as a member of the elite. Calling two estates home was the crowning touch, and that was all due to Unk.

In another letter to Yusha, she urged him to avoid becoming enamored with any one girl, providing insight into her own perception of commitment:

"You shouldn't fall in love more than once or twice in your whole life—and don't ever try to make yourself, for then it won't ever be real. Someday, it will just happen—and be wonderful for both of you. What you should really do is write to several girls and in the summer take out several and rush several at dances or "play the field" to see what they're all like and try not to get too involved with any of them—for you always make it seem like love in your own mind when it really isn't. And after each of those great romances you are left sort of shattered and unsure . . .

"If you are going to fall in love you will just fall—maybe in a minute standing by her at the Snack Bar, or maybe after a long time you'll suddenly realize you love her . . . please don't try to make yourself fall in love with anyone . . . it's so wrong."

And what was right? If her time away was giving her a sense of what type of partner she knew she wouldn't want, some sense of her ideal husband was forming.

"I want to marry a man with imagination," she told her sister. "And that's not easy to find."

5

THE "TERRIFIC" VACATION

November 1949–January 1950

For the first time in her life, Jackie was free to socialize with anyone she liked regardless of their status, go where she wished, do what she wished, and, most importantly, pursue her deepest intellectual curiosities. Now Jackie Bouvier could indulge her desire to explore. She started with the second-largest public park in Paris, the Bois de Boulogne.

Twice as big as Central Park, "le Bois" offered Jackie plenty to discover: lakes, greenhouses, an amusement park, a zoo, a tennis stadium, and racetracks. What had most excited her, however, was discovering that there were stables where she could rent a horse. As the sun began setting early, trotting off into the park's wooded trails with her unnamed beau, the prime minister's aide, was a good way to stay warm as winter neared.

Whether or not her parents detected that Jackie was dating many young men, both seemed increasingly uneasy with what they did know about her life overseas. In late November, when she casually reported her rides through the Bois de Boulogne to Black Jack, he dashed off an angry retort that she had broken her promise not to ride again until she had returned home. At that moment, he went on, the bill from Smith College for her studies abroad was on his desk and he'd nearly shredded it in rage. Her father threatened to stop underwriting her life in Paris if he learned that she'd gone riding again.

Mummy, on the other hand, was paranoid that Jackie would be brainwashed by the openly Communist influence in postwar France, and feared that she was "about to run off for Mao," Yusha noted archly. "Mummy keeps asking me about my intellectual life!" she wrote Yusha. "What will I say?!"

Her newfound freedom was something she'd never experienced and would be loath to relinquish. In Paris, she came to understand who she was and what she wanted. "Being away from home," she wrote a year later, "gave me a chance to look at myself with a jaundiced eye."

That didn't mean she had begun expressing her every thought. On the contrary. She learned the power of silence and acute observation. To her friend Vivi, now the Countess Crespi, whom she was planning to visit in Rome, she offered what proved to be among the most fundamental of her numerous mantras, perhaps the best clue to who she was at her core. Assessing Vivi's typically rash reaction to uncertainty or unpleasantness, Jackie suggested to her that, in general, it was always wise to "Read, then think. Listen, then think. Watch, then think. Think—then speak."

Those skills of patience and contemplation helped Jackie raise her awareness of the growing Vietnamese resistance to France's colonial control. In one letter, she mentioned a Sunday drive in the countryside "with Claude and two boys she knows, who I met at a dinner she gave for us all." Claude recalled that one of the young men was Jean-François Deniau, a fellow student with Claude at the Sorbonne's political school, Sciences Po. Deniau, who was elegant and witty, and would go on to become a distinguished author and statesman, was then on leave from active duty fighting to help France hold control of its Southeast Asian colony Vietnam. The French were combating especially strong resistance from guerilla forces in the north who, supported by Communist China, were seeking independence. Despite its small size, this country nevertheless represented a large financial interest to France.

Over a half-century later, Claude remembered the dinner, although the details of what Deniau told them about the Indochina War were too casual to recall. Still, it was the first known instance in which Jacqueline Bouvier met someone who held forth about Vietnam.

Journalist Gloria Emerson, who also lived in Paris and became an expert on the human cost of the war in Vietnam, recounted a brief but stark episode that Jackie shared with her years later. Down a narrow street, Jackie glimpsed two Vietnamese restaurant workers hauling trash to the sidewalk. "All of a sudden," Gloria reported that Jackie told her, "one guy pulls out a corkscrew and begins jabbing a tire of a parked car with some official insignia identifying it, puncturing it. She couldn't believe her eyes! She feared they'd seen her and didn't know what to do but when a policeman [later] passed her at a nearby corner, she decided not to say anything. Why she chose to stay silent she never said. I teased her. 'You were a subversive deb!'"

If being a Catholic in a Catholic nation gave Jackie a sense of inclusion, she resented the presumptions the French made about her as an American. "I was galled at the patronizing attitude towards America," she later emphatically wrote, "annoyed by the complaint 'but no one would think you were American' if one showed a knowledge of literature or history."

Americans in Paris might have been proud that Eartha Kitt and Josephine Baker were the toast of the nightclub scene, but both Black women were there because racism prevented their performing in clubs and theaters back home, a fact Jackie later recognized.

When she learned that fellow student Martha Rusk planned to travel to Bavaria during the holiday break, she asked to join her, after which she would make an overnight visit to Vivi in Rome. Before Christmas, she went to England, where she visited Anne Plugge, her father's East Hampton wartime mistress, now married and living in London. Based on her January 6, 1950, report to her father about the visit, Jackie was curious to see Anne's twins, believing a later disproven claim that she was their half sister, Black Jack never having refuted it.

In a letter to Yusha, she recorded details of her first Christmas Eve in Paris. After placing her shoes out for "Père Noël," she went to midnight Mass at the Invalides, attended by "old soldiers with their medals, some crippled in wheelchairs," the walls hung with tattered Napoleonic battle flags, music played on hunting horns by men in riding coats and hats. She then attended a *réveillon*, where "you dance and drink wine—but never sing a Christmas carol." After it ended at seven in the morning, Jackie returned to the de Renty apartment "feeling more energetic than I have all winter," and finding her shoes stuffed with a gift of seven handkerchiefs, "one for each day of the week!" By nightfall, she was on a train speeding to Vienna, "with my nose to the window watching Germany go by." Of course, she brought along her Leica. Weeks earlier, Jackie had seen the film *The Third Man*, a contemporary spy story set in postwar Vienna, which fired her imagination. After the war, the former Nazi stronghold had been divided into four zones, each controlled by military police from the various Allies: France, England, the United States—and the Soviet Union. In central Vienna, where police from all four nations roamed, the Soviet ones developed a reputation for defying rules. American military policeman Robert Farley recalled how "the Russian drivers had an annoying habit of ignoring stop signs when they came to intersections." In 1946, 90 percent of all Vienna crimes were committed by "men in Soviet uniform," usually drunk. Conduct in their own zone, however, posed dangers beyond ignoring traffic signs and committing petty crimes.

The Soviets patrolled the streets enforcing curfew at gunpoint. If they seized a person for questioning, it could end in violent interrogation, for which there was no recourse. They also did as they wished, committing "systematic sexual violence against women." Once a person walked into the Soviet quadrant, there were no other police to turn to for help. And once in Vienna, curiosity led Jackie Bouvier—and her Leica—right into the Soviet zone.

Her destination was the Palais Epstein. Built in 1871 as a home for the merchant after whom it was named, and known for its lavish interior architecture, it had served as headquarters for the Soviet *Kommandantura* since 1945. Obscuring its baroque exterior were massive red-starred banners depicting Vladimir Lenin and Soviet leader Joseph Stalin. By 1949, it was "a place dreaded by many Viennese," as the Austrian government now describes it, "the starting point of the suffering of many deportees on their road to Siberia."

Soviet police stood on every corner, carrying Thompson submachine guns, a weapon made popular by gangster movies and FBI gumshoes. They weren't intimidating enough to prevent Jackie from raising her Leica and snapping away at the building.

She apparently didn't get many photographs. As she told Yusha, "[T]he Russians with tommy guns in Vienna—they stopped me for taking a picture of their building and tried to get me to come in their hotel for questioning but I wouldn't as I was afraid I'd never get out."

In fact, she didn't reveal the full story to him, vigilantly preventing any chance Mummy would learn the truth. (If she entirely trusted anyone, it was Yusha, but Janet's inquisitions were famously unrelenting.) Not until 1967 did she disclose the truth in writing, to her friend Robert

McNamara, Kennedy's secretary of defense, with whom she maintained a dialogue on the realities of the Cold War. Jackie significantly described the encounter as "the only time I have ever been scared—because they kept us inside three hours."

After a few days in Vienna, Jackie and Martha Rusk stopped in Salzburg, and Berchtesgaden, in southeastern Germany, which Jackie identified as "where Hitler lived," the only remaining structure from his time there being the Mooslahnerkopf teahouse, which he visited daily. (Jackie was one of relatively few tourists to lay eyes on it before it was destroyed, so that no building associated with Hitler endured.)

Rather than learning history through her classes, where the priority was on memorizing facts, she had developed a passion for the subject through art and literature, consuming countless biographies of British, Irish, and French monarchs and their powerful spouses and paramours. She further recognized that it was important to preserve and witness the sites where history had unfolded. From Munich, her last stop before Rome, she and Martha took a ten-mile trolley ride to the medieval town of Dachau, site of the first Nazi concentration camp, where it was estimated that 41,500 people were killed.

The swastika and imperial eagle that had adorned the camp's main gate had been removed, but the facilities of mass murder and cremation were still in place. Some fifteen thousand prisoners were buried there without markers, other than warning signs of infestation and infection to those who got too close to the burial site. Weeks earlier, the new German government had agreed to preserve it as a memorial.

Jackie did not discuss Dachau with Claude when she returned to Paris, but to Vivi in Rome, she defended her visit. As Vivi explained, "She had wanted to see it. She wanted to know. She was so appalled . . . my Italian husband thought . . . 'why would you want to see something like this?' *History*. She wanted to know about these things."

Celebrating New Year's Eve in a Munich nightclub with Jackie and some friends, Martha Rusk felt a stark incongruity between the city's shells of bombed-out buildings and the boisterous beer halls, as if nothing had ever happened there in the past few years. Yusha would maintain that while his stepsister was "appalled and outraged" by the Holocaust, she "always saw the Nazis as distinct from the German people." He pointed out that she was fascinated enough by Germany's first chancellor, Otto von Bismarck (who engineered its 1871 unification), to later visit northern Germany to "touch his grave." That may be what she later wished people to think, but in an early 1950 letter to Yusha, she gave her unvarnished assessment that "the Germans are still Nazis and have secret meetings and just think the Americans are a bunch of suckers sending them dollars."

Europe was more than museums—her trip east, with her three-hour detainment in Vienna, had provided a glimpse into how apocalyptic life could be under a repressive regime. As she told McNamara, she struggled to maintain her composure while being interrogated by the Soviets, who were seeking to determine whether she was on an espionage mission, while she was kept seated, staring at a wall, blank except for a large, menacing photograph of Stalin.

In recalling it all months later to Yusha in person, she flippantly called her experiences at Dachau and Vienna "the most terrific vacation," adding that she'd "really got in there and saw what it is like." Whatever fear she had harbored about being sent to Siberia, however, was nothing compared to the imminent threat coming her way in a month.

"Stalin," Jackie cracked, "doesn't scare me half as much as Mummy does."

6

AUTONOMY

January–June 1950

In the winter of 1950, Jacqueline Bouvier heard her International Relations Since 1870 professor at the Sorbonne's political institute, Pierre Renouvin, make a remark so profound that she "dropped her pencil and just let it roll down the steps" of the staggered class seats: "Once oppressed people have experienced freedom, they can never again be truly controlled."

The subject was French colonialism in Vietnam, but as she repeated the story to Yusha several months later, she believed the remark was true of anyone who experienced a period of autonomy after having been controlled. As her spring term ensued, it was obvious that her own subversive resistance to parental authority was accelerating as she neared legal adulthood.

While admitting she "did not much care" for diplomatic history, her instructor and the setting in which he taught were too compelling to ignore. The amphitheater classroom held a thousand students. Entering in a formal suit and accompanied by an aide, Renouvin proceeded to the front center, drawing attention because he had lost his left arm in World War I, the conflict on which he was a renowned expert. He read his lectures like a monologist, expecting students to memorize every word if they hoped to pass the final exam, the sort of academic challenge Jackie Bouvier had liked since grade school.

Renouvin was speaking about France's current battle to retain its Indochinese colony of Vietnam, against a native foe fighting for sovereignty, led by Ho Chi Minh in the north. Backed by Communist China, this "North Vietminh" army was proving to be formidable against the French army. France had colonized the peninsula in the 1880s, but during World War II Japan invaded and seized control. With their investments—in infrastructure and numerous businesses—in mind, the French regained power after the Japanese were expelled. Among Jackie's readings for class was Renouvin's 1946 book, *The Far East Question, 1840–1940.* In it he made clear that French political leaders considered Indochina a "necessary part of the Republic . . . convinced that French national identity, international grandeur, and economic expansion" depended on maintaining it as part of its empire. But Renouvin believed that while France might technically control the land, it did not control the people.

Just as Jackie began her second term at the Sorbonne, in January 1950, the Soviet Union joined China in support of Ho and the Viet Minh fight for Vietnamese self-rule. France responded by claiming it would commit to a reform of its control of the country, but without giving it independence. In their battle against the Viet Minh, the French were backed financially and militarily by the United States.

Around this time, Jackie was avidly reading the three-volume *The Psychology of Art*, by André Malraux—the final installment was published the year she arrived in France—which may have been the gateway to her blossoming interest in Malraux's political theories. His earlier writings advocated Vietnamese autonomy, but by the late 1940s, when he was minister of cultural affairs, he was unwilling to defy the government. His caution may have been warranted. The year that Jackie arrived in France, Paul Mus, who had been raised in Vietnam and ran the French Colonial Academy in Paris (a school that trained colonial administrators), was fired for disavowing French colonialism—a dismissal that made headlines.

If Renouvin had subtly influenced Jacqueline Bouvier's concepts of a people's right to individual freedom, she already would have grasped the connection between the Vietnamese people and American democracy through studying the writing of Voltaire and Diderot in Uncle Lefty's library; both were Frenchmen who vigorously attacked European control and enslavement of indigenous peoples. (Indeed, when writing about American democracy's founders, her "three geniuses of the eighteenth century" were Jefferson, Franklin, and Diderot. Sometimes she swapped in Voltaire for Diderot.)

Yet she was canny enough to already recognize that while democracy was an ideal form of governing people, the most precious commodity was life itself. While nobody would ever accuse Jackie of being a Communist sympathizer, she would later express empathy with the Vietnamese people, believing that human life was ultimately more important than the form of government they existed under. As she would remark to Gore Vidal in 1961, "Yes, it would be better to be Red than dead, not maybe for oneself, but for the children."

At this point in her young life, however, Jackie responded to global events through the lens of how they emotionally affected her. Five years earlier, when President Franklin Roosevelt suddenly died, she didn't calculate how it might change the fight to end World War II, instead writing to Yusha: "Isn't it awful about the President? I'm so worried about what will happen now that Roosevelt is dead. I think he was really great and I know the only reason I didn't like him was because Daddy was always moaning about what he did to the Stock Exchange. . . . I feel so sorry for Mrs. Roosevelt. It will be awfully hard to leave the White House after all these years!"

Learning that Mummy and Unk had taken Lee to witness the late president's funeral procession through the streets of Washington, Jackie remarked that she "would have given the world to have been there."

IN THE NEW YEAR, Jackie Bouvier had one goal in mind: to never return to Vassar. The reasons seemed both simple and complicated. "I can't figure out what Vassar meant to you," a family friend later remarked to Jackie. It appeared that neither could she.

Jackie wrote Yusha that at the beginning, Vassar was "wonderful," with "so much freedom," and that having to find her own way on campus and keep to a schedule was making her "responsible," which was "very good for me." She enthusiastically joined a theater group, a riding club, and the school newspaper. Just two weeks in, however, she was deflated by student apathy regarding those interests, bemoaning that "hardly anyone else tried out."

If any one incident in her first weeks suddenly upset her, it was when a junior, "troubled for a long time," had "jumped out of the window and committed suicide." It "made me wonder if I'd ever do that." She'd once joked that boarding school was a "prison," and that "if school days are the happiest of your life, I'm hanging myself with my skip-rope tonight." She now considered how unhappy a student would have to be to kill herself. "You hear of people in other places doing that," she continued, "but when it's so near you—there just isn't anything funny about it at all." The trauma of it, she ended, "makes you want to go to church."

Earning As in Shakespeare and history, she helped individual students struggling with those subjects but joined no study, campus, or dormitory committees. As the 1947 Debutante of the Year, she was a campus celebrity who "could be a leader," one instructor remarked, "but never wanted to," making another instructor "cross because she wouldn't expand her potential." Her college friends consistently recalled how she stood out for her intelligence and sophistication but rejected the responsibility of being a leader, hating being a "schoolgirl among schoolgirls." Jackie complained to Vivi that she felt "suffocated" on Vassar's isolated campus, adding, "Once classwork is done, I need stimulation." As 1950 began, Jackie had been reveling in the sophisticated urban life of Paris for four months, and had affirmed her conviction that she belonged in a city.

During prior visits from campus to see her father in New York and now in her letters to him from Paris, she complained about Vassar, but since she had completed nearly half her college education there, he insisted she return that fall to finish it. After making her appearance at the New York Debutante Cotillion and Christmas Ball in December 1947, she had posed with several other debs for a *Life* magazine photo. Although the image was not ultimately published, she had nevertheless earned her first paycheck, prompting her to suggest shortly thereafter that she quit Vassar and try to make a living as a print model. Black Jack objected. When, in early 1950, she raised this idea again, from Paris, he snapped that "you don't waste a college education and a year at the Sorbonne to be a model in New York City—so forget that idea." Now, in a January 10 letter, responding to one she had sent four days earlier affirming her decision to leave Vassar, he hammered his case to her: "You may hate the thought of going back to that damn Vassar as you call it, but perhaps going back as a senior and one who can relate all her travels, you may not find it half as bad as you think." Unable to get his approval, she dropped the matter for the time being.

Black Jack's more immediate concern was the imminent visit to Paris of Janet and Unk (or "dear mama" and "Toot Toot Tootsie," as he sarcastically nicknamed them). He framed his jealousy as concern that they would interrupt her studies, because Janet "thrived on interfering."

Mummy and Unk arrived for their three-week visit in the third week of February, during a long spell of heat and rain. When they saw the elegant but simple apartment where she lived, they were "taken aback," apparently having been expecting luxury lodgings. Jackie made clear how much she loved her Paris residence; she would not relocate. Unk "muttered about the price of everything," and Jackie suggested they travel to see other places in Europe by taking second-class rail. As one biographer put it, "Janet's horror was overcome by Hughdie's enthusiastic endorsement of the idea." Her daughter was obviously provoking her mother; Janet was not accustomed to second-rate accommodations.

Jackie did raise the subject of Vassar. According to Jack Davis, who had access to letters between her and her father, Black Jack promised that if she graduated from Vassar, she could come live with him and work at his Wall Street office. That potential scenario prompted Mummy to offer no resistance to Jackie's decision to leave Vassar. Her support may have been calculated not only to deny Black Jack their daughter's presence but to avoid revealing a deeper secret as well.

A later Vassar dean stated that by entering the Smith program without first obtaining permission from Vassar, she had forfeited her place and that Black Jack had met with the dean while Jackie was in Paris, unsuccessfully insisting that she be permitted to return. It may well be, however, that Jacqueline Bouvier was actually expelled.

In a 1987 interview with biographer C. David Heymann, Edie Beale recalled going on a date with a boyfriend and their being joined by another couple. The woman said she'd gone to Vassar with her cousin and both had been expelled. Edie balked at this: "Jackie kicked out of Vassar, are you crazy?" The former student further explained, "We went away on all these weekends. Finally, they caught up and we were expelled." Students weren't permitted to leave campus without reporting their whereabouts, and when the dean discovered that Jackie and her friend "went with boys," both were asked to leave Vassar. However, the woman continued, "Jackie had so much pull and her mother had married such an important man. . . . Jackie was re-instated."

According to Jack Davis, Jackie had traveled to New Haven for a date with a Yale student, who "purposely kept her with him until after the last bus had gone back to Poughkeepsie." She had to instead take a New Haven train to New York, then a midnight one up to Poughkeepsie, long past Vassar's 11:30 p.m. curfew. Black Jack would have learned of the incident from the dean, not his daughter. He reprimanded Jackie to "[n]ever make a boy think you are easy," and declared that the Yale man was a "bastard."

Several facts give the story veracity. Despite Vassar's rigorous archiving of paperwork on all its previous students, Jacqueline Bouvier's entire record, including "biweekly letters to her father, and personal things," vanished from the Vassar archives, suggesting that some incident was willfully expunged.

If true, the story would also explain why Janet Auchincloss so readily agreed to Jackie's not returning to Vassar. Janet had prized the status conferred by her daughter's enrollment at the exclusive college, which would explain why she wanted her immediately reinstated. Having her return to campus for her senior year, however, would only increase the chance that humiliating gossip about her earlier expulsion would circulate. Cutting all ties with Vassar would be expedient. When later pointedly questioned as to why she didn't return to Vassar, Jackie gave an answer that might vaguely confirm the general account, saying, "I wish I had gone away less on weekends or had less callers on weekends." While on another occasion, she stated of the school, "I would have gone back there had not all my friends left," this might have applied not only to those who dropped out to marry but also to the friend who was expelled.

Mummy and Unk sailed home on the *Île de France*, arriving on March 11. Once back in Washington, Mummy learned that George Washington University, a short drive over the Potomac from Merrywood, offered an undergraduate degree in French history and literature and accepted women students. According to Jack Davis, she went directly to the dean there and "persuaded him to accept all of her daughter's previous college credits." It meant Jackie would have to live at Merrywood, with its stable of horses for her to ride. She accepted the offer.

If Janet considered Jackie's decision a victory over Black Jack, she didn't realize how much more attentively and meaningfully her ex-husband had been engaging their daughter about her future. Mummy might have been influential about practical matters, but Jackie's father held her heart. She announced to her mother her decision not to return to Vassar as a fait accompli, but knowing how it would sadden Daddy that she would no longer be just two hours away from him, she had delayed telling him about her change in plans until the last possible moment.

Although secretive with both parents, she was usually more forthcoming with her father. When she told him about her diplomatic-attaché beau, he warned her to beware of charmers like himself and avoid any romantic commitments until she had been out of college for a year. Unlike Mummy, he tacitly approved of the unconventional path she seemed inclined toward. "He always encouraged her artistic talents—in every field," recalled her cousin Mimi Cecil. Impressed by her colorful letters, Black Jack was the very first to suggest she might well have a promising career as an author. "I honestly think you could write a book on your travels," he wrote to her. "All you have to do is to take the time and you could get out a book that would be a best-seller."

Realizing how much her year abroad was costing him, especially given what she sensed was his diminishing income, Jackie offered to forgo the monthly allowance increase she'd been asking of him. Surprised by her unselfishness, he nevertheless framed his appreciation with a bit of mockery, calling it "one of the most generous offers . . . made in many years."

Still, he was crushed when Jackie finally confirmed that she wasn't returning to Vassar. He blamed Janet for manipulating his daughter away from him. He was not entirely wrong. What he didn't know—or want to face—was that Jackie had played her mother into the position of supporting her Vassar departure.

His sister Maude believed her niece's decision made Black Jack sink into permanent despondency and begin withdrawing from the larger world. Her husband, John Davis, said, "[I]t caused him to assuage his pain by drinking too many dry martinis with his customary veal chop at the New York Stock Exchange Luncheon Club, to the detriment of his business."

There was more disappointment. When Jackie wrote in March that she was going to Spain over Easter vacation with "a friend" she did not name, Black Jack did the manipulating. Jealous that Janet had been able to come see her while he paid the bills, he claimed he had been planning on coming to Paris at that time, although "now . . . I would be going around by myself."

In truth, neither daughter nor father was honest about their lives at the time. She had suggested to him that, along with her whirlwind trip to Spain, she had no leisure time to guide him through Paris if he visited. Only to Mummy did she suggest otherwise, writing, "April in Paris, my dream for years & it is cold and raining and I am writing this [while] wearing socks in bed!"

As it turned out, Black Jack knew he couldn't have visited. That winter he'd developed such severe iritis that he was threatened with blindness; he underwent surgery and was forced to convalesce at home from March 12 to April 30. He was isolated except for the routine check-ins by his housekeeper Esther Lindstrom, who indulged his gambling addiction and was a formidable poker opponent. He felt the absence of his daughter acutely, and this period seems likely to have been when Black Jack crossed a taboo boundary. As his sister Edith Beale dared to confirm in a filmed recording in front of his daughter Lee, it was a matter of "incest."

With his elder daughter living overseas and his younger one at boarding school, the desperately lonely Black Jack welcomed the attentive visits of his statuesque blond niece "Little Edie," who was living at the residential Barbizon Hotel for women, eleven blocks away from him. "Every time I went into his apartment," Edie would casually recall of the unconventional relationship, "he was sitting in his underwear with the three phones, bickering with all those bookies." The recorded dialogue makes clear that it was his thirty-two-year-old niece who seduced Jack. "I was madly in love with him," Edie admitted.

"My father wasn't very nice to my cousin," Jackie later said.

JACKIE WAS EXPECTED HOME by the end of June. Mummy wanted her to attend Lee's debut reception. Daddy was renting an East Hampton cottage to share with Jackie through Labor Day, after which Mummy wanted her back in Newport for the summer social season finale. Jackie had plans of her own, concocting a scheme that neither parent saw coming.

She wasn't coming home.

Knowing better than to provoke Mummy's rage by mentioning her intention to linger in Europe, Jackie had tactically let her leave Paris feeling triumphant. Instead, confident in her power to appease and persuade both parents with artfully written words, Jackie waged a subtle campaign by mail. Pushing back her return date by increments would irritate but not enrage Mummy, but there was sure to be an emotional upset for Daddy that required different finesse.

Her letters to Mummy that spring were more than a vivid narrative of her activities. She dropped the first hint to Mummy of her plan to stay longer by expressing frustration that her few days in Spain that April hadn't been enough time to absorb all the history in Madrid, Toledo, and Valencia (and perhaps not given her enough time with her traveling companion, one of her Paris beaux, Paul de Ganay), and saying she wanted to visit again.

By now, Jackie was wading more deeply into a stream of young society types, often with transatlantic educations, from families with inherited estates and unfathomable fortunes. It was a rarified network of privileged prep school and elite college acquaintances, like Vassar classmate Jessie Leigh Hunt, whose mother, Louise de Vilmorin, was the legendary hostess of the Château de Verrières, which Jackie also visited. For his part, de Ganay invited her to his family's country estate, the Château de Courances, forty miles outside Paris. In her letter home, she described the visit:

"I went to Courance, the de Ganay chateau near Fountainbleau. It was built by a minister of Louis XIII and you come up the long, cobbled ride lined with trees and cross a moat and are in the courtyard with fairytale towers of winding stairs and on either side, lawn stretch[ing] for miles and there are statues and lakes and fountains. It is one of the very prettiest that I've ever seen and to spend the weekend in a place like that instead of visiting it with a guide—it was just a dream come true.

"I got there Saturday afternoon and we drove over to their friends—some Russians who live at Fleury in a little house covered with roses and in the garden under a chestnut tree with sticky blossoms we had wine and cake. Then we went to see where they breed pheasants for shooting in the fall. Dinner was such fun—we had snails and red wine and after dinner in the salon, sitting on Louis XV chairs we played South Pacific and Kiss

Me Kate records and afterwards we pulled the raft across the lake in the moonlight.

"Sunday we all went to church—this heavenly little village church with a twelfth century tombstone of Jean de Cavance, who went to the Crusades in his armor. We all sat up in the front as the de Ganays are the châtelaines of the town. There were eight little altar boys in red and lace—so naughty tripping and smiling at you—and a beadle in a funny old velvet costume and in the country, they always have the ceremony of the 'pain beni,' blessed bread and two little altar boys carry loaves of brioche heaped with roses up to the priest on a blue stretcher with lace and then they pass it around and you eat it.

"After lunch we rode their horses for miles through the park and fished for carp and pike and perch and trout in the ponds and moat."

Worldly, ironic, conversant in the Romance languages, Miss Bouvier was becoming so popular among Europe's smart set that Vivi Crespi, thinking she might be lonely, invited her to the French Riviera in the summer, only to learn she was fielding other offers. Becoming absorbed into the social scene, she confessed to Yusha, "I haven't done any work all winter." To Mummy, however, she conveyed the impression of balancing academics and socializing:

"I've had three of my four exams already and all went quite well. My international relations one was on the opposing policies of Austria-Hungary and Russia in the Balkans from 1900-1914. The night before I got in from . . . the biggest ball of the season in Paris in this beautiful old 17th century house on the Ille-St.-Louis . . . I got in at 6 a.m. and had the exam from 8:30 a.m. till noon, then went out to lunch . . . quite a day, but I knew all about the Balkans!"

Jackie's strategy to overcome Mummy's inevitable refusal in the fight to let her stay on was to lure Yusha across the Atlantic as her coconspirator. Only Unk could veto Yusha's going, and it would be harder for Mummy to order her home in June if she was guiding Yusha through Europe. To make the endeavor even more attractive, costs would be reduced by traveling in Claude's sister's car and staying with her relatives and other friends. Since Auchincloss funds would underwrite Yusha's trip, only a small amount more was needed to cover her extension in Europe—essential, since there was a chance that Black Jack would refuse to pay for it.

With Jackie being "wholly dependent" on Black Jack, as his nephew put it, her father knew that the "most effective way of manipulating his daughters was through money," only sending their allowance on time and underwriting indulgences if they did "his bidding." He, however, also felt manipulated, at one point writing Jackie, "You come visit me in New York only when you are absolutely broke . . . then as soon as you collect your check you disappear and spend it like water. Money is too hard to make." Early in 1950, when she simply mused about visiting Ireland, he reacted angrily: "Don't you ever intend to come home? You had better come home sometime if you know what is good for you." She could see Ireland, he ended, "if you marry a rich husband."

As it turned out, Jackie was able to delay telling him her plan because she didn't need his money. Yusha confirmed that he was coming to France, after visiting his ancestral land of Scotland, and Mummy approved her extension, Unk paying for it. "I can't believe it," she gleefully wrote her stepbrother.

However, a month before Yusha's anticipated arrival in Paris on June 22, Jackie pushed her luck even further, cooking up a new scheme, suggesting that she and Yusha visit Scotland *after* France, but that they first go to Ireland. She warned him, "Don't tell Mummy I'm thinking of changing as she doesn't really want me to." He agreed to present the plan as his own, leaving Mummy to simply acquiesce.

Jackie still had to tell her father. As summer neared, his spirits were revived by the prospect of his imminent reunion with Jackie in East Hampton, but he also knew that, as he told his nephew, "Whenever she was determined to get something she wanted she usually did . . . when she wanted something she just kept insisting and insisting and insisting until she had gotten it."

After finishing at the Sorbonne, before Yusha came, Jackie went to Saint-Tropez—"a crumbling little port that is an artist's colony"—guest of the aristocratic du Luart family, in their "lovely little yellow stucco house" within the compound of the luxury estate Le Beauvallon, a Belle Époque palace. The group dined nightly on a terrace, drinking "good Provencal wine by candlelight." Always in shorts, she was up early, helping paint a boat, swimming, sunbathing, and playing with "an idiotic poodle." Some days, she just observed the resort entrance, watching "sunburned Frenchmen roaring up in Delahayes."

"I have never known such peace and I'm not at all bored," she reported to her mother. "[L]eisure is so delicious and it makes me want to paint or write." She declared it a "much better way to spend the summer than cocktails & dances," a gentle rebuke of the Newport scene.

After Saint-Tropez, Jackie arranged her trip home for September 12, demonstrating how fierce her determination could be by pulling off the impossible feat of convincing the Cunard and the French shipping lines to allow her to swap tickets.

As far as the summer itinerary was concerned, Janet vetoed her initial proposal to visit Morocco, to which Jackie so readily acquiesced that it was likely she had suggested it as a red herring, knowing Mummy's mistrust of non-Anglo cultures. She called her daughter's plan to visit Spain with two male friends "a bad idea." Jackie responded, "I don't think it too shocking—with one boy a cripple and the other sort of effeminate—I mean nothing could happen." Her mother gave in: Jackie had won her freedom until the middle of September. Not until she confirmed her return date could she bring herself to tell her father. Since Mummy and Unk were footing the bill for her two-month extension, Black Jack would have to accept the fact—and, he rationalized, at least his ex-wife wouldn't see her, either.

She finished classes on June 16, then flew to London for three days to see her friend Shirley Oakes. On the twenty-second, she was at Paris's Orly Airport, eager to welcome Yusha and begin their adventures.

7

LIBERTÉ

June–September 1950

The breathless, elaborate tale Jackie recounted to Yusha in the Louvre so perfectly characterized her to him that he remembered every detail.

Jackie took him right up to the Grande Galerie, to the eighth panel, between Titian's *Woman with a Mirror* and *Allegory of Marriage*. There she was, with her iconic, enigmatic smile, trapped behind a bench and a low rope against a wall. And right there, months earlier on a dimming winter afternoon, Jackie Bouvier had stood scrutinizing the *Mona Lisa*, about to raise her Leica. So began her story for Yusha.

Jackie was unrelentingly stalking the *Mona Lisa* with her camera, violating the painting's boundaries and threatening its security. An alarmed elderly guard, one of 214 "retired soldiers or disabled war veterans" then watching the entire museum's contents, hobbled over as fast as he could to protect the besieged, beloved icon from the bold girl with the camera. She backed away, apologizing profusely. Her only intention had been to disprove the popular myth that the eyes of the *Mona Lisa* were always gazing directly back at the person looking at her.

The guard glared angrily and pivoted, waddling back to his post at the end of the gallery, muttering "*Américaines arrogantes*," loud enough for her to hear. "*Qui pensez vous être?!*"

Chastised, she maintained a placid facade until he was at a good distance. Then she raised her camera and leaned even closer to the *Mona Lisa*, snapping away. The clicking shutter echoed in the lofty gallery. "*Arrêtez! Arrêtez!*" the guard yelled, in limp chase after her.

Jackie justified her actions by saying that since she wouldn't know if she had succeeded until after the film was developed, she had to keep photographing from different angles, moving her Leica closer to the canvas, ignoring the rope and nearly climbing up on the bench. "She knew she was naughty," Yusha observed, though it seemed warranted to her: "He was mean to say that. What did being an American have to do with it?'"

Finding she had outrun the guard in the hallway, Jackie took a breath, pausing at the top of a curved marble staircase, then descended the steps slowly, as ascending tourists stared and parted to the sides. "Anyone can make an entrance," she declared, pausing with Yusha at the same staircase, "but the real art is making an exit."

As Yusha wrote, they continued "up the Eiffel Tower, up and down the Champs-Élysées, along the banks of the Seine, through the Bois de Boulogne, and the Tuileries Garden, Notre-Dame, Maxim's, having pressed duck at the Tour D'Argent, and Versailles." In the Versailles Hall of Mirrors, she pointed out the spot where she had first spoken French in public. She told him to look around, asking, "What don't you see here?" He stared at the furnishings, and the busts of historical figures. She then declared: "There's not one woman—but they were important too."

All through Paris, she had her Leica, proving how light changed the shape of Louvre sculptures, unveiled the shades of yellow in the dahlia beds of the Tuileries, and revealed the hidden patterns of the Eiffel Tower's interlocked beams. She vacillated on her preferred format. Black and white might record a journalistic truth but, as she told George Plimpton, "the greys and silvers disguise as much as tell."

Having had her name and face in the newspapers since childhood, Jackie Bouvier was already practiced in crafting a persona for public display, knowing how to be "on," to make an intentional impression, to invent herself into a character. Now her storytelling was becoming another aspect of this. Through her narrating, chronicling, romanticizing, mythologizing, and, most importantly, editing, her stories—especially when spoken—assumed an episodic quality, in which she presented herself as the hapless protagonist in some zany predicament, blending what her confidante Nancy "Tucky" Tuckerman called a "sense of the ridiculous" with enough detail to set a stage and capture the essence of the characters she met. It is difficult to distinguish the degree to which her stories were a matter of her real perception of herself as opposed to the image she wanted others to see. How much of her *Mona Lisa* story or any other of her wild stories she may have embroidered wasn't important to Yusha. He found it to be another example of her "capacity for concentration," a trait best "exhibited in amusing storytelling, both real and imaginative."

The beginning of their summer sojourn included a brief separation, with Yusha driving off to the south of France with Claude's friend Solange Batsell, a French attorney who had studied in the United States. The romantic Yusha had fallen hard for her, and the duo planned to spend some time alone together. Jackie made her way to Lyon to meet Claude, who had her sister's car. Starting July 15, Jackie and Claude made a meandering road trip through the more remote and ancient villages of south-central and coastal "deep France." It was a rustic experience for her, as they would "picnic in the woods, swim in a river, go fishing." Facilities were primitive. She used the outhouses like everyone else. They began the trip by a leisurely exploration of the rolling hills of the Auvergne region, "the part of France where very few tourists go . . . covered with fields and old women with cows and hammeux where the butcher and baker pass once in a week with a truck . . . on every hill is a ruined chateau," she wrote Mummy.

At one point, on the outskirts of the medieval village of Salers, they came upon the large public washing pools, with clotheslines holding items drying in the sun. Jackie grabbed some laundry, then "decided to finish the job as a good washer-woman," soaking the clothes, kneeling on the stone perimeter, and cleaning each item.

In the half-deserted village of Conques, they visited the basilica where pilgrims once left relics and ornaments. In the Gorges du Tarn, where there were centuries-old hamlets still clinging to the steep slopes, they fished for trout in the shallow river and rode narrow canal boats drawn by horses along the adjoining path. As the sun set that day, Jackie found just enough water to cool off, slipped into her bathing suit, and mimicked Esther Williams. In Toulouse, there was a legitimate pool and a deeper river in which they swam and sunbathed. "We both realized that it was a time of freedom," recalled Claude, "getting some sense of ourselves."

The only plan on their agenda was meeting up with Yusha and

Solange at the end of July in Saint-Jean-de-Luz, a short drive from the Spanish border. Their friend Donald Coons had rented "Borda-Berri," an elegant manor house, for the summer, where they were joined by other friends, Gordon Wholey, Frecky Vreeland (son of Diana Vreeland, the famous fashion editor), and Demi Gates, the brother of her friend Puffin. It was with them that Jackie marked her transition into adulthood, turning twenty-one years old. Perhaps to dispel any anxiety about the rite of passage, she marked it casually in shorts, playing tennis and winning a bike race.

Jackie, Claude, Yusha, and Solange proceeded north toward Bordeaux, stopping at the Château de La Brède, "where Montesquieu wrote his political works on democracy," Claude recalled, and there was "[a] moment of emotion in his library" as they perused documents which were rudimentarily connected to the creation of the United States.

In Saintes, they toured its famous Gothic basilica before proceeding up to La Rochelle. After seeing the island of Marmoutier off the Brittany coast, they stopped at the Saint-Vincent de Paul Hospital for Children in Nantes, speaking with a nun about "her dedication to lonesome children," Claude recalled. The next stop, La Bretesche, was especially memorable. "We arrived late in the afternoon and wandered until night around the moat and the grounds," Claude recorded. After entering a castle on a medieval drawbridge, they thought they'd seen "the ghosts of the arrowed knights fighting each other behind the cedar trees." Then came Azay-le-Rideau, where they toured the famous fifteenth-century island château that seemingly rose straight out of the water. There was one final picnic—with sandwiches, grapes, and wine—along the Loire. Then they finally returned to Paris.

Jackie still had several weeks of travel ahead but, perhaps to discourage her from concocting any excuse to further delay coming home after that, Mummy made a preemptive public declaration of her certain return. She had her friend Betty Beale, the society columnist (no relation to Black Jack's sister's family), announce in the July 5, 1950, *Washington Evening Star* that "Jacqueline Bouvier, post deb . . . is coming back to the Capital [winter social] scene next year . . . Jackie adores Paris and is loath to leave it but is coming back to take her senior year at George Washington."

Yusha and Jackie arrived in Dublin on Monday, August 14, 1950, in time to attend the final day of the city's annual horse show. Unable to find rooms, they tried to call on a close literary friend of Uncle Lefty's, Father Joseph Leonard, for help, but he was out of town. Jackie went right to the American Embassy and begged for assistance. Aides there not only found them rooms but also loaned them a spare car for their stay in Ireland. The next day, Father Leonard was back in Dublin and chaperoned them to every site they wished to see. He instantly bonded with Jackie over their mutual passion for literature, the gap of fifty-two years irrelevant to his respect for her intellect.

Leonard indulged her curiosity about the lives of Ireland's most acclaimed and politically subversive writers by stopping to see places associated with James Joyce, William Butler Yeats, Samuel Beckett, Bram Stoker, and Oscar Wilde. One evening, he took them to an Abbey Theatre performance of George Bernard Shaw's play *The Doctor's Dilemma*. There was lunch at Restaurant Jammet, mentioned in Joyce's *Ulysses*, and a pub night downing Guinness.

Leonard even arranged for them to meet his friend Irish prime minister John A. Costello, who recalled Jackie as being "full of youthful vivacity and charm" and that she was "delighted with everything she found in Ireland." At the American Embassy, she also met Costello's son Declan, a young attorney three years her senior. Jackie was immediately infatuated, confiding to Father Leonard that the future attorney general of Ireland was "absolute heaven." There was no time for anything serious to develop, but they would remain lifelong friends.

They spent considerable time outdoors, exploring the city's architecture as well as Phoenix Park with its wild deer and cricket, polo, and hurling playing fields. Jackie had two regrets about her time in Dublin: not getting to "shake hands with the mummy" preserved in the thousand-year-old St. Michan's Church and, she told Yusha the day they left, not being there at Easter time, which "would have been so meaningful." Her reference became clearer as she began ticking off the number of Irish citizens arrested, wounded, killed, and executed during the "Easter Uprising" for independence from the "bloodthirsty" English, and she recited lines from Yeats's "Easter 1916." As Yusha noted: "The more she traveled in Ireland, the more she wanted to be Irish."

While Yusha drove (Dublin to Kildare, Kilkenny, Waterford, Cobh, Cork, Blarney, Killarney, Limerick, and Tipperary), Jackie's behavior varied. At times, she fell into silent reading, "always studying the complicated [Irish] history," Yusha recalled, "crazy about the Irish kings." At other times, passing the ruins of fortress castles, she offered a running monologue about Irish history, combining her "knowledge of art and architecture and of military history." She seemed especially mesmerized by the landscape in all shades of green.

Most of all, Yusha wrote, it was "the village people [who] caught her imagination," as they stopped in rural pubs. Much as she had in the French countryside, Jackie enjoyed learning about the lives of a largely peasant population so different from her own. (She and Yusha often shared a suite, raising eyebrows when they claimed to be siblings despite their different last names.)

For every day of what Yusha called "three joyful weeks," as they meandered down one-lane roads, to one tiny village after another, Jackie playfully assigned character traits from history and literature to the real people they saw. A sturdy milkmaid became "Molly Pitcher," a condescending mechanic was "Julius Caesar," a proud, pale young farmhand became "Wilfred of Ivanhoe." Erudite enough to catch the subtlety of her references, Yusha found her quirky, obscure quips hysterical, but also revealing of her ability to spot timeless human commonalities, an increasingly recognizable trademark of her humor.

There remained, however, one subject too off-limits to fully discuss: the truth about Mummy's family. Their first morning in Cork, Jackie was up and out early on her own, returning with a watercolor she had painted of the city center.

"There's a river that runs right through town. Guess what it's called? The River Lee!" she announced with a smiling, lingering stare. It was her cautiously signaling uncertainty about just how much he knew of Janet's being the grandchild of poor Irish immigrants and not the descendant of the Anglo colonial aristocracy that she insisted she was. Both broke into nervous titters, and the moment passed.

The subject was abstractly addressed in their discussion on the schism between Catholic and Protestant Irish. Even before she had lived overseas, Jackie had shown a curiosity about those from different cultures who were ostracized as minorities. She had written Yusha with fascination about an Iranian Muslim girl, "a religion that says you have to be terribly modest," who "wears nightgowns in the bathtub." She had started pen pal correspondences with Afghani students in November 1944. She noted how some Japanese "worship the Gods of Nature."

On the other hand, in her letters she expressed a casual racial insensitivity (not untypical of her era and class), mentioning a "shifty talent scout," referring to a Jewish person, who "spiced up an otherwise dreary [train] trip," and that the names of two Chinese students were pronounced "by making a sound as if you were going to be sick."

Her year in Europe exposed her to so many different cultures that it inevitably diminished a large portion of the lingering prejudice she had brought with her. "Her stay in France had been a broadening experience," Yusha told a journalist a decade later. "She had met so many people who were very different from those she had known before. And she was always interested in everybody else's ideas."

In Limerick they stopped for tea with retired Auchincloss maid Nellie Curtain in her thatched cottage. Jackie delighted in "making Yusha carry my Waterford glass" after a shopping spree in the city famous for its crystal ware. He was eager to participate in the legendary Blarney Castle ritual—ascending narrow steps up a round tower to the castle parapet, then lying down on one's back to kiss the large stone set in the wall, said to bless those who dared to try the dangerous stunt with the gift of eloquence.

Jackie was wary. Many with fear of heights turned back. Any slip and one would plunge down five stories to their death. Yusha agreed to hold her legs down. When she saw that only an elderly guide held down the legs of tourists, it dawned on her that Yusha wouldn't be allowed to do so. In the flash of a moment, Jackie "tilted over backwards" and summoned the confidence to take her turn, "looking forward for good luck."

Jackie seemed less engaged in Scotland. Two months earlier, she had written Mummy for "any ideas of what to do" there, her only plan being to "let loose in moors . . . and firths and *Wuthering Heights* storms [and take] pictures [of] every thatched peasant cottage . . . and to share their gruel." They went up to the furthest point north, John o' Groats, where she climbed out on the sharp rocks overlooking the sea, attended theatrical performances at the Edinburgh Festival, and toured Sterling Castle. In Inverness they bought a Sherlock Holmes cape for Yusha and a Royal Stewart kilt for her. During a brief stop in London, she floated the idea of visiting Wales, in jest. She was stalling. They had to leave.

From colonialism to egalitarianism, Vietnamese restaurant workers to Soviet troops, weekend parties in the French countryside to her amorous night in Florence, Jacqueline Bouvier's perception of both her place in the larger world and her ability to flourish in it had widened. Months later, she reflected: "I loved it more than any year of my life. . . . I learned not to be ashamed of a real hunger for knowledge, something I had always tried to hide."

YUSHA SHARED HER HUNGER, not only for real knowledge but also for experience, and over the three months that they had traveled together, they came to understand each other even more deeply than before; they had discussed serious matters amid the pleasant diversions.

From the moment Yusha had set foot in Paris, radios blared reports (translated for him by Jackie) of the Korean War. He immediately began analyzing the unfolding conflict between northern Korean forces, backed by the Chinese Communists, and those in the south, backed by the United States. For him, that summer would be dominated by his determination to join the fight and prove his patriotism; his dreams of serving during wartime had been thwarted after he enlisted in the Marines in April 1945 and World War II ended just five months later. As Yusha aired his desire to reenlist and fight in Korea, Jackie, who, though "ashamed" that her view of military service could be seen as "very unpatriotic," called out his visions of heroism: "There isn't [as] much glamor to it as you think . . . In fact, I don't think there's any."

Her concern was that it might deepen his inclination toward gloominess. She expressed it all in an extraordinary letter which offered insight into her own character, written when she was only thirteen years old:

"I just know that being in the Army is bound to make people different . . .

"I know you think and philosophize a lot—and sometimes get almost morbid—But when you're in the Marines realize that you're just seeing one side of things—and when you see underprivileged men and intolerant, race conscious ones, and bullying sergeants—don't let all that get you down and realize that there is such a huge and beautiful and good side of things.

"There are so many people who get lost in pessimism and seeing the worst—but that is so wrong when there is good and beauty in the world—and it's so much happier being optimistic—even if you're wrong—you're happy and you make other people happy and isn't that what's important?"

As they deconstructed how to defuse the threat of Communism in Asia, their conversation also inevitably turned to Vietnam, and a new development that would now directly involve Americans. That very week, planes, Jeeps, and a thirty-five-member U.S. Military Assistance Advisor Group arrived in Saigon. Jackie agreed that intervention to stem the Communist threat and support an ally was the right thing to do. However, one truth she'd learned that year lingered as she ended her transformative year in Europe and readied herself to return to America: "Once oppressed people have experienced freedom," she told Yusha, echoing Pierre Renouvin's observation, "they can never again be truly controlled."

ABOARD THE S.S. *LIBERTÉ* for three days, Jackie felt a dread of returning home that emerged in her humorous threat to hide on the boat and return to Paris. She mused about writing a book but made no mention of marriage. "I don't want to just live for pleasure, I want the satisfaction of being creative and some larger purpose," she told Yusha. Having been away from the United States for just over a year, Jacqueline Bouvier was now coming home to a country that had become one of the most powerful political, economic, and cultural forces on the globe. With her new firsthand grasp of internationalism, she would soon express a desire to play some part in exercising that influence, in some as yet undetermined form.

On her last day at sea, Jackie accepted the inevitable reality, wiring her father that the *Liberté* would dock at four in the afternoon on September 15, 1950, at Pier 88 on West 48th Street in New York. He gleefully responded: "Can't wait. Hurry. Hurry. You can leave everything at my apartment including yourself. Love Dad."

As the ocean liner neared New York, Jackie slipped into a black dress and white wrist gloves, as if assuming the costume of a familiar character she was ready to play. Predictably, among the expectations soon to be faced was the societal pressure to marry, made all the more intense with the passage of a year.

Looking over the ship's railing as it neared the dock, Jackie focused on a gent who looked like Clark Gable leaning against a convertible. It was Black Jack. But unseen by Jackie was Mummy, who had been waiting inside the hangar on the dock, where trunks and luggage were conveyed from the ship's lower deck. Jackie had written to Mummy asking that she not "meet me" because Daddy was "so mad" at her delay that "it might assuage him a little to think he's the first I see on arriving home."

Mummy willfully ignored Jackie's wishes and pushed her way to the gangplank to surprise her daughter, immediately greeting her with the news that her Vassar friend Lucky Showker had recently gotten engaged to the grandson of President Theodore Roosevelt. Jackie deflected her mother's marriage obsession with humor. As she wrote in her letter to Lucky, "Mummy handed it [the engagement announcement] to me in a bunch of mail as I stepped off the gangplank and I nearly fell in the water." Mummy justified her presence at the dock, ostensibly, as a necessity so that she could retrieve Jackie's trunks, even though her daughter had also specifically told her, "I'll send my trunks to D.C. & [then] come up to Newport." Instead, after smiling for the ship's photographer while Jackie sat on her luggage, Mummy abruptly ordered some trunks sent to Washington and took the rest with her to Newport. Black Jack kept his distance, making Jackie come to him, and off they went.

The period from her return from Europe to the start of her senior year would encompass only a few weeks in September and October 1950, but would bring up many memories of the colorful family members who had so influenced her.

Part III

FAMILIES

We were all . . . a bit eccentric.

—JACKIE, ABOUT THE BOUVIER FAMILY,
TO HER AUNT AND COUSIN,
EDITH AND EDIE BEALE

8

EAST HAMPTON

September 1950

As the duo drove to the Triborough Bridge, then into Queens along Northern Boulevard, they finally began the four-hour crawl eastward, the only distraction being an occasional billboard touting one of the new Long Island suburban communities and shopping centers.

By the time they began passing the Polish farmers working in potato fields and caught their first whiff of Long Island's famous duck farms, Black Jack and Jackie had begun a venture into their past and the once-glorious summers of the formerly grand Bouviers.

To come down Main Street in East Hampton in the late summer of 1950 was like entering a cathedral, the arching ancient elms offering dark, cool shade, the road an aisle leading toward a social altar. Upon arriving in town that day it would have been acutely obvious to both father and daughter that *their* East Hampton was no more. They did not arrive at tiny East Hampton Airport, a converted World War I barracks, because it was cheaper to drive. They didn't ride the ancient steam-engine railroad train from New York, nicknamed "the Cannonball," because there was no longer a fleet of family cars and a chauffeur to retrieve them at the station.

St. Philomena's Catholic Church was full with summer residents; three summers before, the entire Bouvier clan would have attended together. Jackie never forgot walking to church with Grampy Jack and how kindly he engaged with children they met. Now he lay alongside Grandma Maude, in the church cemetery on Cedar Street.

Then, as they had for nearly all the three preceding decades, the family would retreat for a boisterous Sunday supper at their reliable fortress, Lasata. Now it was no longer theirs, having been sold while Jackie was in Paris. Mummy's father still had his Lily Pond Road Estate, on the lawn of which her parents held their wedding luncheon. Black Jack wouldn't bring Jackie to see Gramps Lee; the two men despised each other.

Instead, Black Jack drove east of Ocean Avenue past the old Sea Spray Inn to one in a row of its thirteen small beach cottages on sixteen acres of beach grass, Hook Pond behind them. This was where he would now spend his East Hampton days with Jackie. As later guest Lynn Douglass recalled, it was essentially a "grey driftwood beach shack," with a wood-planked floor, entered through sliding French doors, with a wraparound porch. Facing the ocean, window shutters rattled in the breeze, and the scent of salty sea air blended with that of mildew. They swam, played tennis, and took meals at the Maidstone Club, where Black Jack maintained a membership.

The Bouvier family history was deeply integrated into the life of East Hampton. Jackie's great-uncle Edgar Sergeant first summered in East Hampton and drew his sister Maude Bouvier out to the far end of Long Island. In 1915, she bought Wildmoor, retaining it even after buying a grander, wood-shingled manor house within sight of the ocean in 1926. The couple named the manor house "Lasata," a Nepali word for "place of peace."

Maude developed the landscaping with a manicured lawn, flower and vegetable gardens, and groves of trees. Her husband, John Vernou Bouvier II, an active leader of and committeeman on civic, educational, banking, political, patriotic, and Catholic organizations, hosted meetings for the people involved in his multitude of public endeavors there. (Little Jackie especially loved Lasata's riding ring and horse stable.)

"Grampy" Jack Bouvier was initially a Democrat and a friend of New York governor Franklin D. Roosevelt, but once FDR became president, he turned on him, fearing the New Deal would make the country socialist. Always pontificating, Grampy delivered an address each July 4 from the East Hampton village green, which his grandchildren were trotted out to hear. "Nothing is more important than independence," granddaughter Little Edie recalled from one such speech. "Don't give it up—you'll never get it back."

Grampy Jack had been enjoying summertime on Long Island since his parents were able to begin leasing a clapboard Quogue beach house, in 1888, merely one sign of the success his family had achieved in just two generations. His grandfather Michel Bouvier emigrated from France to the United States in 1815, settling in Philadelphia, where he prospered as a skilled furniture artisan and married fellow French immigrant Louise Vernou.

Their son, Grampy's father, the first John Vernou, served heroically with the Union Army before marrying Caroline Ewing, of a prominent Philadelphia family. He moved to New York to become one of the first New York Stock Exchange members along with his bachelor brother Michel Charles (M.C.). The brothers' wealth mushroomed after buying eight hundred thousand acres of West Virginia coal lands. When M.C. died, in 1935, he left Grampy nearly $6 million.

Born five years after the Civil War ended, Grampy earned a master's in political science and a law degree at Columbia University. More engaged in practicing law than stock brokerage, he had a proclivity for theatrical and scandalous cases, defending wealthy men against breach-of-promise claims and blackmail by starlets. He delighted his granddaughter Edie by joining the defense team of actress Mae West, accused of "corrupting the morals of youth" as writer and star of her 1926 Broadway comedy *Sex.* Sex was a common topic among Grampy's thousands of narrative ponderings. "It is a biological truth that all rapacious animals, including the vulture, are monogamous," he noted in one entry. "Not so, however, with humans."

Perhaps this belief helped Grampy justify keeping a mistress, Mabel Ferguson. Despite committing adultery and having four divorced children, he considered himself an exemplary Catholic. French Catholicism was elemental to his identity, and something his granddaughter Jacqueline embraced for herself, although through his mother they were also part English Anglican, German Quaker, Dutch Reformed, Swedish Lutheran, and Scottish Presbyterian.

Being French Catholic defined Jackie's most essential quality: individualism. In midcentury Anglo-Saxon Protestant Eastern Seaboard society, being a Catholic was a declaration of being proudly distinct, especially since religious bigotry still lingered. "Catholics had no standing," Maude Bouvier Davis stated. Maude further claimed that her brother's "Black Jack" nickname was far from affectionate, used to disparage him for "being different." Within the ranks of even Jackie's peers, however, the nickname was attributed to racial bigotry and gossip that a Bouvier ancestor was African. Jackie's Newport friend Charlie Whitehouse stated that "[t]he story one heard was that he was called Black Jack because he was black." Her cousin Shella Scott recalled that when Jackie welcomed her father to Miss Porter's campus, a friend asked, "Why is that Negro kissing her?" The novelist Louis Auchincloss, Unk's distant cousin—who declared that the Bouviers were "not really 'in' anywhere"—observed that Black Jack "looked like a big sexy Negro."

Ironically, in his effort to link his family to a noble branch of the Vernou in *Our Forebears*, Grampy Jack gave currency to the rumor, falsely claiming to have an ancestor who had spent most of his life on the island of Guadeloupe, where enslaved people were brought from Africa in 1650, many intermarrying with French residents once slavery was abolished there. Jackie knew about the story, and when later approached with a genealogy linking the Bouviers to the Muslim Afro-Dutch Van Salee family of New York, she sarcastically dismissed it by vaguely referencing unspecified ancestors, saying she had thought they were Jewish. The pervasiveness of the rumor was such that Jackie's friend Puffin Gates recalled their high school English teacher Miss Watson labeling each student as a flower. Puffin was named a pansy while Jackie was declared an "orchid," because she was a rare flower "blooming . . . in a jungle."

While never overtly religious, Jackie later spoke of Catholicism's sustenance in times of grief, but she was far more immersed in the faith's theology than has been previously assumed. Vassar sophomore Joan Ellis recalled that after a philosophy class, where she had become incensed about the "rigidity of the Catholic Church," she returned to the dormitory seeking someone who "could possibly explain and defend this tyranny to me." She was directed to Jackie, who "roamed wonderfully through the fields of philosophy, religion, and history and quietly talked about her faith." Ellis concluded that Jackie was "reading things I haven't even heard of."

Whether or not Jackie took church doctrine literally (or even fully comprehended the liturgy, which was spoken entirely in Latin), she grasped the value of discipline and ritual. She recalled how Grampy "snapped his cane in and out during service," to keep her attentive, and "would never allow me to rest my backside against the seat when it was time to kneel." Although Jackie so rarely spoke of being Catholic that her lifetime confidante Tucky would perceive her as "not very Catholic," she was highly conscious of being different. She would reveal to a friend in their social milieu who had a Jewish parent that "we both live and do very well in this world of Wasps and old money and society. It's all supposed to be so safe and continuous. But you and I are not really of it. Maybe because I'm Catholic and my parents were divorced when I was young—a terribly radical thing at the time—I've always felt an outsider in that world."

EVEN MORE THAN PUBLIC speaking, Grampy Bouvier loved to write, whether it was hundreds of poems and essays for the *East Hampton Star*, thirty-three diaries, or the nearly four-hundred-page *Pocket Agendum* privately published in 1939, a compendium of quotations from civilization's great thinkers—including himself. "Only those who have tasted better conditions revolt," he recorded, echoing the mantra about the Vietnamese people demanding independence from France after being freed from the tyranny of wartime Japan, which Jackie had taken to heart in Paris. Among the *Agendum*'s hundreds of observations, Rousseau's definition of history stood out: "The art of choosing, among many lies, that which most resembles the truth."

Jackie admired her grandfather's passion for writing and attended to him closely. Flattered to be the focus of his favorite grandchild, Grampy bragged to his mistress that the "fragrant Jacqueline" was "one of the most charming and beautiful young girls, quite aside from her alert intelligence, that I have ever encountered." As her sister Lee noted, "He really adored her and I think felt that she had enormous potential in the field that he cared about, which was literary." Without the "exceptional bond" Jackie had with Grampy, observed Lee, she "never would have gained the particular strength and independence and individuality she had."

Grampy committed to helping Jackie, getting her published for the first time by submitting one of her poems to the *East Hampton Star*. She also began consulting him on her writing, which gave Grampy an opportunity to share his thoughts on art and the creative process. "It was wise on your part not to attempt a poem on Russia," he advised at one point, "poems fall within Art. The essence of Art lies in the power of forming images, which are its only wealth. It does not classify objects, but feels them. Accordingly, one is an artist as soon as he imagines, and long and long before he reasons." He concluded that she should choose subjects for which she had a visceral, familiar sense. The element that most characterized her writing, Grampy thought, was its descriptiveness. Critiquing a poem she named "Smoke," he offered the highest praise the young writer could read: "You really possess a wealth of imagery that is distinctly unusual, particularly in a girl of your years, and you have expressed your thoughts in rich and vivid terms."

He also prompted her lifelong passion for crafting long, narrative letters by first writing to her, despite their living within walking distance of each other and seeing each other weekly. Even as a busy teenager at boarding school, she vowed to maintain their correspondence, to his apparent delight. Grampy told his granddaughter that she possessed "a buoyant spirit and a courageous heart," and that these were "qualities which it is evident you are intent on developing." By disciplining her mind, he advised further, she could be an example: "I discern in you more than passing evidence of leadership, but before leading others we must guide and direct ourselves. This is the true way of usefulness in life. . . . Thus, you will observe that those who are useful are the best contributors to the correct leading of life and in the last analysis are the most efficient and contented members of all God's creatures."

Grampy offered a subtle feminism in his passing remark that working on her personal development now would prove to be "adequate preparation for future feats of work and responsibility," encouraging her eventual pursuit of a profession while pointing out the necessity of humility to success for both genders: "But don't be pretentious or labor under the false impression of indispensability—to do so spells the prig, either male or female."

Grampy would leave each of his ten grandchildren $34,000, but Jackie came away with the richest inheritance: a passion for writing. It was something of an accomplishment, too, that she was so valued by *both* Grampy and Black Jack, for no such relationship existed between father and son. Grandma Maude protected her two eldest, Jack and Edith, but three years after her April 1940 death, the hostility between father and son led Grampy to make good on his threat to disinherit his son. Only an eleventh-hour reconciliation would restore him to the will. Aunt Michelle moved in with her widowed father, running both of his households. Just before her scheduled departure to join her new husband, Harrington Putnam, in Brazil, Grampy was rushed into prostate surgery on July 9, 1947. She remained at his side until his death five months later.

During their 1950 visit to East Hampton, Black Jack would bring Jackie to Grampy's grave. It was not for his own sake, but an act of love for his daughter; ambivalence was the best that could be said about Jack's feelings for his late father.

Despite losing half his wealth in the 1929 crash, Grampy had refused to compromise his lavish lifestyle, thereby decimating his principal and accruing debt. He designated Jack as executor of his estate; some relatives felt Jack resented that responsibility, since the twins, Maude and Michelle, had inherited the real estate and would reap the income from its sale. As executor, Black Jack was the first to assess the contents of Lasata in the fall of 1949; only former servant John Ficke remained as caretaker there before it was entirely emptied and readied for sale.

Ficke recalled to Jack Davis that Black Jack spent time in the attic, emerging with only some "old, large envelopes" and telling him that everything else up there was "not worth anything." His nephew would be perplexed when he learned that his uncle had been rummaging through the material, since, as he wrote, his uncle "had never taken any interest in the family's history." As far as the remaining "crates of family papers," Black Jack "tagged these items for destruction."

Ficke made little progress on the assigned task. On the "damp, misty April morning" when a moving crew hauled out furnishings to be temporarily stored at Wildmoor before it too was sold, Davis "climbed up to the attic and managed to save most of the family papers and photographs." There were boxes, envelopes, and folders of financial records and family memorabilia, including Grampy's correspondence. He found letters between Black Jack and Jackie, but "none of the letters or poems written by Jacqueline or Lee to our grandfather. Someone took it all. It would have had to be him."

* * *

THE CAR THAT JACKIE and her father drove to and through East Hampton in September 1950 was a black Mercury convertible with a beautiful red interior that they both laid claim to. Jack taught her to drive in it on weekend excursions to show her where he had lived in Nutley and New Haven. He then gave her the car in June 1947 as a high school graduation gift. Yusha laughed in recalling how she named the vehicle "Zelda"—as in Fitzgerald—because "she was an unreliable beauty."

It was more than a method of transportation for her. In an era when many still considered it improper for young, unmarried women to be behind the wheel, Jackie Bouvier wanted to go places and drive herself. (And she had even before the Mercury entered her life: "I snitched the station wagon . . . I could be the most efficient crook," she confessed to Yusha when she was fifteen. "I swerved so I wouldn't run over a dead skunk and I nearly hit someone else. But I didn't.") She confessed to Gore Vidal, "I plan to lure many a beau in the back seat of my car."

Ostensibly, Zelda was "her" car, but her father kept it in New York for her to use when she was visiting. At some point in the weeks after she returned from Paris, she was able to convince him that she needed the car for commuting to George Washington University from Merrywood. Yet, during the holiday season, he expected her to return it to him, ensuring that she would come to see him at least once during the early winter.

Black Jack's insistence that they continue to share Zelda likely resulted from a reasonable insecurity about how much longer his daughter's dependence on him could last. By mid-September 1950, Jackie had become aware that her father would not be able to provide the funds she wanted. Instead of curtailing his expenditures in response to his diminished income, he had been borrowing money from his own father, which then reduced his inheritance. (His father's will would deduct Black Jack's unpaid $576,000 loan from his portion of the inheritance, though he still received $1.1 million.)

Feeling financially pinched, he sometimes lashed out at Jackie. "About the first thing you should do, young lady," he reprimanded in one note, "is to try and stop being selfish and, at the same time, try and see if you can't make somebody else happy once and [*sic*] awhile besides yourself." When she disagreed with his decision to include someone in his will, it hit a nerve, fearing she had adopted his ex-wife's "want of generosity," repeating his singular perception of Janet as "nothing but a gold digger all her life."

After being away for a year, Jackie likely had gained the perspective to recognize that Mummy's being greedy didn't negate the fact that Daddy created his own problems. He insisted on living as he wished while blaming his problems on his father, his ex-wife, and even Joe Kennedy. Among the valuable lessons that Black Jack taught his daughter was the unwitting one that every person is ultimately responsible for their decisions and how they choose to face the consequences.

Soon after arriving in East Hampton, Black Jack took Jackie to his sister Edith's estate, Grey Gardens. "Mother said she had arrived without anything to wear," her daughter, Edie, wrote in her diary after lending some summer clothes to Jackie. "She had nothing from her pinch penny Mother." They also came to retrieve Jackie's letters to Grampy, which Black Jack had taken from the attic of Lasata in the fall of 1949, brought to Grey Gardens, and then unintentionally left there when he abruptly bolted during an argument with Edith—her "wrangling abuse," as he referred to it—about his management of her trust.

In the winter of 1949–50, he had written to Edith questioning her spending: "Where in God's name does all this money go?" During a subsequent phone call, he admitted to Edith that he was making risky stock investments with her trust money. She accusingly retorted, "Jack, you are using my money and it's just not right!" Edie whispered to relatives about her suspicion that her uncle was using $7,000 from her mother's trust to underwrite Jackie's life in Paris.

During their September 1950 visit, as brother and sister rekindled their argument, Edie took her cousin upstairs to her room, excited to play her "new Cuban mambo" record. Of her eight Bouvier cousins, Jackie had "worshipped" Miche as "the older brother I always longed for," but with Edie, a dozen years her senior, she shared a passion for dancing and composing poetry. They had even collaborated on a poem for Grampy Jack's last birthday, three years earlier. The record they listened and danced to was the 1949 hit *Mambo Number 5*, by Perez Prado; enthralled, Jackie borrowed the album (which, Edie noted, she failed to return).

Like Jackie, Edie aspired to support herself in a creative profession. She also dreamed of living in Paris, concluding, after Jackie told her about her life there, that it had given Jackie a polish that made her "irresistible." But Edie was unfocused, torn between her own dreams and her duty to a mother intent on keeping her as a permanent companion. She never developed a plan to liberate herself. Jackie would soon face similar uncertainty. Shortly after her time with Daddy at summer's end in 1950, she would begin her final months of formal education, after which she would be confronted directly with the stark choices that society's dictates caused many young women of the time to believe were their only options: attempt to employ her talents in some practical professional work that satisfied her aspirations; marry a husband who would be expected to financially reward her in exchange for her sacrificing those aspirations; or remain dependent on family. Her father had already begun urging Jackie to come live with him after college. Edie's relationship with her parent was a warning for Jackie. She needed a plan—to escape, and then to flourish.

There was another lesson learned at Grey Gardens: thoughtful consideration for another person's experience. Jackie maintained her composure with Edie, even when attacked, out of an understanding of the significance of her challenges. After once enduring a hurtful monologue by Edie about Black Jack, witnessed by family friend Doris Francisco, who then apologized on Edie's behalf, Jackie explained, "Oh, Doris, it's so much more complicated than you realize. Forgive Edie. She had reason for being angry at Daddy . . . She's had so much struggle but no way to overcome it." Jackie did not elaborate as to whether she was speaking about money or intimacy, and Doris did not pry.

Jackie left Grey Gardens with more than a mambo album. She carried out "a thick stuffed envelope" of letters, according to Edie, the one Black Jack had originally retrieved from Lasata and left at Grey Gardens the autumn before. In the weeks ahead, Jackie made reference to those writings, recalling several weeks later how Grampy "would praise a poem I had written for him at school and explain how all the lines should have the same number of syllables." She would also write a short story about his wake, barely disguising the identity of family members.

Jackie's great affection for her Bouvier family was lasting. She would eventually write the Beales about her "nostalgia . . . for those sunny days when all the cousins were growing up in East Hampton and there were the great trees at Lasata to shelter us—and you, Aunt Edie, would come in and sing a beautiful song to us." She may not have ever cut pajamas into short-shorts like Grampy or worn sweaters as headscarves like Edie, but like them both, she didn't hesitate to enliven the mundane with a touch of the dramatic or hyperbolic, particularly when it came to her written stories. "I guess we were all on the same wavelength," she wrote the Beales, "which probably means a bit eccentric."

Reviewing her early writings during her train ride from New York to the Kingston, Rhode Island, station, near Newport, would remind Jackie that she not only had a gift for adapting the events of her life into fictionalized stories but had always relied on doing so, particularly as a way of responding to the unpleasant incidents of her life, including her parents' divorce. "It amuses me," she wrote at that time, to craft fairy tales. When her balance was thrown off or her boundaries were crossed, Jackie would retreat into the role of imaginative chronicler, casting allies as heroes, violators as villains, artfully transfiguring reality. She often illustrated her fanciful chronicles with caricatures of friends, family members, teachers—and herself, literally turning her real life into an absurdist cartoon world.

As she would later confide to Richard Nixon, "I always live in a dream world."

9

NEWPORT

September–October 1950

New York. Washington. Boston. New Haven. Hartford. Poughkeepsie, Kingston, Rhode Island. Penn, Grand Central, or Union stations. *The Senator* or *The Patriot* train. Holiday or weekend, coming or going. Jacqueline Bouvier had been riding the rails along the Eastern Seaboard for a decade, and knew the schedules. She could leave New York after lunch and be in time for dinner in Newport.

Seated in the back seat of a family car as it purred in front of the Kingston, Rhode Island, rail station, Mummy impatiently and agitatedly paged through her magazines. If the train was late, she tended to personally blame Jackie, as if she had ordered the conductor to hold the train for her. "I don't know what else may have been troubling her," Yusha recalled of Jackie's Newport arrival that fall, "but her mother was not very nice to Jackie when she came in." Not only were her moods not always attributable to something Jackie had done, but their causes were often unknown even to her. "During cocktails," Yusha recalled, Jackie mentioned the River Lee in Cork, and "what a coincidence that was her mother's family name." Assuming her daughter was suggesting that she was of Irish ancestry, Janet stood up angrily as though to slap her (as she often did)—until Unk came to the rescue. "I always thought they were the Shanghai Lees," he dryly quipped.

Janet *was* Irish, no matter how much she tried to hide it. Her mother, Margaret Merritt, was born and raised in the overcrowded tenements of

New York's Lower East Side, among Italian and Irish immigrants, herself the daughter of County Clare immigrants. As a child she brought in money for her widowed mother, "Mum Maria," by mending clothes.

Janet knew her grandmother well, since, once out of the tenements, the old woman came to live with the family. Always in black, Maria felt she had to earn her keep by housecleaning but, ashamed of her brogue, dashed out of sight into the servants' quarters when guests arrived; her social-climbing granddaughter told friends that Maria was just the old Irish maid. Maria died at age forty-nine, forty days before the Lee-Bouvier wedding. She was buried in Calvary Cemetery in a working-class section of Queens.

It wasn't merely having a mother who was raised in poverty that embarrassed Janet; it was simply *being* Irish. Even more so after marrying Unk, Mummy was forever striving for acceptance by the Eastern Seaboard ruling class. It took more than wealth. Unk's great-grandfather had immigrated from Scotland in 1803 and his family had intermarried with Vanderbilts and Rockefellers, but Janet had to do better. While she was enrolled at Sweet Briar College, one of her Southern belle classmates assumed that, given her name and residency in the Old Dominion, Janet belonged to the famous Lees of Virginia. Mummy not only embraced but also bragged of this faux ancestry.

It's unclear just when Jackie learned of the fallacy, but she made light of her mother's pretense, remarking, "I wish I'd had a Puritan father for an ancestor so I'd have some of their strength of character." Gore Vidal marveled, "I don't know how Janet got away with this . . . it was just nonsense." *Social Register* types who took genealogy seriously were suspicious, the whisper soon trailing her that, as diplomat Charlie Whitehouse put it, "she was Jewish, that Lee was really Levy." (Unk, known by some in the family as a quiet but sincere antisemite, simply dismissed the story as untrue.)

Unk was typically caricatured as disengaged, the caricaturists never putting in context his having lost his father when he was sixteen, leaving him in a household of three women, or his having had to leave one wife due to tragedy while another divorced him due to his sexual impotence. He was a man of few words, perhaps due to a stutter (unknown is whether his stuttering caused him shame or vice versa). Jackie detected his vulnerability. They first bonded over his eighteenth-

and nineteenth-century collection of English caricatures and drawings by Hogarth, Gillray, Rowlandson, and Cruikshank, which she began referencing as she developed her own whimsical cartooning style. Their fondness for each other could not be made too obvious, since Mummy might react jealously if Jackie drew too close, but he served as an essential buffer between her and Janet.

By extending her stay in Europe, Jackie had missed Lee's debutante dinner, Unk's Guernsey-cow competition, Mummy's receiving a blue ribbon for her gladioli, dancing with Uncle Lefty at the Clambake Club, and Nini competing in Tennis Week—all social rituals that bored her. Now Mummy insisted that Jackie's presence was of vital importance and saw to it that her return was heralded in the September 12, 1950, *Newport Daily News.* Jackie's Washington friend Claiborne Pell, whose mother-in-law had a Newport estate, recalled that Jackie spent "as much time outside smoking" as she did socializing with the "appropriate" men Mummy wanted her to dance with, "and there were plenty."

What Jackie loved most about Newport, however, was Hammersmith Farm. There, Jackie shared a bedroom with Lee, sleeping in twin beds on the third floor, where all the children lived in "sunny, drafty rooms." It had, Nini said, "yellow wallpaper, big border of flowers against white ceiling, white wood furniture, caned inset chairs, a little shelf with tiny china animals" that was painted green.

Hammersmith and Merrywood were ruled by Janet to a standard of perfection. She hired more than two dozen household staff to keep the properties in pristine order. Once, when she glimpsed the maid who had the sole task of emptying and cleaning wastebaskets holding one of them unattractively, she slapped her face. Alan Pryce-Jones, a Newport acquaintance, recalled Janet's "explosive, temperamental outbursts," elaborating that "she had a vicious temper. She once pulled a knife on a maid during an argument and threatened to use it."

In marrying Unk, Janet also took charge of her three stepchildren. Besides Yusha, the household included Nini and Tommy. Their half brother Gore Vidal left a scorching account of her: "[S]he was a small woman, with a large pouter-pigeon bust that neatly balanced large low-slung buttocks set atop sandpiper legs. The sallow face was all great curved nose-beak set between small, fierce dark eyes. With me, she was her usual rude self . . . her unconscious jet stream was more than usually turbulent . . . the cawing of Janet's voice [was] like that of some dark crow." When the Newport household got tense, Jackie escaped to Uncle Lefty and Aunt Annie in the "Castle," a smaller house on the property, as she had to their Farmington home during her years at Miss Porter's.

Despite his daughter's closeness with her stepbrother, for an inordinate amount of time, Jack had refused to meet him. Jackie persisted, telling Yusha before he made a trip to New York from boarding school in Groton, "Daddy will be terribly glad to have you." Yusha was uncertain. "I had heard uncomplimentary things about him from my stepmother," he said, "but never from my father."

In 1945, with Unk's discreet permission, Jackie had finally brought her father and stepbrother together, stopping at Black Jack's apartment for a drink before they all went to dinner. As Jackie dressed, her father thanked Yusha for "always supporting her in what she wants to do with her life." He asked Yusha to call him "Uncle Jack." (Eventually, one of Black Jack's girlfriends told Yusha, "Jack thought of you as his son. He never had a son, and he almost thought of you as Jackie's brother instead of stepbrother.") He invited Yusha for dinner on his next trip to New York. On that occasion, Yusha recalled, he "expressed his appreciation for making Jackie feel a part of my family coupled with some resentment towards her mother for taking her away from him." When Yusha told Mummy about the dinner, it "did not sit well."

Still, Jackie pressed forward with her next goal, to have her father and stepfather "get to know each other and get along." As fellow Yalie stockbrokers, both men had previously met and were willing to meet again. But it "never had a chance due to the resentment felt by Janet," Yusha wrote, when she refused to let Unk follow through. Unk "preferred to remain passive" and acquiesced.

As had been the case when Janet wouldn't let Jackie call him during the separation, Black Jack's jealousy of Jackie's time with the Auchincloss produced a series of new edicts. He declared that Jackie could only ride her beloved Danseuse at the East Hampton Riding Club, where she was boarded, and refused to ever let the horse be transported to the Auchincloss homes, a tactic similar to the one he pulled with her car. He delayed sending her monthly allowance unless she sent more letters to him, "that is if you care enough about your father to do so—sometimes I wonder."

She retaliated by writing him idyllic descriptions of the Auchincloss estates, making him feel he was losing her favor. Whenever she mentioned seeing something in New York that she wanted, it triggered Janet to fear that Jack would buy it and *she* would lose favor.

Mummy, however, exercised harsher control over Jackie as she matured, thinking nothing of opening her mail and listening in on her phone calls. During one holiday season, she told Jackie and Yusha that they would be "hosting" a party of guests whom *she* had already chosen and sent invitations to. This prompted Jackie to lament, "[I]t might be nice to know just who is coming to your own party." Mummy scheduled it, of course, for a weekend Jackie was meant to see Black Jack.

Mummy could also needily demand Jackie's attention for dubious reasons. When Jackie had only just started at Vassar and Janet was in New York City, she suddenly claimed to have become ill, calling on her daughter to come and be with her. "Anyway, it's one of those awful things again," Jackie reported to Yusha; "she thinks they'll put her in the hospital and give her transfusions." Whatever the diagnosis, if Janet even bothered to get one, the fact that she fell ill on a weekend when Jackie was supposed to be visiting her father was hardly coincidental.

Mummy wasn't an entirely negative force; her control expressed a desire for her daughter to conform to Janet's own concept of success, and she took her rejection of it as a grave insult, even on matters as inconsequential as Jackie's refusing to play bridge, her favorite pastime. Yet she could also be quite thoughtful. While Jackie was celebrating her birthday in Europe, Janet sent her an unexpectedly moving letter, to which she responded with effusive appreciation: "How can I ever thank you enough for my heavenly birthday letter—you don't know how much it made being far away from home feel like a birthday and especially when I know the frenzy you are in now and it was so sweet of you to write it."

And stepdaughter Nini found Janet to be "steadfast, very dependable," with "common-sense intuition" and a passion for art history. While Nini helped Jackie create her albums of drawings, poetry, and photography, Nini observed that "[p]utting together a scrapbook develops the editorial eye, how to look at things for a purpose." Sharply examining each image and then composing visually appealing layouts was a skill for which Nini felt Jackie could give credit to her mother, who had been scrapbooking herself since she was young, and who asked her children to make them for her as gifts. "By looking at yourself and other people you learn how to be looked at."

Janet's friends emphasized her sociability and gift for creating "havens of hospitality," praising her "poise and dignity" and saying she simply "demanded a certain standard of behavior and good manners." Jackie's friends characterized it differently. Calling Janet a "tough lady," Charlie Bartlett said that Jackie "probably had an anxiety to get out of that house." His wife, Martha, was blunter: "She cared more about her dogs."

There were times, even, when Mummy would hit her adult daughter. Michael Canfield, who later married Lee, disclosed that "Janet would strike her [Jackie] in fits of temper . . . they were very violent." Louis Auchincloss confirmed this, recalling that when "Janet had black moods . . . she'd strike Jackie."

It was therefore an act of great courage for Jackie to make an announcement during her brief stay in Newport before heading to Washington to finish college. After graduating, she told Mummy, she was returning to Paris to live there more permanently. It set Janet off into a hysterical rampage, recalled Yusha, screaming that Jackie was ungrateful for the time she had just spent there. "Jackie usually backed down if her mother challenged her, but not always," he stated. "She was determined to go back to Paris after finishing college. Well, she [Janet] sometimes threw things at her. I did not see it, but Jackie later said her mother . . . threw a magazine at her and said it was the only way she would ever get back there, because she wouldn't help and she wouldn't let her ask my father for help either."

The magazine in question was the August 15, 1950, issue of *Vogue*. In it was an article about its annual "Prix de Paris" writing contest, open to female college seniors. The winner would be "judged on writing ability, grasp of subject matter, and evidence of a special talent."

That year, 1,280 applicants from 225 colleges submitted enrollment applications, due on October 10, 1950. All accepted applicants would be invited to submit the first round of essays, due November 1. For the second round, the field would be winnowed to two hundred contestants, who would choose from a list of topics in the December 1950 *Vogue* with essays due on January 15, 1951. Essays would be graded on "writing style . . . general awareness . . . evidence of ability to think clearly . . . an interesting taste and a ranging mind . . . ability to sense relationships between her subject and others outside it, to use her knowledge of history, the arts, politics, news, persons and places to enliven and to extend the boundaries of a theme."

From there, the contest would be reduced to twelve finalists, who would each submit a 1,500-word essay, the list of topics from the February issue with a March 1 deadline. This one dozen would then be personally interviewed by *Vogue*'s New York editors, from which the winner would be chosen and notified on May 15, 1951. She would then train for six months in New York before leaving for Paris as a junior editor.

In the *Vogue* contest, Jackie found a tangible goal, giving shape to her abstract inclination toward writing. Completing the required essays would be a formidable challenge, but one she was eager to take on.

"Somewhere under heaven today, unknown and unsuspecting, is a girl with Paris in her future," rhapsodized the announcement.

Jackie was determined to prove she was that girl.

Part IV

WRITING

I could be a sort of Overall Art Director
of the Twentieth Century, watching everything
from a chair hanging in space.

—JACKIE, IN AN ESSAY FOR *VOGUE*

10

GEORGE WASHINGTON UNIVERSITY

October–December 1950

On October 2, 1950, Jacqueline Bouvier began her first day at George Washington University, navigating around the urban campus in D.C.'s Foggy Bottom neighborhood. Its buildings were a hodgepodge of converted nineteenth-century homes, dormitories built in the 1930s, and a new Student Union Hall. She was, again, "an outsider."

Most American college students attended one school; this was Jackie's third. Most seniors had already taken general study classes. She was changing majors, which meant a heavier workload. Her class was 40 percent women, but her commitment to graduating made her an anomaly in an era when those who got a diploma instead of a fiancé were considered socially unsuccessful.

Despite her having to live under Mummy's thumb and commute to school, GWU proved an ideal environment. Many of her striving middle-class classmates were the first in their families to attend college, often on the G.I. Bill, and she shared their view that education was the path to success. By not returning to a college dominated by her social peers, most focused on marriage, she spared herself their judgment. During her year at GWU, she unapologetically demonstrated her intellect and drive.

Academics were of paramount importance to Jackie, yet while at Miss Porter's she had felt the need to downplay this. Not until her senior year had she finally confessed just how rigorously she worked, because, as she wrote a friend, "fall term marks this year count most towards getting into college. . . . I'll go on for hours once I get started."

Jackie began GWU purposefully, in the office of an assistant dean, seeking approval to switch her major from English to French literature with a minor in art, consulting on what courses she needed to fulfill this. That settled, she engaged in her studies immediately. In art history class, she illustrated her presentations with color slides she'd photographed in the Louvre, then donated them to the art department. In her French literature class, where students were required to study and compose reports in English on works by France's greatest writers, Jackie secured permission to go beyond expectations and do all her assignments in French.

The Deb of the Year turned heads on campus. "She was so striking," remembered musician David Amram, who was then a junior. "She [had] such a spirit, even then as a very young person, such a dignity, and a bearing, and a feeling, that while none of us would come up and speak to her, we all knew who she was." Finding their "common interest in the arts in America," they attended an international concert at the new Lisner Auditorium: "Jacqueline enjoyed . . . music from another part of the world . . . and to celebrate what we now called 'a worldview.' She always had that."

"She was always very quiet and in the background," recalled a female classmate. "In the Student Union Hall when the other students would be noisy or boisterous, Jacqueline would just stay in the background and look on. She didn't take much part in school activities. . . . She dressed just the way the other girls did then."

Former Vassar classmate Jessie Leigh Hunt said that Jackie had a "reserve without being cold." Despite her having "a lot of friends," Hunt had "a feeling she was alone" and that there were "few that know her well." In contrast to classmates who "were set" in their thinking, she "was evolving, [and] has become more interesting because of it." The characteristic Hunt found most distinct about Jackie Bouvier was that she had an "imagination off-beat."

Jackie admitted that "[m]y life was not connected with the college. In the evenings I would go out with friends and beaux or stay home and study. That was the year I was trying for the Prix de Paris—so between term papers and Prix papers . . . there was lots of studying."

* * *

ON OCTOBER 10, THE day of the deadline, Jackie finished her application to enroll in the *Vogue* contest and mailed it in, along with a note to the contest director, Mary Campbell. She lied to explain what would be the late arrival of the application, writing, "I returned from Europe only a week ago and then it took me several days to get hold of an August issue of *Vogue* as there were none left on the newsstands." In truth, she had returned on September 12, and Mummy had thrown that *Vogue* issue at her within two weeks after that. She told a second fib, saying she "completed three years at Vassar," but not mentioning the Sorbonne, perhaps thinking editors would favor contestants who'd never lived in Paris.

Fearing *Vogue* might deny her application because it was late, she tried to prove her worthiness by saying she would just "go ahead" and write the first round of essays—due November 1—even before they determined whether the application would be accepted. To her relief, her application was accepted, but two and a half weeks later, on October 31, she wrote Campbell again, "ashamed to be asking for an extension" for her first round of essays. While admitting "it was stupid of me not to have gotten them done way ahead of the deadline," she blamed the delay on a student she paid to type the four essays. In claiming to have already handwritten the thirteen thousand words of flowing prose in just four days, she clearly forgot her earlier claim that she'd begun writing weeks before then. Whether or not Campbell caught this, she accepted Jackie's essays when they arrived on November 3.

Despite her uncertain start, her willingness to risk disqualification by telling a few lies attested to just how intently Jackie now wanted to write—and return to Paris.

For her essay on those she wished she had met, Jackie chose men of poetry, playwriting, and ballet: Charles Baudelaire, Oscar Wilde, and Serge Diaghilev, respectively. In it, she disclosed a deep discernment about the creative process. Her analysis was that "a common theory runs through their work, a certain concept of the intersection of the arts," and she provocatively observed that these artists shared "a belief that beauty in art has nothing to do with the questions of good or evil."

Baudelaire and Wilde were "idealists who could paint their sinfulness with honesty," and Wilde could capture the late Victorian era "with the flash of an epigram." She pinpointed what she called Baudelaire's "theory of synesthesia, a tendency to associate the impressions given by one of the senses with those of another." It was something that Jackie herself did, as evidenced in her vivid descriptions in her essay of the "sensory images" of Wilde's poetry: ". . . the yellow liquid light pools in the street cut by the stiletto tree branches outside the *Harlot's House*, the musk of gold heat that emanates from a vase of flowers in the *Music Room*."

She included Diaghilev for how he blended Eastern and Western cultural elements in his ballets. She would also famously emulate the singular quality she admired about him: "[H]e possessed what is rarer than artistic genius in any one field; the sensitivity to take the best of each man and incorporate it into a masterpiece all the more precious because it lives only in the minds of those who have seen it and disintegrates as soon as he is gone."

Jackie concluded with a fantastical declaration of the role she would most like to play in the larger world, "Overall Art Director of the Twentieth Century, watching everything from a chair hanging in space."

More personal was her biographical profile, necessitating objectivity about her attributes and deficiencies. After admitting, "I do not have a sensational figure but can look slim if I pick the right clothes," she delineated her literary heroes as *The Jungle Book*'s Mowgli, *Gone with the Wind*'s Scarlett O'Hara, *Little Lord Fauntleroy*'s Earl of Dorincourt, and Robin Hood.

In her beauty-care essay, she announced that "good grooming" was "more important than beauty," and urged a "vinegar rinse" for hair sheen, cologne to save on perfume costs, and Dorothy Gray's Dry Skin Mixture—which contained radioactive particles. Known for biting her nails, Jackie suggested using polish only on long nails. She suggested using two hours each Thursday for grooming because "you should never have to scream in anguish . . . when told that your best beau has arrived unexpectedly and is waiting downstairs." Admitting that she'd been smoking ever since a friend gave her a Longfellow "in the balcony of the Normandie theatre in New York" (and was kicked out for loudly coughing), she advised smokers to rinse with peroxide because "nothing will be counted against you faster than a dingy smile."

She identified three outfits featured in the August issue of *Vogue* as her ideal wardrobe for college—a "dark grey suit" for daytime and traveling, a sleeveless plaid wool dress for casual wear, and an orange-rayon taffeta skirt with a black velvet top for evenings out, none of which would "look outdated next winter when I might be working in the city." Instead of buying new dresses, she said she'd keep wearing the grey suit and "spend my money on carefully chosen accessories." She thought the plaid dress was perfect for "beer and pretzels at the Dutch Cabin," and the evening gown would "look delicious" with "an apron that you don't take off after you've shown him that you can cook too."

Often writing into the early morning, completing the essays must have been a relief. Since high school, she'd always found comfort in her "radio and cigarettes" while working late, finding that music "always does something to me," especially *Your Hit Parade*, which played songs from the best-selling records. Although taking a typing class, Jackie confessed to Mary Campbell at *Vogue* that "it still takes me ten minutes to peck my way through a sentence," so she drafted and composed in her clear, loopy penmanship.

Although Merrywood was home to nine family members, in the weeks before Thanksgiving 1950, Jackie was often the only one in residence. Yusha, Lee, Tommy, and Nini were away at school. Unk and Mummy returned from Newport in mid-October but left by month's end, attending Lee's debut in Tuxedo Park, New York, staying in the city and, at year's end, Boston.

Jackie's relationship with her siblings varied. As their letters attest, Yusha had long been her emotional confidant. She felt a maternal instinct toward her toddler half sister, Janet, and half brother, Jamie. Her most elusive bond was with stepbrother Tommy, who had been sent to boarding school at eight years old and spent his entire summers at camp. Although Jackie was protective toward Lee, her stepsister Nini was a more natural companion. Nini also rode well and read voraciously; she later earned a master's degree in journalism from Columbia University, worked as a reporter, and wrote a novel, all while raising three sons. When Nini, Lee, and Jackie went out together, they were dubbed "the Nini, the Pinta and the Santa Maria." Her Auchincloss siblings, however, lived with the security of knowing that they would each inherit around $2 million when they reached twenty-one years of age, along with trust dividends.

Jackie's room in the massive Georgian-revival brick mansion was at the foot of the first-stair landing, "not much larger than a closet," as its former occupant Gore Vidal described it, with an adjoining white-tiled bathroom. Its most inspiring feature was a big window that looked out beyond the lawn and woods to the Potomac River. Jackie spent hours here, writing and drawing, but also had two other places on the verdant forty-acre estate that offered solitude.

The property had terraced lawns, tennis courts, a swimming pool, a pool house, a riding stable and ring, and covered garages, encircled by thick woods. The sound of the gushing Potomac River could be heard inside the house when it was empty and silent. It was dangerous beauty. Beyond the lawn was a sheer wall of jagged rock, which dropped precipitously to the river below. Poison ivy grew wild along the path to a boulder at the furthermost point, which she christened "Lookout Rock." Returning home by dusk, she would find a moment of peace by rambling to the spot, as she "watched it grow dark" and looked at "the river through the dogwood trees."

Her other secret place was Unk's library, where she pored over his old volumes of literature, history, philosophy, and architecture. When she first arrived, Jackie fixated on a shelf of multiple leather-bound volumes by Alexandre Dumas, reading each in order. "I can remember a slight commotion when I lost volume twenty-one," she recalled, "but I found it somewhere."

She formed friendships with the household staff, who were often her only companions in the house; she brought each a gift after her first trip to Europe, from rosary beads blessed by the Pope for the Irish cook to gloves for an elderly butler. She liked hanging out in the stables with Doc, the family's handyman and horse groomer, because he was "wonderful at spitting tobacco." She named a Scottie dog she gave Mummy in a hatbox "Corkscrew," a sly reference to Doc, who, she noticed, would take sips of whiskey from a flask.

About six dogs lived with the family over time. At Merrywood, besides Corkscrew, there were poodles Caprice and Gally, Great Dane Ellita, and Welsh terrier Woofty, and she scrutinized their individual personalities; she felt calmed by having them in her room when she worked.

It was Merrywood's broader natural world that most soothed her. Beyond "the rock," she scaled down a short ravine to stare silently at the churning Potomac, where "the most peaceful feeling comes over me & I forget the hectic little life of parties." She even went down there when it rained, and during snowstorms and thunderstorms, finding it "wet and fresh and beautiful." The ineffable metaphysical sense she experienced in silence, Yusha suggested to her, was her "inner self . . . which is the guiding light of your life."

The holiday season at home kicked off with Mummy's December 3 birthday. Jackie's annual present was a piece of original writing. Her most elaborate was the first one she composed after Mummy married Unk in 1942, a metaphor of their marriage told through her short story about Woofty of "Merrybone" longing for Caprice, "French countess from New York." More typical were poems, like the 1940 one she composed after the divorce. In it, she teased Mummy about "telling the elevator man your age," recalled how she cried during Jackie's First Communion, and cooked them steaks "that were blue inside." There was even a poignant reference to Janet's taking them to Nevada to divorce their father: "You were sick on the plane with us going out west." Her 1945 birthday poem, the first after half sister "Little Janet's" birth, predicted that Janet would be the first woman president and win five terms, leaving FDR "jealous in his grave," while the other children "failed in every walk of life, are now in jail or on relief."

That Christmas, Jackie's creativity was in evidence. She staged the family's annual Nativity play, a tradition she began as a child, handwriting the programs and listing which sibling played which character. As gifts, she made them caricatures or wrote poems. For her young half-siblings, she wrote and illustrated a children's book. She gave Mummy her painting of Cork's River Lee, which Yusha thought was her unsubtle statement about Mummy's ancestors from that city. He recalled his stepmother snapping, "I thought you were a writer now, not a painter." All Jackie said about it was that she liked to "paint things that my mother doesn't put in the closet until a month after I have given them to her at Christmas."

Her creativity was now being harnessed in pursuit of a significant goal. She upset Lee by missing her New York debutante ball on December 18, but Jackie had to begin work on the next round of four *Vogue* essays, which were due on January 15. An early holiday present had come for her just after Thanksgiving: Jacqueline Bouvier had made the first cut of two hundred semifinalists. She would not grovel again for an extension. She might impress the editors with her work, but she knew that missing another deadline would be a mark against her. As she wrote to the *Vogue* editors, "a career on a magazine is what I have always had in mind and this seems the perfect way to start trying for it."

11

LAST SEMESTER

January–March 1951

While the social columns that winter chronicled how Mummy helped host a debutante tea at Washington's Sulgrave Club and that Lee headlined a formal dinner at Baltimore's Mount Vernon Club, Jackie was consumed by her *Vogue* essays, pausing only to invigorate her body and mind by riding horses and devouring books.

Except for tennis, Jackie preferred exercising alone. She excelled at swimming. Not so much at skiing. "I slide down the hill backwards just when I'm halfway up," she confessed, "and fall down and my skis come off in the middle of a great leap and I freeze to death." Riding, however, was her meditative discipline, practiced in solitude except for a beloved horse.

With Washington temperatures averaging 48 degrees in the first two months of 1951, Jackie would dash outside in slacks and a turtleneck sweater and mount the formidable Chief or the unpredictable Sagebrush to gallop hard or meander slowly across Merrywood, from the shooting range to the forest of black walnut trees, which had supplied the library's wood paneling. Afterward, she appreciatively brushed her beloved beasts in their stable. While Janet judged horses by how well they carried her from one silver trophy to the next, Jackie considered them friends.

If she could ride regularly only at Merrywood, Jackie could indulge her other primary escape anywhere. Jackie liked reading two books at a time, usually in different genres. She consumed works by Hemingway,

Twain, Poe, Hawthorne, and Maugham, but also obscure new authors. George Plimpton recalled her recommending *The Town and the City* long before its author, Jack Kerouac, earned acclaim. She loved rereading "my treasures," she told Yusha the previous fall, asking him to fetch her "tiny little art and ballet books—Shakespeare, etc." from storage in Newport. She was familiar with most French literature. When journalist Richard Lemon told her about an obscure new translation of François-René de Chateaubriand's works, she not only already knew about it but declared to him that "his novels were romantic and fluffy."

Her intense focus on the *Vogue* essays, however, upset both of her parents.

On New Year's Day, Black Jack waited for the phone call she usually made to him, but it never came. The "thoughtlessness was crushing," his nephew remembered, and left him "feeling abandoned and alone." And Mummy argued that Jackie was unwisely investing her time, because no wealthy man would marry an intellectual woman. It was not only, as one of Jackie's chroniclers later put it, that Janet "criticized her love of books and learning," but she maintained that if Jackie did not start to "conceal how bright she was" she would never "land a husband."

Mummy might have been correct if Jackie had been striving to become a wife rather than a writer. Her next set of essays, though, required a shift. The first set had given a sense of who she was, but the second round required a technical and professional tone, suggestive of just what type of *Vogue* editor she might be.

She wrote an original short story about Grampy Jack's wake, one opinion piece on how to best visually present new women's fashions, another opinion piece on men's fashion, and then a critique of *Vogue*'s December story on perfumes, paired with her own alternative version of it.

She opined in her first opinion piece that *Vogue* should primarily feature a professional model to show new fashions, who must "efface herself and call attention to her dress," and use photographers who captured "the cut, fabric, and detail of a dress." Revealing her breadth of artistic knowledge, she suggested the magazine give its fashion illustrations a "moved-up-to-the-1950s" look by emulating the work of early-twentieth-century artist Kees van Dongen, whose style she admitted to copying in her own paintings. Conceding that it would be occasionally "fun to come across Marlene Dietrich brooding in a great black cape," she concluded that "offensive as the clink of silver may be, *Vogue* could not exist if the clothes it featured did not sell."

In her second opinion essay, she gave a "new approach for *Vogue* on the subject of men's fashions," reflecting an attentiveness learned from her fashionable father and her savvy for technique, branding, and marketing. *Esquire* would always dominate men's fashion, so *Vogue* articles on men's fashion should be "directed at women" who might help men with a wardrobe that, although "bound by convention and good taste," could reflect "color, variety and elegance." She proposed articles on shirts, collars, cuffs, ties, suspenders, and suits, and a regular feature of two facing pages of photographs of one well-dressed and one badly dressed famous man. She argued the feminist point that women should not be held responsible for the way men dress, and that men should learn to do it for themselves.

Jackie's final essay was a critique of *Vogue*'s December feature, "Famous Noses, Famous Scents." She complimented the "eye-catching, appropriate and original" layout of noses in black-and-white photographs at the page's top. She warned that, though it had such "shock power," readers might forget the drawings of perfume bottles at the bottom. She offered her own detailed version, blending her knowledge of history and literature and the senses. She began with a theory that perfume was "analogous to wine," since both "act upon the closely related sense of taste and smell to produce an intoxicating effect," and suggested blending poetry about perfume and literature about wine, from "Omar Khayyam to Colonel Cantwell and Renata."

For her section on perfume and poetry, she envisioned a two-page spread. Quite specifically, in the upper-right-hand corner of the left page, she wanted some brief text connecting perfume and literature, and "a full-page photograph of a finely-grained bookshelf filled with thin bound and tooled volumes," with bottles of perfume between the books. "In color it could be quite effective, with the red and green and gold of the books, the sheen of the wood and the liquid amber sealed inside beautifully cut bottles." On the right, she envisioned a photograph of an open book "with parchment pages for texture interest," alongside an open perfume bottle. She wanted three quotes about poetry, across both pages: from Milton's *Samson Agonistes* ("Coveted by all the winds that hold them play / An amber accent of odorous perfume / Her harbinger"); Shakespeare's *Hamlet* ("A violet in the youth of my primy nature / Forward, not permanent sweet, not lasting / The perfume and suppliance of a minute"); and a poem of Oscar Wilde's ("And the perfume of your soul / Is vague and suffusing / with the pungence of sealed spice jars").

In her haste, Jackie made a few errors pertaining to these quotes for her essay. In the correct Milton quotation, "Coveted" should be "Courted," while the poem that she identified as being written by Oscar Wilde was in fact an excerpt from Amy Lowell's "A Lady."

She envisioned a similar layout for her take on wine and perfume, with the suggested headline of either "Intoxicating Liquids" or "The Petal and the Grape." As on the first spread, she wanted some brief introductory text on the left page's right-hand corner, with a large background image of wine-cellar compartments with perfume bottles labeled like wine bottles in each. She suggested that this be in black and white, with "the black depths of the compartments pointing up the reflections of the glass bottles." On the right, over black, she wanted "strewn flower petals," with a blurred impression of a woman pouring perfume out of a "diorama bottle" into a thin-stemmed crystal wineglass.

She submitted the essays by the January 15 deadline, and began her last semester of college.

IT WAS A HEAVY course load for a graduating senior. She took a writing class in journalism because, she later told Molly Thayer, "I wanted to know people better. I thought that studying journalism would be a great chance." Other courses included Man in Modern Society; Readings for the Major in French Literature; and Development of European Civilization—she found the last one's instructor, Dean Elmer Louis Kayser, to be a "most incredible teacher." After a few weeks in an economics class, she "decided I wasn't up to [it]," as she later admitted. Finance and business bored her.

The class in which she most thrived was her advanced English composition course, Short Story, taught by Muriel McClanahan, who fondly recalled how Bouvier "always sat in the back of the classroom" next to a French-Canadian student, Joe Metivier, so they could whisper during class, "always in French." She and Jackie formed an affectionate mutual respect.

"She was an extremely intelligent young woman, but she also possessed a brilliant imagination," said McClanahan. "This was coupled with a genuine talent for the craft of writing. She had a gift as a writer and might have become prominent in her own right as a writer had she followed another path." She covered many different subjects, including "the beauty and peace of her family's home in Virginia" and "the purpose and excitement of art to the soul. She was beautiful, and she could write like a million. She didn't need to take my class." For an assignment to write "a simple activity," Jackie submitted "In Florence," on February 16, 1951, her sensuous tale of a romantic night with "Monty," earning an A+.

George Washington University was Washington, D.C.'s, last segregated college, and President Cloyd Heck Marvin was waging a losing battle against student groups who wanted it integrated, which finally happened three years after Jackie graduated. The controversy made national headlines. When she resumed residency in the Washington area, in late 1950, its segregated restaurants, theaters, and stores were just beginning to be picketed and boycotted. Jackie left no record of how she viewed segregation, but fellow alumna Jane Lingo reflected that "it would have been impossible" for her to be unaware of the campus debate. It also would have been easy for her to ignore it from behind the gates of Merrywood.

Although her free time was limited, she wasn't entirely without a social life. She took a vacation in Nassau in April, and hosted a weekend of activities in Washington for visiting Princeton students. Tucky, who didn't go to college but instead went to work at a travel agency, was a frequent weekend visitor. She did make a new friend in Lorraine Rowan, an older divorcée, and would visit the small Georgetown home of newlyweds Charlie Bartlett and the former Martha Buck, both of whom she had known independently. Martha found that although Jackie usually "looked out for herself," she made an effort to see Martha, being the only friend the newlywed had in Washington. Charlie, a journalist, "felt bad" for Jackie, who seemed to have "a lot of problems from her parents and the divorce," but was fascinated by her "wonderful imagination."

As always, Yusha was her ballast. After finishing at Yale, he returned to Merrywood in the new year while pursuing rank placement in the Marine Corps. He was quick to engage her in conversations about his favorite topic of world affairs. Southeast Asia, he told her, was where the most dramatic changes were occurring. Although the United States was enmeshed in the Korean War, Yusha recalled that Jackie remained fixated on "the French war" in Indochina.

Introduced to the works of André Malraux while in France, Jackie had "already read his famous book," *Man's Fate*, according to Yusha; that winter she was poring over much of his writings on both Indochina and the relationship between the arts and government. Yusha was amused that Janet asked Jackie if she was "reading communist material, and Jackie rolled her eyes and said, 'Oh, Mummy it's art and philosophy.' Of course, she never said anything about Malraux starting a paper and organization that led to Ho Chi Minh creating the Viet Minh."

If either found himself or herself without a date to social events, one was always available to accompany the other. Jackie loved dances but felt insecure going on her own. Yusha detested and avoided them. "Well, you promised you'd go," she implored in one letter, "couldn't you come with me? I need you desperately." She was always able to "drag" him out, and they often passed the time observing pompous guests.

With a stepbrother as her daughter's primary social companion, Mummy's worries about Jackie extended beyond Communism. In just months, her daughter would graduate from college and turn twenty-two. While no definite deadline had been set for when she was expected to fly the coop, Jackie didn't want to linger under Mummy's hawkeyed gaze.

As she would explain to a *Vogue* editor, ever since 1944 she had been functioning "without ever having a home base, which Mummy seems to feel is important" and thus "feels terrifically strong about keeping me 'in the home,'" which "is why I went to George Washington this winter." Jackie's conflict was simply that she "would rather work at what interests me than have a home base." She was eager to declare soon that she had "escaped being frozen here for the rest of my life!"

Not that she was self-sufficient. "The cook is out & I have to make my lunch," she once admitted to Yusha of her cooking skills. "I've burnt five pieces of toast & I tried to make a fried egg but it stuck to the pan & I can't get it out . . . now I'm eating sort of pink Jellowy soup . . . I'm starving." As the self-admitted "messiest creative on earth," it was only on her "last day" of her semester that she had "a great splurge to clean everything up . . . I'm sure I shall go to heaven."

With only her monthly $545 allowance from Black Jack, Jackie would not have been able to afford rent on even a modest apartment and be able to cover her living expenses at the same time. Neither was she capable of living on a budget. Overdrawing her account by unwittingly writing bad checks at boarding school, and reminded that there was a potential $1,000 fine and jail time if caught doing so, she covered her embarrassment with humor. "I'm patiently waiting for the cops to nab me," she told Yusha, "but I only had about 50 cents anyway." She may have griped about Mummy's "keeping me in the home," but it was an estate with servants to cook and clean for her.

Many of her friends now had rich husbands—rather than parents—who supported them. For her to sustain her privileged life by marrying, her potential husband would need to have great wealth. If he was a contemporary, like most of her beaux had been so far, he would have to be either unusually successful in his profession or heir to a fortune, or an older, independently affluent man. This did not even take into account what would be, for her, the primary issue of compatibility: given her unusual degree of intellect for a woman of any class at that time, Jackie would have been happy only with someone with an equal or greater intelligence, curiosity, and passion for knowledge. Complicating this was her Catholicism in a dating pool that was mostly Protestant; families of both faiths still largely expected their children to marry someone of the same denomination. Further, the pressure of expectation from both parents meant that her ideal prospective husband would have the status by which they judged success—ancestry, selective boarding school and college educations, exclusive club memberships, powerful social and business connections, and a favorable position in a respected profession with a high income.

While Jackie didn't overtly acknowledge her calculation of men as commodities, she had been inculcated with this perspective by Mummy's words and deeds. Her Auchincloss stepsiblings and half-siblings, secure about their future financial stability, had less need to think about the wealth of their potential spouses. When Jackie once echoed Janet's transactional view, Yusha called it out, saying, "[Y]ou seem to so emphatically imply in your last letter that love goes with fortune."

The second option was to pursue a career. If Jackie took this route, she would have to determine whether a steady commitment with a set salary or a series of freelance contracts with unpredictable earnings would be the better option.

The former Deb of the Year was no stranger to certain forms of work. In East Hampton, she'd volunteered for the Red Cross during the war. At

Hammersmith Farm, which provided the local navy base with dairy products, she performed farm chores. (Her primary assignment was to gather eggs from the henhouse; she called the chickens "mean" and played ball with some eggs that broke on her.) She hated milking the cows; although she joined 4-H, she never entered their competitions. Jackie also had a summer job working at a local hospital maternity ward, where she liked to "watch the fathers see [the babies] for the first time." At Miss Porter's, she'd worked as a waitress—albeit not a very good one. "I waited on the tables and broke five cups and one butter plate and the plate broke on an old girl's head . . . I wanted to sink through the floor." At Vassar, she worked as a switchboard operator for pin money. After she got a paycheck for a modeling stint, her father shut down her idea of it as regular work, saying it was for "a woman on the make."

So what to do? As a young teenager realizing "I couldn't be a ballet dancer" for lack of the necessary physicality, she thought that a costume designer was "what I would like to be," so she could "be connected with it [the ballet] through costumes." As part of her high school drama club Jackie worked on scenery design, but "the whole darn set of the apple orchard fell on me—and pin[ned] me down for hours." Hoping for better luck at scripting and producing original musical comedy for the senior class proved frustrating: "I am writing it and no one will come to rehearsals."

Acting was soon to follow. After auditioning for the Dramatic Club Players, she wrote to Yusha that she realized "what a strain" being an actress could be, sarcastically adding that it was more "down my alley" than being a math teacher. She bragged to Gramps Lee, "I think I'll be an actress . . . I'll be the toast of the town." She nevertheless remained intrigued by acting as a profession even after marriage, once asking Gore Vidal, "Do you think it's too late?" More enamored with the fame it could bring than the craft of it, she ultimately admitted, "I'd never be willing to starve and tramp the streets day and night for the sake of art!"

Fame also factored into her writing aspirations. "Someday I'll send him a literary masterpiece," she wrote to Yusha about a boy who demeaned her ambition when she was fifteen, "that will make him swallow his braces." And writing remained her primary passion, where she could so eagerly indulge her imagination and lose herself for hours on end. She even wrote when she had other tasks to perform, once allowing a switchboard to light up with unanswered calls, another time so distracted by it while working as a tennis match scorekeeper that she would "yell scores which I get all wrong." So, by 1951, embarking on some type of writing career was what Jackie really wanted to do. She made her first declaration of this ambition that spring, to *Vogue*'s editors: "I have always known that I wanted to 'do something' with my life but I could never visualize just how to go about it. I have vague little dreams of locking myself up somewhere and turning out children's books and *New Yorker* short stories."

Jackie made clear to Mummy that she was inclined toward the option of finding work instead of a husband, though not specifying the field of writing. Mummy discussed the matter with Unk. One can only speculate about the mysterious chapter in Jacqueline Bouvier's story that followed.

Over the previous two years she had mastered French, and now she excelled at speaking, reading, writing, and translating the language. It has been assumed that Unk, with his network of powerful figures in government and the defense industry, introduced his stepdaughter to an official who offered her a job where those skills could be used at a new federal department, created four years earlier amid the rising Cold War tensions: the Central Intelligence Agency.

Several of Jackie's Vassar peers, also skilled in linguistics, were going to work for the CIA as translators on short-term contracts. Jackie indicated that she intended to do the same in a letter she wrote to the *Vogue* editors later that spring, in which she said, "I have talked to the man in [the] CIA who would be my employer. I pestered him for the job, promised I would take it . . . and the government is spending money clearing me," meaning her background investigation was already under way. The only reason "why I applied for a CIA job," she elaborated, was because her mother wanted her to continue living at home and would allow it due to the fact that it was only "a special job on a certain project," to begin in October and end in January 1952.

Despite Jackie's agreeing to her mother's mandate of living at home even if she was commuting to a CIA job, Janet was unsatisfied. She had acceded to Jackie's choice of Vassar College, despite its putting her closer to Black Jack (and, albeit indirectly, leading her to the Sorbonne). Even though she saw no real need, other than academic prestige, for a woman to earn her degree, she had gone along with Jackie's intention to graduate. She even arranged for her to do so, via GWU, although Jackie had to accept Mummy's home rule. (There would be no scandalous late night at a boy's apartment as there had been while at Vassar.) Now it seemed that Janet felt the time had come for Jackie to do as *she* wanted and find a husband.

Jackie was well aware of how many of her peers were engaged without the anxiety of Mummy harping on the subject of potential spouses. At the end of February, she served as a bridesmaid for Jessie Leigh Hunt. Two weeks later, she was at the wedding of Bow Bowdoin's sister Julia. (Bow was already married.) Tension with Mummy grew sharper that winter. She began discouraging Yusha's long talks with Jackie, then suggested it was best if she went to dances without him so she would appear available. On one particular night, Janet demanded that Jackie join her and Unk at a formal event in town. Her daughter seemed to give in. Yusha recalled that as Mummy was then getting ready, Jackie suddenly announced she wasn't going and Janet "went berserk." Not quite so mature that she no longer feared Janet's slap across her face, she returned to her room and began dressing. "She resisted in subtle ways," Yusha noted of that night. "She kept changing her mind about what to wear . . . She really wanted to make them late." With Unk keeping the peace as they finally began their drive into the city, Janet began criticizing Jackie's lipstick and suggested she was overdressed. "It never ended," he added with a sigh, retelling her account of the evening. Janet's more eviscerating critiques were about Jackie's looks, especially her "kinky hair."

Instead of lashing back, Jackie used evasion, subversion, and placation. She veiled Janet's criticism in a sarcastic passage of her *Vogue* autobiographical sketch, writing that "often my mother will run up to inform me that my left stocking seam is crooked or the right-hand top coat button about to fall off. This, I realize, is the Unforgivable Sin." In a short story for her composition class, Jackie depicted Mummy as wasting hours at her vanity.

Janet's criticism may have dented Jackie's self-esteem, but it didn't destroy it. Asides in her letters suggest that she had found a delicate balance between insecurity and confidence about her appearance. She despised most of her photos yet also wanted copies of them: "I know it's a revolting trait—but I love to see pictures of me!" She worried about getting varicose veins and sunspots, but as far as "having to wear glasses for reading, I wouldn't mind at all." Her suspicions were easily aroused by "fake flattery." And she criticized men who judged women by a single attribute or deficiency: "Even if they don't like her face—you really can't have everything and isn't her figure enough?"

HER IMAGINATION HAVING BEEN fueled by Jackie's 1950 letters, Lee Bouvier was now, Jackie wrote to Father Leonard, "dying to go to Europe next summer—she has never been." The Auchinclosses agreed to send Lee as a present for her graduating from Miss Porter's that June, and "mapped out the most studious trip . . . every cathedral and museum on the Continent." This gave Jackie a potentially improved angle to get herself back to Europe (at least briefly) over endeavoring to win the selective Prix de Paris competition. "I am trying to persuade Mummy that it wouldn't be fair to send her with a Latin [teacher] [for] the first time and that I would really be a much better guide."

Janet might control her daughter's deeds but she could never control her thoughts. Like all tyrants, Janet was blinded by her arrogance. She believed she was determining what her daughter was becoming. Yet, crafty as Jackie could be in giving the impression that she would follow the course Mummy laid out, Jacqueline Bouvier never relinquished her right to the larger future she intended to have. It drove her on.

Following Black Jack's advice, Jackie had learned never to be entirely vulnerable or offer her full thoughts. She adhered to an edict about dating she once related to Yusha: "[M]ystery always helps." So expert was she in conveying the impression of a prospective dutiful bride that few recognized *she* was the hunter in search of an equal partner.

During the winter social season, elite Washington families sent their adult children to the weekly Mrs. Shippen's Dancing Class at the Sulgrave Club on Dupont Circle. As Gore Vidal recalled, students were taught "to deport themselves in such a way that in due course they would marry someone from the dancing class . . . and settle down to a decorous life."

One Shippen's event Jackie attended with Mummy and Unk that winter was the St. Valentine's Day dance. There she met John Husted, a tall, blond, handsome New York banker, and a guest of his aunt, Helen Husted. His parents knew the Auchinclosses and also Daddy. John had gone to St. Paul's prep school in New Hampshire, then Yale; served in the war; and worked on Wall Street. Jackie knew two of his sisters from Miss Porter's. "I was immediately attracted to her," he readily admitted. Mummy approved. And while Jackie may not have taken John's instant ardor with great enthusiasm, she soon recognized that his mere existence had put a stop to Mummy's badgering.

That night, John asked Jackie to dance. He seemed to think she accepted because she liked him, but Jackie, who loved dancing when she was in a celebratory mood, may have had something else on her mind. A few days before, she had received a letter from Condé Nast, informing her that of the two hundred contestants invited to participate in the final round of essays, she had been chosen as one of a dozen finalists. She was now invited to compose and submit what would prove to be the most ambitious and intense of the contest assignments: a narrative version of her vision for an entire *Vogue* issue.

12

VOGUE

April–June 1951

Jacqueline Bouvier's final *Vogue* submission was a small masterpiece. Using "Nostalgia" as her theme, she composed an introductory editorial and then outlined six fashion and five feature articles. She was "evoking the past," not re-creating it, suggesting a cover image of a drawing by frequent *Vogue* artist Eugene Berman to "capture the romanticism of the far-off and the bygone." She justified her "backward glances" to "other countries, other times," in her introduction:

"There is a loveliness in the whisper of another era, a softness and a shadow that have not had time to settle on our spanking-new decade . . . we are none of us insensitive to an echo of the past. We think Nostalgia can be cloying when evinced in cluttered rooms with crochet[ed] antimacassars . . . in a weepy feeling at the mention of the 'good old days,' but we think it can add a grace and a nuance . . . when it is hinted at occasionally." Even in their "own very U.S.A. living room," readers wearing the "harking-back clothes" she described in her issue would indulge in coquetry, and "when subtly done, that is never bad."

She began with six types of fashion articles.

The largest of these featured clothes that resembled costumes: a Scottish Sherlock Holmes cape; an Imperial Russian fox-collar tunic coat; a trumpet skirt and bolero jacket resembling a Spanish riding habit; a buttoned cape cut like a priest's cassock; a massive red taffeta dress, coat, and pillbox hat that looked like it could belong to a Venetian cardinal; a tight-fitting jacket with bows like those worn by a Directoire dandy; a hanging, belted dress and coat with mandarin collars that looked like it might be worn by "a Myanmar pedestrian"; and a boxy, tapered jacket with wide lapels and a carnation boutonniere that suggested a gigolo.

The second, "Echo the Ages in the Evening," presented colorful gowns worn by famous women of the time, such as Nehru's wife, Kamala, in a stylized sari on an Indian prayer rug; Princess Alexandra of Greece in a calla lily tunic next to a classical statue; and socialite Babe Paley in an Edwardian-style gown beside a Sargent portrait.

"Moments for Memories" was her third fashion article, consisting of a two-page spread of white "enormously full skirted" wedding and debutante dresses photographed against a black background with white type, clothes that would be forever preserved in "folds of tissue paper" to be "your own very special piece of nostalgia." The next one, "For the Girl with More Taste than Money," aimed at those unable to buy *Vogue*'s expensive couture, used a "sleeveless sheath with scooped neckline" and, in a three-page black-and-white layout, showed how it could be transformed via nine imaginatively different accessories: a long-sleeved striped blouse with white collars and cuffs worn over it would conjure "the schoolgirl blouse." Worn with a "great dip brimmed black hat," it would give the impression of a "femme fatale one takes to hear tangos at teatime." By attaching organza balloon shoulders to it, a woman could look like a member of "the Corps de Ballet of *Giselle*." Twining a red chiffon scarf through necklaces and dozens of arm bracelets would make a woman in the sheath ready "to dance the Charleston." Slipping a short-sleeved ribbed turtleneck over the dress and donning wrist gloves and a beret would have the wearer "swagger like D'Artagnan." A red petticoat peeking out beneath the hem would "bring Andalucia into the living room." A large "Alice in Wonderland butterfly bow" with long streamers would turn the sheath into a cocktail dress. Draping it with a black-fringed red cape referenced the Gay '90s, while a striped taffeta apron worn over it would make the wearer "feel as if you stepped out of *Tales of the Arabian Nights*."

In her fifth fashion article, Jackie suggested a spread of contemporary hats inspired by historical imagery—a Renaissance page's beanie, a matador's bicorne, a sailor's cap, a flapper's cloche, a clerical calot. Her final article used photos of colored dresses set in larger images of colorful paintings—like gray in a Whistler, blue in a Persian miniature, yellow in a Gauguin—to provoke a nostalgic feeling.

Finally, Jackie created five feature articles with the theme of nostalgia. The most intriguing proposal was for an article to be written by an authority on Proust who could explain his "exact science of evoking the past," using "sensory perception" (which she used herself), wherein if "one concentrated upon [an object] intensely" it could "set off a chain of thoughts that will put the thinker back" into a similar past situation.

The second feature she suggested was the obscure F. Scott and Zelda Fitzgerald story "Show Mr. and Mrs. F. to Number—," which she deemed "beautifully written," about the series of hotel rooms the couple lived in, with "echoes of the twenties." Her third feature was an assortment of excerpts from humor pieces by writers of an earlier generation, such as H. L. Mencken. A "Gossipy Memo," another to be written by an unspecified social critic, referencing historical events such as the *Titanic* sinking, Lindbergh's flight, Shirley Temple, and the Teapot Dome scandal, was her fourth contribution. Finally, she conceived "*Vogue* Nominations for Nostalgia," taking bits of recent pop culture that she predicted would induce nostalgia in twenty years, like "television fever," the comeback of prizefighter Joe Louis, and the Broadway musical *South Pacific*.

Bouvier's submission made the rounds of a dozen *Vogue* editors through April. The first review, by a Mrs. Gleaves on March 9, was sour: "Flat footed. Biography uninviting. Other papers are sensible and thorough. No flair." The next three put her on an upward trajectory. Miss Talmey, on March 16: "Would definitely consider this girl—has range; easy writing; bright mind." Miss Daves, on March 26: "Wonderful possibility. We must consider her seriously." Miss Heal, on April 5: "A. Intelligent, good background, fashion flair." After a mixed review ("Uneven—but some of it isn't bad") came supreme praise from Carol Phillips, the managing editor, on April 12, who gave her an "AAAAAA," declaring: "This is IT - for my vote. A most impressive set of papers. Each paper is excellent. There is no exception. She *is* a writer; she definitely has the editorial point of view. My only worry is that she might *marry* someday and go off on one of those horses she speaks about. But I'm *counting on her* for the copy room team!!!"

Meanwhile, *Vogue* sought a background review of Jackie from GWU, with the director of "Women's Activities" responding that she was a "very pleasing, attractive young lady," while Muriel McClanahan opined that she "writes much better than do most students and that her critical sense is perceptive . . . very worthy of any honor she might win."

Waiting to graduate and for her CIA security clearance to be finalized, Jackie was ready for action. "Nothing very much has been happening here. It is dreary winter weather and we all have colds," she wrote to Father Leonard. She was flattered by lovesick John Husted's unflagging attentiveness, but she still considered him "immature and boring."

On Tuesday, April 24, the Prix de Paris director Mary Campbell telegrammed Jackie that "you are among the top finalists," from among whom the winner would be chosen. Not unimportantly, Mary Campbell offered praise (something Jackie was unaccustomed to receiving from her own mother): "[Y]ou have done a swell job and deserve a lot of credit for the hard and painstaking work you have done." Campbell emphasized that the editors felt "you had one of the most interesting papers submitted."

The finalists were invited to a May 10 dinner with *Vogue* editors and a luncheon the following day with Condé Nast top brass. Jackie's final comprehensive exams conflicted with the date, but she arranged to go up instead for a lunch on May 3.

When she arrived at the Condé Nast offices in the Graybar Building at 420 Lexington Avenue, Mary Campbell whisked her up to the *Vogue* offices. Entering a workplace where words and photographs were a professional endeavor immediately excited her, especially "how alert everyone had seemed." It was the first such setting the young woman had seen.

Then it was off to lunch along with Carol Phillips and Miss Heal. Jackie mostly listened, and as the editors described their paths to *Vogue*, she found their enthusiasm "about everything" infectious. She had "grand ideas," but although encouraged to ask any questions, she remained largely silent, later fearing this left such a bad impression that she would be out of the running.

At this crucial meeting with potential colleagues, when she would have wanted her brightest self to be shining, she had good reason for being distracted. As she would explain to Mary Campbell, without details, "[M]y father, whom we haven't seen for quite a long time, was in the hospital and my sister and I had to go together to see him."

Except for flying in and out of Black Jack's apartment to change into a bridesmaid dress the last weekend of February, Jackie hadn't given her father much attention that winter. It was unfortunate timing. His drinking and depression had worsened. By spring, he had also begun suffering from physical debility, writing his sister that "my arm is still very bad and the pain seems to have spread to my neck and collarbone." Although he left no medical records, it may be that he had some early sign of cancer, which would take his life six years later. Likely at the insistence of his physician, he went from Miami to a private sanitarium, which helped individuals "dry out." In early May, however, he contacted Jackie to come fetch him.

Jackie had originally told the *Vogue* editors that she would fly to New York for her lunch meeting with them, but she drove up instead. She hastily left lunch to speed north for about ninety minutes to Farmington to retrieve her sister, who was then more focused on her imminent first trip to Europe, with Jackie having been approved as chaperone by Mummy. The sisters headed south to New Canaan and pulled into the driveway of what looked like a New England country club. It was the Silver Hill sanitarium, where Black Jack was waiting with his packed bags.

One account of the episode was from Jackie's close Washington friend Lorraine Shevlin. In a 1977 interview, she recalled that Jackie told her that she and Lee had "secretly managed to get him out of the hospital where he was drying out, and Janet became furious because in her eyes things could never be bad enough for Black Jack Bouvier." Once Jackie had returned Lee and Black Jack home to his apartment after an exhausting day of driving, he requested that she return the car to him when she finished college in a few weeks. According to his nephew's wife, who later briefly lived with Black Jack, Jackie finally stood up to him. He had "given" her the car as a graduation gift four years earlier; now she "stole" Zelda, declaring her full ownership of it.

Jackie feared that her "running off so soon" left the impression she was "blasé and apathetic" with *Vogue*, but she was determined not to let her father derail her professional plans. Three days after returning home, "thinking very hard about 'my career,'" she wrote in a May 7 letter to Mary Campbell that she felt "relieved to have decided on something definite that I can start working for." She boldly asserted that in a decade "I would like to be a top editor in Condé Nast." Most revealing of how

Jackie perceived her own creative "bents" was her observation that magazine work was ideal for those who lacked any one talent "pronounced enough," but "love keeping up with new ideas."

In a bold move to assure the editors of her seriousness, she declared that she was "satiated" with Paris; what was more important to her was the work. If she won, she hoped to start in January, by which time her commitment to the CIA project would be fulfilled.

The most enlightening revelation in Jackie Bouvier's letter was an awakening sense of purpose she began to strive toward: "I suddenly realized what an exciting thing it must be to have something important to do."

Finished with her final exams, set up with the CIA job that fall, her duty to Daddy fulfilled, and eager for her forthcoming trip to Europe with Lee, Jackie Bouvier relaxed. She accepted an invitation from Charlie and Martha Bartlett to an informal Sunday supper on Mother's Day, May 13, in their narrow 3419 Q Street house. They promised her that another guest would be there whom they insisted she just had to meet, whom Charlie had tried but failed to arrange her meeting earlier in the year. He kept trying, and "got to be quite a bore about it," Jackie recalled. In fact, Charlie Bartlett had first tried to introduce them at his brother David's 1947 wedding, where they were both guests. His friend was the war hero, author, and Democratic congressman John F. Kennedy, known to his family and friends as Jack. A Harvard University graduate and a Catholic, he was running for Congress when he met Charlie in 1946, and they became close the next year when he was a freshman congressman and Charlie was a Washington newspaper correspondent.

As she joined the other guests in the small garden of the Bartlett home, the college senior was unintimidated by the presence not only of Congressman Kennedy but also of Senator Albert Gore and his wife, Pauline. "She was the odd young lady and a beautiful one," Albert Gore remembered. "He, the odd young man and surely a dashing one. It was a most enjoyable evening." He recalled there being a total of eight or ten guests; Charlie said it was six.

When she arrived at the May dinner, Jackie Bouvier knew more about the congressman's father, Joseph P. Kennedy, than about him. Joseph P. Kennedy had been in the papers and on newsreels since she was a child. Now sixty-two, he was a millionaire former U.S. ambassador to the Court of St. James's and a movie studio mogul with connections to the nation's media and business leaders, and also a father of nine children, with expansive properties at Cape Cod and Palm Beach as well as a New York residential hotel suite.

Even the most superficial facts about Jack, however, made immediately clear their substantive similarities, despite their generational difference; Jack would turn thirty-four three weeks after their meeting, while Jackie would be twenty-two in July. He'd lived and studied in London and explored Europe with passionate curiosity. His first ambition was to write, for which he also had a genuine talent. After publishing a book in 1940, *Why England Slept* (about the British government's failure to recognize the global threat posed by Hitler), and his heroic wartime service in the navy, he briefly pursued a career in journalism, for the Hearst newspaper syndicate. Working in Europe the summer after the war ended, he reported on England's failure to reelect Winston Churchill as prime minister, observed the personal interaction between American president Truman and Soviet leader Joseph Stalin at the Potsdam Conference, and also covered the first session of the United Nations in San Francisco. In later examining a diary Jack kept during his time as a journalist, historian Fredrik Logevall was struck by two significant qualities that were likely apparent to Jackie at the May dinner, because they also defined her: an "inquisitive mind" and "curiosity about the world." After a year as a journalist, Kennedy had determined to make news, not write about it, whereas Jackie Bouvier hoped to make news by writing about it. A mutual interest was clearly sparked.

Mummy had met Jack Kennedy at a Washington dinner without Jackie, declaring him a "purposeful young man," but she didn't consider politics a dignified profession for a potential husband for her daughter. As Jackie was always eager to defy Mummy, it may have even made Jack Kennedy more appealing to her. "My mother used to bring around all these beaus for me," she later observed, "but he was different."

Nine years after their initial meeting, she would share her unfiltered written account with Molly Thayer, who would later sanitize it for her 1961 biography of Jackie, *Jacqueline Bouvier Kennedy*. In her original statement, the former Jackie Bouvier accidentally disclosed that she did have marriage a bit more on her mind than she admitted at the time: "When I met Jack Kennedy, that strange, laughing, amused and intelligent inquisitive—rather irreverent face—I remember him so well that nite [*sic*] at the Bartletts—I knew that man would have a profound and disturbing effect on my life. I was rather frightened of him—because I knew if he came towards me, I wouldn't have the power to run away—though it would probably be better if I did. He didn't look like someone who wanted to get married and I pictured heartbreak but it seemed worth it. . . . That is how we met and parted."

A man of many girlfriends, Jack Kennedy showed an especial interest in her. As the dinner party broke up, Charlie walked Jackie out to her open convertible, and recalled that Jack followed, "muttering shyly about, 'Shall we go someplace and have a drink?'" Yet there in the back of her Mercury was one of *her* boyfriends.

Jackie's "friend" had slipped into the car to wait for her. In Molly Thayer's published account, the identity of the "friend" remained anonymous, but he was almost certainly John Husted. When he was down from New York to see his relatives, he always checked in on her, and his ally Mrs. Auchincloss likely directed him to find Jackie at the Bartlett house.

Intrigued as Jack and Jackie were by each other, it was "an awkward time," as Charlie noted. She was leaving the country for three months, would not be back in Washington until October, and then, if things at *Vogue* went her way, she would be moving to New York and possibly Paris. The next year, as rumors already circulated, he would be undertaking a campaign for the U.S. Senate. He was only in Washington when Congress was in session, and even then he spent most weekends in Massachusetts. They parted, and made no plans to see each other again.

Then there was the other: John Husted was originally planning to be in Europe at the same time Jackie was there, but a family wedding prevented him from going. Before she left, however, another door opened, promising access to a world that was hers for the asking, and it involved neither Jack nor John.

Two days after the Bartlett dinner, on May 15, a telegram arrived at Merrywood for Jackie from *Vogue*'s editor in chief, Edna Woolman Chase: "Delighted to announce you have won first prize Vogue's 16th Prix de Paris." Curiously, it took Jackie three days to respond by telegram: "Can't believe I have won Prix. Will be in New York all day Monday. May I come in and see you? Will call you Monday morning."

Even before Jackie responded to *Vogue* after winning, Janet had proudly called Betty Beale to have the *Washington Star* announce on

May 17 that her daughter won first prize in the *Vogue* contest. Only four days later, however, Janet's attitude radically changed. By May 21, when Jackie went to New York to complete paperwork and make her employment at Condé Nast official, Janet had started a war she intended to win. Seven months earlier, when Jackie declared her plan to return to Paris, Janet had snapped that the only way that would happen was the farfetched possibility of her winning the *Vogue* contest. Now that Jackie had actually won, Janet opposed Jackie's working for *Vogue* entirely.

Numerous reasons were given for Janet's adamant stance.

Stephen Birmingham, a biographer of Jackie's who spent time interviewing Janet, explained, "In Janet's mind, there was something a little undignified about accepting the *Vogue* prize. It was like accepting a scholarship and that was something that poor people did." Molly Thayer stated that "the family" had "thought it was enough" for her to have already lived in Paris for a year.

But in her May 7 letter to *Vogue*, Jackie made clear she didn't care about returning to Paris; she wanted "a foot in the door" at Condé Nast. It was the prospect of the six months working for *Vogue* in New York that alarmed Janet. "That, of course, meant that Jacqueline would once more fall under the potent influence of Black Jack," Janet thought, according to Jack Davis; "she might even spend those six months staying at Jack's apartment."

When Jackie went to Condé Nast's New York office on May 21 to pose for distinguished photographer Richard Routledge and complete her paperwork, she also went to see Black Jack. He was reportedly "delighted" with her win.

In her employment application, she gave the curator of the National Gallery of Art as a character reference. She could not take shorthand and barely typed. Her favorite study was literature, her least favorite "Sciences, Math." She'd never been bonded, owned a home or hospitalization plan, been a Communist or advocated overthrowing the government. She had no "Business Experience." Her amusements were "Riding, theatre, and tennis," her hobbies "Drawing, making up children's books, collecting ballet books and photography." Her most recent read was *From Here to Eternity*, and she regularly devoured *Life*, *Time*, the *New York Herald Tribune*, *The Washington Post*, *The New Yorker*, *Harper's Bazaar*, *Atlantic Monthly*, and—of course—*Vogue*.

Six days later, Jackie explained in a May 27 letter to Mary Campbell that she needed to turn down the *Prix*: "I have been discussing it with my mother all week," claiming that Mummy still insisted on keeping her "in the home," and negotiations had "taken all this week to arrive at definite plans."

Two weeks and three days after her day at Condé Nast, Jackie and her sister were leaving for their three-month summer trip to Europe, paid for by Mummy and Unk.

"My mother was extremely apprehensive about letting her daughters go alone on such a venture," Lee Bouvier wrote in their later published travelogue, *One Special Summer*. "It took a lot of persuasion. For months in advance, I talked of nothing else but the trip as my graduation present, and Jackie was dutifully convincing about how well she would look after me and how wisely she would behave."

Jackie told Yusha that Janet threatened to cancel their trip if she refused to forgo the Prix, which would devastate her fragile sister. Jackie conceded. She would not start at *Vogue*. Janet had won. Or so it seemed.

Had Janet read Jackie's May 27 letter she would have learned that Jackie was still angling for a position at the magazine. Jackie had her own discreet scheme to first placate, and then undermine, Mummy.

In her letter, she proposed that she start in the New York offices in the new year, "positive" she could "get out of my CIA job," which she had recently agreed to begin in October. "I will stay here next fall—and learn to type I guess—and then in January . . . I can move to New York. I know I will still want to work for you then—in fact it is a definite plan of mine to come in and ask you about a job in January—though I don't think Mummy realizes that!"

Within a matter of thirty-five days, Jacqueline Bouvier's life had undergone a tumult of change and with it an understandable range of emotions. She had withdrawn her father from an alcohol recovery center—and seized full ownership of her car. She kept a man in love with her on a string, then met one who excited yet frightened her, without any promise of getting to know him well. She was leaving for Europe. She won the job she'd spent a year working to attain—and was then forced to reject it. She learned how dedicating herself to one clear goal led to accomplishing it, but also how easily the best-laid plans could fail. A year before, she had vowed to live again in Europe. She was returning not to live, but merely to visit. In the midst of the drama, Jacqueline's graduation from George Washington University on Wednesday, May 30, 1951, seemed almost like an afterthought.

Yusha, sensitive to her every nuance, speculated that having to turn down *Vogue* must have "devastated, then enraged" her, but she "wouldn't have trusted herself to really let her mother know how angry she was." She had admitted as much to him eight years earlier, writing, "Being mad comes and goes so quickly with me. I'm afraid I'll hurt someone when I've forgotten that I was ever mad."

Her default mechanism for handling darker emotions, however, was humor. "Sometimes a day is so unbelievably awful," she observed, "that it finally becomes funny"—to her, at least. Jackie was fiendishly delighted when pipes burst and flooded Merrywood, ruining some of the chintz furnishings Mummy had chosen with her decorator Elsie DeWolfe. Jackie's humor often manifested in practical jokes, but sometimes those antics had a bit of figurative ground glass in the cake. When Yusha tired of rising to feed the chickens with her at Hammersmith, she once came to rub his head with a wet towel—soaked in peroxide, turning him embarrassingly blond. Another time, Tucky recalled, she "accidentally" dumped pudding on the lap of a teacher she despised. Her stepsister Nini recalled how Jackie would send her to the barn to retrieve dead chickens—which she then packaged beautifully and sent as gifts to unspecified "enemies."

One similar stunt, however, really stood out. This time, Jackie sent Nini to get a different, specific dead animal near the stables. She wrapped it exquisitely in a hatbox as a special gift for a certain person.

Experience had taught Jackie to retaliate only passively in response to her mother's behavior and thereby spare herself the possibility of enduring another hysterical outburst and slap. When the personal violation was so egregious, however, Jacqueline Bouvier had the capacity to strike back with artful assertion. "The whole *Vogue* thing, not letting her reap the reward of such effort," Vivi Crespi reflected, "that crossed a line, so spiteful."

Jackie left the special gift for Mummy. The box contained a dead snake.

13

LEE

June–September 1951

The Bouvier sisters set sail for Europe from New York, on the *Queen Elizabeth*, on June 7. The laughs began immediately, when they discovered they were sharing a cabin with an elderly woman whom Jackie accidentally glimpsed nude in the middle of the night. Except for a few weeks during holidays and vacation, the sisters had not lived together in the same place since Jackie went away to boarding school in 1944. (By the time Lee began at Miss Porter's, Jackie had left for Vassar.) For the next one hundred and one days, from June 7 until September 15, Jackie and Lee were never apart.

They had only begun to cross the Atlantic when Jackie started defying the rules, convincing the more obedient Lee that they could pull off all her schemes. They charmed the crew into letting them switch their shared room with the old woman for one of their own. When they encountered a salacious Lebanese man, Jackie depicted the "quirks in the sex lives of Near Easterners" in one of her cartoons for her naïve sister. "You should see us sneaking into first-class, getting stuck on the gate in our tight dresses," Jackie wrote Mummy as they ignored a "Please Observe Social Barriers" sign.

Their seven days at sea together, without the distraction of museums and sights, focused the Bouvier sisters all the more on how different they were. The trauma of the divorce would always bond them, but even before it Jackie had recognized an acute vulnerability in Lee. In her copy of *Book of Dogs*, which illustrated different breeds with a photo and description, the six-and-a-half-year-old Jackie focused her attention on the entry for the "keen, active" Yorkshire Terrier, with the notation that it "requires much care." Beneath the photo of the needy, staring, big-eyed dog, Jackie scribbled "Lee."

Unlike with Jackie, whose every word and deed she judged, Janet seemed to neglect Lee. When the Auchinclosses left Lee, then about ten years old, alone at Merrywood while they went on a deep-sea fishing trip to Chile, the lonely girl took a taxi to a nearby convent, naïvely seeking to adopt an orphan for companionship. Other parents might have found such a story upsetting, endearing, or amusing. "When my mother came back about a week later, I got just such hell for this," Lee recalled. "How you could upset me? How could you torture me the way you have? We were so worried about you!" was Mummy's lecture. "I could not figure out quite why that was," she quipped, "as they were in Chile on a motor boat."

While less apt to be hit by her, Lee never forgot how Mummy joked that she would be the daughter to bear children, while Jackie was the intellect—a perfect distillation of the impossibility of pleasing Janet.

Lee recalled the most singularly damaging of Mummy's criticisms being that she was "fat." A year after the divorce, her eight-year-old sister's sudden thinness concerned Jackie, who devised an illustrated diet plan with cookies, cake, candy, and ice cream to get her to add weight. A year later, she reported on Lee's continued obsession with her weight to Yusha, asking him to encourage her: "Did you get the picture Lee sent you. She is terribly jealous, so you must reassure her. Lee weighed herself before & after [dinner] and she is 3 lbs. heavier."

By 1943, the problem was becoming a serious worry for Jackie, after Lee's "new height of dieting," with a regimen of lemon juice and one rye crisp cracker for breakfast, bouillon and six rye crisps for lunch, and tomato salad and one rye crisp for dinner. She thought it "pathetic," noting how she and Tucky ate far too heartily. Mummy was oblivious to Lee's problem, but when she learned that Jackie had told her to suppress her appetite by smoking rather than starving, she was "raging," firing off an "epistle on the Perils of Nicotine for the Young." Mummy hadn't known that "Lee took up a cigarette when she put down her first rattle."

Just as Lee began boarding school, she sent a "sad letter" to Jackie at college. Alarmed that her sister's blue mood might trigger a dangerous cycle of starvation, Jackie sent her a box of canned food, but the problem persisted, and two weeks later, with Tucky and Black Jack retrieving Jackie at Vassar, they rushed up to intervene with Lee. The relief was temporary. Six months before Jackie left for her year abroad, she told Yusha that Lee looked "like a starved Greek orphan and has lost about 15 pounds and just can't seem to eat." One classmate later recalled Lee as "anorexic-looking."

It wasn't just Mummy. While Black Jack indulged both daughters during their weekends in New York and summers in East Hampton, his preference was obvious. As Lee recalled, "[M]y father favored Jackie." She thought it was because Jackie had been an only child for four years, that she was named after him because he'd wanted a son, and that "she actually looked almost exactly like him." He also found the elder more interesting to engage. As Lee further admitted, "He adored her more than anything in the world and would talk to her endlessly about life. I was never allowed in on those conversations as I was told it would be another few years before I was up to it. He was so proud of her that it was a very touching thing to see—and this was since the day she was born." Lee claimed that she did not resent his favoritism, but it's hard to imagine that it didn't sting, sometimes.

Since both parents neglected Lee, Jackie assumed a protective responsibility toward her. Lee recounted to a family friend: "I often wonder where I would be if she hadn't been such a tremendous comfort and strength to me. I have asked of her and depended on her so much, and she has endlessly given her love, patience, support, and encouragement."

At the same time, despite her protectiveness, Jackie sometimes resented the responsibility and took it out on her. "I was constantly forced to play horse with her (naturally I was the horse!)," Lee admitted. "We had some really violent battles and I was quite sure she would be the death of me! Once she knocked me over the head with a croquet mallet and I was unconscious for quite a while." Jackie backed off only after Lee dared to push her down a staircase.

To others, Jackie also lamented what she considered her sister's superficiality. When Yusha was seriously considering the ministry, she advised him, "You know Lee wouldn't approve of you being anything except a movie star or a night club singer—so don't pay any attention to her." In a diary entry concerning Lee, Yusha recorded: "Jackie said she was selfish and lazy."

The only quality Jackie claimed to share with "my adored sister" was that "we have similar tastes." Lee, however, believed their three months in Europe would mark a change, when they would start "to become so extremely close."

After docking in Southampton, England, on June 13, they headed directly to London. Lee wisecracked, "We look like two criminals arriving off the boat." So began what Jackie called "our three-month odyssey" to England, France, Spain, Italy, Austria, Germany, Switzerland, and Luxembourg.

Socializing consumed as much of their time in England as did seeing the sights. There was a weekend at the Cliveden estate, seat of the British Astor family, and in London they attended a cocktail party hosted by Mummy's friends Guy and Jane du Boulay and a dinner dance hosted by a Mr. Bevan. (Jackie reported to a mutual friend on Lee's complaint that reticent British men "never give anyone any compliments which is why all the women seem dehydrated and just chatter shrilly away.") A Francis Brake intervened to find them a room at the Savoy when their reservation at another hotel was canceled. They bought a used Hillman Minx, crossed the English Channel by ferry, and hit the Continent.

Jackie's letters from abroad, reflecting "how fascinated she was by the history," had inspired Lee to want to see Europe. Now Jackie's talent for storytelling, fused with her "enthusiasm, passion and knowledge," only left Lee further in awe. "Her feeling for history is so strong and familiar that when she speaks of endless, various facts, it is as though she were talking of her family," Lee explained. "It is a source of great pleasure to her and her memory of every word she has read or heard is extraordinary."

In Spain, they were almost arrested and put in prison on the border for trying to cross without ownership papers for their car, and later got a flat tire in the dead of night in the countryside. They encountered a frenetic friend who scolded them for missing a concert by Pablo Casals—"the greatest cello player that ever lived," according to the friend. In an ancient villa they jitterbugged beneath masterpieces and sat in Christopher Columbus's chair, they climbed the Pyrenees, and they cheekily asked the American ambassador how the dictator Franco was doing. When they encountered a junket of American senators, one advised them to "size up the national situation" in each country by going to embassy cocktail parties. At a bullfight, Lee covered her eyes, while a nearby Spaniard tried to get her to watch, prompting another man to tell him to leave her be. This provoked a fight and "minor riot" as "everyone in the grandstand took sides" until a policeman moved the Bouvier sisters.

In Austria, at the Salzburg Music Festival, the sisters took in Verdi's *Otello*, and were taken backstage to meet the conductor, Wilhelm Furtwängler. The following evening, they went to see Leopold Stokowski, the conductor made famous by Disney's *Fantasia*. Jackie was admittedly bored by "dreary Switzerland," but she loved how "everyone is . . . so intrigued with the idea of 2 sisters" traveling together.

In a letter to Mummy, Jackie made a subtle reference to her mother's frequent criticism of her hair, noting that she was "sitting here under ten kinds of strange machines having the front part of my hair decurled and the back curled . . . I had it ALL cut off . . . it is hardly as long as my eyelashes! . . . at least you won't have to tell me to keep it out of my eyes." She added, "I know you are right about us representing our country and that we must never do anything that would call attention to us and make people shocked at Americans. We . . . never go out in big cities except in what we would wear to church in Newport on Sundays." And with the description, Jackie included a photo of herself in sandals and Lee in short-shorts.

At a military training field outside Paris, the sisters interrupted French Army gun and tank maneuvers in order to find their friend Paul de Ganay, now serving in the army, though they failed to "kiss him on both cheeks the way they do in newsreels," and "just wandered around Paris being in love with that city."

In Italy, the sisters zigzagged from village to city—Venice, Rome, Naples, Florence, Sorrento, Pompei, Ca' d'Oro, Capri, and Torcello—some deserving of several days, others fewer. "There is so much to see in Italy," Jackie would write. "I feel stupid even trying—in one summer."

Venice was pure mirth, especially when they "capsized in a torchlight procession on the Grand Canal." While there, according to Lee, Jackie became enamored with a handsome Italian art teacher "who has a lot of experience and she takes sketching lessons from him every day." In a poem about their time in Venice, Jackie crafted a fantasy pastiche of them slipping down a vine from their rooms, their real identities masked as dominoes as they attend a costume ball, where they encounter Molière and Watteau and Jackie takes "*a lover* named Olio 'Delmonico.'"

Italians proved to more substantially influence Jackie's life, one profoundly so.

While he didn't recall the exact circumstances of how he came to informally photograph the Bouvier sisters that summer in Rome, Benno Graziani, who had been a *Paris Match* editor for two years at that point, became a lifelong friend of Jackie's. While Jackie had been seen on the GWU campus with her Leica, she hadn't used it often since her year abroad. Now that she was back in Europe, she was again never without it, and now she had a new photographer friend. She asked Graziani less about the technicalities of lighting and angles than about the impact an image should ideally have. He sometimes thought that she "tried to do too much in one photo."

"A good photograph tells a story in two seconds," he told her. "You can see immediately if the picture is good or not. The picture must speak to the spectator."

That summer in Rome, Graziani introduced her to the emerging Italian filmmaker Federico Fellini. "His English was not that good; her Italian was not that good." But they too remained friends (in November 1965 Jackie would host a dinner party at her apartment for Fellini to celebrate the New York premiere of his film *Juliet of the Spirits*).

Her time in Italy also led Jackie to learn more about abstract and contemporary art. Her education unfolded over the weeks of August, on "the sleepy little pink street hidden behind the taxi tooting shopping swank of the Piazza di Spagna," in the courtyard studio of sculptor Pericles Fazzini. As he sculpted figural works in metal, the sisters sat and smoked and talked with an American G.I. and his wife who spoke only of going home to Brooklyn, "Romeo the poet," and "wild Carlo," the artist's assistant. After exploring the city each day, the sisters would take espresso in a "bamboo-curtained cafeteria," then repair to the crew at the studio. While teaching Lee to make jewelry, Fazzini drew eight pictures of Jackie, which she said were "slightly more abstract than I imagined myself—but I loved them—splotches and lines." Jackie was overwhelmed by Fazzini's openhearted generosity, how he welcomed the curious who poked into his studio, even paying for their lunches. "When we left for Naples in our groaning car—they all came out into the pink street and waved goodbye."

The pinnacle of their trip took place in Florence at Villa I Tatti, the residence and base of operations of art critic and collector Bernard Berenson—Lee having arranged it by writing him. The world's leading Italian Renaissance scholar, Berenson was a Jewish immigrant from Lithuania who grew up in Boston, graduated from Harvard in 1887, and moved to his beloved I Tatti in 1901.

Berenson made the villa a refuge for friends, artists, and lovers. He cultivated a theatrical presence, but his wisdom, drawn from experience, observation, and study, seemed authentic to those who came to pay him homage, from Gertrude Stein to Harry Truman.

As Jackie recalled of their first encounter, he "immediately talked to us of love." She was stunned to learn that during the war, despite his pioneering work on Italian art history, the fascist Mussolini government forced him to flee the country simply for being born Jewish. It was, she said, another example of "intolerance trying to crush the spirit." She would credit the conversation with Berenson for widening her grasp of art, "by using your eyes, by focusing your whole attention on a work of art, to try to understand the message the artist wants to convey."

But it went beyond that. Berenson considered his views on "humanism" his "most enduring legacy," promoting and developing equality, dignity, and the right to individuality inherent to every person. Both sisters were overwhelmed as they attempted to remember or write down as many of his rapidly delivered aphorisms and declarations on how to thrive in society as they could catch.

Berenson frequently referenced a phrase he had coined, "life-diminishing and life-enhancing people," advising, "Don't waste your life with diminishing people who aren't stimulating, and if you find it's often you are with unstimulating people it must be because you yourself are not stimulating." (For all his talk about artistic sensibilities, he also offered them contradictory advice: "Never follow your senses.") Several of his proverbs spoke directly, such as, "Anything you want, you must make enemies for and suffer for"—a welcome if formidable truth. If there was a singular adage that Berenson told them that day that would most immediately impact Jacqueline Bouvier's life, however, it was his advice that "[t]he only way to exist happily is to love your work."

Upon returning to Rome, the sisters wrote Berenson, Jackie wishing they could be "constantly eavesdropping" on his wisdom as "maids in your house." Both corresponded with him until his death, in 1959. In Jackie's case that meant ten letters, reporting on interesting people she met, changes in her life, and musings on history and the arts, once wishing she'd "lived at the turn of the century . . . and seen La Belle Otero dance and Oscar Wilde and have everything mauve and crystal." Lee's three letters carried regrets about returning to the United States and living in London rather than Rome, "thoroughly disgusted with myself" because she didn't see him again. She felt that "if I could see you again, you would help me, as like many other people I can't seem to find a path that leads anywhere."

In early September, the sisters drove their "aching" car back to Paris to sell, Jackie wrote, to "a missionary who is taking it to the Sahara but he looked like an opium smuggler to me and was just about to give me money in a shoebox on a dark corner but I dragged him to a bank."

The sisters were flush with genuine gratitude. With self-deprecating wit, a narrative scrapbook chronicling the sojourn was assembled. "We split the fun," Lee would state, conceding that Jackie executed the elaborate watercolors, poetry, and comical caricatures, while claiming, "I described most of our adventures." In fact, she did dictate some of the incidents that were chronicled, but of the fifty-seven pages of painstakingly handwritten narrative, only two were done by Lee.

They sailed back on the *Coronia*, landing in New York on September 15. With "two or three days before college opens, instead of having to tear straight to it with no chance to tell you about everything," Lee went to her mother in Newport before beginning at Sarah Lawrence College in Bronxville, New York.

Jackie did not go see her mother. Nor is there any record of her having begun work in the job she claimed to have secured with the CIA. Instead, it seems she got settled at her father's apartment in New York and then, buoyed by the confidence instilled in her by winning the Prix, she headed to the nineteenth floor of the Graybar Building, striding into the offices of *Vogue* magazine. While she had indicated in her late May letter to *Vogue* that she hoped to begin work with them in January, she suddenly appeared much sooner, eager to get started.

"[I] thought I would be miserable to come home," she confided to Father Leonard, "but [I] . . . have all sorts of plans for a wonderful winter."

14

OFFICE CLERK

September–December 1951

Beset by numerous ailments, the increasingly reclusive Black Jack was ecstatic about Jackie's plan to be living in New York for the next six months—*Vogue* had agreed to her plan of starting at a later date—before leaving for the second part of the Prix in Paris.

When Janet discovered Jackie's plan, she was not happy. Her anger was mostly fueled by the fact that the arrangements threatened her objective of getting Jackie properly married, especially after her daughter mentioned that practically the entire staff at *Vogue* were women. She began interrupting Jackie at her new job with frantic phone calls, waging an incessant battle to make her quit.

Janet's unrelenting focus on her daughter's having to marry began to sow some doubt in Jackie's thinking. When she raised her concern about not meeting a potential suitable husband over lunch with Carol Phillips of *Vogue*, the editor found her "confused and uncertain about her future, a sweet darling girl with not a great deal of confidence." She advised her to succumb to Janet's advice, declaiming, "Go to Washington, that's where all the boys are."

She had poured her time and attention for nearly a year into winning the dream job. Her May 27 letter to *Vogue* had made clear she felt no remorse about willfully misleading her mother about her intention of taking it. Why would she surrender it so readily?

The answer involved her father and her beau.

Jackie could see for herself that beyond his usual possessiveness, her father had become more isolated. It's unclear how much her father disclosed about his health, and he still maintained an image of virility, but his emotional neediness was all too evident. Black Jack enjoyed gambling with Esther Lindstrom, yet she was his housekeeper. He would take his young girlfriends to dinner or a show, but none were social equals; he tired of them quickly. His nephew Miche and his wife, Kath, especially compassionate to him, would eventually move to New York, but were then living in South America. While Lee was now in college nearby, she had none of the exuberant dynamic with him that her sister did. "We all loved him; he was our uncle Jack," recalled Janet's niece Mimi, "but I know he became very lonely. He seemed restless without Jackie, as if nothing really mattered."

When Jackie told him she had quit *Vogue*, he immediately offered her a position in his brokerage firm at a salary in the same amount as her monthly allowance. Without having to pay rent or other routine expenses, and added to her allowance, it would have given her a monthly income of around $1,000, hardly enough to live extravagantly but double what she had to live within at Merrywood. Yet the prospect of putting aside whatever sort of writing work she might want to do while also having to assume the role of her father's emotional caretaker felt perilous to Jackie. She declined her father's offer but did all she could to show love for him. As Lee put it, "She felt a great responsibility to him in his extreme loneliness."

Black Jack's disappointment at the plan's falling through was mitigated by the fact that Jackie would still be visiting New York and staying with him, though coming, ostensibly, to visit John Husted. Seeing both when in New York helped obscure the intent of her visits. When they'd last seen each other, in the spring, Jackie and John were dating regularly enough to halt Mummy's quest to find herself an ideal son-in-law until at least her daughter's return from Europe. Having fallen in love "at first sight," Husted remained mesmerized by her "sensitivity," "originality," and "expression of eternal surprise."

By the fall, Jackie seemed to have come to appreciate his unstinting devotion. "What I hope for you," she wrote to her former beau Bev Corbin, "is for the same thing to happen as quickly and as surely as it did with me. It will when you least expect it." As if to convince herself, she further claimed to Corbin that John was not at all the "sensible boy next door" when, in fact, he was highly conventional.

SOMETIME IN THE FALL of 1951, upon her return to Merrywood, Jackie was riding her horse Sagebrush especially hard and was thrown from her mount and knocked unconscious. Reminding her that she'd broken her collarbone and developed a pinched nerve in her neck from previous accidents, Black Jack yet again ordered her to give up riding or he would cut off her allowance. She didn't stop riding, nor did he cut her off. Her father's dissipated power over her was made all the more obvious by the rare but crucial move made on her behalf by her stepfather.

Black Jack still derisively called Unk and Mummy "Uncle Toady the Naval Hero and your Goddamn Mother," but in the nearly dozen years since he'd been her stepfather, Unk had gained Jackie's trust, and then her love. On more than one occasion, he prevented Janet's attacks on her daughter from escalating. Jackie emulated his implacable, often remote calm.

While Janet had triumphed in getting Jackie to leave New York, Yusha thought that it had "only made her more determined to work in the writing field." Seemingly more appreciative of her ambition than his wife was, Unk interceded. He asked if he could share some of her stories and drawings with his friend Arthur Krock, Washington-bureau chief of the *New York Times*, who had a history of helping talented or connected young women pursue journalism careers.

Krock later told reporter Dorothy McCardle that after reading "some of her writing and [seeing her] sketches" he called his old friend Frank C. Waldrop, executive editor of the capital's leading newspaper, the *Washington Times-Herald*, adding that "Jackie was smart in school too."

"Are you still hiring little girls?" Krock asked Waldrop in his October 1951 call about Jackie Bouvier. "Well, I have one for you. About the best one—round-eyed, clever—want[s] to go into journalism—what can you do[?]"

Waldrop told Krock to send her to his office. Waldrop—a forty-six-year-old father of three—was a passionate newspaperman. He grew up in Alabama, graduated from West Point and Columbia, then started at twenty-four as a reporter for the Nashville *Tennessean* the year Jackie was born, becoming an editorial writer, editorial page editor, managing editor, and political editor. He had come to Washington in 1933 to work for the *Washington Herald*, part of William Randolph Hearst's syndicate. In 1939, Hearst sold it and his other city paper, the *Washington Times*, to Cissy Patterson of the McCormick-Medill publishing family. Three years before Jackie arrived, Patterson died, and the combined *Washington Times-Herald* paper was sold to her cousin Robert McCormick. Putting out ten daily editions, it had the city's highest circulation.

Headquartered at the original Herald Building downtown, two blocks north and three blocks east of the White House, at 1307 H Street, the enterprise occupied four stories. The newsroom was on the ground floor, its windows facing out onto the street. Here, as executive editor, Waldrop had a large glassed-in office, which was where Jackie first came to meet with him in early October 1951.

Initially, Waldrop recalled she "mumbled around saying something about pictures," immediately mentioning photography. He bluntly asked, "Do you really want to go into journalism or do you want to hang around here until you get married?"

"No, sir," Jackie replied. "I want to make a career."

"If you're serious, I'll be serious. If not, you can have a job clipping things."

"No, sir. I'm serious."

"I don't want you to come here in six months and say you're engaged."

From that point in Waldrop's well-honed story, retold in about a dozen interviews over thirty years, he often obfuscated the precise timeline or withheld seemingly insignificant details ultimately necessary in delineating the full arc of Jackie's newspaper career. He likely did so as an act of loyalty, in coordination with her; the fuller version made her drive more admirable, but at the point when her story was first being told, she didn't want to be cast as ruthlessly ambitious nor have it disclosed that she had started not on the reporting staff but on the clerical one.

A congratulatory message she received from Mary Campbell at *Vogue* suggests that Jackie began work at the *Times-Herald* on Monday, October 15, 1951. She started with a sense of entitlement but learned quickly that she still had to prove herself despite getting the job through a millionaire stepfather. She began as a "gofer," getting coffee for the clerical staff and sitting at the front desk as a receptionist. Said Waldrop, "I didn't care how well she'd written in school; she was not being hired as a reporter. I'd seen her type. Little society girls with dreams of writing the great American novel, who drop it the minute they find the great American husband."

If he began to detect that "they were serious," he promoted them "as secretaries to get the feel of the place—get acquainted and see what they could do. . . . Really, they answered my phone. . . . It got me curious. How would these girls fit into the newspaper environment?"

By week two, Jackie Bouvier began applying "persistent charm" in reminding Waldrop that she was there to write, willing to employ her skill for any mundane assignment he saw fit. "She could see around corners. She put her head down and got to work," he recalled. "Never complained about secretary stuff. She couldn't type 'cat' but she . . . [w]ore me down."

By week three, he made Jackie his personal assistant. "I did ask her to write some routine letters for me—but she couldn't take dictation or type, so it wasn't worth the time. I just had her answering the phone and taking messages. Thorough. Asked a dozen questions to anyone who called . . . self-sufficient, good at listening, handling it efficiently."

As word got out in the newsroom that Waldrop's new aide was the former Deb of the Year, she became something of a novelty, especially because she was unrelentingly thrilled to be working at the paper. "I never imagined the daughter of a millionaire could be so cock-a-hoop getting a lowly-paid job like this," one colleague observed.

She seized her opportunity on the last day of October.

After touring Canada, twenty-five-year-old Princess Elizabeth of England arrived at National Airport from Montreal, wearing a cloth coat with two diamond lapel pins in the shape of the Canadian maple leaf, accompanied by her husband, Philip, the Duke of Edinburgh. Some two thousand invited guests attended the welcoming ceremony, after which the motorcade began its four-mile drive into Washington, the open lead car with the princess and President Harry S. Truman, followed by the prince, First Lady Bess Truman, and the Trumans' daughter, Margaret, to roaring cheers from the half-million citizens on the sidewalks. Among those pushing forward in hope of glimpsing the princess was Jackie. Mr. Waldrop had let her go down to see it all, as a spectator. She saw it as a chance to prove she was a journalist.

The first event on Elizabeth's packed three-day schedule was an invitation-only press reception at the Statler Hotel, where nearly a thousand reporters crowded into the ballroom, including Mummy's friend Betty Beale, the *Washington Evening Star* society columnist. "I know everyone in town and I've known Jackie since she was a teenager and I saw that right in the middle of all the *invited* press was Jackie," Beale said. "She didn't belong there. She wasn't press. She was a secretary! That's Jackie! Pushes to get what she wants, ignores rules when they don't suit her. She must have snuck in saying she worked for the paper—without saying she was filing papers and delivering messages! Oh, she was that girl!"

Waldrop recalled that Jackie had returned to the office with a handwritten, witty article filled with quotes showing how infatuated the government bureaucrats cheering on the sidewalks were with a monarch. "I told her I couldn't use it. She was shocked. I snapped, 'You're not a reporter!' And she put her head down . . . 'Oh . . . Mr. Waldrop. I'm so sorry.'" But her attempt gave Waldrop an idea.

There was a young man working as a freelance "stringer" for the paper (his name was never published), writing the "Inquiring Photographer" column for the paper—a feature column familiar to the readership since the paper had been just "the *Herald*." The column, published six days a week, consisted of responses from half a dozen random people to the same question, and included their names and pictures, requiring the columnist to snap them with a large Speed Graflex. Jackie's story had essentially done the same thing, in narrative form. Waldrop told her to tag along with the stringer and listen, then to figure out her own question about Elizabeth's visit and ask it to whomever she wanted. Waldrop would then decide which to publish in the next day's column.

On November 2, 1951, Jackie Bouvier's first column appeared in the *Times-Herald*, her question being "Is Princess Elizabeth as pretty as her picture?" She questioned six men—Berkeley Payne, Byrd Ferneyhough, William Luers, James Zimmerman, Wellner Streets, and W. Paul Dennehy—all of whom were *Times-Herald* staff photographers. For the faces always behind the camera to stand in front of it was novel and flattering—and tactically clever on Jackie's part.

The paper had a history of publishing an unusually large number of women columnists. Waldrop, who edited them all, found they were best "able to tell things in very concise short terms." The timing was also right.

"I knew I needed a new Inquiring Photographer—the kid who was doing it was a stringer who was quitting to go to law school," Waldrop recalled.

The problem was that nobody wanted the job. "We used to joke about being in the dog house when we were assigned to the Inquiring Photographer spot," recalled one reporter. "They preferred to sit in a bar someplace rather than snap mugshots of people standing on street corners answering stupid questions. Nobody could fathom anyone wanting the job and agreeing not only to pose the questions but take the pictures." In fact, the "Inquiring Photographer" never carried a byline, because the columnists were always rotating; nobody did it regularly enough to make it their own.

"I'll tell you what we'll do," Waldrop told her. "You can try out for this thing." He told her to keep going out with the stringer but ask her own question once a week and submit the responses on a trial basis.

Jackie recognized she could do something interesting with the "Inquiring Photographer" column that nobody else at the paper wanted. For what was likely her next published column, on November 9, Jackie asked a question that showed it could serve as an outlet for all that she was then ruminating on: "Should a girl live at home until she gets married, or go out to see how it is to live alone?"

At that time, Jackie was considering whether she could afford to rent her own apartment. According to managing editor Sidney Epstein, Jackie Bouvier was first hired at the weekly salary of $25 (around $270 in today's dollars). She spent a good part of it on her twice-monthly train or plane tickets to see John Husted in New York, the gas to drive Zelda round trip from McLean, Virginia, to downtown D.C. five times a week, and parking in a covered garage rather than fighting for an open space on the streets, as the other employees did. She would have little extra if she were to rent her own apartment, but money wasn't the only reason she hesitated.

Living at Merrywood, where there was an uptick in the maternal carping about her need to find the right husband, was a situation from which she was desperate to escape. Yet a single woman living on her own was still viewed with disdain, at least by the conventions of her class. Her concern over whether she should break such a taboo was revealed in the question she posed for the column.

Of the five women and one man she asked, four essentially said it really depended on the individual. Mrs. R. W. Bradley, however, seemed to best speak to Jackie's dilemma. A girl should stay home until married, she said, but "go out and have a good time, meet boys, and go to . . . dances and nightclubs."

That column brought an epiphany. Jackie Bouvier knew not to seek advice from Black Jack or Mummy; each would respond in a way that favored him- or herself and disparaged the other. She could correspond with Yusha or Father Leonard, but their response would be delayed by mail. Seeking advice from a diverse demographic of strangers who had neither a vested interest in her choice nor knowledge that the questions might be about her personal life could help clarify whatever concerned her. It was an early sign of what became a defining characteristic of Jackie's as an adult, being simultaneously overt and covert.

Jackie went to see John Husted in New York on the weekend of November 10. While there, he took her home to Bedford Hills to meet his doting mother. When Helen Husted pulled out his baby picture to give her as a gift, Jackie recoiled, insisting she could take her own photo of him. She would later tell a friend how John "adored mama maybe a bit too much," and found it "weird how he praised her as this ideal, old-fashioned wife." For her next trial column, on November 14, her question sarcastically referenced what John seemed to want from her: "Is it possible to now find a girl like the one who married dear old dad?"

Her column published on November 23 perhaps reflected an uncertainty about her skill for the job ("What is the silliest question anyone ever asked you?"), but also revealed her already artful efforts to make it compelling. She targeted some switchboard operators who'd never been asked such a question and chose unpredictable responses. Olive Frazier answered that she'd once been asked by a caller for the day, year, time, and location, joking, "She really must have been mixed up—or well mixed." Shorty Shipe was angry at being repeatedly asked why he seemed to be a sociopathic liar ("I get a kick out of it."). Pauline Stafford was befuddled when asked to explain the difference between a horse and a mule. Joe Mercillott got defensive about being asked why he flipped an auto while driving ("I didn't turn the car over deliberately.").

Jackie spent Thanksgiving weekend with the Auchinclosses at Merrywood, then went to New York to see Black Jack and John. Typically, Jackie responded to unwelcome and excessive declarations of romantic love with, as John recalled, her "devastating, cutting wit." That only seemed to make him fall deeper in love; what he saw as her "very good sense of humor" was a primary quality that kept him besotted.

As if it were part of the approaching holiday season's festivities, John now sprang a cheeky dare on her. Based on his presumption that they "had sort of declared our love for each other," he suggested she "prove it" by marrying him. Before she could say anything, however, he made a game of it. She would be returning to New York the weekend before Christmas to exchange gifts with her father. "I told her to meet me at the Polo Bar of the Westbury Hotel at noon on [that] Saturday," where she could "tell me your answer." She was grateful to be spared any expectation of an immediate reply to his proposition, since she seemed unable to muster inspiration for sharing her life with him. He just wasn't the man she had imagined marrying.

The questions she had to pose in order to write her column now served as a way to learn how others felt about her ambivalence. On December 6 she posed her most highly personal question yet: "Should a girl pass up sound matrimonial prospects to wait for her ideal man?" Of the five people questioned, only one advised holding out. Eleven days later, on the seventeenth, her uncertainty remained as she asked six servicemen, "What was the closest you've ever come to being enticed into matrimony?" Five were relieved to be single and one admitted he'd married "in a weak moment."

The holiday season was approaching—Jackie was about to leave to see her father; then she would come back to Merrywood to celebrate Christmas with the Auchinclosses and, finally, travel with them to Florida, where they would stay until the new year—when Waldrop asked to see her. He told her to "come back after the first of the year," when he'd have a final decision about giving her a permanent writing position. Her questions about marriage may have made him suspicious, and he reminded her of his warning during their initial conversation in October. "If you are just marking time until you get engaged, don't come back!"

"Being a journalist seemed the ideal way of both having a job and experiencing the world, especially for anyone with a sense of adventure," she would explain to Gloria Steinem years later. "Journalism has variety. . . . Being a reporter seems a ticket out of the world."

Her continuing to badger Waldrop about a writing job right until she left for the holiday, however, finally led him to snap. "She went silent and looked down . . . but she was thinking. I asked if she knew the departments at the paper, and the different beats—the courts, theater, crime. 'What interests you enough to do it day in and out, Miss Bouvier?!'

"She looked up, right in my eye and had one word: '*Everything.*'"

And then she seemed to throw it all away.

15

PALM BEACH

December 1951

It was snowing heavily on the Saturday before Christmas. Jackie's train was delayed getting into New York, arriving so late that she didn't know if she would still find John at the Westbury Hotel, but she told the cabdriver to take her up to Madison Avenue and 69th Street anyway.

Bruised but perhaps not surprised, the tall Yalie who had been sitting inside at the hotel's Polo Bar by himself since lunchtime was about to pay his bill and leave. With fateful timing, Jackie Bouvier "breezed in," came up to his table, and simply said, "Yes." That moment, as John Husted told it, seemed more like she was playfully accepting a dare rather than joyously taking the first step toward sharing her life with someone she loved.

They hastily made their way to Black Jack's apartment. John had seen him once before, when he and Jackie had played in a father-daughter tennis tournament at Miss Porter's in the late 1940s. As the first to hear their news, he was elated not so much because his daughter was marrying but because she would be moving to New York. With proper formality, John asked him for his daughter's hand in marriage. The old man's reply left the gentle John Husted bewildered: "Sure—but it will never work."

Neither Black Jack nor Jackie offered an explanation for his odd remark.

Shortly thereafter, she wrote Father Leonard that she was now "terribly much in love—for the first time—and I want to get married. And

I KNOW I will marry this boy. I don't have to think and wonder—as I always have before—if they are the right one, how we'd get along etc. . . . I just KNOW he is and it's the deepest happiest feeling in the world."

Joining her family days later for Christmas, Jackie sensed that her decision confounded Mummy. She had initially approved of her dating John. She'd accepted him as a potential son-in-law during the preceding months, making no effort to guide her daughter toward some other potential suitor. Now, however, after Jackie accepted John's proposal, Yusha reported, Janet darkly joked that it was due to her daughter's being knocked unconscious when she was thrown from Sagebrush. It all seemed a bit too easy.

Janet's growing objection to the marriage would be attributed to her discovery that John Husted's net worth and salary did not meet her expectations. Thus, Mummy had, through her own encouragement, ended up with the opposite of what she'd wanted: an insufficiently rich husband for Jackie, who lived in the same city as her ex-husband. Janet's disapproval, Lee thought, fueled Jackie's passive determination to defy her, but it's hard to imagine that she would sacrifice her happiness just to spite her mother. Instead, the fact that she was "extremely anxious to leave home" seems the more valid reason. She was perhaps influenced by Janet's fearful projections that she was on the precipice of a lonely, impoverished future as a single woman for which professional satisfaction could never compensate; that she must grab a likely last chance to secure a comfortable future.

Yet Waldrop's threat that he wouldn't make her a columnist if she became engaged was not part of the sexist postwar belief that a married woman shouldn't work on the presumption that her husband earned enough to support her, or that her holding the job prevented a man from having it and earning an income. There were many married women writers at the *Times-Herald*; Waldrop simply did not want to invest the effort in training her if she was planning to leave soon. John Husted never insisted that Jackie quit her job, but moving with him to New York after marriage would rule out her working at the paper in Washington.

What set Jackie apart from most girls of her background had been her belief that she had a chance of earning her own income, perhaps even a large one, by becoming a renowned writer. She seemed alone in this, supported by remembering Bernard Berenson's exhortation that working at a career one loved was the path to happiness. John Husted had given her a deadline by which to respond to his marriage proposal, and she didn't yet know if she'd be hired as a columnist. She may well have felt she had no option but to marry.

One other factor that has largely been ignored, however, is a better explanation for her decision, given what she said at the time about her excitement—but also self-doubt—about the possibility of becoming the "Inquiring Photographer" columnist. If she were to defy Waldrop's unambiguous warning that she would be denied the job if she became engaged, Jackie would then have an explanation for why she wasn't hired. It would be a shield for her ego, albeit one that would require her to sacrifice her best chance yet at becoming a professional writer. As Carol Phillips of *Vogue* had observed of Jackie three months earlier, when they discussed her career as a junior editor, she had "not a great deal of confidence." The same insecurity was later discernible in her fear of pursuing an artistic career, when she confided to a friend at his photography exhibit, "I wish I could do what you're doing—but I can't." A powerful insecurity about her ability to be hired and retain the job may well be why she abruptly decided to surrender to social convention and get engaged.

A BALMY FLORIDA VACATION promised to at least temporarily distract Jackie from whatever anxious uncertainty she was enduring. After Christmas, the Auchincloss family headed to the exclusive community of Hobe Sound, guests of Unk's cousins.

Charlie and Martha Bartlett were at his parents' Hobe Sound home. It was Charlie who apparently invited the Bouvier sisters to join him in visiting friends in Palm Beach for the day: the Kennedys. He may have done so with intention. "Jackie was engaged to a fellow whom we didn't think much of," he recalled. "He was a nice fellow, but he didn't seem to be worthy of her hand."

One entered the high white stucco wall at 1095 North Ocean Boulevard through a massive wood door that looked like the sort found at castle drawbridges. Once inside, Jackie and her companions strolled down a covered colonnade, overlooking tennis courts. Inside was a buzzing hive, where guests were expected to compete in displays of athletic prowess, barbed wit, and knowledge of current events and world history.

On the emerald lawn behind the house, a touch football game usually included all of Ambassador Kennedy's active and attractive adult children. Jackie knew some of them, although the details of how and when remain unclear. She already knew the "star" of the family, Jack, with whom the Bartletts had been "shamelessly matchmaking." The two hadn't spoken since they first met in May, when Jackie had turned down his offer to join him for a drink after dinner at the Bartletts', but she may well have seen him recently—on national television. Both of their lives had taken unexpected turns in the intervening months.

Jack's siblings, gathered for the holidays, included thirty-year-old Eunice, a Stanford University graduate who'd been working as a social worker in Washington when Jackie started at GWU. (Her first memory of Jackie was that she played tennis and spoke French and did "both well.") Jackie had met Bobby and his wife, Ethel, through mutual friends, likely the Bartletts. Bobby, then all of twenty-five years old, was a Justice Department criminal division lawyer, and father of five-month-old Kathleen. There was also television producer Pat (twenty-seven), Jean (twenty-three), and Teddy (nineteen), on leave from basic training. Typically, the gatherings included their prep school and college pals and navy friends of Jack's. As Charlie recalled, activities at the Ambassador's revolved around the "swimming pool, movies, tennis courts, family games, lunch [on the] patio." When they were gathered for lunch at the white wrought-iron tables and chairs in the stone-floored courtyard, conversation was mostly light, punctuated by joking, needling, and one-upping about the morning's competitions, but also included serious discussion of world affairs.

The 1951 holiday was the first time the family had been together since summer. Eunice and Jean had recently completed a tour of Mediterranean and Middle Eastern nations. Eunice, who was focused on political developments, observed to the *Boston Post* that continued U.S. support for Greece's monarchy was a factor in retaining it as a Cold War ally, being "the one stabilizing permanent influence of the nation." Earlier in the year, Jack had been to England, Germany, France, and Australia, but the seven weeks he spent visiting Israel, Iran, Pakistan, India, Singapore, Thailand, Vietnam, Korea, and Japan, from October 7 to November 30, along with Bobby and Pat, changed him—and perhaps the prospects for his political rise. Kennedy had been determined, preparing to become a foreign-relations expert since entering Congress, and home movies showing the trio at the Taj Mahal and the Bangkok shopping district belied the political nature of their travels. Jack met with each nation's leaders, learning of the danger of Iran's falling under Soviet influence unless oil revenues were restored, India's needing U.S. food aid, and rising anti-Americanism in Pakistan. He wrote a *Boston Post* story about his interview with Pakistan's prime minister Liaquat Ali Khan just before Khan was assassinated that October.

The congressman was intent on redirecting America's Cold War foreign policy. He connected the dots between U.S. foreign aid and winning over the nonaligned developing nations as allies before the Communist Soviet Union and China did, but not merely to elevate American world dominance. He was also determined to lift the people he'd engaged with out of poverty. In an era when most U.S. representatives rarely made foreign trips except to fancy European capitals, the trip blew open his concept of global politics. Vietnam interested him the most. On October 19 the three Kennedys arrived in Saigon, where Jack angered both the French general there and an American Embassy official by questioning the wisdom of their entire military strategy.

Jack's falling deathly ill, with a fever that reached 106 degrees, during their last stop, in Japan, where he was hospitalized on Okinawa (he had neglected to take medication which helped keep his adrenal-gland deficiency in check), was barely mentioned in media reports. Instead of taking time to recuperate, however, from the moment he returned until he hit Palm Beach, Jack engaged in an intense public speaking schedule, blending charm and knowledge before crowds that might have gathered for cozy tales of his famous family but came away learning about the far reaches of the world, from the Pittsfield Chamber of Commerce to the Lowell Service Club to the Framingham Catholic Women's Club. With extemporaneous recall of detailed facts from his trip notes, he discussed foreign aid and Cold War policy, using only a map to illustrate his itinerary.

The effort culminated in his appearance on the national news show *Meet the Press* on December 1. His criticism of U.S. Embassy staff for being more interested in "tennis games and cocktail parties" than learning about the problems facing the people of their host nations made headlines, but more important was his assessment of the situation in Vietnam. The United States, he argued, mustn't blithely continue to provide heavy military support to the French against the North Vietnamese insurgents, who were backed by Chinese Communists and seeking control of Vietnam. Instead, it must convince France to relinquish its possession of that nation as its colony and let it become self-determining and sovereign. The Vietnamese, said Kennedy, aspired to be independent, and, increasingly, viewed the American alliance with France as supporting the continuation of their colonization. The consequences of not making this policy change, he concluded, would be the eventual domination of Communist China in the country. His November 15 radio address, nationally syndicated by the Mutual Broadcasting System, crisply articulated his observation that Vietnam, Cambodia, and Laos, as "French principalities," were "as typical examples of empire and colonialism as can be found anywhere," and that the United States' role in continuing to ignore their "nationalistic aims spells foredoomed failure."

Thus, the Jack whom Jackie met at the end of 1951 was different from the carefree flirt she'd met seven months earlier at the Bartletts', in May. He was intense. He was serious. He was in perpetual motion. He sought out General MacArthur to confer on classified Korean War developments. More nationalistic than partisan, he defied President Truman, lobbying him to revise his peace treaty with Italy and permit the country into the United Nations. As columnist David Rudsten observed in a June 1, 1951, editorial, "In the field of foreign politics [Kennedy] early recognized our weakness through disarmament and urged larger expenditures for national defense," developing "a liberal foreign policy that recognizes America's leading position and responsibility in world affairs." The congressman had also "studied federal legislation procedures quietly and efficiently," and "his efforts on behalf of education, labor and veteran's housing won him wide recognition."

Despite his play for national attention on foreign affairs, Jack paid assiduous mind to every matter affecting Massachusetts. Instead of using congressional breaks to relax, Kennedy spent hours every day of the week each summer and fall visiting the cities and towns of the Bay State, speaking before any civic organization that would invite him.

His high profile in the state caused some to speculate that he wanted to become governor, but his intent was to challenge the popular Republican U.S. senator Henry Cabot Lodge. As Kennedy had calculated, becoming senator was a necessary step to becoming president of the United States.

"He really wasn't normal—he had a drive, and intense interest in everything," noted businessman Lemoyne "Lem" Billings, Jack's best friend and confidant since their Choate days. His "brightness" had always been there, revealed less by his school grades than by his curiosity and reading habits. Even as a teenager, Billings noticed, Jack "read the *New York Times* every day."

That "interest in everything," Vietnam included, also characterized Jackie Bouvier—Kennedy's observations about his time there would have drawn her curiosity. She knew well the French colonial attitude, even if her own views on it hadn't fully formed.

Years later, Teddy Kennedy offered that, on that day Jackie visited, Jack surely discussed Vietnam, "since it was so much on his mind right after that trip," and recalled as well the fact that she "had a long history of interest in the conflict there," speculating that it was likely they "would talk about it."

Jackie was also immediately impressed by the powerful Ambassador, a fact putting her at odds with both Black Jack and Gramps Lee, who were united in their hatred of him. As Securities and Exchange Commission chairman, Joe Kennedy's crackdown on specialist stock brokerage commissions resulted in Black Jack's catastrophic 1936 decline. The year Jackie was born, according to Jack Davis, Jim Lee and Joe Kennedy had been such good friends that the former told the latter he was about to make a lucrative investment in a piece of Chicago real estate known as the Merchandise Mart, then the world's largest building, with four million square feet of retail space. Kennedy acted fast and bought it himself. Being "double-crossed" like that caused Lee to have "eternal enmity" for Kennedy.

Despite the outrage it would cause her father and grandfather—or perhaps because of it—Jackie was unrepentant in later declaring that of the entire family, Joe was her "most adored." The feeling became mutual quickly. "Papa Kennedy," recalled Charlie Bartlett, "thought she was great." In time she would learn of his unsavory business maneuvers, antisemitism, and manipulation of the media and political system to benefit Jack, but she turned a blind eye to these. "I am sick of all the mean stories of old Joe," she would later tell a friend. "No one knows the great heart that man has." This may well be how she felt about him, but it also showed her opportunism—even if it didn't work out with Jack, having

Ambassador Kennedy as a friend could prove useful in her professional ambitions.

Jackie didn't meet Jack's mother when she first visited. "The first I ever heard of Jackie was sometime during the winter of 1951," Rose Fitzgerald Kennedy would write, noting that Jackie was working at the paper. When she soon after received a thank-you note signed "Jackie," she recalled wondering, "[W]ho is Jackie?" She would come to know the answer soon.

Part V

THE PAPER

Would you rather have men respect or whistle at you?

—JACKIE, IN HER "INQUIRING PHOTOGRAPHER" COLUMN

16

THE BLUE ROOM

January 1952

With the memory of the active, worldly Kennedy household fresh in her mind, Jackie walked assuredly into Waldrop's office "the first week of January," bracing for his certain anger at her breaking her promise not to become engaged. Their interaction, in the way Waldrop told it in two interviews he granted later in life, proved him a colorful storyteller.

"Well, I'm sorry," she said flatly, "but I can't take the job."

"Why not?!" Waldrop recalled snapping at her, "a bit angry."

"I got engaged over Christmas."

Her candidness had an unexpected effect. "I've always liked her for this because it was an honorable thing to do," said Waldrop. He also appreciated her "straightforward manner in dealing with me." She told him that she'd known her fiancé, John Husted, for a relatively brief time.

"It won't last," he replied confidently. "Get out there and go to work."

It was a bit of artful reverse psychology on her part. Waldrop had not yet officially offered her the columnist job, but in unexpectedly declaring herself ineligible for the position, she got him to insist that she continue her training.

While pleased with her trial columns, Waldrop hesitated to finalize her hiring: he'd been angry to discover that "these bastards in the photographic department were all going out and taking the pictures for her."

"I'm also a photographer and used a Leica at the Sorbonne," Jackie had assured managing editor Sidney Epstein. He laughed. "Kid, we don't have anything that fancy. You'll use a Speed Graflex here." When he first handed her the large, clumsy camera, he noticed her "puzzled, worried look." He gave her a day to learn how to use it.

"She didn't know one end of a camera from the other when she came to us," cracked Waldrop. Her "pictures were awful." Several staff photographers determined to teach her the right distance to stand at in order to get clear thumbnail pictures of her interviewees, close enough to capture detail, far enough to be clear. It wasn't enough to take pictures from the right distance; she had to handle the Graflex and the big, round flash affixed atop it. She went to the Yellow Pages, found the Scurlock Studio's Capitol School of Photography on the second floor of 1813 Eighteenth Street, and signed up for intensive, abbreviated training. As Waldrop later told reporter Dorothy McCardle, "She was smart. She learned fast."

Although the fact that Jackie attended a photography school would occasionally be mentioned in her later biographies, the particular one she chose to attend revealed something of her progressive views on racial integration. Addison Scurlock, famous for chronicling Washington's African American community, had originally opened the studio in 1911, and his son, Robert, a former Tuskegee airman, had started the school in 1948. A photojournalist whose work appeared in national magazines, he was an expert with the Graflex. Among Jackie's fellow students were African Americans on the G.I. Bill. It also welcomed women, its brochure declaring their "exceptional skill in Child Photography, Fashion Work, Retouching and Oil Coloring."

Photojournalist George Thames, later with the *New York Times*, heard "many amusing stories" about Jackie from staff photographers, who formed an instant camaraderie with her. "The first time that one of her pictures appeared in her column, the other photographers said: you should buy us a drink . . . she went out and bought a quart of milk, to tease these fellows."

Thames said, "[S]he had her own ideas about what made the best picture," but she harbored frustration about her inability to take outstanding images. In thanking an acquaintance for a "beautiful colored picture," Jackie acknowledged that "you are a fantastic photographer—which makes me very jealous." She would maintain a lifelong admiration for the work of female photographers she came to know, including Berenice Abbott, Lily Emmet Cushing, and Toni Frissell.

Her search for the most varied material moved Jackie a wide distance outside her privileged comfort zone. Invested in her success, Waldrop sent her "on a brief tour of police and hospital spots to get a look at the life of the city." She walked the streets, strolled the parks, weaved through hotel lobbies, dove in and out of taxis and city buses, popped into neighborhood stores, and lingered outside office buildings and government agencies, interacting with bureaucrats and clerical, service, and domestic workers and familiarizing herself with their lives.

Despite being engaged, on Monday, January 21, 1952, Jackie was officially made the "Inquiring Photographer" columnist. She was given a raise that was nearly twice her starting salary, to $42.50 a week (around $500 in today's dollars, the annual equivalent of $19,656). "The column improved immediately," said Waldrop. "She was soft-spoken and shy, but she wasn't afraid to go out onto the street and get her columns. The kid we used before, I think he would go into a bar and interview the first five people he met." Waldrop didn't consider her camera skills as important as her insight into human nature. "Everything turns on how well the interview was handled—not the picture," Waldrop said. "She didn't know anything about taking photographs. But she certainly knew how to get to people."

That same day also brought the dreaded newspaper announcement of her engagement to John Husted, although Waldrop discouraged her from feeling that she would have to sacrifice the job in six months to become a stockbroker's bride, never believing she would go through with it.

In fact, their engagement party at Merrywood became legendary for its grim atmosphere. Sherry Geyelin, daughter of Unk's brokerage partner Chauncey Parker III, deemed it "chilly . . . no warmth there." When John's aunt Helen moved some flowers, she set off Mummy's temper and an argument broke out. To Unk's distant cousin, the author Louis Auchincloss, Jackie admitted to feeling gloomy at the inevitably "peaceful but dull" life that becoming Mrs. John Husted promised to be.

It was quickly obvious that her new job consumed more of her attention and generated greater pride than her engagement. During a visit with her friend Mary de Limur, who knew Husted, Jackie arrived with gloves on but removed the left one to show her the engagement ring, which had belonged to John's mother. De Limur noticed a green discoloration to her fingernails, and Jackie explained it was due to the chemicals she used to develop her column photos. "She immediately launched into a lengthy and very detailed account of her job at the newspaper. She went on and on," de Limur recalled. "Finally, almost as an afterthought, she mentioned that they had scheduled the wedding for some time in June . . . she seemed rather blasé about it."

Shortly thereafter, Jackie was out on her beat when a call came in for her. No sooner had the caller's name and number been left than word got out in the newsroom. By the time she returned, Waldrop himself delivered her message, with a wry warning to "stay away from the guy if she wanted to avoid trouble." He knew the caller well, but it wasn't his reputation that provoked the fatherly caution: it was concern for what going out with other men might do to a newly engaged woman's reputation. It was Congressman Kennedy, inviting her to the dinner and orchestra dancing held most evenings at the Shoreham Hotel's Blue Room.

When she arrived for dinner, there were two men waiting for her: Jack had brought along his Boston ally Dave Powers, who would help plan Kennedy's senatorial campaign strategy later that year. It's unlikely he invited Dave to join them as a chaperone; Jack Kennedy didn't worry about the conventions of polite society. Even if he hadn't learned of her engagement from Jackie during her Palm Beach visit, the announcement had hit the papers before their dinner. Jackie was unlikely to seriously pursue a man who was not interested in dating, as she had ascertained about Jack when they first met, but she was curious enough about his intentions to accept. Even though she was engaged, she didn't find it inappropriate to go out with a single man.

Although Jackie recalled it as the "first time I went out with him," and also recalling their intention "to dance," the moment she saw Jack's "political friend from Boston," as well as crutches to alleviate his back pain from compressed nerves (the result of a war injury), it was clearly more a meeting than a night of romantic dancing. The Blue Room's "Supper Dance" offered an eight-course dinner, from celery and olives to after-dinner cordials. There would be no interruptions, since the hotel did "not page in the Blue Room." Dinner was served until ten, with a choice of broiled bluefish, breast of capon, roast lamb, cold ham, turkey, or beef, served with potatoes, Jackie typically going for something light,

Jack invariably liking his red meat. They likely discovered their mutual fondness for ice cream over bowls of "Shoreham Desire." With their early work hours, they likely left before the Barnee-Lowe Orchestra floor show.

Given that, while Congress was in session, there were some weeks when Jack Kennedy would make a same-day round trip between Washington and Boston, flying north and taking the sleeper train back to the capital for a day of work (during which he liked to challenge himself by reading an entire book), he had to be highly motivated to arrange seeing Jackie Bouvier. He was then also barnstorming the Bay State, making a half dozen appearances from Springfield to Pittsfield to the Berkshires in late January and early February.

Most assumed Kennedy's attempt to unseat Lodge was just to expand his name recognition, but he liked the seemingly impossible challenge. "There wouldn't be much enjoyment in life without an obstacle," his close friend the writer and investment banker Chuck Spalding observed. The potential contest "was one obstacle . . . [he] enjoyed and talked about . . . and laughed about."

"He had the wealth, he had the education, he had the political acumen," Massachusetts political figure Wilton Vaughn noted, but "perseverance more than anything else" defined him. In Congress, his colleague Olin Teague was struck by his drive, and how "he was very much his own boss. He had very positive ideas on what was good and what was bad for this country . . . he didn't hesitate to express them . . . Jack studied very hard. . . . He was concentrating on trying to inform himself . . . he was an independent person, he was completely honest intellectually."

He hardly looked or acted like a millionaire. His ill-fitting suits and wrinkled shirts marked him as a man in need of the sort of wardrobe guidance Jackie had written about in her *Vogue* essay; still, if seeing the family's Palm Beach mansion hadn't been evidence enough, a January news story about his sister Jean's jewelry having been stolen, containing the disclosure that it was valued at $357,000, made the family's staggering wealth clear.

His casual demeanor belied his ruthless ambition. As a Harvard student before his first congressional campaign, Jack even had his own driver and valet, George Taylor, an African American Cambridge resident who knew the local "bigwigs" well. Taylor attested to the fact that upon his 1940 graduation, Jack Kennedy planned to pursue a political career and asked him to "introduce me to all the politicians in this area," contradicting the popular myth that his father persuaded Jack to run for office upon the death of his older brother, Joe, for whom Joe Senior had harbored similar ambitions. "I never saw anyone so enveloped," said Taylor. "He just loved it—he talked politics all the time."

Jack had begun by seeking out one man: "He'd always look up Dave Powers to get information as to the possibilities of what was the future in store for him," Taylor explained. A son of immigrants, the precinct worker from Boston's Charleston working-class neighborhood had befriended Jack and helped win his three consecutive congressional campaigns since 1946. Powers had a legendary memory and "recognized talent and people who were able to get things done," said Kennedy biographer Terry Golway. Powers was now developing campaign strategy for Jack's likely challenge to Lodge.

Jackie left no record of her first impressions of Powers, but he was immediately impressed, he said, by her "intelligence and utterly original insights," and recognized an "iron determination when she saw something could be achieved."

Jackie recalled that Powers had been "rather left out of the conversation," but told by Jack that she was Republican "old society," Powers hoped she might offer "insight" into how Lodge, from the same milieu, might respond to political attacks intended to break what political columnist Mary McGrory called his "bland adroitness." Her family didn't know Lodge, and she didn't tell Powers anything he didn't know, but he found her observation and suggestions of help she could provide unexpected: "Jackie is a perfectionist; anything she did, she wanted to do very well—and she became very, very good at it. That went to politics, too."

She realized that her aptitude for languages could help Kennedy with the mail that came into the Boston office from Massachusetts Italian, French, and Spanish speakers. "I was shocked that she knew there were many French Canadians in the old mill cities Lawrence and Lowell," Powers recalled.

"I have never met anyone like her," Jack would tell Dave Powers in good time, "she's different from any girl I know."

17

OUT ON THE STREET

February 1952

Her desk was a mess. She had a typewriter sitting on top of it on which she pecked out her bundle of daily quotes, a tedious exercise for someone untrained as a typist, accustomed to handwriting everything. A jumble of pencils and pads were strewn around the machine. She was, by Waldrop's account, apparently too focused on meeting her daily deadline to worry about keeping a neat desk. "She concentrated on the question of the day. She listened carefully," he said. "She treated it as a business, small, but important enough as a start in a writing career. She was just very serious." Picture editor Larry Jacobs shared her desk, where she kept transcripts of interviews to be used for future columns, bits of factual research, or provocative quotations for future questions in a bottom drawer. He recalled it as being "pretty full" and "looking much as though a recent hurricane had hit it a good deal of the time."

Running late for filing one day, she coaxed an acquaintance and NBC Radio employee, Everette Severe, whom she also interviewed, back to her office to help her compose a column. Observing her process from interviewing to finalizing, he described her as "very efficient" with "energy and initiative"—the "kind of girl you could play stickball in the street with."

Following her own advice to Vivi Crespi to "become distinct," Jackie invested considerable time in determining how to turn the confines of a traditionally mundane column into a refreshing bit of wisdom, wit, poignancy, and news. In a relatively short time, she would develop a rhythm that captured her quirky sensibilities and make public the unpredictable person who always lay beneath the veneer of glamour.

As she later reflected, "Like politics, there was no routine. No two days were ever the same. I loved every minute of it."

"If something interesting happened" in the news, according to Waldrop, she would address it in real time with a column question. Rushing to file for the next day's paper, she would dash back to the office, develop her photos, determine her final six choices among the ten or so people she interviewed, and do her daily battle with the typewriter to transcribe her quotes.

Jackie, like many creative types, stayed at it until all hours to get her best work done—an unstructured schedule was her way of pulling the column together. Published six days a week, the column averaged 144 individual interviews monthly—a total of nearly 2,600 people by the time she left the job. Although each day meant interviewing new people, the memory of some lingered with her, she told Waldrop: "I wonder what's happened to them. I stopped them for a moment—and they trusted me to answer. . . . Sometimes, they haunt me."

A large percentage of her income was spent on round-trip transportation to see John in New York. While flying was faster, airline tickets every other weekend quickly became too expensive for her. Apart from this, however, she still preferred taking the train. "She loved the efficiency of taking the plane, but it was never as relaxing for her as the train," a friend later observed. In fact, one of her early columns asked Washingtonians, "Do you prefer to travel by train or plane?"

In early 1952, the Senator regional passenger train had been upgraded to include a "parlor service," featuring a car with large windows and plusher seating, where she could comfortably read. She used the time well: at Christmas she had received an unexpected gift of about a half dozen "precious books" from Father Leonard, to whom she then expressed the depth of value they held for her:

"You know the most wonderful things about these books—I was really scared once I left college I would never learn anymore—just read best-sellers and maybe a couple of things like history I'd never learned and bit by bit forgot so much. And you're keeping me learning and opening up so many new worlds.

"I could never do that by myself no matter how much I wanted to because I just didn't know those books and those authors existed—but it seems to me you know everything and from all you've read and learned you can pick and choose the most lovely things for me—Does it give you a sense of power to think you're molding someone else's mind and taste? I hope it does and certainly no one ever had a more willing piece of putty to work with."

Being in New York seems to have been less pleasant than traveling there. Black Jack was thrilled to be seeing her more frequently, but he couldn't help being disappointed that once she'd dropped off her bags and embraced him, she had to change and run out to dinner with John Husted. While John's suggestion that they spend weekends with Unk and Mummy in Newport after their honeymoon was intended as an incentive, it made her "stomach drop," said Yusha, because she hoped to return to Europe.

John was also frustrated with her. Taking the train to save money meant less time together; they could share only Saturdays and Sunday lunch together before she had to leave. Failing to please either her fiancé or her father began to discourage her. It wasn't long before she confessed to a friend that seeing John involved "too much long distance."

Unbeknownst to him, she more eagerly returned to Washington and the company of a radically different John.

Eighteen years her senior, John B. White had an armful of tattoos and a passion for history, reading, politics, and journalism. He dubbed himself a "frivolous scholar." A wartime combat correspondent, he'd written for the *Boston Herald Traveler* as well as the *Times-Herald*. He'd recently gone to work at the State Department but remained close to his former *Times-Herald* colleagues; he first met Jackie when he dropped by to see them.

White and Jackie immediately bonded over their range of interests, and in the winter and spring of 1952, his basement apartment, with walls of books, became her haven.

"I had the distinct impression she felt weary shuttling back and forth to New York," White recalled, noting that she never mentioned Husted. "After a while she started spending her weekends around Washington, and she and I went out occasionally."

Jackie was ecstatic to learn White was a mythology expert. When he took her to the city's mental institution, St. Elizabeth's, to interview its director, the trio engaged in a dialogue dissecting the psychology of

Hercules. She educated him, too, with her passion for the ancient lyric poetry of Sappho.

White was attracted to her, but found that an "undigested, renegade toughness lay at the very core of Jackie's personality . . . [she] intimidated lots of people." He "certainly never tried anything" with her except to once hold her "big strong hand." He detected that she did not have "much, if any, sexual experience," but wasn't "particularly afraid of it." Instead, they talked ideas and work.

"We discussed her Inquiring Photographer column," he recalled. "She was good at dredging up questions. She was curious-minded and gifted at gaining people's confidence—she elicited frank answers from her interview subjects. And she loved to talk with her high-class friends about questions to put to people in her column."

In order to turn out a column that was provocative enough to satisfy a diverse readership, she drew her inspiration from a variety of sources, pulling from her personal interests or breaking wire-service news. She'd take an argument debated in the office and see if it would similarly incite pedestrians. She acknowledged editing some responses to draw out drama and pithiness but knew she could take only a degree of liberty with remarks attributed to people identified by name; there is no evidence that anyone objected to how they were quoted. (There was one known instance in which she pushed the envelope. To her stepsister Nini she attributed an answer to her question about whether boarding school and college students were eager to return to campus, declaring that she liked being home and able to "throw your clothes around the room in utter piggishness." Later, she revealed, "I never said that—Jackie answered it for herself.")

Waldrop recalled that she had both an unpredictable way of thinking that led to provocative questions and an instinct for asking what would have been on the minds of most readers. Sometimes he thought, "Where does she come up with this stuff?" concluding that her reading a random range of topics fed her imagination. When the newsroom encyclopedia "B" volume went missing, he found she'd kept it at her desk, studying the entry for "Bolivia." Telling her he'd teach her how to play the so-named card game, she responded, "No, the country."

This unpredictability would help build and maintain a strong following for her column. Jackie's colleague Glen "Zeke" Hearin advised her to always "dare to deviate" in her questions. One way in which she did so was by searching out the most incongruous demographic possible for particular questions. Instead of asking ladies at luncheons, for example, "What do you think of Dior's spring fashion line?" she waited on a street corner for truck drivers to stop at a red light and shouted out the question. Other times she poked at what might lie beneath the surface of those with strongly defined personas, asking circus clowns, "Does your smiling face hide a broken heart?" and "Are you funny at home?" She waited in a hotel lobby during the American Psychological Association convention to confront respected mental health professionals and ask, "How do you think you're maladjusted?"

Jackie sought to do more than entertain. She wanted to inspire and educate, consistently offering readers a chance to better understand exasperating behavior ("Why do you think people put off Christmas shopping until the last minutes?" "Why do you think so many people crack corny jokes in elevators?" "Do people welcome constructive criticism?") and develop greater empathy ("What is the greatest need of people in the world today?" "What are people most living for?" "What do you first notice about people when you meet them? Do you find that you often have to change your first impressions?"). She even managed to pose a few existential questions ("What came first, the chicken or the egg?" "What is the best age?").

The effort to draw out the best in strangers by pausing and encouraging them to think for themselves and own their brief moment of public attention was a small gesture, but it nevertheless lifted the dignity and respected the individuality of otherwise overlooked citizens and, vicariously, engaged the minds of thousands of similar readers. While some columns might have been intended to encourage erudite pursuits ("If you were put in solitary confinement and could only take one book, which would it be?"), she never avoided esoteric questions on the presumption that a cleaning lady or clerk was uninterested in the topics ("In *The Doctor's Dilemma*, George Bernard Shaw asks if it's better to save the life of a great artist who is a scoundrel, or a commonplace, honest family man. What do you think?" "Do you think modern art mirrors our times as much as Renaissance art did for that time?") The way she composed the question let even those unfamiliar with an author or historic period offer a valid opinion. She did not talk down to the largely working-class people she interviewed—she listened to them.

She recalled, "You could make the column about anything you

wanted to. So, I'd find a bunch of rough, salty characters and ask them about a prizefighter just so I could capture the way they talked." The process called on her best editing skills. Intent on preserving the variety of cadence, dialect, and language she heard, she printed responses that often read like script dialogue, with colorful euphemisms, dialect, or aphorisms. In fifty or so words, she sought to encapsulate her respondents' personalities; visually aided by a snapshot, each answer essentially presents a distinct character.

In one column about southern charm, she interviewed Senator Richard Russell of Georgia, Governor John Battle of Virginia, and actress Tallulah Bankhead, whom she met at the home of Alice Roosevelt Longworth. Daughter of a former Speaker of the House of Representatives, the actress did not disappoint: "My magnolia-scented southern charm has served me well, both professionally and privately. It has melted many a manager, chilled many a carpetbagger and confused many a swain. Exercise of it in lavish doses has brought me from Huntsville, Alabama, dash—that's [Senator] Sparkman's hometown—dash, you heard me—dash—to New York, London, Hollywood and other spots it would be indiscreet to mention."

Jackie loved live performances—whether it was the theater, opera, or dance—and the column gave her a chance to put her inquiries to the artists. She cornered actors in a National Theater musical to ask, "Why is there 'no business like show business'?" She went backstage to ask the Metropolitan Opera Company's *Madama Butterfly* cast, "Do you think foreign language opera should be sung in English in this country?"

She later reflected that children were the best interview subjects because they "gave better answers than anyone," but she "most enjoyed" the interviews involving dance performances, because they let her spend "so much of the day with dancers at rehearsal." (Several times she interviewed Ballets Russes dancers who let her sit in on rehearsals. "What do you think about while dancing?" she asked them.)

Jackie's column ideas were never censored, although Waldrop threatened to fire her when she asked pedestrians what local newspaper they liked best and printed responses that chose the competition.

Jackie was also savvy enough to draw attention to the column by interviewing members of the Senate, cabinet, Supreme Court, and armed forces, and even actor Jimmy Stewart when he visited town.

Despite what would emerge as a timeless style, Jackie Bouvier had been eagerly following popular culture since she was a young adult. In boarding school and college, she tumbled her chestnut mane over one eye like movie stars Rita Hayworth and Veronica Lake, and she loved swinging in a "wild jitterbug" to the big band music of Glenn Miller and Benny Goodman. Like millions of Americans, as a high school student she was bitten by the "Latin Craze" of the late 1940s, enamored with fashion, furnishings, and music inspired by South American cultures.

Now, as a young reporter, she was equally attuned to what was trending. She balanced her highbrow inquiries for the column with those about pop culture, from the rage for pinball machines to the cartoon character Li'l Abner getting married. When a flying saucer was widely reported over Washington, she asked what people thought it really might be.

A subject of particular intrigue for her was the popular actress Marilyn Monroe, who had become a sex symbol by popularizing the bikini five years earlier and was breaking through as an actress and singer: "What would you talk about if you had a date with Marilyn Monroe?" "Do you think Bikini bathing suits are immoral?" "Are women's clubs right in demanding Marilyn Monroe be less suggestive?" "Do you sincerely think that diamonds are a girl's best friend?"

Washingtonians quickly began talking about the column's changed tone to the point where the *Times-Herald* advertised it as a featured benefit of subscription. The column gave her a sense of doing "something useful." She had no regrets about not staying at *Vogue*, telling her dressmaker Mini Rhea, "Not that clothes aren't important, but a career like that would be limiting to me." Perhaps the highest praise came from the generally critical John White, who said that he thought her column "represented the best escapist literature then being produced in the District of Columbia."

Less enthusiastic was John Husted. When he came to Washington for weekends, he quickly grew weary of tagging along as she went out to ask her column questions on Saturdays and then spending Sundays with her family. Her driving him to and from the airport was the only time they had alone together.

Jackie captured John's stuffiness in his appearance in her February 19 column. Husted was asked which historical era he'd liked to have lived in. Others Jackie interviewed chose the lusty, heroic, and wild periods of Henry VIII, La Belle Époque, the Civil War, the Roaring Twenties, and the American Revolution. John replied with "Vienna in its heyday," because it offered "the best of food, wine, music, and surroundings accompanied by the elite of Europe" and the chance to wear "a red tunic and polished cuirass," using an archaic term for *breastplate*, "while dancing the gavotte."

It was perhaps telling that Jackie never took John to any social events in the city or even out with her friends.

18

BYLINE

March 1952

When John Husted wasn't in town, Jackie enjoyed a frenetic social life. Betty Beale reported Jackie's attendance at a "Leap Year Dance," waiting in line to dance with an air force general, going strong until four in the morning—but the most impactful was an evening she shared with the young congressman from Massachusetts.

In the last weeks of winter, she was invited by Jack Kennedy to a dinner party at his brother Bobby's house in Georgetown. It marked the fourth time they had met up, and as with all their previous interactions, they were joined by others. "Everything was done in groups," writer Page Huidekoper recalled of socializing with the young Kennedys and their pals at the time.

Among those she met as part of the entourage heading to Bobby and Ethel Kennedy's gathering was Lem Billings. In an era when a person's homosexuality often led to his or her being ostracized, neither Jack nor any of his family in any way rejected Billings for being a "confirmed bachelor."

"I didn't know anything about Jackie until the first time I met her," Billings recalled. "I can remember we were going to Bobby's for dinner . . . I was staying with Jack at the time and we drove out to Merrywood and picked up Jackie. . . . That was the first time I'd even heard of Jackie Bouvier. I remember he told me this was an attractive young girl and that she was engaged to somebody else. . . . In fact, she was even wearing an engagement ring when I met her. Through all the years that I had known Jack, I had met many of his girls so, to me, this was just another. It was rather interesting that this girl was engaged. . . . Frankly, he didn't know her too well when I met her. . . . At that time, it wasn't anything special, except that she was an awfully pretty girl, younger and prettier, I thought, than most he dated."

Jackie recalled their early encounters to Molly Thayer: "Saw Jack occasionally that winter when he would come down to Washington." It was a rare evening that the congressman was then in town. While waiting for Governor Paul Dever to decide whether he would seek the U.S. Senate seat, Kennedy doggedly forged ahead with his intense speaking schedule in Massachusetts, convinced he could beat Lodge. When John White tried to persuade him not to run, Jack snapped at him. White was stunned: "I never saw such passion in him."

Having met a decade earlier, John White admitted to being jealous of Jack Kennedy for having already published a book, but was won over when the congressman "said that the most beautiful book he's ever read was *Seven Pillars of Wisdom* by T. E. Lawrence . . . the way he said it, it suddenly came out of nowhere and it was, it seemed to lift him out of being just . . . hard-driving to a thoughtful, somewhat compassionate man." The men had met through White's great companion, Kennedy's late sister Kathleen. At the end of 1941, shortly after White came to work at the *Times-Herald*, Kathleen Kennedy and Inga Arvad (both having made their way to the paper on the recommendation of Arthur Krock, like Jackie) became chums and Kathleen helped Inga write her column "Did You Happen to See?" Kathleen introduced Inga to Jack, then a navy ensign working in Washington. Although married, Inga began a passionate affair with him. The foursome publicly socialized to convey the impression they were all just friends.

Since his days at boarding school, Jack Kennedy had rarely dated any one woman seriously; they were his companions, sometimes sexual partners but not intellectual ones. In this case, Inga's talents fused with her physical appeal. As her biographer put it, "He had fallen in genuine love with her because she had listened to him as a way to understand him, as a person, as a writer."

Arvad, a Columbia School of Journalism graduate, had earlier worked as a freelance reporter in Berlin, making inroads in the Third Reich hierarchy and even interviewing Hitler, who thought her a Nordic ideal and invited her as his guest to the 1936 Berlin Olympics. By the time she was working for the *Times-Herald*, the FBI was trailing her as a possible Nazi spy, apparently after suspicions were raised about her to its director, J. Edgar Hoover, by Frank Waldrop. Weeks before the United States went to war, Hoover learned that she was dating Jack Kennedy. Fearing she might seek to obtain sensitive information from the young navy ensign, Hoover wiretapped the couple. Joe Kennedy was informed; he grew alarmed at how the affair might threaten whatever career Jack pursued.

On January 12, 1942, gossip columnist Walter Winchell reported: "One of ex-ambassador Kennedy's eligible sons is the target of a Washington gal columnist's affections . . . Pa Kennedy no like." Inga's biographer concluded that it was, in fact, Joe Kennedy who tipped off Winchell, to force the relationship to end. As Jack's later letters to Inga make clear, their intellectual bond and his love for her persisted.

After the split, it had comforted Kennedy to still have his sister's companionship. The two resembled each other so much that they were called "the Kennedy twins." Kathleen left for Great Britain to join the Red Cross in 1943. In May of 1944—as Jack lay in a Boston naval hospital recovering from a severe back injury that resulted from the PT-109 boat he commanded as a lieutenant being rammed by a Japanese destroyer—she married William Cavendish, the Marquess of Hartington. Four months later, Cavendish died in the war. Living in England as a widow, Kathleen died in a May 1948 plane crash.

With her writing a column at the *Times-Herald*, in the same newsroom where Inga and Kathleen had worked, and her own association with John White, Jackie would inevitably evoke memories of the two women who had meant more to Kennedy than any others—a significant factor in Jack Kennedy's early perception of her.

JOHN HUSTED HAD NO fondness for Jackie's work on the *Times-Herald*. His displeasure ran deeper than the limits it imposed on their time together—he seemed to resent the passion she had for it. "You take it too seriously," he told her, according to Yusha. He certainly did not. In a 1978 interview, he claimed that he would "help her with the Inquiring Camera Girl business, which was an insipid little job. . . . We'd go to supermarkets and ask people stupid questions." He said they laughed together as she worked, but he knew well that she worked hard to craft what he demeaned as "stupid questions." Perhaps Husted was embarrassed by having his fiancée's imagination on public display six days a week. His hostility ridiculed the most defining element of her life at that moment, her writing.

Such belittling nevertheless forced her to—as she had often told Yusha during his vacillations about important decisions—"figure it out as soon as you can." In fact, previously unpublished remarks evidence that Jackie had found Husted intolerable even at the time of their engagement; "a disaster," her friend the lawyer Walter Sohier thought. "She said, 'You know what I like about him . . . He looks so good in tails.'" To Molly Thayer, Jackie would later confess that when she "realized that the most important thing in his life was making a dry martini," she knew she "didn't love him," and "broke the engagement." On Sunday, March 16, 1952, she drove him to the airport and returned the ring.

Husted forever maintained that Janet learned that he didn't have great wealth and forced the breakup. In a letter he claimed Jackie wrote to him (which he never showed anyone), he said that she suggested he ignore the "drivel" linking her to Jack: "[I]t doesn't mean a thing." From all she said, Jackie Bouvier loved being *in love*, but she did not love John. She later sought to erase the episode from her story, declaring, "John Husted's name must never be mentioned . . . I refuse to drag his name into the history books." Janet ensured that the world knew her daughter was again available by getting Betty Beale to explain in her March 23 *Washington Evening Star* column that she "decided they were rushing things a bit" and "called off their engagement."

In a letter to a British friend, Dan Samuel, Jackie admitted that the decision had left her "rather confused," but, she added, "I know it was right to break it," admitting the pact "seemed very wrong." She was more reflective in her letter to Father Leonard:

"I am ashamed that we both went into it so quickly and gaily, but I think the suffering it brought us both for a while afterwards was the best thing—we both needed something of a shock to make us grow up. I don't know if John has—I haven't seen him and I don't really want to, not out of meanness—it's just better if that all dies away & we forget we knew each other—but I know it's grown me up and it's about time! The next time will be ALL RIGHT and have a happy ending."

Jackie had learned not to rely on wishful thinking. Certainly she wanted no end to the privileged lifestyle she had been afforded, but judging by her efforts to launch larger and potentially more lucrative writing projects, she had not abandoned her conviction that she could eventually earn a comfortable income from a career she cared about, if not a large fortune. She increased her career chances by focusing on the column, with the bonus that her focus on work left her "doing just fine" after the breakup.

For her March 17 column, she went to the Irish Embassy to ask about the significance of St Patrick's Day. Ambassador John Joseph Hearne declared it "first and last a religious feast," and one of his aides said it "brought into Ireland the civilization that was to mold western Europe." For Jackie, however, their brogues "made me so homesick, he [a staff member] could hardly get me out of the place." She proudly sent the column to Father Leonard.

Her column nine days later was more routine, asking for opinions of musician Johnny Ray, but more momentous was the day's conversation in Waldrop's office: though it was only eight weeks after she'd been named a columnist, he had decided to give her another raise, to $45.50 a week (for an annual salary of $26,000). Eight months later, she had so made the column her own that its title was changed, from the "Inquiring Photographer" to the "Inquiring Camera Girl." More important than the raise, or the title, or the fact that she was the first woman to write the column, was that she became the first person to write it who was given a byline. Every day, everyone in Washington saw the name "Jacqueline Bouvier" in print.

In her letter to Father Leonard, she allowed herself a moment of quiet pride, and a wink of self-deprecation: "I have my name on the column now. Jacqueline Bouvier, the 'Inquiring Photographer' staggering around the streets clutching her 50-pound camera about which she knows nothing except how to click the shutter.

"It's really ridiculous," she admitted, "but it's fun."

19

WORKING WOMAN

April 1952

Mummy never let Jackie walk out of Merrywood and make her ten-mile drive to work in downtown Washington without scrutinizing her appearance.

It wasn't just that she would point out that "the line of my stockings was not straight," Jackie recalled; it was also criticism of her wavy hair ("a little bit wild") and the revealing plunge of Jackie's neckline, as well as her insistence that Jackie wear a hat and gloves before being seen in public. Only after dutifully adhering to Mummy's decorous arbitration was Jackie let free.

Just before she turned onto the George Washington Memorial Parkway, the real Jackie manifested. She lowered Zelda's convertible top, ditched her scarf, hat, and gloves into the glove compartment, and blasted the radio loud enough to hear the hit songs of late spring 1952, pushing the gas pedal and not letting up until it seemed she was flying along the scenic drive.

More than once she prompted a policeman's motorcycle siren. Speeding might cause an accident but paying for a ticket would break her budget. She almost seemed delighted by the challenge of getting out of it. Once, she was racing along with Yusha when they were stopped by a state trooper. "Jackie leaned over," he wrote, "her wide spaced eyes looking seriously at his and in her soft voice politely informed him, '[E]xcuse me, officer, but your fly is undone.' Embarrassed, he thanked her, and neglected to give a speeding ticket."

She had technically "owned" her car, Zelda, for six years, but had only begun driving it regularly in the fall of 1950 when commuting to GWU. Her driving experiences had mostly been confined to summers at the beach or meandering through Europe; now she had to maneuver through unnerving downtown traffic, and her frustration made it into the column ("Should all cars have directional lights?" "Should Washington adopt the system of loudspeakers embarrassing jaywalkers?" "What is the biggest traffic problem the local area communities have in common?").

Traffic and policemen were not her only worries. With dents and scrapes, Zelda had become an unpredictable jalopy, which made Jackie alert to even the slightest off-kilter sound. She would arrive at the parking garage near her office with relief. Longing for a new model despite being unable to afford it, she justified browsing the models at the annual car show and popping into dealerships as part of her job ("What do you look for in a new car?" "What has your car got that no other car has got?" "Does the car make the man?").

Once, after leaving an appointment with dressmaker Mini Rhea, she hurried back and asked politely, "Mrs. Rhea, where can I get a pitcher of water?" Unsure of what was going on, Mini filled a pitcher and handed it to her. Jackie left quickly, returned with the pitcher, and smilingly asked for a refill, casually remarking, "I think one more pitcher and I won't have to call the fire department." Mini ran to her door to see smoke billowing out of Zelda at the sidewalk as Jackie calmly dumped water through the car window, explaining, "I set my car on fire with a cigarette."

The unlikely collaboration Jackie formed that spring of 1952 with Rhea was a result of her slight rise in income and her reappropriating funds that had previously been used on her New York commutes to see John Husted. Whatever the amount she spent on Mini's dressmaking services and bolts of expensive fabric, however, the pleasure it gave her proved inestimable. She was finally able to fulfill a fantasy she had been nurturing through years of creating her own designs. Jackie's recognition that a woman should dictate her appearance but would also be judged on it was evident in many of her column questions: "Would you want women to discontinue wearing makeup?" "What do you think of the poodle cut?" "Do you dress for men or women?" "If you were a judge, what type of femininity would you choose for Miss America?" "How long should a woman try to look young?"

Mummy had introduced Jackie to the dressmaker, who turned out original clothing for the conservative tastes of the capital's political and social set. Seventeen years Jackie's senior, Mini Rachel Sells Rhea hailed from rural Mississippi. In 1947, after losing her husband in the war, the fervent Methodist moved to Washington with her two daughters, first working in a dry-cleaning business doing alterations and repairs, then teaching herself dressmaking. With her impressive handiwork she was able to establish her Georgetown shop in the English basement of her home.

Jackie's original sketches were "bold and positive strokes," recalled Mini, who then made paper patterns and fitted them to her. She sewed the garments with fabric Jackie bought. The dressmaker observed that "Jackie was never intimidated into wearing what others were wearing." What struck her was that "in following her own thinking . . . [s]ome sixth sense told her where fashion's trend was leading." All of this was not merely an exercise in creativity for Jackie, but economy—along with original designs, she sketched her adaptations of expensive designer clothes from the pages of *Vogue* and *Harper's Bazaar*.

Despite coming from such different worlds, the two women worked well together. Rhea was impressed by Jackie's "depth and understanding and sympathy for the highest and the lowest." Whereas many of her matronly clientele "treated me like a maid," dropping their clothes on the floor for her to pick up as they watched, "Jackie didn't want a lady's maid and she had great respect for every individual. . . . [She] was self-sufficient, didn't want me to fix her hooks or help her with a zipper," she later wrote in a memoir. "She hated to tell other people what to do," Rhea concluded, and "while she was always very sure of what she wanted for herself, she was very careful never to impose her opinion on others."

It wasn't her clothing but her hair that made Jackie self-conscious at the time, regretting that she got a mid-length haircut right before posing for a *Times-Herald* publicity image. She tried pinning it up but thought she looked mannish and called it "that lesbian picture." She soon cut her hair into a pixie style and frosted it with blond tips.

The few other photographs of her at work show her wearing long, wraparound "New Look" skirts, sweaters, plaid shirtwaist dresses, and sweater vests with Peter Pan collar blouses, well-groomed but inconspicuous. The utilitarian nature of her look was dictated by her job. On her beat, she carried a work badge and a massive leather shoulder bag jammed with pads, pencils, flashbulbs, and film.

"She didn't have any froufrou in her style. Very simple," Waldrop recalled of her appearance. "She never dressed fancy," added one colleague. "She didn't dress as well as most of the other women on the paper," said another. When someone asked the meaning of the gold words on her black belt ("*Honi soit qui mal y pense*"), she translated the Middle French maxim with a straight face as, "Love me, love my dog." The real meaning: "[S]hame on anyone who thinks evil of it."

With a bit of condescension, Jackie characterized her colleagues as "such rough diamonds it's almost trite." But she also found them "the most fun and the kindest" and, importantly, "the most different I've ever met." None were from her milieu nor, reporting aside, exposed to it. The gulf of social class defined their relationship. As she told Father Leonard, "[T]he toughest reporter of all didn't think he'd like me at all at first because I'd been to a 'finishing school,' etc.—but he finally decided he did—and the only way he could think of showing it was to offer me the highest treat he could think of—he told me that the next time he got 2 tickets to an execution he'd take me! I'm afraid I didn't look quite as thrilled as he expected."

Jack Schneider recalled that some of the "staff tried to discourage her by giving her a hard time," while he and others, such as Bob Mulligan, "helped her get going." Some politely said she was "shy and aloof," or that she was "friendly enough," but "few felt they really knew her." Photographer W. Berkeley Payne said she was "very quiet and pleasant . . . did her job well." Larry Jacobs recalled that while she "wasn't the least bit snobbish," she was also "not at all outgoing or the extrovert type" and "never talked about her personal life." Among the staff, the warmest words that Joe Heilberger could offer were "awfully nice" and "friendly."

Her most critical colleagues were city desk writer Estelle Gaines and assistant managing editor Jack Kassowitz. Gaines's recollection was that Jackie was "untrained and very scared," "awkward in movement as well as assignment," "couldn't handle a camera," and produced photographs that were "perpetually out of focus." This was all true, but only during her early months on staff.

Kassowitz was more eviscerating. "As a reporter she was at best mediocre," he declared to one of Jackie's biographers. This was a fair assessment, considering she was a columnist and employed a different writing skill than that required for a traditional straight news story. (She would ultimately write a total of six full-length feature stories for the paper; these were unusual pieces, reading more like storybook chapters, complete with caricature illustrations.) Kassowitz further asserted that Jackie "found it difficult to approach strangers"—a fact she herself admitted to—and "simply refused to go out"—a claim that seems specious. She had to turn out a column six days a week or she would be fired. Her name was on the column, and she didn't have an aide or staff to write it for her.

Gaines added that Jackie was "primarily interested" in interviewing members of the Social Register, which is disproven by a survey of her interviewees. This does suggest, however, a class resentment at the root of the staff hostility toward Jackie. "She landed the job only because she was the stepdaughter of 'Take-a-Loss with Auchincloss,'" Gaines said. "Very few of us were intrigued by the Washington and New York social scene. We didn't socialize with Jackie, because she wasn't one of us. The rest of us had grown up on the crime beat. We weren't likely to serve Jackie tea and crumpets." Kassowitz echoed the sentiment, calling Jackie "a poor little rich girl" who lived on an estate and "enjoyed dancing, fancy restaurants and meeting people who were famous and had money."

Among the male staff, there was another reason Jackie was resented. She "got her share of attention on the paper," is how W. Berkeley Payne politely put it. Kassowitz bluntly explained: "In the grim atmosphere of a hot, cluttered city room it was pleasant enough to look up and see an attractive girl like Jackie. Many of the reporters and photographers were after her, but she constantly deflected their invitations. . . . When they realized she wasn't available to them, they ganged up on her."

Frank Waldrop recalled a vague incident which seemed to involve Jackie's turning down "a fellow who wouldn't take no for an answer" as she pointedly lectured him in a side hallway. While she could capably fend off unwanted attention with a firm turn of phrase, she did her best to avoid the more aggressive harassment. Dubbing the men who worked on the printing and mechanical floors three flights up and made comments about her figure the "4th Floor Wolves," she sought refuge in more enlightening conversation with the International News Service bureau chief William K. Hutchinson, who took an interest in her "keen mind."

The conservative *Times-Herald*'s articles and other columns disseminated the era's gender expectation that women acquiesce to men, a norm to which Jackie seemed to behaviorally adhere. However, not just her questions but often the leading way she worded them, disarmingly couched in sarcasm, suggested a subversive feminism: "Would you rather have men respect or whistle at you?" "A Boston University professor said women marry because they're too lazy to go to work: Do you agree?" "Should a wife let her husband think he's smarter than her?" "Chaucer said that what women most desire is power over men: what do you think women desire most?" "What do you think of wrestling as a sport for women?" "Should single women be permitted to join social clubs as single men are?" One question was a startling, perhaps even bitter, reflection on the permissiveness of violence against women: "Noel Coward said, 'Women are like gongs; they should be struck regularly.' Agree?"

Asking the questions as she did often put the men on the spot, forcing them to either disclose their sexism or condemn the paternalistic status quo. "When did you learn that women were not the weaker sex?" was the most overt example of this, but she drew this out even within questions ostensibly on other topics. When she asked what the future might hold for the first American transsexual woman, Christine Jorgensen, four men understandingly responded without judgment of her decision, but also with sexism in that they pondered why anyone would choose to live with the second-class status of a woman.

With her name now publicly attached to the column, Jackie's previous insecurity began to melt away. "When I'm really famous and syndicates are fighting for my every word and I feel like hopping over and seeing you—I'll just do it and write about Dublin," she wrote half-jokingly to Father Leonard, "or a profile of you for the *New Yorker*." The column was the public platform she needed to achieve her loftier writing goals. It instilled the daily discipline to write. The column's word limit trained her to communicate succinctly. It forced her to capture a distinct narrative voice with the economy of poetry. It taught her to write for an audience. The column was making her a better writer.

But she wanted to expand in a variety of directions, from newspaper feature stories and magazine profiles to "the great American novel" and children's books, which she intended to illustrate herself.

Jackie's first attempt at expansion was initially promising. The photo scrapbooks and illustrated poems she had been producing in her early teens had evolved into little books with original stories and watercolor illustrations. One in particular, a children's fairy tale for her young half sister titled "The Red Shoes of Janet Jennings," had been enthusiastically lauded by everyone who had read it. John White, for one, praised it as a "beautiful piece of work," and believed it could be published, but ultimately his contacts in the publishing business couldn't determine a marketing strategy and turned it down.

One coworker admitted that some of the staff teased Jackie about how she was able to fly to New York or lunch at the Willard on her salary, not realizing she often used it all on such extravagances. There were times when she would write several columns ahead of time and take a Friday or Monday off from work, but she lacked enough of her own money to pay for traveling (pleasure trips being underwritten as gifts from Unk and Mummy) and sometimes food. On more than one occasion, Waldrop noticed that she didn't eat lunch. He'd ask her to walk with him to a nearby deli, where he bought a sandwich for himself—and one for her.

"She was always a little short on money," Waldrop recalled. "She always had to be careful how she spent, about paying the bills. She would always be looked after [with housing and meals] by her stepfather, but he had his own children. She certainly wasn't going to get anything substantial from her father. She worked, and she earned her own living."

Jackie was responsible for meals out, clothing, accessories, incidentals, and all costs related to her car. Her father kept her small inheritance from Grampy locked in investments, but still sent her a monthly allowance, which supplemented the money she was making at the newspaper. Modest though it was, her salary was a point of pride she would reference to counter the "myth that I am just a sheltered socialite," as she put it. "I proved that I could support myself by holding a newspaper job for a year and a half."

And at her immediate disposal to bring in extra income was her imagination. A clue to her next move was dropped one morning when she strode purposefully into Waldrop's office and asked point-blank, "Do we own a television station?" He was bewildered. "She could be kooky. 'No!

We're a newspaper,' I told her. 'Well—we should.' See, she saw around corners. She knew the power was shifting."

Days after her byline first appeared, Unk and Mummy would become largely absent from her life, leaving for trips to North Carolina and Nevada, then a lengthy one to see Lee, who had dropped out of college after a semester and convinced Mummy to let her study music and art in Italy that February. Little Janet and Jamie were cared for by a nanny, and Nini and Tommy were in boarding school. Mummy and Unk would return for two weeks in June before moving the entire household to Newport for the summer, where Lee joined them. Jackie was left alone and in charge of Merrywood that spring, briefly joined there by Yusha in summer.

Before they left, Mummy and Unk had agreed to be interviewed for her column, and Jackie's version of what they said offers a glimpse into their dynamic. Asked which movie star their spouse most reminded them of, Unk suggested Janet's domineering personality. "I think I'd better refuse to answer that on the grounds it might incriminate me. How about Myrna Loy, *The Perfect Wife*? She may not be Myrna Loy to everyone, but she's the perfect wife to me. Who were some of the silent screen ones? No. I'd definitely say my wife is no star of the silent screen." Janet initially mentioned a "sour-looking creature" from the silent era but instead compared Unk to Harpo Marx "because he's garrulous. Except he's a little better than Harpo Marx because he can say, 'Yes, dear.'"

Without any parental control of her time, Jackie began to linger in the city. The Washington area had been her home base for nearly a decade, but the column now gave her the excuse to explore its many historic buildings and cultural institutions—all in the hope of finding new material that could facilitate her ascent as a writer.

At the end of April, Jackie was interrupted by an unexpected call from Martha Bartlett. She and Charlie had invited her to a May 8 dinner. Needing an "extra man" to balance the guest list between men and women, Martha urged Jackie to invite Jack Kennedy. At a confident point in her life, Jackie called the congressman's office. Having announced his Senate campaign on April 6, he was almost always in Massachusetts, but he would be in town that night. He accepted.

20

A SECOND DINNER

May–June 1952

By all accounts, it was during the May 8, 1952, gathering at the Bartletts', in the same house where Jackie and Jack had met almost exactly a year earlier, when their deeper connection took hold.

Not long after the dinner, Jack Kennedy would regale anyone who would listen with the story of how he "leaned across the asparagus and asked her for a date." Her retort: "There was no asparagus that night." It was a bit of stagy banter, like two actors playing against type, Jack the romantic and Jackie the realist.

Martha Bartlett did not recall any magical turn of events which had sparked their mutual interest, but the evening—marking the fifth occasion, according to the record, on which they spent time together—would become the start of a romanticized public narrative, pulled from an arsenal of polished anecdotes to be used repeatedly in press accounts. It was a tactic already pioneered by Kennedy's father. His frequent claim to the press that the death of his first son, Joe Jr., had led him to draft Jack into politics was a "trite story," Jackie would explain, to be used whenever "you get so tired of people asking for anecdotes."

It was after this dinner that Jack began mentioning Jackie to his family. All of them, except his mother, had casually met her in Palm Beach five months earlier. Jack made no mention of her appearance or social status but rather "the column she wrote," as Teddy recalled. "He got a real kick out of it and he had a few he clipped and showed members of the family. It showed her utterly unique way of thinking about the world. He told her that he read it all the time."

The couple saw each other more frequently after the second Bartlett supper, though with Jack on the campaign trail, scheduling was a challenge. Jackie would recall of that period, "My courting with Jack [was while] he was running for the Senate, so he was in Washington rarely. He would call me before from Massachusetts and arrange one evening. It was always very private, either dinner at the Bartletts' or Ethel and Bobby's. Either we stayed there until he took me home or sometimes saw a movie." His driving her home was, as she put it, their "only private time."

One oft-repeated anecdote involved Jack's car breaking down in the driveway of Merrywood in mid-June, when Unk and Mummy had returned from Europe but before they left for Newport. Jackie recalled: "He came tramping back to the house and I gave him the keys to Uncle Hugh's car to get him home. Uncle Hugh was rather severely surprised the next morning leaving for the office to find his own car gone—and a broken down one with a Massachusetts license blocking his driveway." Implicit in the story is that Jack had returned her to Merrywood far too late into the night for them to tell her stepfather. But Lem Billings suggested that the extent of the couple's intimacy was kissing in the congressman's parked car.

By all accounts, Kennedy, by late spring, was already creating a unique classification for Jackie, introducing her to his most trusted and closed of circles, that of his family. As journalist Laura Berquist, who would become close to them both, observed, "[N]ever once did this suitor propose they go off for a night or a weekend," as he had with others. But neither did it mean that he stopped seeing other women.

"Oh, there were several [girls he was dating]," Jean Mannix of his campaign staff recalled. "No one specifically. Now, Ann McDermott he dated. That was during the [1952] campaign. She came down to Washington with the idea of getting a job in government. Nothing really seemed to appeal to her, and she went home in May. He did see her, but he was dating Jackie at this same time. And they [McDermott and Kennedy] had a wonderful relationship." Still, Mannix believed that Jack Kennedy realized by 1952 "that he wanted to marry Jackie Bouvier." True or not,

Jackie seemed flattered enough by his attention that she enjoyed seeing him without concern for the outcome.

Kennedy's primary distraction from Jackie, however, was his campaign. He was in Massachusetts every summer weekend and then daily, once Congress was in recess. Social columns at the time suggest their continued independence, even when he was in Washington. Jack attended that year's April 14 Cherry Blossom Ball, for example, without a date. She frequented Billy Martin's Tavern in Georgetown alone, "with her camera," recalled John D. Lane, an administrative aide to Connecticut senator Brien McMahon.

Kennedy's first major campaign event was held on May 18, 1952, in the Worcester, Massachusetts, Hotel Sheraton, at what became a trademark format: a "tea party," which depended on the presence of his sisters Eunice, Pat, and Jean, but especially his mother, Rose.

The Worcester tea party was attended by an estimated four thousand women. First, Rose Kennedy ascended a low platform lined with flowers and thanked the audience for coming; she then introduced Jack, who spoke for around thirty minutes, after which the family received an endless line of women.

For the next six weeks, until the Fourth of July weekend, they repeated the event, in Holyoke, Springfield, Quincy, Fitchburg, Boston, and Brockton, Jack unable to make only the last one. The events generated massive mailing lists of women voters of both parties.

Just as doggedly, Jackie was calculating her own moves to advance her career. She'd been the official "Inquiring Photographer" columnist for only two months but was already eager to break out of the column's confines and begin writing full feature pieces for the paper. When she learned from a colleague that the famous Boston Red Sox outfielder Ted Williams would be in town for an April 15 game against the home team, the Washington Nationals ("Nats"), she became determined to somehow interview him. The goal was all the more challenging because Williams could be hostile to the press.

With feigned naïveté, she had asked a male colleague how she could best corner the ballplayer. It was impossible, he told her; the only place she could be sure to meet him was in the locker room at Griffith Stadium—a place to which she knew she wouldn't be admitted.

While April 15 came and went, her colleague's warning that she wouldn't be permitted into the locker room stuck with Jackie, as if it were a dare. On May 10, 1952, she was able to push her way as far as the door to the locker room, but she was denied entry in the run-up to Washington's game against Philadelphia. Some players considered the presence of a woman even just near the locker room before a game to be bad luck, but she created enough of a stir by begging for interviews that the home team president, Clark Griffith, and manager Bucky Harris came out to speak with her. Soon, first baseman Mickey Vernon, right fielder Jackie Jensen, shortstop Pete Runnels, and center fielder Jim Busby were coaxed out, as she asked them all, "Do you think the Nats will pull out of their hitting slump?"

As the game got underway, Jackie headed back to the office, where she learned that fate had played into her hands that day, the Nats breaking their losing streak with thirteen hits. Some players hailed her as a good-luck mascot. "Jacqueline seems to have been what our ball club needed," the *Times-Herald* boasted of its columnist to its sports fans. "A short time after she sweetly asked the Nats when they were going to start slugging again, the club exploded with thirteen hits and defeated the Athletics, 5-3."

For someone like Jackie Bouvier, who enjoyed defying rules and decorum, to slip uninvited into union conventions or venture along loading docks or push her way backstage at theaters was a delightful adventure. As a reserved person, however, she found that the most basic task of her job provoked dread. As she would confess, it was "sheer agony to stop perfect strangers to ask them questions."

Even before opening her mouth, the odd sight of the young woman with the big camera roaming the streets drew stares. To cope with her anxiety about violating personal boundaries, Waldrop recalled that Jackie crafted a well-timed tactic of hiding her own face from her subject by raising the camera just as she finished asking the question and then snapping their picture, often momentarily blinding them with the flash. After transcribing their response, she had to coax them to disclose their name, occupation, and sometimes even address. Everette Severe distinctly remembered that she was already wearing sunglasses (tucked atop her head when she was indoors). Her camera and the soon-to-be trademark sunglasses both served as shields.

Jackie was also further developing her inimitable, enigmatic persona. Severe's NBC colleague Mac McCarrick recalled her conversational voice as evenly modulated; yet, at other times, she'd employ a girlish, whispery tone, misleading many into assuming she was helpless. This duality of vulnerability and confidence hid her true self—which was warm, earthy, informal, and inclined to absurdity—from full public view. But it was also a way of gaining power in social interactions and taking control of how people saw her. Jackie was less an actress who shifted roles in front of different audiences, as many cynically believed, than the director and producer of the scenes of her life.

That spring, Jackie's professional life continued to blossom, as did her social life—cocktail parties and receptions and further integration into Washington's most powerful circles.

Her biggest splash, showing how quickly she'd risen in journalism circles, was being invited to the annual Gridiron Club Sunday reception. In the reception line into the Statler Hilton's Congressional Room, where cocktails were served, were political celebrities such as Republican senator Bob Taft and his wife, Martha, former commerce secretary Averell Harriman, Nancy Kefauver (wife of the influential Tennessee Democratic senator Estes Kefauver), Alice Roosevelt Longworth, Chief Justice Fred Vinson, and Senator Margaret Chase Smith.

The Inquiring Photographer herself even earned a mention in a *Washington Evening Star* social column that spotted "Arthur Krock talking to pretty, young Jacqueline Bouvier."

As further proof of her ascent, with Unk and Mummy gone, Jackie began hosting her own bustling Merrywood parties. John White was as startled by the powerful positions of the mostly "highly intelligent" male guests as he was by their being thirty to forty years her senior. He observed that she had "a great knack for inspiring [good conversation] and loved to see people enjoying themselves and being bright." As he watched her move among the men, White concluded that "Jackie took pleasure in dealing with and being close to men who were doing important things, not necessarily as advisor so much as confidante . . . her interests in people tended to be in direct proportion to their importance. . . . Power and charisma seemed to override all other qualities in her estimation of people."

In the last days of June 1952, a British friend of the Kennedy family, Dinah Bridge, was a houseguest of Robert and Ethel Kennedy's. She recalled that one morning during her visit Jack and Jean were joining them for breakfast when "around the corner of the front door came this beautiful girl in riding clothes to pick up Jean to go riding. And very shortly after that, I think even one night later, or two, she was invited to supper."

Days later, Jack asked Jackie to join his family for the Fourth of July weekend at their summer home in Hyannis Port, on Cape Cod, Massachusetts. Jack Kennedy would have first cleared with his father any of his intended weekend guests. In the intervening six months since the Ambassador had first met Jackie Bouvier in Palm Beach, far more than her hairstyle had changed.

Jackie's ambitions had become ever more extravagant. She had won the byline on her column, then stamped it with her unmistakable imprint. Her sights were set on writing headline stories for the *Times-Herald*, yet it was clear that this would not be enough. She wanted even more. Even being a *New Yorker* writer—which she mused about several times as her ultimate perch—would not be enough. What she wanted, though she did not know how she would get there, was real influence. She had hinted at that vision, subversively, by the questions she chose for her column and the answers she chose to print, which communicated to the public what was on her mind, and what she thought of as societal and political progress. But a popular local newspaper column, even in the capital of the world's most powerful nation, hardly constituted a global platform. Jackie Bouvier was intent on bigger things.

Before Jacqueline arrived in Hyannis Port, Joe Kennedy almost certainly had a sense of her intended trajectory. As his daughter, Kathleen, had confirmed to John White a decade earlier, the Ambassador informally, but carefully, investigated anyone who was becoming close to one of his children, discovering not just their status in the world but their attributes and deficiencies. Having already given each of his children a million dollars (around $17 million in today's dollars) so they could "tell me to go to hell," he was alert to con artists, grifters, and frauds who might be seeking to exploit them. "My father was impressed by her," recalled Eunice Kennedy, "which impressed me." It didn't matter to him that Jackie was neither the heiress her demeanor suggested nor as French as her surname, Sorbonne education, and linguistic skill convinced people she was (she was in fact only one-eighth French). What likely dazzled the Ambassador even more than her sophisticated facade was his sense that she was covertly angling toward something greater. "It's not what you are that counts," he famously declared, "but what people think you are."

Part VI

THE CAMPAIGN

Maybe I'm just dazzled and picture myself in a glittering world of crowned heads and Men of Destiny . . . very glamorous from the outside—but if you're in it—and you're lonely—it could be a Hell.

—JACKIE, TO HER FRIEND FATHER JOSEPH LEONARD

21

HYANNIS PORT

July 1952

Two days before Jackie left for Cape Cod to join the Kennedy family for the Fourth of July weekend, the film studio Metro-Goldwyn-Mayer reported the results of its poll of three hundred Washington news correspondents: Jack had been chosen as "Handsomest" congressman. Months earlier, a nationally syndicated piece hinted at his happily playing the field. "Attractive as any current Hollywood movie star," Associated Press reporter Jane Eads wrote. "He entertains a lot and gets around, but so far he's resisted the march to the altar."

Jackie's focus that weekend, however, wasn't Jack but Joe. "I had already met Jack's father when I'd gone for a weekend at the Palm Beach house [in December 1951]," she recalled. "He was the same—so welcoming and kind. I adored him." Unless he thought an individual worthy of his energy and, even better, that they might offer some type of quid pro quo to serve his larger purposes, the ruthless titan was not inclined to gratuitous benevolence. He immediately recognized that she had all the qualifications to be an ideal partner to Jack, and thus very much worth his time.

For her part, Jackie was riveted by Joe's tales of FDR and his advisers Harry Hopkins, Cordell Hull, and Harold Ickes, as well as Winston Churchill. Jack and Jackie's friend Bill Walton, who knew them individually, observed of Joe and Jackie, "They would talk about everything. She relied on him completely, trusted him and soon adored him."

It was a two-way street. "Joe soon became Jackie's most ardent supporter," said Lem Billings. "He admired her because of her individuality. She wasn't afraid of him. She cajoled him, teased him, talked back to him. . . . By conquering him, she was conquering his son."

One chronicler characterized their symbiosis as a "sense of fun that almost excluded the rest of the family." A jealousy of this newcomer's immediate bond with the Ambassador may, in fact, have been an overlooked factor in the frosty attitude Jack's sisters and his sister-in-law, Ethel, exhibited toward her rather than the traditional narrative that they found her a bit too precious. There was no confrontation, but at times there was unmistakable tension.

"Meals were much fun, never dull, and very noisy," Dinah Bridge reminisced about Kennedy dinners, "so many laughs the whole time." Added Chuck Spalding, "There was a tremendous amount of exciting discussion about everything that was going on," the Ambassador dominating. "[T]here wasn't any question about his own view. He stated that, as you can imagine, extremely powerfully. They were not afraid to disagree, but they weren't insubordinate about it."

Arthur Krock observed that "while there was tremendous respect for the head of the family, always at dinner or in any company—if he had anything to say, and they would wait for him to say it—they all felt perfectly free to express, in very respectful terms, complete differences of opinion with their father. . . . He would sometimes say he thought they didn't have any sense or were 'idiots,' and . . . 'Jack is saying everything I don't believe in.' But it didn't seem to bother him very much."

Initially, Jackie may well have misunderstood how strict the rule against contradicting the Ambassador was, leading to an incident which, ironically, would further endear her to him. Joe Kennedy kept clocks in every bedroom, so there was never an excuse for being late for meals, which especially irritated him. When Jackie appeared a full fifteen minutes after lunch began, Joe was not pleased. "So," recalled Spalding, "he started to give her the needle, but she gave it right back. Old Joe was always full of slang and so she told him, 'You ought to write a series of grandfather stories for children, like, The Duck with Moxie, and The Donkey Who Couldn't Fight His Way out of a Telephone Booth.'"

The room fell into immediate, grave silence. None of his family ever dared respond to him with such sarcasm. Then suddenly, he broke out into laughter, easing the tension, won over.

There were other differences between the Kennedy household and those Jackie knew. At the Bouvier and Auchincloss summer weekend gatherings, both dress and menu were formal. The Kennedys wore informal beach attire, and, along with grilled steaks, hamburgers, and hot dogs, Rose Kennedy always served Boston baked beans and brown bread on Saturday nights, the leftover beans then warmed up for Sunday breakfast.

After dinner, they played games such as Telephone, Charades, Sardines (a variation on Hide-and-Seek), and Ambassador (in which the assumed famous identity of one member of a team must be guessed by the other team). "It's incredible how good Jackie was at these games," Billings recalled. "Jackie's background of constant reading and her quickness of thought in these areas made her much better than [Jack]," he continued. "It always irritated him, because she was obviously better in these things than he was and it just absolutely drove him out of his mind."

That weekend, she also joined Jack and his siblings in sailing, perhaps their favorite activity. For the first time she experienced the waters off Cape Cod, colder than East Hampton and with a less rocky coastline than Newport.

Jackie would later write about the weekend, leaving out any difficulties she encountered: "It was the first time I'd seen all of Jack's family together. . . . How can I explain those people? They were like carbonated water. . . .They'd be talking about so many things with so much enthusiasm. Or they'd be playing games. At dinner or in the living room, anywhere, everybody would be talking about something. They had so much interest in life: it was so stimulating. And so gay and so generous and so open and accepting to outsiders. I thought they were wonderful."

During the weekend, Jackie met Rose, who also had a passion for European history and was striving to improve her French and German. Mrs. Kennedy credited strict, archaic Catholic dietary rules (Friday abstinence from meat and fasting before taking Holy Communion) with teaching her discipline. She expected the same from her children, driving them to be as "morally, mentally and physically as perfect as possible," and admitted to having used rulers and coat hangers on them when they were younger, if they got out of hand.

Rose felt that Jack had "[a] great interest in people and social issues. He was reading all the time. . . . Good looking. A very good athlete." Yet she also singled him out for the fact that he was always late for family lunch, "every day." It wasn't just "poor discipline," she said, but "deliberate."

In some ways, Jackie may have found Rose to be a bit like Mummy. Whereas Janet derided her daughter's "wild imagination," Rose said, disapprovingly, that Jack "did things his own way, and somehow just didn't fit any pattern[, which] distressed me." Jackie was also given to intensive reading and being willfully late for family dinners, defying maternal regulations. And Rose could fixate on her son's appearance, just as Mummy had with Jackie, complaining that he was "careless about his clothes."

Of the family dynamics she observed, Jackie wrote to Father Leonard that Jack had "so strong a personality—like his father, who has so overpowered Mrs. Kennedy he doesn't even speak to her when she's around and her only solace now is her religion. I don't think Jack's mother is too bright—and she would rather say a rosary than read a book."

Jack "had a shyness about him," his mother's relative Polly Fitzgerald thought. "He liked people but it wasn't that easy for him to put himself in the limelight." So, too, his visitor. Around the Kennedy house, Jackie looked at the childhood books, notably *King Arthur and the Knights of the Round Table*, that Jack had relied on as a boy when he was isolated during a series of early illnesses; for Jackie, it had been the divorce and acrimony between her parents that had inspired her to seek consolation in literature. The compulsion for in-depth reading they shared was striking. Whereas Jackie had read the complete works of Shakespeare and Dumas, Jack had pored over Winston Churchill's five volumes on World War II, and his father's multivolume *The World's Great Orations*, covering every period onward from the ancient Greek philosophers, and she recalled, "[H]e read that set through from beginning to end."

She instantly got on well with Teddy, the youngest of Jack's siblings. Their relationship was uncomplicated as they freely engaged on a range of American historical topics, from colonial Boston to the Civil War. He told of how eagerly Jack had "bragged" of Jackie, before she had joined them for the holiday.

Whatever Jack confided to Jackie about the late Joe Jr. left her considering him as "a bully for an older brother." The worst indictment in her mind, however, was the single most important quality she felt a man must possess. "I've got a feeling, from what I think of Joe [Jr.] and everything, that he would have been so unimaginative, compared to Jack," she bluntly admitted. "I don't think he had any of the sort of imagination that Jack did."

All of the family, however, was united and absorbed in one great compelling crusade: to get their adored Jack elected to the U.S. Senate. Dave Powers and political operatives Larry O'Brien and Kenny O'Donnell were the nucleus of the campaign team, but the Ambassador insisted on acting as king of it all, his volatility during meetings leading the others to avoid him. And it wasn't just in private that the Ambassador proved challenging. Public allegations of his antisemitism threatened Jack's support with Jewish voters. He also espoused political views that put him at odds with his son. In January, he'd written an editorial for Waldrop, calling on Democrats to support Republican senator Robert Taft if he gained his party's presidential nomination that year as a way of rooting out what he considered to be the "socialist-labor czars who have gained control of [the Democratic party]." He had also earlier declared, again contrary to his son, that the United States must withdraw from Korea. When asked about his father's isolationism, Jack bluntly affirmed his right to his opinion but said that he formed his own.

By summer, Bobby Kennedy assumed leadership of the campaign, hanging a wall-sized map in Jack's Boston apartment (then functioning as headquarters) which showed every city and town where the candidate had spoken. When complaints of Jack's absenteeism in Congress began appearing in early June in the *Springfield Union*, the *Haverhill Gazette*, and other Massachusetts newspapers, because he seemed only to campaign, he canceled his speeches and sent Bobby on the trail in his stead.

Bobby controlled every action that propelled his brother's campaign toward victory. Even the anecdotal claim that his wife had dubbed Miss Bouvier "the Deb" may have been rooted in the larger, unspoken strategy formulated to turn Jack's single marital status to his political advantage. Any public suggestion that he was dating a woman who might be important enough to be considered a potential spouse, the thinking went, would reduce the enthusiasm of thousands of women voters who had crushes on him, and might even dissuade them from going to vote.

On Jackie's first day back at work in Washington after her weekend on Cape Cod, the Republican National Convention opened in Chicago.

By week's end its delegates nominated General Dwight D. Eisenhower for president and U.S. senator Richard Nixon of California for vice president. Two weeks later, in the same arena, Democrats nominated Illinois governor Adlai Stevenson for president and U.S. senator John Sparkman of Alabama as vice president.

Jackie began to almost immediately ask column questions on a range of opinions about the presidential race, from "What do you think of General Eisenhower's winning the nomination on the first ballot?" and "What do you think of the nomination of Governor Stevenson?" to "With which Presidential candidate would you rather be marooned on a desert island?" and "How should health care for the aged be provided?" and many others.

While this sudden embrace of political subjects for the column seemed obsessive, with one question after another, it was all new to Jackie. The Bouviers, Lees, and Auchinclosses had been rabid Republicans; when she was naughty, the two names used to scare her into good behavior were Bruno Hauptmann, kidnapper of the Lindbergh baby, and President Roosevelt. The extent of her young interest in politics was collecting presidential campaign buttons promoting the Republican candidacies of Wendell Willkie in 1940 and General MacArthur in 1944. But by 1952, she appeared to have become a genuine independent, judging candidates by their ideas; later her friend Arthur Schlesinger discovered that Stevenson was "the first political voice to whom she listened."

However, she couldn't help but hear another one.

22

SUMMER IN THE CITY

August–September 1952

When Jackie returned to the office after the holiday weekend, Waldrop was gone, away for the summer, with Sidney Epstein substituting as her direct boss. A dullness set in. Washington's notorious mugginess intensified, presenting a challenge to productivity. Although the newsroom was on the first floor and its large windows could be opened, there was no cross breeze except for what was generated by large floor fans. Without the relatively new phenomenon of industrial air-conditioning, working inside was miserable. Hitting her beat on the pavement was even worse.

"How do you keep cool?" she asked that summer "in various hot spots" around the city. Short-order cook Bobby Donaldson said watermelon; little Mark Miller said ice cream (and when his mom didn't give him money for it, "I ask my dad"); model Betty Jean Cullen relied on iced tea; student Susan Shephard went swimming; fair-skinned housewife Carey Brent wore a large, protective hat ("You can remove freckles with buttermilk you know"). The answer that Jackie surely loved most was from bookseller Thomas Fitzgerald: "Are you being facetious? You are conversing with the Supreme sufferer. I do not keep cool, dear lady, I sweat. I sweat and I paraphrase those deathless lines of Omar Khayyam: 'Oh paradise, what I wouldn't give for a piece of ice.'"

Times-Herald society reporter Angela Gingras observed how the job could become "something of a grind" for Jackie Bouvier, though she "managed to maintain a sense of humor about it." She recalled running into her out on the steamy streets, "wandering around with her camera slung over her shoulder, searching for interesting people to photograph and interview." Jackie knew that Angela had also lived in Paris, "so she grinned and asked me how business was going—as one lady walking the Washington equivalent of the Boulevard des Italiens to another." Miss Bouvier was referring to the street prostitutes of Paris.

Adding to that misery, with so many she knew escaping the inferno for cooler destinations, her social life ground to a halt. Having a pool at Merrywood gave Jackie an enormous advantage that summer. She resisted the entreaties of Jack Kassowitz and other reporters who wanted to leave the office and head to "your pool this afternoon," but let John Husted's three Washington cousins go use it. Once home, Jackie was back at work—and not just on her column.

In June, Jackie had heard rumors about an obscure brick building with an odd shape called Octagon House, on the corner of New York Avenue and 18th Street. Two blocks west of the White House, it was one of the city's oldest structures—built in 1798, it had withstood the city's burning during the War of 1812—and was, some said, haunted. She'd been so intrigued with the supernatural folklore about the place that she'd decided to write a TV script for a documentary about the possibly haunted house. After outlining her script into six segments with an overview, Jackie began writing the voice-over narration about the original owner, the architect, the interior, the history of its use over the centuries, events which had taken place there, and five specific ghost stories.

As she had with her *Vogue* essays, she conveyed acutely detailed visual sequences, this time accompanied by suitably eerie narration. The script included ghost stories about the first mistress of the house's hearing peculiar bell-ringing, her daughter's suicide over an ill-fated romance with a British officer, her niece's stumble over a black cat that caused her to fall down the sweeping staircase to her death, and the murder of an enslaved woman.

Once completed, Jackie sought direction in getting her script produced. Despite Unk's influential network, she had no contacts in the film or television world, and as friendly as she was with the Ambassador, she didn't feel familiar enough with him to ask for his help.

Although she was not formally a member of the National Press Club, many of her colleagues were and she often joined others in journalism and its related industries for drinks there after work. It was at the club where she first met utilities lobbyist Stephen M. Walter, president of his own public relations firm. Sixty-two years old, he was a native Kansan and former reporter familiar with Jackie's column. Despite his conventional veneer as a farm state Republican, Walter moonlighted as an inventor, and agreed to act as a producer by seeking broadcast outlets and funding for her project.

For the previous three summers, Black Jack and his daughters had forgone their time together in East Hampton. He may have skipped going to avoid his sister Edith, who had continued to spend without any budget, given to charging things directly to her trust, which Jack then had no choice but to pay from her principal. He had even begun to spend his own money to cover some of her bills, to keep from dipping too deeply into the Beale trust. Already dealing with extraordinary stress related to squabbling with Edith over the family inheritance, in August he was hit by such debilitating pneumonia that he claimed he nearly "kicked the bucket." After the market value of his Stock Exchange seat rose, he planned to sell it "because my health will not permit my continuing in this business any longer." He had been a broker for thirty-three years at that point, but work "has taken its toll on my health during the last three years."

While Jackie had been trying to balance her column and her documentary script, her sister Lee was reveling in the sunny days and cool evenings of Newport. Coaxed by Mummy, Jackie finally came up for a few days at the end of August. The sisters hosted a cocktail party and modeled in a fundraising effort for Newport Hospital.

After Labor Day, Jackie joined Mummy and Unk for the seventh World Bank Conference in Mexico City, beginning on September 5, 1952—her first visit to that country. Based at the Del Prado Hotel, the conference was a full week. Having written a week's worth of columns ahead of time, and after exploring all of the city's museums, Jackie was itching for an adventure. Mummy exploded angrily after discovering Jackie's plan to "roam wild" and explore the beach city of Acapulco. Despite their argument, Jackie went.

Jackie recalled, "[I] loved Acapulco"; it would become one of her favorite destinations. While exploring the area, she was captivated by the sight of a pink stucco house, with staggered green slate, rising above the aqua sea. The "charming house" was the one "I always thought I'd like to spend a honeymoon in." The idea of marriage, evidently, was on her mind again.

While Mummy returned to Newport to work as arrangements chairman of a mid-September opera lecture there, Lee's competitiveness was still in evidence. Jackie had lasted only a week working at *Vogue*, but sometime after Labor Day, Lee would manage to get herself a plum position at the fashion magazine *Harper's Bazaar*, hired as an assistant to its legendary editor, Diana Vreeland, whose son Frecky was a friend of Jackie's.

Jackie returned home to the welcome company of Yusha. Having completed his second tour of duty with the Marines, he was in town to take a class at the School of Advanced International Studies, a division of Johns Hopkins University based in Washington, preparing for his courses that coming school year at the American University of Beirut.

Yusha helped rejuvenate Jackie's social life during the hot tail end of summer. After his class and her day at the paper, they'd invite two "interesting" friends chosen for stimulating conversation to join them for dinner and a swim. "After we finished, we'd talk about the questions she had asked during the day, and who'd she seen that she found particularly enlightening," he wrote. Once they were alone, however, he was troubled by her darkening mood over her perceived lack of romantic desirability. He later observed of this time: "She never understood her own charm or her beauty. She never thought she had a good figure. She didn't know whether anybody was going to be attracted to her."

Jackie's admission of spirals of depression and harsh self-analysis seems less surprising when one assesses the number of her columns focused on self-reflection and mental health. ("What compliment would you most like to receive?" "What are the best and worst things about yourself?" "When were you the most scared?" "What have you learned from experience?" "What is your cure for the blues?" "Do you believe there is a Dr. Jekyll and Mr. Hyde in all of us?" "Of all the wickedest things you've done, what's the one you're most ashamed of?")

Her mood was linked directly to the fact that, by the time she had returned from Mexico, she felt a growing insecurity about the ambivalent nature of her relationship with Jack Kennedy. It had been two months since they'd last seen each other.

Others were catching on. When she was slowly typing her question of the day, "Who is the most fascinating man in the world to you?" a colleague asked for her own response. She hedged, enigmatically replying, "He's already left town to run for something or other. And if I told you, you'd only laugh. And besides, he couldn't be less interested in me."

The best she could say about the relationship was that it was "spasmodic." It wasn't a matter of jealousy. There were women he might take to dinner and others, it might be assumed, he slept with, but there were no women he was dating in any serious way at the time. After up to fifteen-hour-long days of speeches and public appearances, he was typically found alone in Schrafft's on Boylston Street enjoying a double-chocolate soda, or flounder at the Union Oyster House.

Two days after Jackie had returned from Mexico, Jack Kennedy won his party's nomination for the Senate seat, and there was a brief lull in his campaign schedule. She recalled that he called her "from some oyster bar up there, with a great clinking of coins to ask me out to the movies the following Wednesday." While he was in town, she invited him to join her and Yusha for an evening at Merrywood.

Before Jack Kennedy arrived, Jackie lectured Yusha: "I don't want you to get into any argument with him because you're conservative, he's a liberal. You went to Yale. He went to Harvard. You went to Groton. He went to Choate. You were a marine. He was in the navy. But . . . you both have an interest in foreign policy." She told him to make the lime daiquiris that she and Jack both liked to drink, while she flipped hamburgers on the grill. Jack impressed Yusha, who wrote: "I liked him very much. And we didn't argue . . . he always asked questions and he was a great listener . . . [and] very gracious person. . . . Jackie always looked for . . . chivalry, grace and charm and courage [in men] and . . . he had all four." Kennedy returned the next night, Yusha recorded in his Tuesday, September 23, diary entry: "Jack cooked our supper and took me to the train. Picked up John White along the way." But with her stepbrother's departure to Beirut, which happened shortly thereafter, Jackie was again alone in her thoughts.

Just as quickly as he had returned, Jack Kennedy vanished, eager to get back to campaigning in Massachusetts. Jackie began considering whether their lifestyles were too different. As she confided to Father Leonard, Jack's presence in her life gave her "an amazing insight on politicians—they really are a breed apart."

It was, perhaps, not so much the path into politics he had chosen which gave her pause, but the aggressiveness with which he pursued his goals. She considered Jack to be "consumed by ambition 'like Macbeth.'" But she, too, had a fierce determination—once she set her sights on something, she chased it relentlessly: acceptance into the Sorbonne, an extended stay in Europe, winning the *Vogue* contest, and her columnist job.

In one of the most revealing letters of her early life, she confided everything to Father Leonard. Perhaps distance afforded her the comfort to "write all this down and get it off [my] chest—because I never really do talk about it with anyone." After she reflected on her time with the Kennedys, she first put in writing what she had not yet felt comfortable speaking about with anyone else, even Yusha. She was thinking about marriage with a degree of certainty and seriousness she never had before:

"Maybe it will end very happily—or maybe, since he's this [35 years] old and set in his ways and cares so desperately about his career, he just won't want to give up that much time to extracurricular things like marrying. . . . If he ever does ask me to marry him, it will be for rather practical reasons—because his career is this driving thing with him. . . . Maybe I'm just dazzled and picture myself in a glittering world of crowned heads and Men of Destiny—and not just a sad little housewife. . . . That world can be very glamorous from the outside—but if you're in it—and you're lonely—it could be a Hell."

The five most telling words in her confessional to Father Leonard were "I think I'm in love."

23

MASSACHUSETTS

October–November 1952

"Worked on the paper [*Times-Herald*] all fall," Jackie noted of her typical days in the months after Labor Day, 1952. "[I]t was an election year and I didn't see too much of Jack." When she did see him, however, it would significantly shift her understanding of him.

Along with the column, she was redrafting her documentary script. That past spring, she had intimated to Waldrop that the burgeoning power of television as a medium for entertainment might just hold for news, too. By autumn, she was enthusiastically embracing that vision. Everyone was. By the end of 1952, some twenty million American households had a television set, an increase of 33 percent from a year earlier, when Jackie first came to work at the newspaper. Over the same one-year period, American advertisers were spending 38.8 percent more money on television commercials, a total of $288 million.

The fifteen-page length of her script indicates that she intentionally wrote her Octagon House documentary for television, the standard rate being one page per minute of broadcast to be slotted into a half hour; half of the airtime was allotted for commercials. According to his wife, Martha, Stephen Walter "only made suggestions" to the script. He then approached several of his public relations clients and found one interested in underwriting her project; meanwhile, Jackie made her own connection with the local affiliate of CBS Television, WTOP, as a potential venue for broadcasting it. (She hadn't been off base in asking Waldrop if the *Times-Herald* owned a TV station; two years earlier, the *Washington Post* had become part owner of the station.)

WTOP was known for its high-quality and early transmission of color programming. CBS Films had been created that year as a syndication service, capable of carrying local-affiliate programming to hundreds of other stations around the country. She submitted her rewrite to Stephen Walter, cheekily suggesting that, if a TV deal eluded them, she was willing to reconceptualize it as a two-hour dramatic feature-film script:

"Here it is. I have 50 million more facts but it would be a little heavy if I put them all in. I tried to put OOMPH in it with romantic suicides and lovers' meetings . . . but I don't think I jazzed it up enough. Don't you think if CBS doesn't want it, we could really pile it on and sell it to Louis B. Mayer as a co-starrer for Errol Flynn and Marilyn Monroe?"

Paralleling Jackie's eagerness about television was Jack's simultaneous foray into it. He'd already twice appeared nationally, on NBC's *Meet the Press* on December 2, 1951, and on CBS's *Longines Chronoscope* show, on March 12, 1952. Recognizing the potential of television to reach into every home in the state, Jack had conceived of a television show, *Coffee with the Kennedys*, to be aired in the late morning, targeting housewives. Cards were distributed to the thousands coming to the teas, encouraging them to sponsor "coffee hours" at home and invite their friends to come watch. Perhaps not coincidentally, in her column among the questions Jackie asked were "If both were on TV at the same time, which would you watch, the convention or the World Series?" and "Do you think that televising the convention will lead to more intelligent voting?"

On October 15, Kennedy turned up at Boston's WNAC-TV studio with his mother and sisters. Eunice wore a poodle skirt with his name printed across it. "The Yankee Network" had Rose, Jean, and Pat seated before a large silver coffee service on a low coffee table, the mother pouring some into china cups for her daughters. Jack and Eunice sat at an adjoining white-cloth-covered table, taking live telephone calls from viewers.

Though Black Jack had inculcated in Jackie the belief that "[p]olitics is no place for women," Jackie's columns that summer and fall showed her beginning to question that precept: "Should women become more active in politics?" "How has the League of Women Voters affected your community?" "Would you support a woman for President of the United

LEFT: Jacqueline Lee Bouvier as a Vassar College student, circa 1948; the following year, according to her cousin and a fellow classmate, she was expelled for breaking campus curfew, failing to return the night she visited a Yale student in New Haven (though she was reinstated). (Copyright unknown)
RIGHT: Posed with her father, John Vernou "Black Jack" Bouvier III, shortly after her July 28, 1949, twentieth birthday, Jackie modeled a traditional Mexican *china poblana* dress in an East Hampton fashion show. Within the month, she left for her year abroad. (Getty Images)

LEFT: The Paris apartment building on the Avenue Mozart that Jackie called home from October 1949 to June 1950. (Maria Buglione)
RIGHT: The Countess Germaine de Renty. (Claude du Granrut)

LEFT: Claude de Renty, the countess's daughter, with her friend Jean-François Deniau, on leave from the French Indochina War. (Claude de Granrut)
RIGHT: Sorbonne Institute of Politics professor Pierre Renouvin, who first interested Jackie Bouvier in Vietnam's fight for independence from France's colonial control. (Claude de Granrut)

Soviet headquarters in Vienna, Austria, where Jackie Bouvier was held by soldiers for questioning when she photographed the building. (Austrian National Library)

Jackie exploring rural France with Claude the summer she turned twenty-one years old: swimming in a lake, enjoying wine and grapes on a riverbank, and winning a bike race with friends. (Claude de Granrut)

Jackie Bouvier and her stepbrother Yusha Auchincloss in Newport, Rhode Island, with a friend in the late 1940s. (John F. Kennedy Presidential Library)

Yusha in Scotland during his and Jackie's trip there. (John F. Kennedy Presidential Library)

Jackie welcomed home from Europe by her mother, Janet Auchincloss, at a New York dock in September 1950. (European Photos)

Black Jack Bouvier and the entrance to his New York apartment building at 125 East 74th Street; this was Jackie's home in the city from 1942 until 1953. (Library of Congress; courtesy of the author)

TOP RIGHT: "Lasata," the East Hampton estate of the Bouvier family, was sold after Major John Vernou Bouvier Jr.'s death in 1948.
BOTTOM RIGHT: A Sea Spray Inn cottage of the type Black Jack rented for his brief reunion with Jackie in the summer of 1950. (Copyrights unknown)

TOP ROW: Jackie Bouvier's paternal grandparents, "Grampy" Jack Bouvier and Maude Bouvier. (Jack Davis)
BOTTOM ROW: Her maternal grandparents, Jim "Gramps" Lee and Margaret Merritt Lee. (Mimi Cecil)

Jackie's maternal grandmother was born and raised in the crowded immigrant tenements of New York's Lower East Side before she rose in status through education and teaching; Jackie's great-grandmother, Irish immigrant "Mum Maria" Merritt, endured poverty by mending clothes and selling sewing items. Later, Maria lived in her son-in-law's Park Avenue apartment, and her brogue embarrassed her granddaughter Janet, who told people she was a maid. (Library of Congress)

Hammersmith Farm, the Newport, Rhode Island, summer estate of Jackie's stepfather and mother. (Copyright unknown)

"Mummy" and "Unk," as Jackie's stepfather, Hugh D. Auchincloss, was known, here in undated images from the mid-1940s. (Both photos courtesy of Yusha Auchincloss)

In Newport, the 1947 "Deb of the Year"; Jackie loved dancing. (Copyright unknown)

Jackie biking with her friend Lallie Lewis in Newport, 1945. (*The Social Spectator*)

"Merrywood," Unk's McLean, Virginia, estate, which was home to Jackie during her senior year at George Washington University and her employment at the *Washington Times-Herald*. She shared her life here with a "cobbled" family of six siblings: sister Lee, half sister Little Janet, stepsister Nini, stepbrother Yusha, half brother Jamie, and stepbrother Tommy. (Library of Congress; courtesy of Yusha Auchincloss)

Jackie driving her sister, Lee, in her 1947 Mercury convertible, which she called "Zelda." Although her father gave it to her as a high school graduation gift, he insisted she drive it back to him in New York on occasion, until she "stole" it for good in the spring of 1951. (Copyright unknown)

LEFT: The urban campus of George Washington University, where Jackie Bouvier completed her higher education. (George Washington University)
RIGHT: She graduated with a bachelor's degree in French literature in a May 1951 ceremony. (Library of Congress)

Charlie and Martha Bartlett and their Georgetown home, where they introduced Jackie to Congressman Jack Kennedy in May of 1951. (Martha Bartlett; Nancy Hackscaylo)

Congressman Kennedy, seen here in his office circa 1951, shared Jackie Bouvier's passion for exploring foreign countries, and also like her had had an earlier ambition to write professionally. (John F. Kennedy Presidential Library)

Jackie and Lee in a circle of Italian men; the 1951 summer trip gave her a particular love of Italy, as her year abroad had done for her love of France. (Photo from *As We Remember Her*)

Jacqueline, Fille Naturelle de Charlemagne

In her imaginative drawings, Jackie liked casting people she knew as historical or literary figures, even spoofing herself in this 1951 drawing as a fictional daughter of Charlemagne. (Reprinted with permission)

PRIX WINNER'S VIEW OF THE PRIX DE PARIS

BY MARGARET COLLETTE,
winner of the 14th Prix—1949

FIRST PRIZE, 1951
JACQUELINE LEE BOUVIER
GEORGE WASHINGTON UNIVERSITY

CO-WINNER SECOND PRIZE, 1951
QUINERA SARITA GOUDSWAARDT
BARNARD COLLEGE

CO-WINNER SECOND PRIZE, 1951
ANNE ROBINSON HOPKINS
VASSAR COLLEGE

SPECIAL AWARD, 1951
JULIA WIENER
COLLEGE OF MOUNT ST. VINCENT

The idea of the Prix de Paris is to dissolve the "no experience" barrier that exists between the young and the professional world; a contest that gives The Condé Nast Publications an idea of where the talent lies, then gives Vogue the opportunity to train that talent while it's still fresh. No contest, in that those who don't win, lose; the aim is to sort, rather than sift, the contestants, taking on those the company can use, passing on numbers of the others to interested companies in allied fields, through introductions and recommendations.

You could make the Prix de Paris your plan of attack on the world-beyond-college; the only way we know of to cover the hot pavement between magazine and advertising agency, magazine and department store, while sitting of an evening, in your college room, with your feet in a pair of slippers. The Prix has been the plan of over 17,000 college seniors in over 300 colleges since it was first started in 1935 with 563 contestants, a number that has grown to a yearly average of about 1,500 entrants.

That the Prix idea is a sound one is proved by the countless careers still rocketing with the momentum given to them by the first Prix push. And it is proved daily by the twenty-three Prix girls now on the staffs of Vogue and the other Condé Nast publications, *House & Garden*, *Glamour*, and *Vogue Pattern Book*. Two of the top Prix winners are now Vogue copy writers. Others who did or didn't place among the top twelve have jobs that range from art assistant and secretary to associate editor, senior copy writer, and fashion editor; in departments that include merchandising, promotion, patterns, photography, feature writing, and production.

Your part in the Prix is outlined on pages 75 and 96. First, you answer two quizzes. Then if you pass these, you are eligible to write a 1,500-word paper, on subjects to be announced in February. The rules are reasonable. If the dates the entries are due coincide with the due-dates of your term papers, write the Prix Director and something can be worked out. None of the questions is "tricky." Thoughtful answers can give a good three-dimensional *(Continued on page 193)*

Left: The four top winners of the 16th Prix de Paris. To each: a beginning job as a Junior Editor on Vogue.

Vogue magazine's Prix de Paris essay contest announcement appeared in its August 1950 issue. Jackie entered the contest in October 1950, won in May of 1951, and began work as a junior editor, but was soon pressured to quit by her mother. (Condé Nast)

Jackie Bouvier's first boss, newspaper editor Frank C. Waldrop, and the Washington Times-Herald building. (*Washington Times-Herald*; Library of Congress)

Princess Elizabeth during her first visit to Washington, in the autumn of 1951, greeting reporters at a reception, where Jackie managed to sneak in. (Courtesy of the author)

On his heavy speaking schedule as he began his Senate campaign in the late winter of 1952, Congressman Kennedy brought a map of the world to educate his constituents on international affairs, focusing on his late-1951 fact-finding mission to Vietnam. (John F. Kennedy Presidential Library)

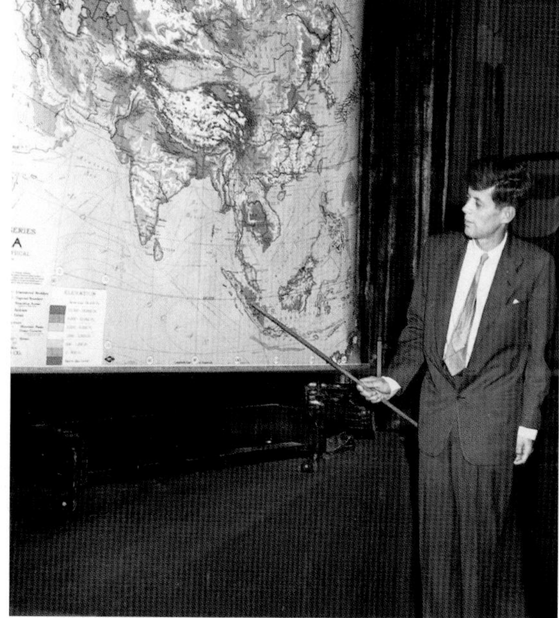

The 1952 engagement photos of Jackie Bouvier and her first fiancé, John Husted. (Copyright unknown; European Photos)

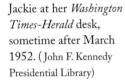

Jackie at her *Washington Times-Herald* desk, sometime after March 1952. (John F. Kennedy Presidential Library)

A drawing advertising the Blue Room's "Supper Dance" at the Shoreham Hotel in Washington, where Jack first took Jackie on a date, in January of 1952. (Copyright unknown)

Inquiring
Camera Girl

By JACQUELINE BOUVIER

CLOCKWISE FROM UPPER LEFT: Jackie Bouvier's byline as it appeared in the *Washington-Times Herald*, her camera, and her cartoon of herself as a photographer. (Reprinted with permission; *Washington Times-Herald*; John F. Kennedy Presidential Library)

Jackie photographing a London bus driver during his visit to Washington for her April 14, 1952, column. (John F. Kennedy Presidential Library)

THE QUESTION

Who will be Washington's No. 1 hostess now that the Republicans are back in power?

THE ANSWERS

Mrs. Richard M. Nixon: Why, Mrs. Eisenhower, of course. I think her friendly manner and sparkling personality immediately captivate all who see or meet her. She is equally gracious in small groups or long receiving lines, where she has the knack of getting acquainted with each person, instead of merely shaking hands with the usual phrase, "How do you do?" The people of America will always be proud of their First Lady.

THE QUESTION

How do you feel when you get a wolf whistle—flattered or embarrassed? Asked in downtown Washington.

Eugenia Stathis, secretary, Jacksonville, Fla.: Well, I'm not particularly flattered because I think most men when they're standing around will whistle at anything. They do not do it because you're pretty—just to see if you get embarrassed. I bet if you whistled at them they'd be so embarrassed they'd step off the curb and get run over.

THE QUESTION

How do you get by the day before pay day?

Junius Willis, cab driver, 900 block Irving St NE: I don't get hard up before payday now because I keep something in reserve. I've got a wife and children, but before that when I saw financial distress coming I'd stay in a whole week, not spending anything. Some folks always stay behind pay week. That's a bad habit.

THE QUESTION

Do you think a wife should let her husband think he's smarter than she is? Asked at Center Market City, Fifth and K streets northwest.

THE ANSWERS

John R. Pankey, accountant, Clinton, Md.: I certainly do. It boosts your ego. When you come right down to it the husband knows he's not the smartest, women rule the roost, but if a woman goes about it the right way, not laying the flattery too thick, she can make a man actually believe he's the smartest.

THE QUESTION

Malenkov said all issues between the U.S. and Russia are solvable by peaceful means. Do you think he means this?

THE ANSWERS

Bessie Reznick, housewife, 760 Seventh St. SE: You can't believe in people; you have to believe in God. Round and round the world people are the same. I lived under the Russians in Poland. Some of them were bad. They would come in and kill you and take everything in the house. Some of them were very nice and would save you. Even in America there are bad people. How do I know if Malenkov means it? I hope he does.

QUESTION

How should health care for the aged be provided? (Asked at a conference of the American Public Welfare association.)

ANSWERS

Raleigh C. Hobson, Richmond, Va., director: I think it should be done thru adequate clinics and increased numbers of specialized institutions. These would be supported by the community. There has to be more care for the chronic ill and aged, and we need more public buildings for them. This is only for those who cannot care for themselves.

THE QUESTION

Do you think hope ever dies? Asked at Goodwill Industries, Washington's Workshop for the Handicapped, 1218 New Hampshire Ave.

THE ANSWERS

Bill Chapman, upholstery dept., 1600 block L St. NW.: As long as a man lives he has hope. I lost my sight in an industrial accident, but when I got discouraged I'd look under the bottom of discouragement and see someone worse off than I. You must have belief. I can upholster furniture as well as anybody on the outside.

THE QUESTION

What are some things most people don't know about Lincoln's assassination? Asked at Ford's theater.

Violet E. Vaughan, clerk-stenographer: Occasionally people turn up with a playbill or shawl they claim is stained with Lincoln's blood. But Lincoln's wound did not bleed. The bullet entered behind his left ear and lodged above his right eye. Doctors who examined him had trouble finding the wound. They took off his coat and loosened his collar and vest, believing he had been shot thru the heart.

THE QUESTION

How do you think you're maladjusted? Asked at the American Psychological association convention.

THE ANSWERS

Fred McKinney, University of Missouri: I think my giving out this interview just to get my picture in the papers is sufficient evidence of maladjustment, don't you? It's a partial symptom of exhibitionism and narcissism. It's a bad sign, all right, but I hope that I'll be able to integrate it into wholesome channels.

THE QUESTION

Will Indochina turn into another Korea? Asked in the Silver Spring shopping center.

THE ANSWERS

George Hewitt, advertising artist, 1200 Myrtle Ave.: Two weeks ago I'd have said yes. Now I don't know. In the past week the Communist side has begun to look as if they're going to quit and go away. Maybe this is just another one of their bluffs ... You can't trust those people

THE QUESTION

When did you discover that women are not the weaker sex? Asked in downtown Washington.

THE ANSWERS

E. H. Valentine, tobacco auctioneer, Fairhaven, Md.: The rude awakening came to me after about one year of marriage. Then the wool was pulled from my eyes. I found that women are really meek during courtship. They act real quiet and do everything you want. Then you get married and then they take charge—of the money, of the house, of everything.

THE QUESTION

How much of your success do you attribute to Southern charm?

THE ANSWERS

Tallulah Bankhead, actress: My magnolia-scented southern charm has served me well, both professionally and privately. It has melted many a manager, chilled many a carpetbagger and confused many a swain. Exercise of it in lavish doses has brought me from Huntsville, Ala., dash—that's Sparkman's home town—dash, you heard me, dash—to New York, London, Hollywood and other spots it would be indiscreet to mention.

In her column, Jackie used wit to address contemporary issues from sexism to mental health, asked opinions about topics from income to world peace, posed personal questions both poignant and prescient, and interviewed celebrities from Pat Nixon to Tallulah Bankhead. (*Washington Times-Herald*)

Jackie's May 10, 1952, interviews with the Nats' (Washington's hometown baseball team) president, Clark Griffith, and manager, Bucky Harris (both standing to the immediate left of the flag), coincided with the team ending its losing streak, and led Jackie to earn her first notoriety as a columnist. (Library of Congress; *Washington Times-Herald*)

‹Jacqueline seems to have been what our ball club needed a short time after she sweetly asked the Nats when they were going to start slugging again the club exploded with 13 hits and defeated the Athletics, 5-3. —Ed.›

Congressman Kennedy campaigning for the Senate in 1952 at one of the "tea parties" hosted by his mother and sisters. Part of his campaign strategy used his status as a single, available man to appeal to women—hence the need to distance Jackie. (John F. Kennedy Presidential Library)

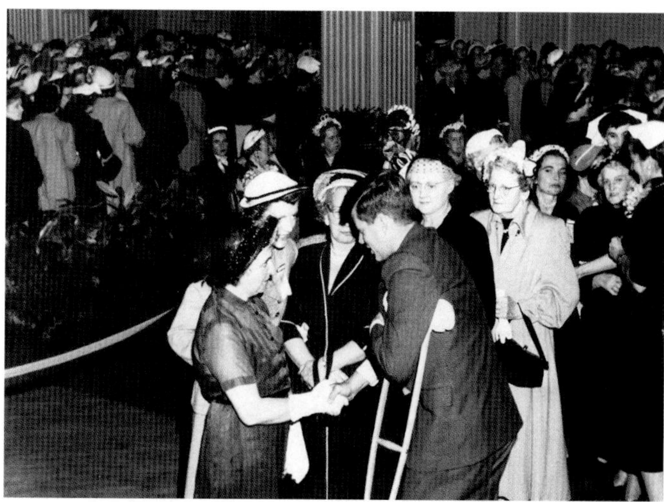

Jackie Bouvier's foray into television documentary writing focused on the historic Octagon House's alleged haunting by the ghost of First Lady Dolley Madison. (Both photos Library of Congress)

As a U.S. Senate candidate, Jack conceived of a television special that encouraged Massachusetts housewife voters to gather and watch together as they enjoyed morning coffee. *Coffee with the Kennedys* included his mother and sisters. He shared with Jackie a sense of the increasing importance television would play in public life. (John F. Kennedy Presidential Library)

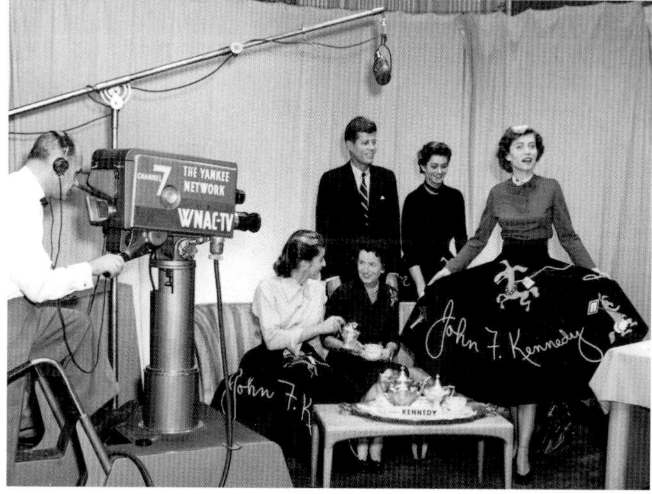

Jackie Bouvier, seated between Jack Kennedy and his best friend, Lem Billings, in early 1954; a closeted gay man, it was Billings who made clear to Jackie that Jack was unlikely to adapt to monogamy. (Peabody Institute)

An image of Jackie in the white gown and red "Bouvier stole" that she designed for dressmaker Mini Rhea to make, along with Senator Kennedy. This may be a photograph of their first public appearance together, attending President Eisenhower's 1953 Inaugural Ball. (Copyright unknown)

Jackie's *Washington Times-Herald* cartoons of President-Elect Eisenhower and his niece (November 1952), a hot dog salesman (January 1953), and pampered dogs during her crossing on the SS *United States* to cover Queen Elizabeth's London coronation (June 1953). (*Washington Times-Herald*)

This is lovely – I dare you to say in your speech that we should give Indo China to the communists because they are the ones with the most integrity!

ABOVE: An excerpt from the handwritten portion of Jackie Bouvier's Vietnam report, written for Senator Kennedy's use in preparation for his July 1953 speech, daring him to declare that if Communists secured Vietnam its independence, they should rule there. (Reprinted with permission)

ABOVE: In the months before their engagement, Jackie became a regular presence in Jack's Senate office. (Peabody Institute)

LEFT: Jackie photographing her colleague Dale Chestnut feeding goldfish on the roof of the Washington Times-Herald building in the summer of 1952 (as an unidentified colleague looks on); before she left her job, Jackie trained Dale to take over as the second woman to pen the "Inquiring Photographer" column. (Copyright unknown)

Jackie and her father at the April 1953 wedding of her sister, Lee. (McInnis Auctions)

Jackie with her mother and Jack's father, Ambassador Joseph Kennedy, in January 1955; as Jackie watched Joe approach Janet, determined to convince her that the wedding should be a public spectacle and thus useful for Jack's publicity needs, she recalled thinking, "Oh, Mummy, you don't stand a chance." (CSU Archives/Everett Collection)

At staged media events during their June 1953 engagement weekend, Jackie photographed Jack with her Graflex camera (as well as her Leica) while press photographers snapped away. (Copyright unknown; John F. Kennedy Presidential Library)

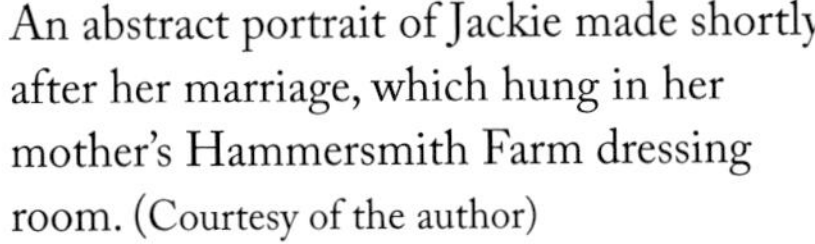

An abstract portrait of Jackie made shortly after her marriage, which hung in her mother's Hammersmith Farm dressing room. (Courtesy of the author)

States?" "Should a candidate's wife campaign with her husband?" Certainly all of the Kennedy women Jackie had come to know were in the news, doing their part for Jack. Ethel Kennedy was photographed in a hospital bed, holding her newborn son, Joseph, in the morning, and back campaigning later that day, while Jean Kennedy was shown welcoming presidential daughter Margaret Truman to Massachusetts. The papers announced that Rose would fly straight from Paris to share the fashion trends she saw there with the women of Massachusetts, which boosted attendance at a September tea.

Jackie went to Newport the last weekend of October, where Mummy and Unk were preparing to move the household to Merrywood for the winter. It's unclear whether she called Jack to let him know she would be relatively nearby or he initiated, but the result was an invitation to come and see him on the campaign trail. The experience would show Jackie just how central women voters were to the strategy of getting him elected to the Senate.

On Sunday, October 26, Jackie turned up in Boston. Presidential candidate Adlai Stevenson headlined the day's events, but Jack was his costar. They drove in an open car from Boston to Quincy, where the candidates spoke on a platform outside the local high school. They then headed to Cambridge for a Unitarian church service and back to Boston for lunch, followed by stops in Taunton and New Bedford for an Israel-bond rally. Jackie accompanied Jack's sisters to Fall River for the most publicized and enthusiastic of the campaign's tea parties, at 2:45 p.m. Four thousand attendees turned up at the vast armory. The *Boston Globe* reported that few ever "reached the tea and cookies."

As evening set in, the vanishing sun leaving behind a sudden New England chill, the motorcade made its way back toward downtown Boston. Along the way, hundreds of people packed the sidewalks cheering Stevenson and Kennedy. The Kennedys and their entourage, along with Governor Dever, who'd retrieved Vice President Alben Barkley at the airport, proceeded through a shower of confetti to a massive night rally at Boston's Mechanics Hall. Jean and Pat were given seats of honor at the front of the platform and introduced by the mayor of Boston. Humphrey Bogart and his wife, Lauren Bacall, warmed up the crowd. Thousands of supporters yelling "Adlai!" spilled out onto Huntington Avenue from the overcrowded hall, listening to Stevenson's speech, broadcast by loudspeaker. It was a three-ring circus the likes of which Jackie had never seen.

Afterward, she and the sisters retreated to Jack's two-bedroom apartment on the third floor of 122 Bowdoin Street, across the street from the gold-domed state capitol building. Rose had furnished the place with some of her cast-off chintz chairs and curtains, a floor lamp, a federal-style bureau, a bookcase, and a desk. Jack was rarely there alone; his siblings were often in and out, while their parents stayed in a suite at the Parker House hotel when in town.

Although Jack had an official congressional office on Kilby Street, his apartment was where the initial strategy meetings for his campaigns since 1948 had always begun. The living room was cluttered with card tables where mailing lists of donors and supporters were being drawn up, an effort undertaken by Jean. At times, members of his Washington staff would also work from the apartment. Jackie found the space crowded, later telling Eunice she thought it suggested how his public life dominated his private one.

The Kennedy campaign was, as the October 3 *Congressional Quarterly News Feature* put it, a "frank play" for the women of Massachusetts, estimated to be 52 percent of the state's total electorate. As campaign staff member Edward Berube awkwardly expressed it, he recalled Jack saying that "the woman was the one that was going to put him in." Jack declared as much at one of the tea parties, hoping he was "impressing the feminine electorate." He and his team still thought that if it got out that he had a special person in his life, let alone the former Deb of the Year, it would likely considerably reduce his appeal to women voters. As campaign volunteer John Droney said: "Every unmarried woman had that hope and dream that lightning would strike."

On election night, Kennedy's strategy paid off. With a record 90.94 percent of the state's eligible voters casting a ballot, and over 90 percent of women voters in major cities going to the polls, he won by a 1.5 percent margin, only 70,737 votes more than Lodge. It's estimated that nearly twice that number of women had attended the teas. The thin victory was all the more remarkable given that Eisenhower trounced Stevenson.

Meanwhile, Jackie and her big camera managed to infiltrate Republican election night headquarters at Washington's Statler Hilton. The party faithful had brought an end to two decades of Democratic hold on the presidency, and she asked them (including Stevenson's Republican cousin Ashton Embry), "How do you feel now?"

In Jackie's mind, the overnight shift in power was as visceral as a coup, and over the next dozen weeks she managed to interview for her column the outgoing Democratic attorney general, the U.S. Treasury secretary, the secretary of the Senate, a presidential assistant, and Ambassador Perle Mesta about what they planned to do their first day out of power. She also interrogated civil service employees about how they'd feel about working under Republicans and members of the general public about who they wanted to see appointed to the Eisenhower cabinet.

Whether or not it was the result of the influence of Jack, her column noticeably maintained a focus on current political subjects. She raised the issue of Eisenhower's controversial appointment of Clare Boothe Luce as ambassador to Italy but also pushed for more women to be named to executive positions in the executive branch. Shortly after Jack endorsed President-elect "Ike" Eisenhower's trip to Korea in response to a press inquiry, Jackie posed Jack's follow-up question (without crediting him): she asked people if they thought Ike should meet with General MacArthur before going, and most of her respondents were against it.

Her own prospects were looking up. An executive at the local CBS affiliate who read her Octagon House documentary script found it promising and "bought it," as Stephen Walter's wife Martha recalled. The network planned to have it made for one of the half-hour shows produced by the station. Around this time, Jackie also apparently managed to get a small piece published in *Time* magazine, though it didn't carry her byline and the subject remains unknown, the only known reference to it being in a letter from Yusha, "to congratulate you on the clipping in *Time*." He offered an afterthought that characterized her exact intentions at that point in her career: "[I] expect you shall be receiving a much more interesting and enviable position in the paper in the very near future. You certainly deserve it."

Early on at the *Times-Herald*, Jackie Bouvier realized that no matter how novel or engaging she made the column, she needed some type of jump-start to advance her writing career. Her column on the Nats gave her more attention, but it proved ephemeral. She needed a scoop that might land her on the front page. One local beat offered the best potential for national, perhaps even international, news. So Jackie began lingering outside the nation's most famous home.

"Jackie was especially intrigued with everything about the White House," recalled Mini Rhea. "She was always asking the White House reporters, male and female, about their jobs and telling them they were lucky to go there. Everything about the White House was exciting to her." She stopped guests, members of the press, and workers exiting 1600 Pennsylvania Avenue, looking for something she could turn into a bigger story. Her questions were usually general—"What are your memories of Presidents?" "Would you like your son to grow up to be President?" "Which First Lady would you like to have been?"—but some were sharper and more politically direct, such as mentioning Truman's ordering tidewater areas to be set aside as naval reserves, asking, "Should these oil reserves be held for national defense?"

Significant attention during the campaign had been given to Ike's running mate, Richard Nixon, and Jackie knew readers were curious to learn more about the new vice president. (Over the summer, she had asked his four-year-old daughter, Julie, "Do you play with Democrats?" prompting her to pose her own inquiry, "What's a Democrat?")

Three days after the election, with interest in Richard Nixon ratcheting up even higher, Jackie learned the location of his private home and went there, lurking outside the house long enough to ask a number of neighbors, "What do you think of Nixon now?" They were a housewife with a baby on whom Nixon's children doted; another whose dog played with Nixon's dog; the daughter of a Truman undersecretary with a direct view of his home; a five-year-old playmate of his eldest child, Tricia; and then six-year-old Tricia Nixon herself. The child's response was unfiltered: "He's always away. If he's famous, why can't he stay home? See this picture? That's a coming home present I made for Daddy. Julie did one, too, but she can't color as well as me. All my class was voting for Eisenhower, but I told them I was just going to vote for Daddy."

After endless months of sobering news about the national election, Jackie's exchange with Tricia Nixon offered a humanizing aside, and the story was syndicated, appearing in newspapers around the country. After a year of voicing her increasing frustration to Waldrop that he wasn't assigning her the feature articles she insisted she was capable of turning out, she'd created her own opportunity. Jackie Bouvier had her first bit of national publicity as a reporter.

She had simply gone where she was not supposed to, just as she had done a year earlier when she had first wanted to write the column and crashed the press reception for Princess Elizabeth. Her ploy of exploiting unwitting children to advance her career crossed an ethical line, but her mild intrusion on the privacy of a public figure had resulted in the sort of brief notoriety that a writer needed in their pack of clippings if they hoped to get larger assignments.

Driven by the response to her syndicated interview with little Tricia Nixon, and spared any censure for her method of obtaining it, she pushed her luck a week later.

Jackie could easily have been taken for a nanny or an older sister as she scrutinized the children pouring out of John Eaton Elementary School in Washington's Cleveland Park neighborhood. Once she identified the ten-year-old and eight-year-old sisters she had come for, Ellen and Mamie Moore, nieces of President-elect Eisenhower, she followed them out of the schoolyard as they began their short walk home. Without identifying herself as a reporter, she approached the trusting girls.

"She had on a pink suit with high heels," Mamie Moore could still vividly remember seven decades later, after having glimpsed Jackie from the corner of her eye in the schoolyard. "She was so beautiful." Mamie continued, "I sort of was whispering to Ellen, I told her 'We're not supposed to talk to strangers,'" as Jackie approached and called for their attention, "but then my sister began to talk with her, and then I just joined in."

They were the daughters of Frances "Mike" Moore, sister of Mamie Eisenhower. Jackie engaged them in seemingly innocent chatter about how the election had changed their lives.

Ellen complained that she only charged fifty cents an hour for babysitting, but, "Now that my uncle is President of the United States, don't you think I should get seventy-five? A girl in my class said that when my uncle's President I should tell the teacher to give me good marks or he'd throw him off the school board." She bragged that her mother told her, "I could have my birthday there [the White House]. I could invite my class, maybe, and have a swimming party."

Little Mamie boasted about having her picture taken standing between President Truman and Uncle Ike, wearing "some kind of melon pin," and looking "as if I was the most important one." She told Jackie her mother said she could take one friend to lunch at the White House, then turned to her downcast friend Carol Jones, who was "still plodding" along behind them, saying she might be the one. Carol "smiled nervously," mumbling, "I think she's lucky." Then the presidential niece boasted of her math skills by determining that Eisenhower would "have to stay there four terms for me to get married because I don't want to get married for years." She was disappointed that "[o]nly three people in my class knew Uncle Ike was my uncle. None of the others would believe me. But I've got brown hair and bangs and everyone says I look like Auntie Mamie, so now they all know."

Arriving at the Moore home, the location of which Jackie had already identified, little Mamie hoped her uncle "won't be so busy being President that he'll forget" to get her a horse he had promised her.

The feature article Jackie wrote, "Mamie's Namesake, 10, Glad Uncle Ike Will Be President," depicted the girls as innocently comical, and was illustrated with three of her own hand-drawn cartoon sketches of Ike and his nieces. It got placement on the front page of the November 17, 1952, *Times-Herald*, an unconventional piece given remarkable visibility, particularly with its drawings rather than photographs. As Jackie had hoped, it set off a buzz in political and journalism circles.

Most importantly, Jackie had again proved her worth to the boss. Two days after the article was published, Waldrop rewarded Jackie with her first assignment of a full-length feature article on the crowds that were expected to gather along Pennsylvania Avenue to catch a glimpse of Eisenhower, who would travel the road to meet at the White House with President Truman. Heavy with interviews, it was like an expanded version of the column but now with narrative context. As people amassed, waiting to see Ike, Jackie weaved among them, provoking them to reveal what they imagined he was thinking on this triumphant day. It was published November 19, 1952, with the long-winded headline, "Throngs Four-Deep at White House as Ike Appears: Crowd Kills Long Wait with Speculation." In the weeks ahead, Jackie would also nab an interview with Pat Nixon, asking who the new leading hostess of capital society would soon be (Mamie Eisenhower it would naturally be, she responded). Five months later, she would interview Richard Nixon himself, for his perspective on the diligence of young pages working in the U.S. Capitol.

Days after the election, Jackie had lunched with cousin Jack Davis, who'd not seen her since days before she had left for Paris, in the summer of 1949. "I noticed how dramatically she had changed," he recalled; "she seemed much more relaxed, much more cheerful, and far more beautiful. She now enjoyed an added degree of freedom, had some money in her purse, and was meeting many interesting people in her capacity as Inquiring Camera Girl." He presumed that one reason for the change was related to the family rumor that she had a steady beau, the new senator-elect John F. Kennedy, though she didn't disclose her feelings about him.

In fact, after the election, she had heard nothing from Kennedy. It appears that she neither wrote nor called him with congratulations but rather continued waiting to hear from him. This was a pattern. Only to Father Leonard would she reveal the emotional impact of this: "He hurt me terribly when he was campaigning and never called up for weeks." And yet, when they were together, he gave her every indication of attentiveness, suggesting he cared for her as more than just a friend, to the degree he was capable of showing it, or willing to show it. As she continued to confide to the priest, "I think he was as much in love with me as he could be with anyone."

If he had remained a bachelor to keep his appeal to single women voters, she realized that, having won the election, he would marry only to serve his political purpose. As she continued to Father Leonard, "[N]ow maybe he will want to get married because a Senator needs a wife."

Her hurt over Jack's continued silence became frustration, and then resentment, which she couldn't conceal from her cousin. As lunch continued, she shared several embarrassing secrets about Jack Kennedy with Davis, disparaging the vanity of his frequent hairstyling to ensure that it always looked "bushy and fluffy," and his sulking egotism, which emerged when "nobody recognizes him or no photographer takes his picture."

Before lunch ended, however, Jackie made an offhand remark that was not only one of the earliest confirmations of Jack Kennedy's larger, undisclosed plan but an acknowledgment that she was privy to it.

"Oh sure, he's ambitious, all right," she told Davis. "He even told me he intends to be President someday."

24

PALM BEACH, II

November–December 1952

Days after Jackie filed her parade story, her second feature for the *Times-Herald*, she discovered that the first one had put her job in jeopardy.

By making the short three-block walk from the school to the Moore home and continuing to ply the sisters with questions, Jackie Bouvier had landed not only a front-page story but herself in hot water. When the sisters arrived home, their mother, Frances "Mike" Moore, was on the phone. Since the election, it had not stopped ringing and the family would soon need to put three lines in to deal with the unsolicited inquiries now deluging this branch of the incoming presidential family, especially after President-elect and Mrs. Eisenhower had come to the house after the parade that Jackie had written about in her second feature article. Mamie recalled how her mother "became immediately very, very upset" when they told her about the ambush interview.

Days after the article was published, Mike Moore contacted her friend George Dixon, who wrote the "Washington Scene" column for the King Features syndicate. She asked Dixon to "do something to make that brash camera girl, whoever she is, know her place." Dixon suggested she call Waldrop directly, then immediately tipped the editor off about her imminent call. Waldrop called Jackie in to question her about how she had gotten to the children. She "stood there, white as a sheet, was sure I'd fire her."

He made clear to his renegade reporter that what she had done was inexcusable. Not only had she failed to do a reporter's duty of disclosing to the subjects of her article that she might publish what they'd said, and literally turned trusting children into cartoons, but she had also, by publishing their school location and home address, left them vulnerable to potential kidnapping plots.

When Mike Moore called Waldrop "to complain about the interview," she emphasized that it "had been obtained without her permission." She "chewed me out, in so many words thought I should fire Jackie, and 'How could you keep a reporter with such low tactics at a paper that needs to cover a new presidency?'" Waldrop did not think it was a threat, but he had no idea if she had discussed the matter with the president-elect. It was highly unlikely that such a minor matter would warrant Eisenhower's attention, but as Waldrop put it, "you never know."

Waldrop assured Moore that he would take appropriate action. Desperate to keep her job, Jackie even suggested that he give her a lower profile by letting her draw illustrations for the paper, trying to justify the piece and salvage her reputation by pointing out that her drawings of the Eisenhower nieces had been instantly appealing. He told her he "needed her to do the column" and never considered firing her, but put her on "probation" from writing feature stories, reducing her visibility until, as he correctly believed would happen, Moore forgot the issue, already swept into her work on the inaugural committee. Despite this, the chastised columnist remained nervous about her future, because the "bad thing right now is that Mrs. Moore is livid." According to Mini Rhea, when the subject came up, Jackie "told people how sorry she was," acknowledging how her article endangered the Moore sisters: "It must be just terrible to be so prominent that your children are exposed to so much publicity."

Jackie's article had also created a stir in the *New York Times*'s Washington bureau. Likely learning the details of the trouble it had caused from Waldrop, Arthur Krock went into action to prevent her from abandoning her writing ambitions. He passed the clipping to his colleague Bess Furman Armstrong, who had covered First Ladies since Lou Hoover, and suggested she might send an encouraging note to the young columnist.

Armstrong wrote Jackie, seeing potential in expanding her article into an illustrated children's book about the White House, with Mamie Moore as the narrator. Several days earlier, one of Mummy's friends had coincidentally sat next to Armstrong at a luncheon. The reporter had regaled the woman with historical tales of presidential families from her book *White House Profile*. The friend shared some of the tidbits with Mummy, who told Jackie. Jackie became enthused and ordered Armstrong's book.

Armstrong's idea sparked Jackie's imagination: "[I]f I could only do it the right way. It is so funny—you try and think up all these fantastic, rather forced ideas that would make good children's books—and they never quite jell—Then something so simple like this comes along—and is the best of all. I never would have thought of that—or anything remotely like it . . . and now poor little Mamie Moore, whom I bearded coming out of school, just might turn out to be my meal ticket." Jackie added, "I can just imagine what she'd say if I called up and said, 'Could I please take Mamie through the White House and write down everything she says.' I showed Mr. Waldrop your letter and he knows a woman who is a terribly good friend of Mrs. Moore's. He said that in a few weeks, when Mrs. Moore is over being upset about this—he'll get the friend to take me there. Then if she does say I can do it, I would love to see you and ask just how you think it should be done. . . . I would hate to mangle it."

Jackie effusively thanked Armstrong for her letter, impressed that she was a "newspaperwoman all your life." Having the episode conclude with validation from such a distinguished journalist helped keep Jackie dedicated to writing. "I am so in love with all that world now," she ended her November 26 letter. "I think I look up to newspaper people the way you join movie star fan clubs when you're ten years old."

John White's earlier effort to get a publisher interested in Jackie's book, *The Red Shoes*, had ended disappointingly, but she now had a new project in which to invest herself, along with the Octagon House documentary. Typically, few obstacles prevented her from pursuing what she wanted, but more bad news as the holiday season approached seemed to give her pause. The local CBS affiliate which was poised to purchase her Octagon House documentary was shuffling its programming. Before the network could produce it and pay her for the script, the half-hour program they intended to use it for, according to Martha Walter, "went off the air."

As with winning the *Vogue* job after hard months of writing only to be pressured to relinquish it by Mummy, fate again worked against her ambitions as a writer. On December 3, as an early holiday gift, Stephen

Walter sent her a historical architectural study, *Development of the United States Capital*, inscribing it, "For my hopeful Jackie." Despite her optimism regarding other potential outlets, her script would never be produced. The disappointment, coming right after executing an original idea that nearly jeopardized her columnist job, gave her good reason to question her instincts. She decided to postpone developing the new book idea.

Still, her opportunities at the *Times-Herald* were to again rise. As the Moore controversy began to fade, there was no denying that Jacqueline Bouvier was an asset there. In a year, she'd transformed her column into one of its defining features. Three days before Thanksgiving, Waldrop assigned her a third feature story. She would still be responsible for the "Inquiring Camera Girl" column, but he now trusted her instincts to find and write the longer pieces that she wanted to pursue and, furthermore, to illustrate them with her drawings. Besides her cartoon sketches of the Moore sisters, in the article about Ike's parade she had drawn a souvenir vendor, sailors at a monument, and a housewife who brought her own folding chair to watch the procession. Some editions of the paper during that holiday season suggest Jackie also drew at least one uncredited cartoon for the book review section, of a wide-eyed animal—a dog or a sheep—reading a book. Plus, during the deadly summer heat Jackie had surreptitiously sketched her colleagues trying to stay cool in the newsroom, hanging around the watercooler, snoozing across a makeshift bed of several chairs, newspaper covering their faces, with their feet on the desk.

As Christmas approached, she got to work on her third feature, focused on "shopgirls" in the city's department stores, who were seasonal hires "working the Christmas rush," tasked with wrapping just-purchased gifts. Like her two previous pieces, it was essentially an expansion of the column format, reliant on capturing dialect and quirky incidents. Despite access to exclusive parties, once again Jackie Bouvier found the stories of working people more interesting.

In the article, she quoted one clerk complaining of how she was often nearly finished wrapping a gift when a customer would change her mind about the choice of gift and paper. "Do you know what makes your feet grow bigger?" another asked rhetorically. "Having babies and working the Christmas rush." The gift-wrapping process, Jackie concluded, "made whipping up the Eisenhower Cabinet look like child's play."

She illustrated one incident with a hysterical cartoon of a worker struggling to wrap foam rubber pillows because they "keep popping out and hitting the ceiling," and predicted that the recipient of the gift would get a scare when she opened it, as if it were a prank snake in a can. The most absurd cartoon depicted three clerks climbing all over a baby grand piano, trying to wrap it, with one shopgirl being stuck up in the air when the top flipped open.

She ended the piece with a touch of poignancy, chronicling the scenario of a customer bringing a flower corsage to the clerk for wrapping and asking her to pick out wrapping paper and a ribbon she liked. Once the gift was wrapped and paid for, the clerk handed it to the customer, who then handed it back, saying, "That's for you, Merry Christmas!"

"She had real talent as an artist and a writer," Waldrop would declare, approving a third raise for Jackie Bouvier at the end of 1952, up to $56.75 a week ($615 in today's dollars). Combined with her monthly allowance from Black Jack, the raise gave her an annual income of just under the equivalent of $35,000. It didn't put her in diamonds, but with her room and board provided by Unk, it was a large amount for discretionary income.

With her raise, Jackie rushed to her dressmaker with a vision for a ball gown adapted not from any fashion magazines but from her imagination. She brought her sketch for what she called a "terrific idea for a dress," along with eight yards of white satin and two-and-a-half yards each of crimson-red velvet and silk. She insisted on "the complete French construction," with the bra and three layers of taffeta petticoats built into the garment. Costing more than twice her new weekly salary, her creation was unlike anything seen in Washington for one particular feature, a red stole that draped over the white gown and all the way down to the floor. It was forty-five inches wide at the base. It proved so innovative that Rhea first put it on display in her workshop, prompting other customers to ask that she also make them gowns with the "Bouvier stole."

Just before Christmas, an unexpected customer appeared with Jackie in Rhea's dress shop: Lee Bouvier had come home for the holidays. Rhea immediately saw the difference. She deemed Lee "fundamentally more interested in clothes," and said she "always dressed in high fashion" that was "colorful and varied," but lacked Jackie's "continuity," Mini preferring the latter's "less theatrical and more subdued appearance of elegance."

Their contrasting personalities were even more distinct to Rhea. Lee "had more of the grand manner than Jackie. Lee did not talk as much or share her thoughts, or express interest in me—a little dressmaker. It wasn't that she was unkind; it was just that she did not have the special warmth that was Jacqueline's." When Rhea grumbled that Lee reminded her of the stylish but willfully shallow Duchess of Windsor, Jackie "merely smiled."

Jackie remained similarly enigmatic about the unexpected news about her sister that was announced in national newspapers on December 12, 1952. After just nine weeks of work, Lee quit her job and became engaged to Michael Canfield, whose father was the president of the book publisher Harper & Row. The era's societal judgment that her younger sister "beat her to the altar" may have prompted a pang of inferiority only reinforced by the continued deafening silence from Jack Kennedy.

Twelve days after his victory, Jack was a groomsman in the Williamstown, Massachusetts, wedding of his friend Robert Kramer. Ten days later, in the last week of November, he left for a European trip with Torbert MacDonald, a personal friend and political ally since they'd been Harvard roommates. Torb was not only Jack's regular companion on overseas trips that had them both womanizing with abandon but a politically ambitious and savvy adviser as well. (He would seek and win a U.S. congressional seat in 1954.) They went to England, Ireland, Italy, and France, where, in Paris, Jack met with foreign affairs officials to discuss the situation in Vietnam. After three weeks away, Kennedy returned on December 17, and stayed in Boston to preside over a children's Christmas party at the VFW named for his late brother. His next trip to Washington was to interview candidates for his new Senate staff, not to take Jackie to any holiday parties. The Bouvier stole and gown were seen more on the mannequin than on their creator.

Yusha had recently updated Jackie that her former beau, writer John Marquand, had a book that was doing well. "Very pleased to hear his book is to be a Book of the Month," he informed her.

Months earlier, in a letter to Father Leonard that she wrote after her July visit to Hyannis, she had quoted Byron as saying that love is "woman's whole existence," but that men kept it separate from their larger public lives. Her intuition that Kennedy viewed marriage as a political tool was correct. Dave Powers flatly admitted that Jack "wondered about it, whether or not he would have to marry a Massachusetts girl, you know, another Irish girl, this sort of thing. And he waited until he was elected Senator to find out whether there was any loss of votes there." Jackie Bouvier did not yet grasp the extent to which not just Jack but Bobby and the Ambassador would ruthlessly evaluate her as a political commodity. She told Gore Vidal that she once overheard them, recalling that "they spoke of me as if I weren't a person, just a thing, just a sort of asset, like Rhode Island."

In the weeks after winning the Senate election, Jack mentioned to several close friends that his father was urging him to consider the pursuit of the presidency. Observed Charlie Bartlett, "I think Jack knew the race for the Senate was the beginning of a long race for the presidency. I think Joe had the whole thing sort of in his mind and Jack was ready to go." Jackie, however, was never one of those who believed Jack became determined to seek the presidency only after winning the Senate and in obeisance to his father. "I think he was probably thinking about it for an awfully long time, long before I even knew," she reflected. "It was always there."

By year's end, it had been nearly three months since she'd seen or heard from Jack Kennedy. She had no sense of whether he had, perhaps, begun dating someone, found some reason to consider her unsuitable for him, or there was some unspoken issue behind his unwillingness to move forward with their relationship.

Initially, she presumed that, like many men, he would have to be coaxed into marriage, and her anxiety found its way into her column: "How do you expect to get married?" "How did you propose or how were you proposed to? (Asked at the marriage license bureau.)" "What is your candid opinion of marriage?" "Can you give me any reason why a contented bachelor should get married?" "What is the food of romance?" "The Irish author, Sean O'Faolain, claims that the Irish are deficient in the art of love. Do you agree?"

In early 1952, she had asked, "Should girls take advantage of Leap Year?" Now at year's end, she returned to the subject, asking, "What advice would you give a girl who wants to marry before Leap Year is out?" Jackie seemed to take aspects of the advice of barber Tom Lascola—"Stop waiting for him to propose to you. Propose to him"—and bookkeeper Jean Pievyak, who advised, "He'll get scared . . . sit tight and wait until next year."

While Jackie wouldn't propose, neither would she wait.

Ambassador Kennedy was already in residence at the family's Palm Beach home by the time the senator-elect arrived on December 21, joined by all the family by Christmas Day. Before Jack arrived, however, Jackie came to see his father.

Some thirty years later, the historian and former *Newsweek* editor Ralph G. Martin left a brief record of an overlooked incident that seems consequential at this critical point in Jacqueline Bouvier's trajectory. It involved the "mutual affection" that was "quick and lasting" between her and the Ambassador, as Martin termed it: "She was vacationing with the Auchinclosses at Hobe Sound, and dropped in on the Kennedy home in Palm Beach. Only the father was there. The two seemed determined to charm each other, and they did. They went swimming, made each other laugh, talked about everything from Cardinal Spellman to Gloria Swanson. When she left, she had an ally and an admirer."

As Jackie would later observe, "I'm more like Mr. Kennedy senior, than any other members of his family." The family's friend Robin Douglas-Home, the British pianist and author, asserted that "the only one who really knew her worth from the beginning was Joe Kennedy."

Jack Kennedy's friend and colleague Florida senator George Smathers would later claim that Jack "told me that his father told him it was time to get married, and his father preferred Jackie." His more intimate confidant Lem Billings disputed this: "Nobody would have talked to Jack at thirty-five that way, including his father," especially since Jack "had thousands of girls" from whom he could make his own marital choice. If the Ambassador was making arrangements to advance Jack's best interests, however, "Mr. Kennedy didn't ever let Jack know it," Billings added.

Within days after Jackie's meeting with the Ambassador alone, there appeared two items in nationally syndicated gossip columns. In her column "The Gold Coast," appearing in the December 21 *Miami Daily News*, Aileen Mehle reported, "Senator-Elect Jack Kennedy, who is one of the matrimonial catches of the decade, what with being young, intelligent, good looking and rich (but not well groomed) is pretty excited about Mrs. Hugh Auchincloss's daughter Jackie Bouvier, who is young, intelligent, good looking, rich and very well groomed." Two days later, on December 23, Dorothy Kilgallen, who wrote the "Voice of Broadway" column, predicted that "U.S. Senator-elect Jack Kennedy and lovely socialite Jacqueline Bouvier will waltz down the aisle early in 1953."

It was the first time Jackie and Jack were linked together in the press. Had the Ambassador been the source for the tips? If so, it was not the first time that Joe Kennedy had used his wide network of personal contacts in the press to plant a story about his son's private life, without his knowledge, to serve what he believed to be the best interests of Jack's career.

On January 3, shortly after the gossip items linking them were published, Jack invited Jackie out. The previous winter, on their first "date" at the Blue Room, he had requested that Dave Powers join them. This time, Jack asked along Lucy Torres, Jean Mannix, Lois Strode, Mary Gallagher, and Evelyn Lincoln, women on his new Senate staff. The "date" was the Eighty-Third Congress's opening session, when he would be sworn in as a U.S. senator. They, along with his new colleagues and family members, watched as he was escorted onto the Senate floor—certainly more exclusive company than the thousands of women at the campaign tea party when Jackie had last seen him, but it was still a public event, hardly an opportunity for them to reconnect in a personal way.

Further underscoring the point: three days later, Jack attended an annual New York charity ball with the striking Maria Carmela Attolico, daughter of the former ambassador to Germany. At the same time, he was also pursuing Betsy Finkenstadt, sister of one of Bobby Kennedy's groomsmen, though Lem Billings thought it was simply because "he never was successful in interesting her." Asked by a reporter if he was "swamped" with marital offers from women, Kennedy jibed, "You would think so, but nothing seems to happen."

Just as with his carefully plotted long game to win the Senate seat, however, Jack Kennedy was methodically laying out his plans for the next momentous chapter of his life. And just like Jackie, when the issue was serious, he kept his own counsel.

Thus it came as a complete surprise to her when, at some point in the first two weeks of 1953, Senator Kennedy asked Miss Bouvier to be his date to the presidential inaugural ball.

25

INAUGURATION

January 1953

On Inauguration Day, January 20, 1953, Jackie was out early, working her Pennsylvania Avenue beat from morning until the late afternoon, her sketch pad and her reporter's notebook at the ready.

She was there to write her fourth full-length *Times-Herald* feature story with a byline. Once again, she gave greatest focus to the everyday "folks" who had come out to wait for the inaugural parade to go by. The roving narrative she produced ran under the headline "Picnic Lunches Help Crowd Wait for Inaugural Parade." She guided her readers near the Pennsylvania Avenue grandstand from which the Eisenhowers would review the parade of state floats that followed their open limousines as they proceeded from the Capitol Building. In minute detail, Jackie described the "sleek black Rolls Royces," the "dapper ambassadors," the elaborate state floats, and the celebrities she spotted. Her reporting of these incidents was punctuated with a levity provided not only by the individual characters she interviewed but also by her cartoon drawings of them. One was a man who bore faint resemblance to the board game character Mr. Monopoly, buying a hot dog at a street stand. Another depicted a Native chief in a headdress who "did a triumphant war dance for the TV camera." A third had a member of one of the inaugural parade bands, from California, slumping against a tree in Lafayette Square, exhausted by walking on the uneven cobblestones of Pennsylvania Avenue.

After fighting her way through the lingering crowds back to the office, quickly filing her story and submitting her ink pen drawings along with it, Jackie dashed home to Virginia to prepare for the ball, then headed back to the city to Kennedy's new house at 3260 N Street in Georgetown, where he was hosting a cocktail party and dinner for Bobby, Ethel, his sisters, and Lem Billings.

Jack had several family retainers to help manage his life, including Muggsie O'Leary, a former U.S. Capitol policeman who regularly raced Jack to the airport, fetching and delivering packages; George Thomas, an African American Virginia native who served as his personal valet and sometime butler; and Margaret Ambrose, the elderly cook who had begun her association with the family as nanny. (She ensured that he had a steady diet of what Lem called "white food," recipes with dairy, such as creamed soups and chicken potpie, due to his frequent digestive upsets.)

With the new year and new job, Jack had rented the place without much consideration of its amenities. It was only when Ambrose went to start cooking dinner that it was discovered there was no working stove; only a grill was available, so dinner at the party before the Inaugural Ball was hamburgers. Jackie very likely wore the white gown she had designed with the red cape, given that it was new and she had not yet appeared in it.

At one point, before they all left for the ball, Billings signaled Jackie to join him in another room, so they could speak privately. If the conversation that ensued gave Jackie her first clue that she was more than just one of the senator's girlfriends, she was also hit with a stark reality about what she would have to accept were her relationship with Jack Kennedy to go all the way to the altar. Billings recounted the conversation for his John F. Kennedy Library oral history:

"I told her that night that I thought she ought to realize that Jack was thirty-five years old, had been around an awful lot all his life, had known many, many girls—this sounds like I'm an awfully disloyal friend saying these things—that she was going to have to be very understanding at the beginning, that he had never really settled down with one girl before, and that a man of thirty-five is very difficult to live with.

"She was very understanding about it and accepted everything I said. Of course, later I told Jack everything I had said to her—and he was pleased because he felt it would make her better understand him."

Without time to process the breadth of all Billings implied, she was off to the ball.

There were two inaugural balls, actually—one at the National Guard Armory and the one Senator Kennedy and his guests went to, nearest his home, at McDonough Gymnasium on the campus of Georgetown University, now resplendent with "glittering gold drapes." Arriving at midnight and staying for an hour, the Eisenhowers and Nixons sat in a balcony overlooking the tightly packed dance floor, the defeated Henry Cabot Lodge and his wife seated in the box adjoining them.

It was a highly formal affair, men in white tie and many women in tiaras, carrying lorgnettes and wearing orchid corsages. The Howard University Chorus performed at the ball and other Eisenhower inaugural events, one of the first instances of African Americans invited to take part in such festivities. The Guy Lombardo band played popular dance music from the earlier generation, like "Glow Worm," "Jambalaya," and his signature song, "Enjoy Yourself, It's Later than You Think."

Although Eisenhower had become president, there was substantial coverage in Massachusetts of the state's new celebrity senator. The next morning's *Boston Globe* reported, "Looking a little ruffled and young and affable Senator John Kennedy was running interference for his sisters, Eunice, Jean and Patricia." There was no mention of anyone else in his party. Having glimpsed him on TV earlier in the day as he had filed through the Capitol Rotunda out to the inaugural stand, one "televiewer" in Boston kidded, "He looks like a college kid compared to the others."

There was still more publicity about Kennedy, none of it related to his work. From Cedar Rapids to Hackensack, the nation's readers of syndicated columnist Inez Robb learned just how popular the new senator was with women of both political parties:

"He wins the popularity title hands down for the bleak reason that even Republicans have marriageable daughters. And no one in Washington is more eligible than Senator Kennedy. Matrimonially speaking, Sen. Kennedy's social and financial status puts him above and beyond the call of mere party affiliation. In the last few days, I have seen Republican matrons with their marriageable daughters . . . buttering up to the junior senator from Massachusetts with shameless intent to snare. . . . He is so nice and he looks so young that I am certain women of all ages, myself included, will want to straighten his tie, see that he has a clean handkerchief and warn him against the unscrupulous wiles of other women."

While he sharply differed on policy with his father, he had absorbed, and expanded upon, the Ambassador's media savvy. "If I know one thing," he explained to his secretary Evelyn Lincoln, "it is that a politician can kill himself faster by playing hard-to-get with the press. As long as they want to talk to me, I want to talk to them." Kennedy's cultivating of personal publicity could appear immodest, but it was all to advance his political career; in private, his humility was consistent, and he more often focused attention on others, especially his most powerless constituents.

Six days after the inauguration, the senator began dedicating time to frequent interviews with reporter Paul Healy for what would be a lengthy *Saturday Evening Post* profile. During their dinner discussions, Kennedy didn't so much as hint to Healy about the existence of Jackie. The invitation to the inaugural ball had not meant that their relationship was going public.

At the time, Jackie was as busy as she'd ever been. She was constantly conceiving new story ideas and pitching them to Waldrop, who was increasingly distracted by dealing with problems at the paper, including its declining revenue. She also tried to keep the column engaging once the post-inaugural boom had flattened.

Jack's sudden fame immediately led to a demand for him as one of the most popular speakers for the Democratic Party. Not only was he regularly going back and forth between Washington and Massachusetts, but he was traveling farther afield as well. Just weeks after becoming senator, he was drafted as the lead speaker of the Jefferson–Jackson Day Dinner in Topeka, Kansas, with former president Harry Truman looking on—a remarkable appearance for a newly elected senator.

Nevertheless, after the inaugural, Jackie said that she and Jack "went out constantly." It was never in public. She was the only woman he invited into his family circle, asking her to join him for occasional movies out with Bobby and Ethel, or dinners and board games with the Bartletts. Lem Billings concurred: "He began taking her out all the time. Instead of taking out a lot of different girls, he concentrated on Jackie."

The simple notations made by Evelyn Lincoln in Kennedy's appointment books are the best available source for the dates and events when they privately saw each other. On Valentine's Day, for example, Mrs. Lincoln noted that he attended the romantic musical *Gigi* at the National Theater but didn't mark down the name of a guest. While Jack loved going to the movies, he was not especially fond of musical theater and even less inclined toward anything sentimental; given that the subject of *Gigi* is Parisian society, and given her affinity for anything related to Paris, Jackie was his likely date.

Just the fact, though, that Jackie's name did not appear in Lincoln's notations indicated the unique place she was assuming in Jack's life. Lincoln noted down the names of other women whom he met with—for example, a "Catherine Plummer" (along with other information, a numerical code was included, such as "143, x 754," indicating an apartment number and entry code), while a "Miss Bowen" appeared to be strictly a professional appointment and was noted down as being for "a job." But Jackie was set aside. Jack asked Lincoln to telephone other girls he asked out to dinner or the movies. But when Jack wanted to see Jackie, he called her himself. As Billings remembered, "If he were in New York or wherever he would say, 'I've got to call Jackie.' Usually, he would only make calls to girls to arrange a date." Often he called her just to converse.

This was clearly an acceleration from their stagnated relationship of the preceding months. For the time being, it seemed enough for her.

What Billings had said to Jackie at the cocktail party was less an explicit warning to her about what to expect *if* she and Jack decided to marry than it was a condition *to* Jack marrying. In the same oral history recording in which he recounted pulling Jackie aside, Billings added: "Later . . . I talked with Jackie on this subject again, and she said, 'When you discussed that with me, I realized all that, and I thought it was a challenge.'" Wrapped in vague, polite words, Jackie's reference to "all that" alluded to Lem's disclosure that Jack was disinclined to be monogamous in marriage. This statement suggested that she felt that she was up to the challenge of marrying a man who was certain to be unfaithful.

It was the first tangible confirmation of Jack's feelings about fidelity, yes—but that much Jackie may have expected. More than that, it was the first tangible confirmation that Jack was, at the least, considering marriage with her.

Furthermore, what Billings presented to her that night contained a profound statement. Jack Kennedy wanted Jackie Bouvier to know the truth about himself before they even seriously began considering marriage—something presumably uncommon for men who want to be married but not monogamous; most would choose to avoid the risk of losing the potential bride and keep this to themselves. However counter-intuitive the characterization, what Jack did, through Billings, can be seen as a gesture of respect. He had no desire to hurt her. If her backing away from him was best for her, it would be better for him as well.

The earliest evidence of Jackie's familiarity with Kennedy's tendencies comes from her July 1952 letter to Father Leonard. Of Jack, she wrote: "He's like my father in a way—loves the chase and is bored with the conquest—and once married, needs proof he's still attractive, so flirts with other women and resents you."

Black Jack had been explicit with Jackie in discussing his own promiscuity, to the point of inculcating her with the mantra, "All men are rats."

By bringing the two Jacks of her life together in comparison, however, she would see just how different they really were.

Part VII

COURTSHIP

Become distinct.

—JACKIE'S ADVICE TO HER FRIEND VIVI CRESPI

26

LOVE AND SEX

February 1953

At some point that February, while both she and Jack were in New York, Jackie invited him to join her and Black Jack for dinner at a midtown restaurant. Her arranging this, and his accepting the invitation, was a turning point that marked the cautious progress of their relationship, but it also gave her the chance to observe their interaction.

"They were very much alike," she later stated for the record. "They talked about sports, politics and women—what all red-blooded men like to talk about," indicating what she considered expected male behavior.

Apart from "needing a haircut," Jack Bouvier told a friend, "young Mr. Kennedy seemed a decent chap—not what I expected. I thought he'd be more like his old man." He extended an invitation to the senator to be his guest at the Stock Exchange Luncheon Club on his next visit to New York, after which he would take him down through the wild trading scene of the New York Stock Exchange floor. To his delight, Jack took him up on the invitation. On a third occasion, Jack visited Black Jack at his apartment, where they watched a prizefight on TV.

Jackie considered her father a "heartbreaking figure . . . more and more of a recluse." She was pained that he "always felt he was a failure in some way." Still, by befriending Lee's fiancé and becoming enamored of Jack Kennedy, Black Jack could feel part of a growing family, hoping to have two new "sons." He wrote with promise to his nephew Miche in South America about Jackie being "in love." Having Michael Canfield and Jack Kennedy enter his orbit came at a time of family attrition for Black Jack, as he was no longer communicating with his sister Edith except in rare, brief business notes, and had cut off contact with his exhausting sister Maude as well.

Black Jack never openly acknowledged just what lurked beneath his alcoholic numbness. Jackie had seen little of him while establishing her career, but by incorporating him into her life as it was now slowly unfolding, she was proving that she had never forgotten him. Given Black Jack's possessiveness toward his daughter and resentment of those he feared might displace him from her life, the senator's attentiveness proved vital. In making the effort to become a chum to her father, Jack especially endeared himself to Jackie.

While Jackie was investing time and effort to reinvigorate her father, she was divesting herself of a traditional concept of marriage. A monogamous husband could not be expected in the partnership she was pursuing, but the relationship would grant her the opportunity to employ her talents and maintain independence while also giving her the status and stability of a financially flourishing husband and household. That was the scenario Jack Kennedy seemed to offer Jackie with the approach of spring in 1953.

Over time, she would come to see the degree of his compulsive promiscuity to be as much of a chronic condition as his painful back, which occasionally required him to depend on crutches. It would nevertheless prove to be a formidable "challenge," as she seemingly lightly characterized it, to accept his sexual intimacy with other women as an analogous crutch.

In the decidedly conservative early 1950s, dating and marriage were highly idealized. Yet the famous Kinsey reports, done in 1948 and 1953, concluded that about 50 percent of all husbands committed adultery; other studies suggest it was about 33 percent who did so at least once, although these studies did not make a distinction between sexual and emotional monogamy. Based on extensive research, anthropologist Helen Fisher concluded that "[w]e have two brain systems: one of them is linked to attachment and romantic love, and then there is the other brain system, which is purely sex drive." Jack Kennedy was the embodiment of this theory.

Once again, Jackie used her column as a mode of research, with question after question about romance, marriage, and infidelity. What she did not—and could not—know in February 1953 was how differently Jack Kennedy was treating her from other women he'd been involved with. His history with women had patterns—but his relationship with Jackie didn't fit any of them.

As Lem explained, although Jack was "crazy about girls," he "never really settled down with one girl." A big part of the reason, his confidant pointed out, was that Jack had "an immature relationship with girls—that is while he was terribly interested in going out and having fun with them at night, I don't think that he was really terribly excited about having girls as friends." Bill Walton concurred: "He was very attentive, flirtatious; but if a woman bored him, he would drop her quicker than any known man."

Other than suggesting he couldn't help himself and that it was a habit indulged sometimes daily, Kennedy never speculated on what he thought were the psychological reasons for his sexual compulsion. As Chuck Spalding said, "He wasn't by nature given to that kind of prolonged introspection." Jack may have avoided thinking about the root cause because he never felt there was anything wrong with being compulsively sexual. The most frequent explanation given was the example and encouragement of his father. It was not merely that the Ambassador took unapologetic pleasure with whomever he wished, but he had also encouraged his sons to do so at an early age.

Jack's awareness of how suddenly death could come may have been another factor leading him to seek pleasure in life while he could. By the time he met Jackie he had lost his siblings Joe Jr. and Kathleen in plane crashes, and he himself had come close to death three times. The first was when he was only three years old, delirious with scarlet fever. The Latin incantations of the Last Rites of the Catholic Church were shouted above the little boy in bed. He received the Last Rites on two other occasions (in 1947, while crossing the Atlantic, and in 1951, in Tokyo), due to complications from Addison's disease. Perhaps the most acute observation on the matter came from Spalding, who saw that Jack lived with a "heightened perception about the brevity of life." Although Jackie had no such brushes with death, she shared his habit of "surveying the scene with a kind of detachment."

The motives and desires that brought Jack and Jackie together are typically said to have been sex on his part and money on hers. Often neglected, however, has been the full consideration of their mutual ambition. They shared a vision of a free and democratic world and wanted the sort of power that would allow them to encourage its realization.

As the spring of 1953 approached, Jack entrusted a special project to Jackie that served to prove to her that he was the sort of partner she'd longed for but had come to believe was impossible to find. It would demonstrate that he wanted to join forces with her, not merely appreciating her intellectual ability as a sort of trophy but wanting her to put it to use. It would make him irresistible to her, and propel what became, arguably, the most momentous decision of her life.

February 10 and 20 were the first times that Miss Bouvier's name was written by Mrs. Lincoln into the official record of the senator's business schedule, and it may have been on one of these significant dates when they first discussed what the project would entail.

Kennedy intended to become a national leader on the issue of the growing controversy over aid the United States was providing to support France in defending its colonial control of Indochina, most specifically in Vietnam, against the increasing success of Communist guerilla fighters based in northern Vietnam, backed by China. He needed to first become an expert on the issue and fully understand the complex history of France's presence there and its justification for delay in granting Vietnam full independence. He needed the help of Jackie Bouvier.

27

MEETING OF THE MINDS

March 1953

"He was not the candy-and-flowers type, so now and then he'd give me a book," Jackie recalled about the days she and Jack were in a groove, seemingly headed in the same direction.

As someone who came to understand how they both thought, Yusha identified "respect for each other's intellect," which they would discover by working together on a variety of endeavors, as the primary channel through which "love definitely grew."

In addition, both certainly had enough common ground to get on well. She liked opera and he liked Irish-American tunes, but both enjoyed popular music. Neither had an especially developed palate, Jack sticking to a bland diet while Jackie ate light foods in small portions. Both loved movies and Hollywood gossip.

They also shared a biting wit and an appreciation for practical jokes. "He loved to pull a few puns, and he didn't mind being kidded himself . . . he enjoyed getting it as much as he did handing it out," a friend recalled. Jackie tested that suggestion repeatedly: once, she took Jack out in a rowboat and served sandwiches for them—his had shaving cream as the filling. When Ethel Kennedy invited her to a St. Patrick's Day party, insisting that all her women guests wear black while she stood out in a bright green dress, Jackie stole the show, coming late and leaving early in Unk's white Rolls-Royce, while wearing a beaded black evening gown shimmering with silver thread, all for Jack's amusement.

IN THE COURSE OF their own privileged lives, neither Jack Kennedy nor Jackie Bouvier seemed to fully comprehend the limitations that bigotry placed on many Americans. Senator Kennedy did not appear to hold racist views—in all of his known private family letters, for example, he never expressed any antisemitism, even to his father, who did so explicitly in interviews and in his diary—but he often seemed indifferent toward racism.

During his first congressional campaign, his sister Eunice invited white volunteer women to eat whatever they wanted for lunch at a local restaurant, which was not segregated, but sent sandwiches to the headquarters for Black women volunteers. Aides Hilda Higginbotham and George Taylor were shocked by the gesture, the latter bringing it to Kennedy's attention, to which he simply shrugged and said, "George, you're thin-skinned. That's one of the things of the time." Never known to use racial slurs (unlike former president Truman and Senate Majority Leader Lyndon Johnson), Kennedy nevertheless displayed a casual racism in sending a staff member a Florida postcard depicting an African American man being terrorized by an alligator.

Similarly, among letters she wrote while young, Jackie once mildly caricatured a Jewish theatrical agent and, on another occasion, composed one line of a multi-verse poem in the dialect of stereotyped southern people of color. Nevertheless, if anything, she displayed more conscientiousness about individuality than Jack. Although she was never told what individual interviews to publish in her column, she included people of color of both genders and of varying ages and professions. During her first year at the newspaper, she read the landmark novel *The Invisible Man*, by Ralph Ellison, and Yusha recalled her enthusiasm for the book.

Given that homophobia was acceptable in the early 1950s, both of their attitudes toward gay people were more progressive than most. In May 1950, Jackie had traveled in Europe with an "effeminate" friend, and she cherished her friendship with Gore Vidal as well as other men in the arts who were not definitively heterosexual. In prep school Jack had learned that his confidant was gay when Lem Billings wrote him a note on toilet paper, which was then used to indicate interest because it was so easily disposable. "I'm not that kind of boy," was Jack's polite brush-off. Their emotionally intimate friendship continued, and Jackie also easily befriended Lem.

The most significant personal difference between them was their health. Other than having several bad falls from a horse, Jackie had no sense of her own mortality. As for Jack, his many health problems and close brushes with death shaped not only his sex drive but also his personality and his entire view of life.

To what degree Jackie knew the extent of his physical problems as she began thinking of him as a potential husband is unclear. She knew about his childhood scarlet fever, and it was already part of his heroic profile that he'd survived having his PT boat hit by a Japanese destroyer during the war, as well as malaria, which could reoccur. As a result of his public appearances with crutches, his painful back-muscle condition was also known. His most dangerous condition, however, was known only to his family and doctors. At what point Jackie knew the details of it is unclear.

Four years before he met Jackie, after years of baffling onsets of fatigue, nausea, mood swings, and a skin-pigment change that, ironically, gave him the appearance of a healthy tan, Kennedy was finally diagnosed with an adrenocortical deficiency, just short of a technical case of Addison's disease, which can be fatal if left untreated. Eventually it was managed with liothyronine, a synthetic thyroid hormone, and then cortisone pills the year before he met Jackie, as well as hydrocortisone, prednisone, fludrocortisone, atropine sulfate, and diphenoxylate hydrochloride.

With such a compromised endocrine system, he experienced unpredictable physical collapses while campaigning in 1945, and during his 1947 trip to England and his 1951 trip to Japan. It was ultimately determined he had autoimmune polyendocrine syndrome type 2, along with mild asthma. Furthermore, he was initially unable to enlist in the armed services because of one shorter leg and had to wear a back brace for the problems it caused.

"There were stretches of times when he was just out of commission," recalled Spalding. "So that when you did see him or when he came to his friends, he was in a euphoric state and he was always the greatest company: so bright and so restless and so determined to wring every last minute that he just set a pace that was abnormal. He had this sense of not being well and how much time is there. . . . You know, most of us don't realize how fast time is passing, and he did." It was only in retrospect that John White, for example, recognized Jack as being "determined to snatch as much pleasure from life as he could in his allotted time." But one of his treatments had a likely physical impact of even greater importance. Kennedy was once prescribed methyltestosterone to counteract the gonadal atrophy that resulted from the many steroids, wildly heightening his libido.

If the degree to which Jackie and Jack were physically intimate before marriage remained a subject strictly between them, so too did any conversation they had about money. Jack had a casual attitude toward the subject, and there was never any report of his having concerns that she might be pursuing his family wealth. Money was "something that he never understood very well. And he didn't want to," observed Spalding; "he wasn't interested." He had no guilt about its source, no greed for more, and was "generous to give what he could." Kennedy never carried what he jokingly called "cabbage" to cover meals, travel, and incidentals. He sent bills to be paid by his family accounts and so often borrowed cash from his friends that it became "a standing joke" among them. When he once reminded his valet that he owed him $300, George Taylor shot back, "You haven't paid me in four months, so you owe me a balance."

Never knowing the anxiety of financial uncertainty, Kennedy admitted to Senate colleague Olin Teague that it was only a few months earlier, during the campaign, when he first "became acquainted with a lot of people that were in the low-income group," particularly Boston dockworkers.

Despite his enormous wealth, Kennedy spent next to nothing in courting Jackie. They dined at the private homes of friends. He often didn't carry enough cash to pay for the few movies they went out to on occasion. He bought her no gifts for Christmas or Valentine's Day. It made the gifts he did get for her all the more memorable: two books—*The Raven*, by Marquis James, and *Pilgrim's Way*, by John Buchan. They were not random choices. In giving her both books, he revealed just how attentive he was to how she thought, and her habit of casting those in her life as classical archetypes.

The Raven was a 1930 Pulitzer Prize–winning biography of Sam Houston, one of Jack's heroes, the Texas military and political leader who helped forge the state's independence. As he'd done in his biographies of Benjamin Franklin, Andrew Jackson, and Woodrow Wilson, author Marquis James used detailed documentation, colorful prose, and dramatic narrative to animate Houston as the protagonist among a galaxy of other Lone Star State heroes. The publisher even billed the book as "the stuff of which legend is made." It was the way Jackie liked her history—not a bloodless academic study, but the winding, vibrant tale of how one human could lead a movement and symbolize an era. It's easy to imagine that Jack gave her the book as a glimpse into how he hoped he himself might someday be viewed in history.

John Buchan had written *Pilgrim's Way* about his distinguished career as a British diplomat, including serving as Canadian governor general. His sensibilities as both novelist and historian blended in his profiles of famous English politicians from King George V to Raymond Asquith, the latter being one of Kennedy's heroes.

Imaginary escape into the past via reading had provided a safe haven since childhood for Jack and Jackie against the respective traumas of a deathly illness and an acrimonious divorce. They enjoyed books about, or written in, early-nineteenth-century England. Among Jack's favorites was David Cecil's *Melbourne*, about British prime minister Lord William Lamb Melbourne and his unconventional marriage to novelist Caroline Ponsonby, who was also the lover of poet Lord George Gordon Byron, whom she called "mad, bad and dangerous to know." Byron—still Jackie's great literary passion—had sexual liaisons with everyone from a half sister to cousins to other men.

Another mutual passion was Shakespeare. She was struck by Jack's ability to quote from his works "out of the blue." "He knew all the great speeches and the problem of every man in those plays," she recalled of Jack, naming *Henry V* and *Richard III* as his favorites.

It wasn't just what they read but the voraciousness with which they did so that became a point of familiarity. As one of her friends recalled, "Jackie's mind was like a sponge. She liked to read several books at once and give herself a deadline to finish them all." Billings observed the same quality in Jack. "His whole mind could absolutely concentrate on what he was reading and he would block out the world. . . . [H]e was always reaching for something to read." Unlike herself, Jackie later wrote, "Jack did not write poetry. But he always read it: alone and to me."

It was inaccurate to attribute Jackie's aspirations to the formal education that privilege afforded her; most of her friends from the elite class who were similarly schooled (including her sister) were unmotivated to similarly develop themselves or use their intellect to aspire to higher callings. Jackie was excited to discover this similarity in Jack: "He had, which I think he gave himself," she recalled, "a classical education. The Greeks, Romans and the British were what shaped him. All that, he really found in his own private reading."

Both also recognized that intellect was not drawn from reading alone. Intuition about individuals, the masses, and the truth of a reported situation was essential. That came from being out among others and engaging. Both inclined toward solitude, they each made the effort to pull themselves away from the page. Jackie insisted that she not be characterized as a "bluestocking . . . because I'm not. I care much more about people than books. I would rather involve myself in life than withdraw from it like a scholar." She saw Jack similarly, believing that while he loved books, he was also "full of love—for life . . . for the great adventure of politics and . . . what he knew must be done . . . for all the things that nourish his body and spirit," and "love for me."

"We both have curious, inquiring minds," she later simply explained as the reason for why "we chose each other." What she had told Frank Waldrop about herself when he first asked what she wanted to write about at the paper, she now discovered in Jack; he was "interested in everything." She also saw that, his having lived a dozen years longer than she had, Jack could further evolve her thinking. He was, in her words, "not romantic but idealistic." For one thing, she found he helped her to "think objectively." Other differences were profound. "I make ghastly snap judgments of people," she wrote to Yusha. "I don't think that Jack Kennedy ever made a snap judgment of anyone," Lem observed. In listening to his philosophy on how to approach national problems, she would come to call Jack "the man who made me a Democrat."

Yet he also wanted to know what she knew. She was especially impressed by how he'd ask what she was reading and pick up her book when she put it down. "When I studied French literature, he went right along with me."

And with regard to Jackie's skill with the French language, Jack had an idea more ambitious than just having her translate letters from his French-Canadian constituents.

In the early spring of 1953, he had more books for her, as she recalled, nearly a dozen obscure, plodding analyses, heavy with facts about the grim details of the French war in Indochina, and all written in French.

At the same time as he faced more immediate issues of commerce and trade for Massachusetts, Kennedy had begun to focus on Indochina. Since his late 1951 visit to Vietnam, meeting with both French and Vietnamese officials, Kennedy had not lost his urgency about the need to grant the nation independence in not just name but fact. On February 18, he held a morning session with the ambassador from Vietnam. He had numerous meetings with Ed Gullion, a former U.S. diplomat he'd met in Saigon, who shared his view that American support for France was only upholding its colonial grip on a nation of people who were beginning to resent the West and turn against it. He hired Harvard graduate and foreign affairs expert Priscilla Mullins to mine all of Gullion's observations on the subject for a report.

The task he had for Jackie was the most exacting. He needed her to read all the books and determine what passages were relevant to his purpose. Then she would translate these from French into English, and process them all into one definitive report. The report needed to cover the history of the French in Indochina, from colonization onward, with all the official accords explained.

Executing the assignment had high-stakes consequences. It would help establish the senator's credibility on foreign affairs, as well as Jackie's own future with him. It was a substantial request. It gave her pause. "One of my most annoying faults is getting very enthusiastic over something at the beginning," she admitted two years earlier, "and then tiring of it halfway through. I am trying to counteract this by not getting too enthusiastic over too many things at once."

Yet, always drawn to what was most challenging, Jackie couldn't help but accept it eagerly. That Jack Kennedy asked her to do this, and the chance it offered her to demonstrate the power of her mind, made it irresistible. It allowed her to drop any self-imposed boundaries on her knowledge and talents, forget her fears of being labeled as unfeminine and thus unappealing. It proved Jack to be the first beau she'd ever had to honor her with the intellectual respect she desired. If, in July 1952, she had "thought" she was in love with Jack Kennedy, the fullest flush of that emotion must have been blooming along with the spring flowers in April 1953.

Most of all, by entrusting Jackie with delivering a stellar report on Vietnam, he suggested his willingness to invite her into the kind of substantive partnership she sought. Such a partnership would be the adventure of a lifetime, an existence large enough to employ not just her writing ability but all her talents. Even decades later, Jackie would use Jack Kennedy's definition of "happiness" as her own: "complete use of one's faculties along the line of excellence and a life affording one's scope."

By breaking off her engagement to the traditional Husted, in 1951, Jackie had resisted following the conventional belief that she must make a choice between being a wife and being a working woman; by 1953, she was able to envision what once seemed impossible: a unique blend of both options.

The Vietnam project Jack wanted Jackie to do for him was the sort of challenge he might once have undertaken himself. His passion for writing had existed at least as far back as college, when he wrote a thesis that was redrafted into *Why England Slept*, published when he was twenty-three years old. An insightful analysis into prewar British foreign policy and a cautionary tale about the cost of ignoring rising global threats around the world, it demonstrated his adherence to what one of his biographers deemed "unsentimental realism" and "clearheaded and informed calculation" in confronting such challenges. By 1953, however, the range of his writing had become constricted to events "in which he had participated," or about which he "had some firsthand knowledge," Spalding pointed out; he "began to write as a politician . . . involved in political events." His stint in journalism from April to August of 1945 had nevertheless taught him the value of pithy yet descriptive writing.

Jackie's *Times-Herald* work would never have suggested to anyone else that she could produce the kind of report Kennedy wanted, but he knew her well enough to believe she could do it. By April 1953, it also seems likely that he would have known that they shared the same values when it came to human rights, which were foundational to Kennedy's developing views on foreign policy. The premise of what he was seeking and what she ultimately produced seemed not too different from that of *Why England Slept*, though it was not intended for publication but rather to serve as the basis of his first important Senate foreign policy speech.

Kennedy was staking a national—and eventually an international—

reputation on becoming an expert on Indochina, which in turn would further help make the eventual case that he was qualified to lead the United States itself. It was no hollow political scheme, however. The events in Indochina spoke to the very core of his belief in a people's right to independence.

The job Jack had for Jackie didn't require her to review foreign-aid budgets. She was not asked to assess troop and armament appropriations. It was simpler and yet more momentous. It relied on that world of words, which she and Jack occupied and the power of which they understood. She agreed to do the job.

"Once you can express yourself, you can tell the world what you want from it," Jackie would later state. "All the changes in the world, for good and evil, were first brought about by words."

28

THE VIETNAM REPORT

March–April 1953

She was back at it, tucked into the solitude of her favorite private place to write, up in her small room at Merrywood, with the big window that looked out across the meticulous lawn toward the river. In her imagination, however, Jackie was in the streets of Saigon and the rice fields near Hanoi.

Sometime approximately in late March of 1953, Jackie began work on what would result in her eighty-four-page report on France's political, military, economic, and social control over its Indochinese colony of Vietnam. It was the centerpiece of a research file Jack was having assembled, the keystone of his comprehensive study.

She began the work alone, while in charge of the Merrywood household for part of the time. Mummy and Unk left for just over two months on January 28 to visit Yusha in Lebanon, where he was preparing to work for an American oil company. Mummy confessed that it was "nerve-racking" to be away, since Lee's wedding was scheduled for right after her return, on April 18.

Kennedy needed an enormous amount of factual detail at his disposal to present to the Senate an airtight case opposing continued American support of France's war against Communist insurgents in the north of Vietnam. Any work Jackie might have begun on her children's book about the White House was put aside. The Vietnam report—her new "spring project"—was as different from the Octagon House documentary and the *Vogue* essays as could be imagined. It all began, as she would recall more than a decade later, when "he gave me all these French books, and asked me to translate them. . . . And I was working for the *Times-Herald*, living alone at my mother's house in Virginia. And I'd stay up all these hot nights, translating these books. . . . I think I translated about ten books." She mentioned that one book was about the French admiral Georges d'Argenlieu, colonial administrator of Indochina from 1945 to 1947, and another on independence leader Ho Chi Minh and the Ammanites, the ancient tribal peoples of central Vietnam. In her final report, she heavily relied on *Histoire du Vietnam de 1940 à 1952* by Philippe de Villiers.

As indicated by an April 20, 1953, cover note from Ernest S. Griffith, the Library of Congress legislative reference service director, Kennedy requested subsequent materials which may have been the "articles on contemporary French politics" that he would also later ask her to summarize.

Kennedy did not seek out the aid of any government or professional translators to perform even part of the job, there being nothing confidential about the material or his need for it. "Yeah, he could read French," Jackie later said, "but not enough to trust himself for a lot of facts and things." That he asked Jackie to perform the task may suggest he wanted her to do it because she shared his vision of an independent Vietnam, a fact made clear by her final report.

Jackie's initial concern was not her linguistic skill but, as she put it, "I couldn't tell what was important and what was not," and was "really sort of skimming through the pages." The report called for a blend of careful historical chronology and analysis, which meant she needed to read through the texts, determine what material was relevant, perform the "translation" of those passages, and then intricately synthesize all of it into a logical, structured document.

It's clear that she rose to the challenge. The finished report began with an eighteen-page typed, double-spaced document summarizing the history of the French in Vietnam, from colonization to the most recent developments of the war. Based on her own admission of being a poor typist and the fact that the section was not neatly typed, she clearly pecked it out herself. Perhaps because she so disliked typing, the rest of her report was handwritten in her clear, distinct penmanship, and was staggering for the small yet important details she chose to include, and for its sixty-six-page length. In its entirety, the document illustrates just how acute her analysis of human nature could be and her ability to balance objectivity and empathy.

Jackie divided the typed section into three parts. Part I began with the 1860 Franco-British expedition to Indochina, hit on seven turning points, and concluded with the French driving out the Japanese occupation as World War II ended. Parts II and III covered the postwar years, concluding with the defeat of Bao Dai, the emperor of Annam, the central region of Vietnam, covering about two-thirds of the nation.

The handwritten first portion of Jackie's report is a minute analysis of five key accords between France and Indochina that came about between March 1945 and June 1948.

Perhaps the most telling, cogent part of the report was her concluding summary, "Cost of Vietnam War." Set apart from the factual data, and startling in its humanism, this appears to have been her personal verdict, and it would turn out to be prophetic. Jackie believed that the situation had simply become a struggle between the French and the Viet Minh, "each fighting for power." She recognized the absurdity of the situation, asking, "What's the point of the fight with neither side winning?"

In criticizing the fight for power, Jackie often returned to the Vietnamese people being exploited by it: "They want a new way of life—no foreign domination, no corrupt mandarinate. . . . It is to them that we must give the reins." Ultimately, she put the onus on France, which had issued statements that recognized Vietnamese independence, urging that "[s]he should now follow up her words with actions—in letting the people freely choose their own destiny." In addition to the fact that France had lost thirty thousand of its men and its economy had been compromised, Jackie contended that the French government had been dishonest with its citizens: "Propaganda makes this look like a defensive war when it's really a conquest," and the French government "exploits patriotic sentiment to justify a misguided policy." Peace, she further contended, would come only when Vietnam had leaders its people trusted, but "[i]t's not for the French, Chinese or Americans to say who those people are."

While she vigorously took to task the Soviet and Chinese leaders and their motives regarding Vietnam, Jackie did not accept that an independent Communist Vietnam would simply become a puppet of another state. "Nothing has proved that a communist [nation] in Asia is automatically dominated by the Kremlin and closed to all other influences," she asserted.

As she composed her report, Jackie was not ignorant of the danger to any public figure who suggested keeping an open mind about Communism, having asked in one of her "Inquiring Camera Girl" columns, "If you secretly found out you had married a former Communist, what would you do?" She sometimes used the column to provoke responses on aspects of the Soviet system and the Cold War ("If you could send a message behind the Iron Curtain, what would you say?" "Would Stalin's death help or hurt world peace?" "Malenkov says all differences between Russia and the U.S. can be solved by peaceable means, do you agree?" "What four Americans would you name as delegates to the U.N. to match Russia's team of Vishinsky, Gromyko, Zorin and Zorubin?"). But what she was saying in the report could be seen as something rather direct—and dangerous.

On the penultimate page of the document, Jackie overtly identified her own recommendation based on all that she had learned and come to believe, daring Kennedy "to say in your speech that we should give Indochina to the communists because they are the ones with the most integrity!"

Despite the serious subject, her last line on the last page showed that her wit remained intact: "END—Thank heavens."

The behind-the-scenes project had been a tedious, exhausting, and yet illuminating undertaking, fully immersing Jackie in the complexities of military strategy from which she emerged with a firmer grasp of contemporary world politics. It brought her full circle from the Sorbonne class of Pierre Renouvin, whose philosophical view about the futility of France seeking control again over the Vietnamese had so seared itself into her psyche. In 1951, the concept of autonomy had been personal for her, in escaping the dominance of Mummy and, to a lesser degree, Black Jack, over her every thought and decision. In 1953, after her study of the policy behind it, her bedrock belief in self-determined independence became a core tenet.

Jackie had discussed Indochina with Yusha when he had joined her in Europe in June 1950 and the following year as she read works by André Malraux that touched on the colonial dilemma. A December 18, 1952, letter Yusha wrote to her proves that they were then maintaining a dialogue on a similar global situation. While in Beirut, he had been studying the "Palestinian problem," and reading the Koran and *Arabian Days* by St. John Philby. He engaged her on the consequences of colonial domination in the region. "A people so long subjected, extremely diverse, not educated well historically," he wrote to her, "when . . . desperate, [are] easily swayed by mob force and communism. But they believe, as we do, in fundamental human and social rights . . . of liberty, individuality, the integrity of what they respect, of self-defense."

The assessments and information in Jackie's report prompted Kennedy to phone his friend Thurston Morton, assistant secretary of state, with endless and detailed inquiries about the U.S. support of France in Indochina. He wanted to know just how much funding the U.S. government was providing. He asked if the French had a plan "for success" in Indochina—"military, economic and political." He wondered how the French intended to secure the support of the Vietnamese, whether some accords could be revised, and to what degree the various factions had ratified them.

Morton said Kennedy's questions "cover so many aspects of this subject" that it would take "several days to furnish the information." After waiting more than two weeks without a response, Jack fired off a crisp letter to Secretary of State John Foster Dulles. "While I knew it involves considerable research and extensive preparation," he wrote, the ambitious freshman senator wanted answers "at your earliest convenience." The answers he received were vague and evasive, raising a red flag for Kennedy as he plunged ahead.

Jackie's report made a strong case for France to grant Vietnam its independence, and in doing so bolstered the argument that Jack had already articulated after meeting with French, Vietnamese, and American representatives during his December 1951 visit to Indochina, that it was necessary in "support of the legitimate aspirations of the people of this area against all who seek to dominate them—from whatever quarter they may come."

In discovering just how attentive Jackie could be to the complexities already at work in Indochina, Jack's sense that her views and values would make her an ideal partner seemed to increasingly become a conviction. After submitting her report to the senator, she thought so, too.

"He has got to ask me to marry him," she recalled thinking in an interview eleven years later, "after all I have done for him."

29

DATING

April–May 1953

As Easter weekend approached, the first weekend in April, Jack Kennedy thoughtfully made sure that his entire staff would be taking those days off, then left on Thursday, April 2, to spend the holiday in Palm Beach with his family. He sent Jackie a postcard of hibiscus flowers, simply saying, "Wish you were here." Jackie would later claim it was his only written expression of affection during their courtship. (She overlooked a telegram he would send just over a month later, forming a sum total of just two known love notes from him.)

Yet, in other ways, Jack was making overtures to her—and she was accepting them.

While she was reluctant to disclose details of her dating life, both she and Jack were becoming more comfortable with others knowing they were "involved." Charlie Bartlett was among the few with whom she shared stories about her adventures with Jack, telling him how on one occasion, she'd surreptitiously arrived at his office to "kidnap" the senator for a brief spell, taking him to the Glen Echo amusement park.

According to Charlie, despite the increasing frequency of Jack and Jackie's dates, the senator remained dedicated to his primary passion: politics. "One thing at a time," he told Charlie. Jack didn't discuss the possibility of marriage with even his closest friends. "No, he just never talked about it," said Spalding. "He was having . . . success in everything he did and he was moving along . . . fast enough to suit himself. . . . He wasn't worried about the fact that it wasn't a connubial life." He also admitted to being averse to what he saw as the expected behavior of a man in love, telling historian James McGregor Burns, "I'm not the heavy romantic type." The good fortune was that Jackie was similarly unwilling to fully express her feelings, making them a comfortable match. If Kennedy had been overtly emotional, it might likely have discomfited her, too.

Jackie's friend Lorraine Shevlin, who was dating Senator John Sherman Cooper of Kentucky, recalled how she commiserated with Jackie about the enormous time the men invested in work. "We said . . . how awful it must be to be married to a man in politics . . . it was all sour grapes because I don't think either senator had asked us to marry him at that point." Lorraine, a divorcée, gave Jackie some advice: "Should your husband feel compelled at some point to cheat on you, either cheat back or buy yourself a diamond tiara and send him the bill."

Jack tried to fit his personal life in with his public responsibilities, but when he took Jackie out to dinner and brought along an aide or a crony, she was often irritated and sometimes left the table. Unlike Dave Powers at their first dinner, who had asked her her thoughts about Jack's challenging Lodge for the Senate, others seemed to presume she had nothing to add. In time, as tape recordings of conversations with journalists who joined them for dinner would illustrate, she offered her insights if she considered the others to be trustworthy friends. Generally, however, whatever political advice or ideas she offered Jack would be strictly limited to private conversations or written communications between them. Jackie's Vietnam report set the pattern for that.

On the other hand, Kennedy began to seem more willing to make her a priority over his attentive generation of publicity. Several weeks earlier, he had canceled a dinner meeting with Paul Healy, who was nearing completion of their interviews for the *Saturday Evening Post* profile, to instead take Jackie out, as was noted in his business calendar with what appears to have been his own handwritten notation of "Bouvier."

At the same time, Jackie had begun helping his career by introducing him to her own small but significant network. Unk's sister Esther was married to Norman Blitz, a successful Nevada developer and fundraiser with powerful political connections out West; Blitz and his wealthy cohorts would prove crucial to Jack in his future campaigns. Jackie helped

Jack forge a personal friendship with her Newport friend Claiborne Pell, then a Foreign Service officer with the State Department. "I met Jacqueline first," recalled Henry Brandon, chief correspondent for the London *Sunday Times* Washington bureau. "It was really through her that I met him and that I was invited to her house and that I gradually got to know him better. . . . In the beginning it was more a social relationship than . . . a relationship of a newspaperman with a politician."

Such overtures, along with her Vietnam report, increased Jack's fascination with this woman who, he later told their friend Joan Braden, "could really think like a man, rational and had acute insight." (The compliment was misogynistic, but of its time.) Yusha also believed Jack was fascinated by Jackie's "inquisitive, no-nonsense mind," and was coming to realize "how much . . . he needed her advice and her sort of comfort." Even if Jack resisted asking her to marry him, Lem Billings recognized the inevitability of it. "I knew right away that Jackie was different from all the other girls Jack had been dating. She was more intelligent, more literary, more substantial," he reflected. "They were kindred souls. Jack and Jackie, two halves of the same whole."

Still, as the weeks ticked forward, Jack suggested nothing tangible. And while Jackie had been musing about marrying Jack for nine months, she continued to face questions of her own: how her sense of self might be compromised by a life in national politics and by being integrated into the Kennedy family; whether researching and writing for the senator would be worth sacrificing her pursuit of a professional writing career (and just how often he would call on her anyway, given that he had a staff to research and write for him); and of course the most sensitive of all, how she could genuinely cope with an unfaithful husband. Her immediate response to Billings's presenting her with Jack's condition for marriage had been to characterize it as a challenge she was up to, but based on later remarks she made, Jackie hadn't abandoned all hope that marriage might change Jack. In fact, she believed that a libidinous bachelor life tamed men as husbands, once advising a friend that men were "always surer to last if they sow their wild oats first." And yet, she had heard and seen enough of Black Jack to know that no wife could change the behavior of a determined adulterer. What *could* be changed was a wife's acceptance of it. According to several relatives, Jackie was intensely against divorce. The challenge was not to change an adulterous husband but rather to manage herself in reaction to him. She never forgot that Black Jack's infidelity, she had confided to Father Leonard in July 1952, "nearly killed Mummy." Yet to her, even this could never justify how Janet ruptured their family unit.

"She was going to make sacrifices to be a political wife," Yusha reflected. "[S]he would not have permitted divorce." Three obvious facts gave Jackie marital power: the Catholic Church forbade divorce even in cases of infidelity; no divorced Catholic could be elected president; and Jack Kennedy was determined to become the first Catholic president.

In a handwritten draft of a statement that appears to have been either a tribute to Joe Kennedy or a submitted contribution to Rose Kennedy's eventual memoirs, Jackie pointed out that the value of Jack's Catholicism was that their children "would learn that marriage is permanent." In further writing that she would always "thank his father" for providing the example for Jack's "sense of family," one can't help but recognize the irony she may have intended: Jack's marital model was the Ambassador, who, despite his infidelity, never divorced his wife.

Janet and Lee had both expressed their doubts about whether Jack was a good match for Jackie. Jack said that Janet "has a tendency when excited to think I'm not good enough for her daughter and talked too much—talked just too much." Lee recalled an evening when Jack came to retrieve her sister for an evening out: "I kept him company while he waited for her and didn't make his visit a bit pleasant because I didn't think he was paying Jackie enough attention. I just wanted him to know that I thought no one was good enough for her."

The wedding of Lee and Michael Canfield was scheduled for Saturday, April 18, the ceremony to be held at Georgetown's Holy Trinity Church, with a reception to follow at Merrywood. The night before, Unk and Mummy hosted a supper for the bridal party at the F Street Club, the Canfield, Lee, and Auchincloss relatives being the guests. Black Jack and the Bouviers were not invited. Her father did attend the ceremony the following day, coming by train in the morning accompanied by his sister Michelle and her husband, and her twin, Maude, who insisted on joining despite her previous estrangement from her brother.

At the ceremony, Black Jack appeared, facing his ex-wife and the unabashed wealth of her second husband to walk his younger daughter down the aisle. Jackie served as maid of honor, and she, along with Nini and three other bridesmaids, wore "ballerina-length bouffant gowns of yellow chiffon, veils of yellow tulle attached to circles of fern and carried bouquets of fern," as Nini recalled. Kennedy did not attend, being in Massachusetts that weekend.

At the spring reception in Merrywood's sylvan setting, the bride attempted cleverness in thanking guests for their gifts, but the sarcasm was unmistakable. "How did you guess that what Michael and I wanted more than anything on earth was a pair of carving knives with china handles?" she told one guest. "They're so pretty it seems a shame to mess them up with meat. I think we'll just use them on each other when we get mad." Louis Auchincloss recalled, disapprovingly, that Black Jack "danced Janet around when she didn't want it at all. We thought he'd take Janet away with him."

Jackie seemed blissfully removed from the family drama. She asked ushers for remarks to use in her column, teasing them that if they didn't comply she'd make up their response. "But Jackie what is the question?" one asked. "I'll make up the question, too!"

Despite her lightheartedness about the column, frustration at work was creeping in. Jackie was losing her enthusiasm for conjuring up provocative column questions six days a week, and her intention of fully transitioning to feature articles remained unfulfilled. By April of 1953, she'd been able to do only four features in nearly a year and a half on the job. She began to question whether she'd chosen the best venue for her writing. "She insisted she would be a writer for life, but she began to sour on doing it for a newspaper," Yusha would recall.

In a sense, she was a victim of her own success, having made the "Inquiring Camera Girl" so uniquely a part of the *Times-Herald* brand that Waldrop encouraged her to continue focusing on it. She'd become used to his ignoring her requests for feature assignments but was also frustrated that the time necessary to do the column well prevented her from conceiving and pitching a greater number of full-article ideas. What she couldn't know was the *Times-Herald* had continued losing money and Waldrop was looking to reduce overhead costs or face the possibility that the owners would have to sell the paper at a loss. Jackie's column questions at the time expressed her dissatisfaction with her work and her boss ("Does your job use your highest abilities?" "Would you like to be the boss here, and what would you change?" "What subject that you took in school has been the least use to you now?" "What is your secret ambition?").

She was reaching a point of frustration, one day snapping to society reporter Angela Gingras, "I am going to quit this job." Gingras empathized with her, explaining, "Not only did she feel that the newspaper was exploiting us—we were being overlooked and underpaid—but there was a sense of personal indignation. Jackie realized that the editors considered her the Junior League type, useful but not essential. They took her lightly because she wasn't reporting hard news."

Finally, Waldrop called her into his office one morning in April 1953 to offer her an assignment in which her professional and personal lives would merge. Though it was for a column and not a feature, it had the potential to generate national attention. He asked her to interview some of the country's most famous U.S. senators, all of whom he knew personally. He gave her a list: North Carolina Democrat Clyde Hoey, Nevada Democrat Pat McCarran, Ohio Republican Robert Taft, Utah Republican Wallace Bennett, and others. The youngest and newest senator on his list was Jack Kennedy.

Waldrop knew that Jackie had been "seeing" Kennedy, and before she left, he couldn't help piping up to air his paternal concerns. He warned her that many other women, "a whole generation ahead of you," had gotten heartsick over Jack Kennedy, and advised her, "You behave yourself. Don't get your hopes up. He's too old for you—besides, he doesn't want to get married." She "rolled her eyes, said nothing and went off on her assignment," he recalled.

The column would be unique in another way, shaped by the nature of the unconventional question, for it countered the response of each elected official with that of the teenage students who worked as their Senate page messengers. The senators were asked, "What's it like observing the pages at close range?" and the pages were asked, "What's it like observing senators at close range?" It's unknown whether Waldrop or Jackie crafted the dual set of questions, but it seems likely that it was Jackie, given that she was in on the joke inside Jack's circle that he looked more like a college intern than an elected official.

Jackie also managed an unexpected scoop and a sixth interview. After she'd interviewed Jack, he introduced her to the most powerful man in the country she had yet met: Vice President Richard Nixon. Kennedy and Nixon had befriended each other as fellow freshmen in Congress in 1947. Their offices, at the time, were directly across the hall from each other, and when the California Republican ran for the Senate against Democrat Helen Gahagan Douglas in 1950, Jack walked a cash contribution from the Ambassador to Nixon's campaign over to him. By sitting down with the vice president, Jackie had now interviewed all four members of the Nixon family.

Meanwhile, in the *Times-Herald* newsroom, Jackie's assignment to interview Jack turned whispers about their relationship into loud chatter. Some of Jackie's female colleagues were jealous. "We were all young women, most of us unmarried, and everybody wanted to get assignments to talk to young Jack Kennedy," recalled Agnes Ash, who wrote for the women's page. "Everyone knew that anyone who married him would one day become the first lady. It was a given."

Soon enough, Jack made an appearance at the *Times-Herald* office to see Jackie. One story that long circulated among the staff and tenants at the *Times-Herald* building was that the senator pulled up in a taxi and dashed into the newsroom, found Jackie, and asked her for some cash to pay the driver. She coughed it up. He was familiar with the newsroom, having visited Inga Arvad and his sister Kathleen there a decade earlier. When Waldrop quipped about those earlier days with Inga, the senator became slightly uncomfortable. Yet again, Waldrop noticed that Jackie just "rolled her eyes."

Jackie did not let the fact that it was now widely known she was dating Jack Kennedy distract from her ambitions. The column that came from the interviews with the senators and the vice president offered a humanizing view of these men with otherwise remote public personas. It appears that she impressed Waldrop with it enough that he agreed to recast it as a longer piece, and she excitedly wrote to a literary agent, identified only as a Mrs. McCrea in the sole surviving letter that Jackie wrote on *Times-Herald* letterhead, that "[t]he editor liked it so much that we are now going to run it as a Sunday feature. I hope you think it is alright. . . . As soon as the others [interviews] come in, I will let you know when the feature will run. Thank you so much for being so kind—and please excuse the pencil. I'm rather slow on the typewriter—and there seems to be no such thing as a pen in a newspaper office." Little is known of why Jackie was in touch with the literary agent, other than Waldrop's vague recollection that his columnist had an idea of doing a young-adult book on the Senate, an angle perhaps inherent in her having interviewed the pages or prompted by the earlier idea of a children's book about the White House. However, whatever the reason may have been, the piece ended up being printed as a regular column and not a feature, on Tuesday, April 21, and did not become a book.

Once again, it began to feel like she was hitting a dead end, in her professional life as well as in her relationship with Jack. She was becoming as pessimistic about his intentions to marry her as she was about her job. She later told a friend that she wondered "if I'll live long enough to marry him."

Jackie's friend Aileen Bowdoin (Bow's older sister) had recently divorced and moved back in with her mother and stepfather, Emily and Ed Foley. Feeling she was "having a tough time," the Foleys held a surprise birthday party for Aileen on Saturday, May 16. At the party, Aileen said, her mother "announced that she thought it would be fun if I took a trip to the coronation of Queen Elizabeth, which I must say was the last thing in the world that I ever would have done. However, I said, 'Okay, Mom, I'll go [but] I'm not going unless I have somebody to go with because I'm not going to go over and take on the Queen by myself.' So, I called up Jackie and I asked her if she'd like to go. That was probably Monday, and she said, 'I'll let you know tomorrow.'"

Mummy then got into the act, first learning of the idea from Emily Foley, and ambushed Jackie with her arguments for why she must go, because "I felt she really needed it." By her own recounting of it, Janet presumed that her elder daughter felt badly about herself after her younger sister married first, and that she was "awfully tired . . . working for the *Times-Herald* all winter." Janet also recalled that she "suspected" Jackie's initial resistance to the trip was because she didn't want to leave Jack Kennedy, "although she had never really said so because she is the sort of girl who covers her feelings." Janet harangued her, saying that if Jackie were "doing exciting things instead of sitting here waiting for the telephone to ring," then Jack "would be much more likely to find out how he felt about you."

Jackie was interested in going, but for the opposite reason Janet had suggested. To her mind, the trip could be "a chance to do some regular writing." She told Aileen that going to England and the coronation could help her get multiple feature articles for the *Times-Herald* published.

On Tuesday, when she approached managing editor Sidney Epstein about going to Europe, he first thought she wanted a paid three-week vacation and balked. When she explained that she was going to the coronation, his mood changed. Aileen recalled, "[S]he had gone to the editors to see if she could get assignments in covering the events." Epstein explained, "We had been trying without success to get someone into the coronation. I said, 'Go! But you have to write us letters you airmail back. And include a sketch every day.'" On Wednesday, May 20, she renewed her passport, listing her occupation as "photographer."

Later biographies consistently maintained that Janet paid for the trip. According to Mummy, she told Jackie that "if they [the *Times-Herald*] don't want to, I'd like to give you the trip," but Aileen testified to the fact that "Jackie insisted on principle that the paper cover her travel and hotel if she was going to be writing stories for them—or else she refused to go." According to Aileen, the *Times-Herald* agreed to reimburse most of Jackie's London trip with a modest stipend, and she "saved every receipt."

In fact, Jack Kennedy already knew how he felt about her; just before she left Washington, he finally did raise the idea of marriage. Based on what Jackie later told her friend Joan Braden, one night before her departure Kennedy suddenly stopped vacillating. "[H]e wanted to get married and didn't want to get married," Braden recounted, "and then she told me about the night that he finally did. And she went off to the coronation."

Saying he "finally did" want to marry one night just before she left was still not, however, asking her to marry him. In Jackie's constant presence for the next two weeks and five days, Aileen Bowdoin confirmed this, stating that "[h]e had asked her *about* marriage." In his earliest interviews on the matter, Billings would repeatedly state for the record, "Jackie, to my knowledge, was the only girl he ever wanted to marry. . . . Jack Kennedy never proposed to anybody except Jackie." Asked whether the senator did technically ask Jackie Bouvier to marry him, even Lem admitted, "I wasn't actually that sure." In a later interview, he clarified the matter further: "I couldn't visualize him actually saying 'I love you' to somebody and asking her to marry him. It was the sort of thing he would have liked to have happen without having to talk about it."

Regardless, it seems that Jack's calculations had shifted. He had been waiting to marry until he felt it was necessary, and that time had come. "It wasn't until he had presidential ambitions that he felt that marriage was a necessity," Billings continued. "I do think he'd reached the point where he felt it was politically important to marry—fortunately, Jackie came along at the right time."

Accounts casting Kennedy as using Jackie to serve his purposes overlook the fact that she also hoped to use him to serve her own. "She wanted the White House as much as he did," her friend Tish Baldrige flatly insisted. "She wanted to be First Lady of the land." That intention, Louis Auchincloss believed, explained her willingness to wait so long for a marriage offer, saying bluntly, "Jackie had always known exactly what she wanted, and how to get it." Even Yusha admitted that she shared Jack's presidential ambition, though he set it in more noble terms, saying they were "both very patriotic people" who shared a "great sense of duty."

"I wanted Jack to be President," Jackie told a friend. "You often don't recognize greatness when you're up close to it—but I did and I wanted him to save my country."

A long-term pursuit of the presidency was, admitted Bartlett, "really part of the deal going in. I mean, the road [was] sort of laid out and I think Jackie knew she was getting into a race for the presidency probably almost immediately. And, I think the point was that this became a great project which really bound them together . . . [and] they would spend many evenings . . . going through books, looking for quotes that really became famous as Jack used them. . . . And [the] research that they did . . . made Jack a much more dimensional figure."

There was little time to discuss whether they would seriously marry. The only remark Jackie ever made about those days of mid-May was characteristically enigmatic: "Both of us knew it was serious, I think, but we didn't talk about it then." The ambiguity of their status was further confirmed by what she told Frank Waldrop when she stopped in the office before she set sail. As he recalled of their brief conversation, "[S]he expected to marry soon after she returned."

On the morning of Friday, May 22, Jackie and Aileen arrived at Pier 86 in New York at 46th Street, for the 11:30 a.m. departure of the SS *United States*. It was the fastest and longest ocean liner in the world and had made its maiden voyage just the summer before. As the tugboats pulled it from the pier into a foggy New York Harbor, Jackie Bouvier was on her way back to Europe.

30

CORONATION

May–June 1953

Manufactured entirely in America, the SS *United States* was conceived to be a symbol of an ascendant postwar nation, proudly declaring itself the most powerful on earth.

Every aspect of the ship's vision and execution was intended to convey a patriotic aura, starting with its two distinct red, white, and blue smokestacks. The striking interiors featured red, white, blue, and gold walls and draperies, and midcentury modern furniture, rather than faux old-world antiques. Above the grand staircase was a massive metal seal of the United States.

The ship had immediately become the transport of choice to get to Europe for the likes of Marilyn Monroe, Bob Hope, Grace Kelly, Cary Grant, Gary Cooper, Salvador Dalí, and LeRoy Neiman. On board with Aileen and Jackie were the Woolworth heiress Jessie Woolworth Donahue, her son Jimmy Donahue, and his friends the Duke and Duchess of Windsor. The more than one thousand crew and staff were instructed to be attentive to guests, but less formal than their European counterparts. Evening dance music was provided by the popular society orchestra the Meyer Davis Band, which had played at Jackie's parents' wedding. The seven daily meals offered distinctly American fare, from pizza and milkshakes to Long Island duck, Maine lobster, and Virginia ham, some named after famous Americans, from "vegetables à la Herbert Hoover" to

"Clara Barton Salad." It was all a tactile manifestation of the "American Century." The ship's newspaper, *The Ocean Press*, reported on daily activities. Shuffleboard and golf were available on the game deck, and there was an enclosed pool, a gym, massage rooms, three libraries, a hospital, a casino, a movie theater, beauty parlors, and an observation lounge.

Not invited to the coronation, the Windsors would deboard at Le Havre and head to their house in Paris. Jackie would touch on the controversy of the Windsors' not having been invited to the coronation in one of her London columns, with one respondent harrumphing that the duke should just "enjoy himself playing golf." While she was fascinated by the duchess, neither she nor the duke immediately drew Jackie's attention—their pugs did.

Jackie had affirmed to Mini Rhea just before her departure that she was making the trip because "I'll get a chance to do some regular writing." And the moment she stepped aboard, she got to work searching for an unconventional story as her first feature of the trip. "I'm supposed to carry on my inquiring camera girl stories," she sighed to Mini, "but I just may throw my camera overboard."

Jackie went into the storage area in the bowels of the vessel, where she discovered an air-conditioned kennel, providing "first-class service" to all canines making the crossing.

"She loved the dogs on board the ship," Aileen recalled. "She did a whole story with sketches about the lives of these dogs. . . . It was funny and amusing, but you know about her delightful wit—she was imagining them as humans and really writing about the personalities of the people they were with." As she once told her cousin Mimi, "the more evolved you are the more you realize how much better dogs are than people." She airmailed her piece and illustrations to the office as soon as they reached England. "Dogs Have Their Day on Coronation Cruise" was printed on the *Times-Herald* front page, four days after they landed.

Early Wednesday morning, the ship docked at Le Havre, France, where the Windsors disembarked with other passengers. By 5:30 that afternoon, Jackie and Aileen were processed through customs at Southampton, and headed into London.

There they were given use of a South Audley Street apartment in Mayfair by Henriette Abel Smith, the wife of a friend of Aileen's stepfather. Lady Abel Smith was one of Elizabeth's ladies-in-waiting and living at the palace in the weeks preceding the coronation. The apartment had no heat, Aileen recalled. "It was freezing cold in London. . . . It was raining all the time . . . we'd come back to the apartment and sit on the edge of the tub, and put our feet on the bottom, and run hot water over them until we couldn't stand it any longer."

Away from family expectations and work uncertainties, in a city steeped in history, Jackie's imagination was animated. "She was fun to be with because she imagined herself as many of the historical characters like the wives of Henry the VIII, and the first Queen Elizabeth," recalled Aileen. "She could imagine how the lives of the queens underwent dramatic change."

Together, they took on the city in all its celebratory pageantry, though the glitter was joined by the mud. "All over, there were still signs of World War II," Aileen continued. "There were a lot of empty lots with wild flowers growing up through the stones." Still, she added, "Neither one of us had ever, and probably ever again, had been in a city where every single person was happy. There was such a sense of euphoria. It was catching, and you started feeling that way too . . . Everywhere you went people had smiles, and were laughing, and talking, and strangers spoke to each other. It was great."

Jackie, however, was there to work, intent on sending back as many lengthy feature articles as she could, along with some "Inquiring Camera Girl" columns. "She tossed those columns off at the drop of a hat in London," Aileen remembered. "She always had her camera with her and took it out quite a lot." She asked, outside Buckingham Palace, "Do you think Elizabeth will be England's last queen?" In Piccadilly Circus, she asked people for their greatest coronation thrill, one couple answering they were excited about sleeping on the sidewalk to ensure a good view of the procession, a Haitian student piping up, "All the world seems to be here in London—that's what makes me happy." Alongside her London columns, the *Times-Herald* concurrently printed those she had prepared before leaving, including ones she conducted at the circus, the annual Federation of Women's Clubs convention, and with high school students touring Washington's monuments.

Her second (and lengthiest) feature story published from England, "Crowds of Americans Fill Bright and Pretty London," appeared on June 2, focused on the masses of people in the streets, hotels, and nightclubs. With her vivid, colorful narrative, Jackie took her readers from the boat train in Southampton to Waterloo Station, where every window, she reported, had an image of Elizabeth; past the department stores, hotels, and small shops, all covered in bunting and flags. She took them into the crowds gathering in Trafalgar Square, then to the gates of Buckingham Palace, where the diversity of Commonwealth regiments marched. At night she brought readers to a charity theater performance of a Victorian comedy, attended by Princess Margaret, the entire audience in full formal dress. She even nabbed an interview with a close friend of Prince Philip.

Perhaps her most elaborate descriptions were of the Dorchester Hotel facade, designed by Oliver Messel, which represented "theater boxes: pale blue balconets with purple and gold draperies. At night gas-fed torches on long white poles blaze above the main entrance." And a private Mayfair nightclub with a "postage-stamp size dance floor," which she said was "lined with accordion-pleated red velvet" and "looked like the inside of a jewel box."

Despite their connections, Aileen and Jackie weren't able to get into Westminster Abbey to witness the coronation. Instead, they got tickets for front-row seating at Burberry's raincoat store along the procession route. They watched the Queen's gold coach roll by, but the royal who most impressed them was the Queen of Tonga in her large turban.

After attending an American Embassy reception, they went to a massive party at the Londonderry House hotel, given by Washington hostess Perle Mesta. Jackie surreptitiously slipped her pad and pen out, taking notes and sketching images for what would be her third feature piece for the *Times-Herald*, "The Mesta Fiesta—Second Only to the Coronation—Was the Show to See in London Last Week," published the day before she returned to the United States. Her drawing posed General Omar Bradley dancing with actress Lauren Bacall, as the Marquess of Milford-Haven and Humphrey Bogart waited their turns.

Back in Washington, as each story and daily column was published, Mummy would at least concede that Jackie's front-page drawings were "very clever." Mini Rhea saw it as a sign of her drive. "I could see that Jacqueline was making this her real challenge," she observed, "to emerge as a writer." Jack's second and final courtship "love letter" (this time a telegram) proclaimed "Articles Excellent—But You Are Missed."

He wasn't far from her thoughts, either. In London, Jackie scanned bookstores, with a long list of titles in hand by the prolific British author, philosopher, essayist, poet, and mystic Aldous Huxley. She told Aileen they were for Unk, but Aileen said, "I knew perfectly well they were for Jack. He loved Aldous Huxley, and so she had a whole suitcase full of him." She lugged the suitcase of books throughout the trip, paying $105 at customs for the excess baggage. Apart from actual telegrams to Jack, she was telegraphing to him through her column. The day she arrived in England, her column asked, "When did the romance fade out of your marriage?" The day after she arrived in Paris, the question was, "What is your candid opinion of marriage?"

Marriage was a matter he couldn't escape back in the States. The day after Jackie left, he was in New York, along with Janet and Unk, among the 1,700 guests at Eunice Kennedy's wedding to Sargent Shriver at St. Patrick's Cathedral, and the ensuing Waldorf-Astoria reception.

"Something was said there," recalled Jean Mannix, who worked on Jack's staff, "that the senator may be becoming engaged to Jackie. But nothing definite was really said . . . And then there were rumors . . . that he was going to announce his engagement. . . . We knew he saw Jackie Bouvier, and we knew that there was an interest there. . . . I can remember Kenny O'Donnell saying that [previous] fall that within a year that he'd be married." Oddly, Jack's sisters didn't seem to realize how serious it was, the trio chiming in after O'Donnell introduced them to Pulitzer Prize–winning author Margaret Coit, "Oh, we do wish he would meet some nice girl."

So fixated on him that she had his handwriting analyzed, Margaret Coit admitted, "I had designs on John F. Kennedy. . . . Every girl in Massachusetts wanted to date him, and I wasn't any exception." Coming up with a "good excuse" to interview him while she was in Washington researching her new book on financier and statesman Bernard Baruch, despite his not knowing him, she dressed in "pink lace gloves, a little gray bonnet with a pink lace veil, and a pink rose. So, he got the idea right away." She invited him to her rented room in Washington, where Jack "lunged" and "tried to drag me down beside him." She protested, "Don't be so grabby. This is only our first date." He looked right into her face, remarking seriously, "But I can't wait, you see, I'm going to grab everything I want. You see, I haven't any time." When they drove by the White House, Jack declared, "I am going to go there." Coit concluded that he was a dichotomy: "So immature emotionally, so mature intellectually."

Jackie saw her share of men in Europe, too—though not in the manner Jack had with Coit. She and Aileen went to a weekend dance in the English countryside, "to meet men," admitted Aileen. In London, they went out with friends Guy du Boulay and Giulio Pascucci. Arriving in Paris on June 3, Jackie enjoyed racing around with Lance Reventlow, the son of Woolworth heiress Barbara Hutton, in his snow-white Jaguar with black leather seats. When Jackie saw her old beau Demi Gates there, he warned that Jack Kennedy was a "hopeless womanizer," to which she replied, "Look at my father!" She also saw her old beau John Marquand, to whom she explained her motives for wanting to marry Jack: "[L]ife will always be interesting with him, and then there's the money." Marquand was upset by this, later telling one of her biographers that he worried about what "is going to become of you in that awful world" of politics. But she knew where Jack was going and wanted to go with him, telling Marquand, "Read the newspapers."

In Paris, Jackie and Aileen shared a room "with zebra cushions . . . [and] no closet in it," at what Aileen described as the "tiny, Left Bank . . . cheap hotel Bisson." There was champagne with breakfast, a mid-morning meal of coffee, cream crackers, Vita biscuits, and shortbread, and luncheons that began with smoked-salmon sandwiches and ended with sherry cream trifle. Teatime included fancy pastries, chocolate éclairs, cream buns, and gâteaux.

Jackie took Aileen to the Louvre and some of her favorite bookstores and antique shops. Recalled Aileen, "She went out quite a bit just for fun, but she was trying to decide whether or not she really wanted to marry. . . . She was thinking. . . . She did talk about Jack, but not that much in the way of discussion. It was more things that she said inadvertently that showed how she really felt about things. He had asked her about marriage before we left and she was having a very hard time making up her mind. That's what was going on a lot of the time."

If Aileen probed too deeply, Jackie would redirect the conversation, usually with humor. "There's only one man I know more handsome and fun and if he asked me to marry him, I would instantly [accept]," Jackie mused as she led Aileen along the Seine to the spot where she had once painted. Then she stopped and whispered, "Joe DiMaggio is the man for me. That crooked nose, and funny smile. And a lifetime supply of Wheaties." Aileen burst into laughter, Jackie slyly smiling. "She came out with the kookiest things. You never knew what she was thinking."

Jack didn't know what she was thinking, either; he kept close tabs on her throughout the trip. "It seemed that every time we got back to the hotel, there was a message waiting for her from Jack," said Aileen. "I don't think it was settled then, but I remember there were many transatlantic calls from him," said Billings, from Jack's side of the Atlantic. Aileen verified this from the other side. "She had a number of urgent calls coming in from him. He was afraid she had changed her mind. I think he'd reached the point where it was a done deal in his mind, but she really had her doubts."

It was not "indecision about him," Jackie told Aileen. She knew she loved him as an individual. As Aileen explained, "She was worried about being taken over by politics and another family, because she always wanted to be herself, and I think that losing her own personality was what she was most worried about . . . it was a legitimate concern." It was also not new: she'd had similar concerns about being absorbed into the tedious, confined suburban world of John Husted, and earlier, about being doomed to the shallow social world of her young Newport beaux.

Another profound and unresolved concern lurked, too, which arose from a conversation with the senator, who had begun suggesting she would not have time to continue her column. Waldrop conveyed that Jackie felt marrying Kennedy meant "giving up her job." Her writing had become an important part of her development and early identity. What upset her, according to Waldrop, was that Jack presumed he had the right to tell her to quit. She seemed willing to acquiesce, however, because—as the Vietnam report proved—she would be able to continue some type of writing. And while she might not always be credited for the writing she did for Jack, it would be in service of a much larger goal: political influence, perhaps even over the future president. Still, by what Waldrop recalled, she wanted to preserve her standing at the paper and keep open the option of contributing features.

To get home from Paris, Jackie and Aileen boarded their first transatlantic flight; Jackie scribbled a postcard to her newspaper colleague Glen Hearin: "I'm just about to fly . . . on Air France where they give you champagne so you won't realize the engine is broken so maybe this is FAREWELL!"

Zsa Zsa Gabor was also aboard. During the last ninety minutes of the flight into Boston's Logan airport—where the plane would stop before continuing on to Washington—the vain actress locked herself in the ladies' room to doll up her appearance. "Jackie got madder and madder," said Aileen. "[S]he wanted to go in there, and so by the time we landed we were really ready to kill Zsa Zsa Gabor." Despite her apparent ambivalence about marriage, Jackie told Aileen, "I wonder if he will be there."

Meanwhile, Senator Kennedy had called Janet to find out what flight Jackie was on to Washington. "I'm going to meet her there," he told Janet.

Flattering herself, Gabor later claimed Jack first saw and embraced *her* in the terminal before Jackie, but according to Aileen, when she and Jackie arrived, he was "there, sitting on a counter," offering a "very formal greeting."

If he was finally clear in his intention to marry, even without being declarative, Jackie was now evasive in giving him a definite response. In line with his family ethos to always win, having gone as far as he'd ever dared to on a matter of love, Jack Kennedy was not going to let himself be turned down. "I don't know how he ever got himself to do it," Billings mused. "He wouldn't like to say all those things that are important if you want a girl to marry you. He'd just rather have it happen without talking about it. Probably that's the way it happened."

When Mini Rhea asked her directly if Jack Kennedy had "popped the question" in the airline terminal, Jacqueline Bouvier responded characteristically.

"Something like that."

31

ENGAGEMENT

June 1953

Though Jack Kennedy had not officially asked for Jackie Bouvier's hand in marriage, she was certain enough about her future with him to know it was the beginning of the end of her time as the Inquiring Camera Girl. She reported back to work on Thursday, June 11, and for two days, it seems, on the eleventh and twelfth, she hit the streets with her camera and questions, quickly preparing about six more columns. She also trained copy girl Dale Chestnut, who would take over from her. "At that point in my life," she would reflect, "what I wanted more than anything else in the world was to be married to him."

However, evidence suggests that she was not ready to give up hope of staying on with the *Times-Herald* as a contributor. Before she had left for Europe, Waldrop had given her a vague promise that she was welcome back at the paper even if she got married.

In her final months as the Inquiring Camera Girl, Jackie had continued to ask questions that reflected what was on her mind: "What money-saving tips would you suggest to young housewives?" "What feature would you most like to see in a new home?" "What cooking tips would you give to brides?" Probing further, there were some questions that reflected consideration of how Mummy had raised her. "Do you believe in spanking children?" "What changes do you plan to make in raising your children from the way you had been brought up?"

In her penultimate published column, she asked, "What would you like to do if you didn't have to work for a living?" All six of the responses she chose to include echoed Jackie's own ambitions. Corporal Anthony Taglieri thought "it would be exciting and educational to visit the places where all the great historical events took place." Café employee Doug Macy wanted to live on a yacht for a while, but, "Most of all, I would like to spend my time meeting and talking to interesting people." After marrying and raising a family, bookkeeper Myra Rose hoped to "pass my time writing books and stories about the places I'd been and the people I'd met."

For Jackie's last published column, which appeared on Wednesday, June 17, her question was more broad, though still topical: "How has television affected your reading habits?"

AFTER JACKIE'S FINAL DAY in the office, Friday, June 12, she headed up to Newport. There, Jack officially proposed to her on either Saturday, June 13, or Sunday, June 14 (though almost certainly on the Saturday, since he was in Boston on Sunday to participate in a radio forum on the Taft-Hartley Act at 2:30 p.m.), formalizing his intentions in the company of Mummy and Unk. Even after this traditional proposal, Jackie waited until the following weekend before formally accepting, according to accounts in the Sunday, June 28, *Boston Sunday Post* and *Boston Sunday Herald*. She delayed until she had time "to talk matters over," as the *Boston Globe*'s Joan McPartlin put it. With whom and about what? As suggested in remarks she made to *Boston Herald Traveler* reporter Virginia Bohlin and by those she was close to at that time, she was stalling because she first wanted some verbal assurance from Waldrop about what possible arrangements he would commit to that would give her the option of contributing articles to the *Times-Herald*. That said, nobody who knew Jackie expected that Waldrop's answer would stop the engagement from going forward.

Jackie remained in Newport after the formal proposal, and the following weekend Jack returned, this time with his mother. En route to Sunday lunch on June 21 at Bailey's Beach Club, the two matrons, Janet and Rose, sat in the front seat "in their hats and pearls and white gloves chattering away about the wedding," while the couple sat, Jackie recalled, "in the back seat, sort of like two bad children," Jack in an undershirt and slippers, Rose "mortified at the sight her son presented." Later, while the engaged couple were swimming, Rose came to call her son out of the water for lunch, but Jackie thought he reacted like a child by ignoring his mother. Rose persisted, loudly yelling his name with her flat Boston accent, until the thirty-five-year-old U.S. senator emerged, muttering, "Yes, Mother."

Jackie's half brother, Jamie, recalled that the Ambassador had "sent his wife" to open "this really rather difficult discussion" with Mummy about wedding plans, with the Kennedys insisting that a large press contingency must be accommodated at the church and reception. "Her mother was so sensitive to having publicity of any kind," Rose Kennedy wrote of Janet. "She thought it was demeaning and vulgar. Mr. Kennedy said in our case there'll have to be reporters at the wedding because he [Jack] was a public figure." As Jamie put it, however, "[M]y mother stood up to all of the ambassador's demands"—at least, until Joe Kennedy showed up himself in Newport, three weekends later.

Janet's willful strength was formidable enough to frighten most people from challenging her, but as Jack's friend Red Fay put it, the Ambassador was a "dominant figure in almost everything he did." Even Jamie, then six years old, sensed a battle brewing as Joe entered Hammersmith, "an alien force invading our happy isle." Before the talks even began, Jackie cannily predicted the outcome. Observing the Ambassador purposefully stride toward Janet at the airport, she recalled thinking to herself, "Oh, Mummy, you don't stand a chance."

Early in the negotiating, Janet surrendered a key psychological point when, after Jack's father told her she could call him "Joe," she insisted on addressing him as "Ambassador." As her son Jamie would say, it was "a title that was a little bit more fearsome than Mr. President." Early in the conversation, however, he transitioned from formally calling her "Mrs. Auchincloss" in the course of flattering her pride, saying, "These are the most beautiful lawns and gardens I've ever seen—*Janet*." Yusha smiled recalling it. "I think she must have felt like she'd been stung by a hive of bees." The Ambassador's dominance thus established, her acquiescence was inevitable.

Joe led Janet to understand that this was not just the wedding of their children but the coronation of a couple who would become a new force in American life. Inviting influential individuals to the celebration who could help them, from the local to the national level, would win their loyalty for the intended ascent. The engagement and then the wedding would be the opening scenes in the next act of Joseph P. Kennedy Productions' grand drama. He would direct the key actors and ornament the stage, intent on captivating not only the guests in attendance but a national audience of voters who would stay tuned, listening on the radio, watching on movie newsreels, and reading all about it in newspapers and magazines. Like his son, the Ambassador could exercise enormous charm, and to further erode the adversarial dynamic, he made Janet an associate producer of his show, deferring respectfully to her success as a hostess.

Expressing an uncharacteristic reverence for the sacrament of holy matrimony, the Ambassador immediately offered a seeming concession to decorum by agreeing not to permit the press into the church during the ceremony. He wasn't giving much away; it was too dim inside to get clear images without a glaring flash. Instead, one photographer would be stationed just inside the entrance to capture a long view of the exchange of vows, showing the couple at the altar from behind. Only after the married couple emerged into the sunshine would they be exposed to dozens of photographers wielding still and movie cameras.

The reception was another story. "One of his requirements was that there be a separate tent and that tent would have cigars and whiskey served to the working press. And there would be a lot of phone lines and typewriters put in there," recalled Jamie. The Ambassador added one more, seemingly insignificant demand: he wanted the reporters to be served lunch, but only ham sandwiches. That provoked Janet—the press could scandalize society by claiming that the hostess of Hammersmith was stingy. As Jamie recalled, "My mother insisted any member of the press that attended the wedding get the same invitation that anybody else had and that they be part of the wedding party and enjoy the same food and drinks as the rest. And if they really needed to make a telephone call, they could just use our phone. And, as it turned out, she won that demand and the members of the press were absolutely delighted."

Still, during and even after her meeting with the Ambassador, Janet remained resistant to the size of the invitation list. "One hundred Irish politicians! The wedding will be just awful—quite dreadful," she shrieked to her "amused daughter." As late as August 6, the *Boston Globe* would be asserting, "Members of the family have consistently stated that the wedding will be a quiet, simple ceremony with families of the principals and a few close friends present." The Ambassador let Mummy persist in maintaining that public facade of exclusivity, at least until the first of September, when invitations went out to 750 guests for the church and another 1,200 for the reception. As some of Janet's fear of the crowd may have had more to do with cost than numbers, Joe offered to underwrite the entire production. (He never disclosed if, or to what degree, Janet accepted.) To the public, the tradition of a bride's family assuming responsibility for the wedding was upheld. If he did entirely cover the event, the Ambassador's pride was not injured; on the contrary, by affirming the Auchincloss wealth in the public's eye, Joe Kennedy only furthered the impression he was crafting of Jackie Bouvier as an "heiress."

The Ambassador also focused on the bride. The mythic "Kennedy publicity machine" was, in reality, a more boutique operation than it was made out to be. Still, one week after Jackie's byline disappeared from the *Times-Herald*, her name was blaring on its front page in a feature about her "storybook romance." It was all by design.

Drawing on his decades in the film industry, real estate, banking, and diplomacy, the engine that drove the "machine" was the Ambassador's deft judgment on what appealed to the general public. It was enlarged by his network of colleagues, from media moguls William Randolph Hearst and Henry Luce to journalists such as Krock and Waldrop.

Another important component of the machine was a man by the name of John C. Dowd, who headed his own Boston advertising and public relations firm with partner Edward D. Parent. Described as a "trim, dapper Irishman with a pencil mustache," the fifty-two-year-old former newspaperman had opened the agency in 1927, with clients to include the *Boston Globe*, Seagram's, Revlon, the Red Cross, and Alitalia Airlines. The Ambassador first worked with Dowd when he gave him the account of his Somerset Importers, the American firm that received the first rights to distribute British whiskey and gin after Prohibition ended. By 1953, John C. Dowd Inc. was one of the nation's largest advertising agencies, employing some forty people in his Boston office.

Dowd employee Mark Dalton was hired in 1948 to help run Jack's first congressional campaign and was even named as campaign manager, while the Dowd agency also assisted with newspaper and billboard ads brilliantly targeting veterans and their parents. They did an equally impressive job with Jack's Senate campaign. To get around campaign contribution and usage regulations, the Ambassador paid the Dowd agency only in cash.

Dowd appreciated the Ambassador's decisiveness, recalling his mantra, "Do it quickly, and do it with every goddamn comma in place." Every word used in Dowd's press releases about the Kennedys was written with close consideration of its impact. Nothing was haphazard.

For publicity around the engagement, the Ambassador likely proposed the strategy and approved the press release, craftily wording it to state that, "Mr. and Mrs. Hugh D. Auchincloss . . . announce the engagement of Mrs. Auchincloss's daughter. . . ." Only after naming Jackie's prestigious education at Miss Porter's, Vassar, and the Sorbonne (without mention of her graduating from GWU) was her father acknowledged. Her French ancestry was emphasized through her being bestowed with the dual branding of both immigrant and colonial ancestry, with the false statements that her "paternal family came from Grenoble, France," and that one of them fought "under General Rochambeau in the American War of Independence." Her Catholicism was made clear with mention of her being related to "Mother Katherine Drexel of Philadelphia, the distinguished founder of the Order of the Blessed Sacrament."

Jackie was assured that the press release would not be issued until Friday, June 26, to give her more time to reach Waldrop to explore the option of contributing to the *Times-Herald*. Instead, the public relations firm sent it out to the international wire services and national, state, and local newspapers on Wednesday, June 24. Given the precision with which the Ambassador expected his media strategy to be executed, it seemed unlikely to have been a mistake.

In just the sixth line of the two-page release, she may have found a clue as to why the news was being rushed out earlier than she was promised it would be: "Until recently, Miss Bouvier, 23, was employed as a news reporter by the *Washington Times-Herald*." With that statement published across the country, it was a fait accompli. Jackie was being forced to give up her job.

At seven on Thursday morning, June 25, *Boston Globe* reporter Elizabeth Watts found her way to Hammersmith, with the help of a gas station attendant who told her, "You couldn't ask for a brighter, nicer girl." The family chauffeur chimed in, "She's shy but very talented and very clever. Knows a lot about what's going on." Already there had been articles about the engagement in numerous papers and reports on the radio. Watts found Jackie packing her suitcase, having to first catch a twelve-minute flight in a two-seat plane from Newport to Providence and then travel on to New York, where she would stay overnight with her sister, lunch with her father, meet Jack at LaGuardia Airport on Friday evening, then fly to Hyannis with him. The sudden publicity was "a little frightening," and she was "awed by the messages" inundating her. "It's been hard on my mother because the telephone just hasn't stopped ringing."

"Things are a little confusing right now," Jackie revealed about her state of mind that morning. "To tell you the truth I didn't expect the wedding announcement to be made public until Friday of this week. But, now, having read the morning newspapers I find it difficult to add anything to the story."

A *Daily News* piece that appeared the same morning, June 25, contained personal details beyond the bounds of the flattering press release. Written by Ruth Montgomery of the paper's Washington bureau, it stated that "not long after she met the tousle-haired Kennedy . . . Miss Bouvier broke off her engagement to John G.W. Husted," leaving him "just in the nick of time" for the "son of a multi-millionaire," casting a false impression. Montgomery also inaccurately stated that Jackie was "an heiress." Almost randomly it mentioned Jack's "stomach disorder" and the fact that he had once missed a scheduled appointment with British foreign secretary Anthony Eden because he had forgotten about it.

At some point on Friday June 26, Jackie put in another call to the *Times-Herald*, attempting to locate Waldrop, who was still on the road, away from Washington. Years later, he said he did not remember receiving any message she might have left with other staff members, asking him to ring her back. As it turned out, the paper's fiscal issues were severe enough that within a year it would be defunct, and bought up by the *Washington Post*. But Jackie would long associate marriage with being led to relinquish her work. "If I hadn't married, I might have had a life very much like Gloria Emerson's," Jackie later observed about her friend who "started out in Paris writing about fashion—and then ended up as a correspondent in Vietnam."

Jack would joke that he married her to "get rid of the competition," telling her, "One writer in the family is enough." True as that may have been, Joe Kennedy viewed every situation through the lens of whether it furthered his long game of getting his son elected to the presidency or impeded it. Clearly, he wasn't fundamentally against women who worked—his daughters all held jobs before marriage—but even for a family that lived outside the boundaries by which Middle America abided, the patriarch viewed a married woman's primary role as that of wife and mother. More importantly, he held the view that voters would want that role reflected in the family of those they elected to higher office.

The Dowd agency sent out a winsome "engagement" photo of Jackie with its press release. It also released for publication in newspapers a number of other photos that depicted Jackie precisely as the Ambassador wanted her presented. The front page of the *Boston American* for Friday, June 26, for example, carried two large pictures of her, competing in a riding contest and posing in her debutante gown.

Jackie reached out to many friends to personally share the news and invite them to the wedding. In Paris, the now-married Claude de Renty was expecting her first child and unable to make the trip. Having just given birth, Vivi Crespi also sent regrets. Nor would the frail Bernard Berenson come from Italy, but Jackie mailed him photos of her and Jack. Although Father Leonard would be unable to preside at the wedding, she sent a telegram with the news, signing off, "So Happy, Love Jacqueline." John White RSVP'd yes, later recalling that he would only believe she was marrying when he saw her walk down the aisle.

With the engagement, Yusha discreetly conveyed to his father Jackie's one great intention, that Unk and Black Jack use "that occasion to bridge the gap and shared a toast to the bride." Janet stopped the idea cold. "It was a deep disappointment to Jackie that this was not to be and a shock that her father [was] not . . . welcome." According to Lee, Mummy actively discouraged Black Jack from coming at all. "My mother had written him telling him she hoped he realized that he was far from welcome and that he might change his mind and decide not to come," she told Jackie's biographer Sarah Bradford, "and she felt that this would be a far more appropriate thing for him to do. . . . A woman's revenge is relentless."

The next afternoon, according to plan, Kennedy flew from Washington to LaGuardia, where Jackie was scheduled to meet him, and they would catch the last flight to Hyannis together. Alerted to the time both were expected, reporters and photographers were waiting at LaGuardia as Jack arrived, "in plenty of time." Then they waited. The senator waited. As departure time approached, an embarrassed Jack was "craning his neck," looking for the absent Jackie. "Hasn't been seen," airport attendants kept updating him. The Northeast Airlines puddle-jumper to Hyannis was the last of the day and rather than wait for her, he left word that she should fly to Boston, rent a car, and drive to Hyannis. "Guess she won't make it," he sighed. As he strode to the foot of the portable stairs of the small plane, about to enter, a "taxi screeched to a halt," according to the *Boston Globe*. "Out stepped Miss Bouvier, breathless and apologetic." Her cab had been trapped in a traffic jam. Jack turned to the reporters: "Just the first of many, I guess, as you married men must know." Wearing a tan gabardine dress with a lapel buttoned diagonally across her chest as she stood beside the beaming senator at the foot of the plane, Jackie did not smile along with him, looking stunned that such a mundane moment merited press coverage and public attention.

She did know, however, that over the weekend at the Kennedy family home in Hyannis, she and Jack would be posing for engagement photographs as part of a carefully orchestrated media day, with photographers and reporters from across the country in attendance.

Perhaps the most iconic of the images was taken by Hy Peskin for *Life*, the nation's leading magazine at the time. Although the Ambassador's friend Henry Luce was no longer the publisher, Luce retained influence. Likely through Luce, the legendary Peskin was assigned to snap photographs of the couple for a cover story.

On Saturday morning, Jackie, dressed in a sleeveless yellow blouse, pink shorts, and blue ballet slippers, made her way out to the lawn with Jack. She then changed into a checkered blouse and later a bathing suit as alternative outfits and was put through a series of staged scenarios which evoked athleticism. With Jack's brothers, sisters, and sister-in-law, she played softball and touch football. She was seated with his sisters on the lawn and on the porch, then depicted inside the Kennedy family home with Jack, and alone in playful poses with her sunhat.

After these photo sessions exclusive to *Life*, other news photographers were also invited to capture the couple in two other settings. First, Jack and Jackie headed to the beach, photographed from various angles together, seated and walking along the shore, Jack skipping stones. Then she and Jack took off in his sailboat, the *Victura*. One image from this series would make the cover of *Life*, for the accompanying story, "The Senator Goes A-Courting," published on July 20. "They just shoved me into that boat long enough to take the picture," Jackie later confessed.

In the afternoon, she changed into her tan dress, pearl necklace, gold chain bracelet, earrings, black patent leather pumps, and a belt embroidered with the phrase BATS IN THE BELFRY, for more photos. Jack put on a suit. First, the couple posed inside the house again for exclusive *Life* images. A few vignettes, intended to forecast their life together, had Jackie pouring Jack a cup of coffee at the breakfast table, another tousling his hair, another gazing adoringly at him as he spoke while she sat on the floor with him in a chair, and some showing her looking at framed family photos on the wall.

Then it was outside again, onto the green lawn in front of the large clapboard house and porch, an American flag snapping in the background. According to reporters, the couple "obliged news reel and still photographers" for "two hours under a blistering hot sun," as they "held hands frequently and exchanged smiles throughout the proceedings at the request of the cameraman" for a "rapid succession of pictures." They strolled the garden, sat on the lawn, then changed clothes to play tennis and take out a smaller sailboat "just big enough for two." For weeks on end, images of the couple taken that day would be repeatedly published in newspapers large and small across the country.

As planned, the photo session was also an informal press conference, during which the couple "related to reporters some of the details of their love story." Using his trademark self-deprecatory wit, Jack managed to affirm two things that were becoming important to defining Jackie's emerging public identity, while also discussing what they had in common, and what they didn't. "Jacqueline speaks French like a native . . . I speak some French. No, we've never tried to converse in that language. Then there's horseback riding. She loves that. No, I didn't take up horseback riding. But there's movies. We both love movies. We'd have Sunday night supper with Bob and Ethel and then we'd all go to the movies."

When asked about Jack's work, Jackie seemed unsure of what to say. She had already wisely declared herself newly loyal to the Kennedy party, proclaiming days earlier, "I guess I'm a Democrat now." That day, she told the *Life* reporter, "We hardly ever talk politics," but then said she "knew the state's problems quite thoroughly. Jack has kept me well informed on that score." Before she could potentially mention her Vietnam project, Jack interrupted: "I'm quite sure that once we're married, she'll become just as interested in Massachusetts affairs and international problems as I am."

Some newspaper accounts hinted at his womanizing, the *Boston Herald* declaring that many of his friends were shocked at the news because he had "recently been seen in company with several young ladies at different affairs," while the *Boston Evening American* referenced "false reports of a romance between Kennedy and several other girls."

The "false reports" being referenced likely included a Walter Winchell "On-Broadway" column that appears to have first been printed on June 15, in which Jack and socialite Estelle Cordell of New York were said to have been spotted together at Central Park's Tavern on the Green. A syndicated column, the gossip appeared throughout the nation's newspapers, at the same time as columnist Dorothy Kilgallen reported, "Actress K.K. Kensington flew to Washington to keep dates with Senator Jack Kennedy."

Jack Kennedy countered these suggestions with a romanticized narrative of his and Jackie's courtship, though one that was still short on actual romance. At one point, as Jackie told reporters that their dating had been "off and on," he interjected that "this was the only serious dating he had ever done in his life." He crunched the timeline of their relationship, suggesting that as soon as her summer 1951 European vacation was over, he took her out to dinner at the Shoreham Blue Room, when in fact it was five months later. "When she came back, I called her up one day and we have gone together ever since," he said. Asked how she would adapt to his being a senator, he suggested she'd campaigned at his side all through the 1952 campaign, rather than just coming for a few days. As far as his intentions to marry her were concerned, he piped up, "It was just understood we were going to get married sooner or later." With subtle assertions in his seemingly casual responses that Saturday afternoon, Jack Kennedy began shaping the narrative of what he foresaw as a presidential marriage, while the flag flew high behind him.

For good measure, he added that "[t]he folks are all for her." And looking perhaps a bit too rehearsed, suddenly the folks appeared, his mother coming down to briefly speak with reporters. (When Rose Kennedy showed Jackie how to stand with one arm behind her back to look slimmer, a reporter thought that Jackie "bristled at the intrusion.") Before exiting the scene to go to lunch with her friend Marjorie McDermott, Rose told reporters about Jackie, "She's a very lovely girl and so very sweet."

Boston Sunday Advertiser reporter Jean Cole gushed that the "romance has intrigued the nation." When she asked why Jackie wasn't wearing an engagement ring, the bride-to-be shrugged. "We're still looking. Jack and I have looked at dozens of them. Some I didn't like and others weren't the right type." In the end, it would not be her future husband, but rather her future father-in-law, who chose the ring, with his friend Louis Arpels, founder of the legendary jewelry store that carried his name: a 2.84-carat emerald and 2.88-carat diamond on a platinum band.

When it came to the dress, the Ambassador took control once again, this time teaming up with Mummy. Jackie had sketched out her own design for a slim, modernistic gown, but it was allegedly the Ambassador who determined it must be "old-fashioned." Janet did the bidding, hiring native Alabamian dressmaker Ann Lowe, a Black woman who served only the most elite Social Register families. The result had a massive skirt festooned with bows. It was, Jackie would recall, "the dress my mother wanted me to wear and I hated it," joking that she "looked like a lampshade."

Publicity was a matter of primal instinct for Jack. Three months earlier, he had even invited the television cameras of Boston's WBZ-TV into his Washington home for an interview, a move Jackie would consider a violation of privacy. "It makes me uncomfortable," she would truthfully admit seven years later, "to read about myself in the paper."

A *Boston Post* reporter, observing how "reserved" she was, attributed it to the enormity of the stakes she would now be playing for in her imminent marriage. "It was obvious," he concluded, "that she realizes the responsibility she will have in marrying a man whose political potential is unlimited and whose family is one of the first of the land."

As she posed, Jackie struck up conversations with the photographers. "Smile," one of them told her. "Forget the camera." She laughed: "I can't forget it." Another one piped up, "Now you know how it feels to be on the other side of the camera." In an unguarded remark, she told *Boston Sunday Herald* reporter Percy Williams, "Everything has happened so fast that

I'm a bit overwhelmed. I have always been on the other side of stories like this, doing the interviewing and photographing myself."

The idea planted, that's precisely what she did. In an instant she broke from the script and spontaneously retrieved her camera—that trusted little Leica that she had first managed to get for herself in the summer of 1949. Earlier that day, when Jack had pulled out the small two-seat sailboat for a photo op, Jackie had brought her large clunky Graflex, the instrument that immediately identified her in Washington as the Inquiring Camera Girl. It was an attempt to tell her own story, and let people know who she was. But the camera was too incongruous for the scenario; she instinctively saw it made for an odd picture for her to be holding it on a boat, and after taking one or two photographs of Jack, shin-deep in the water, she put it away. Now, however, as she and Jack rose from sitting on the green lawn, she would do it right. This time, she positioned Jack at a slight distance and began snapping away. And the photographers and newsreel cameramen whose pictures would be almost immediately seen around the world snapped Jackie as she snapped Jack.

Jackie had taken control of the moment by making a spontaneous move. She now brought the Leica down from her face and, while keeping the strap around her neck, showed how it worked to her smiling, but seemingly startled, future husband, giving "a few pointers on candid camera photography."

The slight movement was nevertheless a significant shift. The photographs and film of her photographing him and then explaining and showing him just how the camera worked captured a brief moment of the Inquiring Camera Girl becoming an assertively equal partner on her own terms.

32

PARTNER

July–September 1953

Less than forty-eight hours after charming the national press at Hyannis, Jackie was back in Washington with Jack, already integrating her life into his, as he prepared to deliver his first public remarks as senator on an issue of great importance to them both: France's war in Indochina.

On Tuesday, June 30, Kennedy took to the Senate floor and delivered a long, detailed argument which directly drew from the substantial work Jackie had done for him. He was urging an amendment to the Mutual Security Act, which dictated the terms that administered $400 million in foreign aid to France—money earmarked for the fight against North Vietnamese Communists. He explained that the amendment would "encourage the freedom and independence desired" by the people of the three Indo-Chinese nations. His argument was "based upon the irrefutable evidence of the accords and treaties," which Jackie had analyzed and collated. The written copy of his speech reveals that four paragraphs on page two, six paragraphs on page three, three paragraphs on page four, and two paragraphs on page five were all taken directly from Jackie's Vietnam report. Further, the democratic ideals which resonated through his whole speech had been influenced by the ethical arguments and logical rigor expressed by the former newspaper columnist seated in the diplomatic gallery looking down at him. Only he knew it, but it was enough.

Immediately after the speech, Jack and Jackie caught a plane to join the Ambassador in Chicago, for a "Merchants of America Hall of Fame" ceremony at his Merchandise Mart building over which the Ambassador and Gramps Lee had their falling-out. While Joe spoke in soaring platitudes about the drive and progress of the great capitalists who generated the nation's leading businesses, Jack's remarks had a startlingly different tone, his Senate speech of several hours earlier clearly still on his mind. "The greatest peril to a peaceful settlement of the issues in southeast Asia is the white man himself," he declared, perhaps including the British and the Americans along with the French in his judgment. "This is because the white man has not recognized the desire of the people there, particularly in Vietnam for freedom."

It was an unexpected angle on the issue for him, but it revealed the passion with which he was committed to Vietnamese independence. Based on the excerpts Jackie had translated, it was a sentiment with which she agreed.

On July 2, Kennedy's proposal to amend the Mutual Security Act was defeated in a Senate vote of 64 to 17, but he was not to be deterred. He regrouped and waited for another opportunity to challenge the U.S. government's support of the war in Vietnam.

Jack and Jackie returned to Washington, and then on Friday, July 3, Evelyn Lincoln recorded that the Senate adjourned early and Jack intended to go up and play golf in Hyannis. He told Jackie to meet him at the airport, but she spent the day browsing housewares, appearing at his Senate office instead, just as Jack was calling to find out where she was, furious she had made him miss the plane. Lincoln put Jackie on the phone with him. Her face sank as he chewed her out.

After spending Independence Day weekend in Hyannis, they returned to Washington, where on Wednesday they joined the Bartletts and Senator Cooper at Lorraine Shevlin's home for a buffet dinner on her terrace. The star couple of the gathering, however, was not Jack and Jackie, but Vice President and Mrs. Nixon. Pat Nixon wrote in her diary that after dinner they all went to the National Theater to see the popular musical comedy *Guys and Dolls*. "Met Senator Kennedy's fiancée," Pat Nixon wrote, "a darling girl." Having such access to powerful national and international leaders would be another aspect of Jackie's new life, providing an informal social venue for her to lobby on behalf of issues important to Jack—or to her.

There was also a private engagement party held for Jack and Jackie by friends, which indicated to some that Jackie was struggling with aspects of her new life. "I think she was still trying to decide if marriage was the best thing for her," Aileen Bowdoin concluded after talking with her at the party. "I do think she was really worried about her life and the future in politics. And she was still mad about having to quit her job."

The couple returned to Newport on Friday, July 10. Jackie remained at Hammersmith while Jack returned to Washington on Monday, and she was still there on Tuesday when she learned the news that Jack had had to be suddenly hospitalized. It's unknown whether she had yet been informed of the full extent of his myriad health problems, but either way it was distressing to realize that her young, athletic fiancé of just two weeks was sick enough to be rushed to a hospital. His staff told the Associated Press it was for a "war-related malady," and the *Boston Herald* learned he had "recurring malarial chills and fever."

The Ambassador did not seem alarmed, and he was likely the one who called Jackie and told her she needn't go to Washington. That day, she went to her scheduled engagement at Boston's Hotel Statler alone, for a Bastille Day dinner dance, marking the "great French holiday" and posing for newspaper photos with French consul François Charles-Roux. As the Ambassador likely saw, it was a chance for her to make her first public appearances as Jack's representative.

Jack recovered enough to rest at Hyannis the following weekend, while Jackie was sent again to stand in for him, this time posing for pictures as she went to Worcester on Sunday to present a $150,000 check from the Joseph P. Kennedy Jr. Foundation to Assumption College, which had been partially destroyed by a recent tornado. As she was uncomfortable about being on display, it was a blessing for her that the appearances were brief. At the Bastille Day event, she could slip away from the crowds without much notice. When she was with Jack, it would be different. Their wedding had made that clear.

On the last weekend of July, the couple, along with the Ambassador and Jack's siblings, attended a housewarming party in New York for Jackie's sister and brother-in-law. Jackie and Jack returned to Washington that week, then went to Newport, where they were feted at a dinner hosted by Claiborne and Nuala Pell, with Congressman Frank Roosevelt (son of FDR and Eleanor) and his wife Suzanne as guests. For her birthday, July 28, Jack brought Jackie three jeweled bracelets loaned to him from Tiffany, from which he would buy the one she chose.

While Jackie remained in Newport, Jack stayed in Washington after Congress adjourned and attended the funeral of Senator Robert Taft. On Wednesday, August 5, he sailed with Torb MacDonald to, one paper said, "spend his last month of bachelor life traveling through Europe."

Despite Kennedy's having, before the engagement, publicly announced his intention of going to France once Congress adjourned because of his "personal interest in the conversations being held on French Indo-China," he was criticized for going. "No man in love does something like that," Mummy complained to Jackie, egged on by her friend Betty Beale, the columnist, who added, "I told her [Jackie] she shouldn't so readily allow that; she should have gone with him."

Jackie didn't react, because she wasn't upset—she viewed marital partnership differently than her mother. In fact, by accepting Jack's freedom to take trips without her, she signaled her own intent to do so when she wished. Their long periods apart, she would indicate in one of the few extant letters she sent him, written several years later, forced them to recognize how much they meant to each other: "[I]t is hard for me to communicate which you do so beautifully. . . . I can't write down what I feel for you, but I will show you when I am with you—and I think you must know . . . I think it is usually good when we go away from each other as we both realize so much," she wrote, also acknowledging his disinclination to examine how he felt about her, while she was all too eager to do so. "We are so different—but I was thinking this trip—that every other time I've been away, you would write 'don't ponder our relationship too much' etc."

Distinctly unromantic, Kennedy qualified his inability to easily express emotion by claiming it was a result of his mother being unemotional and rarely expressing affection to him. By accepting this deficiency in him, Jackie realized she was just as unusual: "You are an atypical husband—increasingly so in one way or another every year since we've been married—so you mustn't be surprised to have an atypical wife—Each of us would have been so lonely with the normal kind." Jack and Jackie protected the other in times of crisis, but the first instinct of each was also to protect him- or herself, and they each expected the other to do so. "She told a friend that she and Jack were both like icebergs with the greater part of their lives invisible," Kennedy biographer Ralph Martin later wrote. "She felt they both sensed this in each other and that this was a bond between them."

Jackie knew that he and Torb were chartering a yacht to sail the south coast of France, then visit Sweden and England. It's unlikely, however, that she knew that while in the South of France, he first met and declared his love to a Swedish woman named Gunilla von Post. Yet, uncharacteristically, he was not sexually intimate with her, as his letters to von Post documented.

Jackie was secure in her belief that he loved her as he did no other woman. She later offered advice in a letter to the former Joan Bennett, Jack's brother Teddy's first wife, after Teddy had also become a U.S. senator:

"Don't explain apologetically. . . . This is the 20th century—not 19th—where little woman stayed home on pedestal. . . . Your life matters—as much as his—you love him—but you can't destroy yourself—You want a life of sharing . . . [not] . . . to wait quietly in the other room while he & aides discuss his problems—then he can have his girls on the side. . . . You're no prude or fool . . . [but] men under pressure have to let off steam sometimes—that's why even the Catholic Church has carnival. . . . What kind of woman, but a sap or a slave, can stand that & still be a loving wife—& care about him & work like a dog for him campaigning? It is so old fashioned—probably got it from his father. . . . Forbidden fruit is what is exciting.

"It takes much more of a real man to have a deep relationship with the woman he lives with. The routine of married life can become boring. . . . Get out of the house. . . . Don't explain where you will be, don't speak of yourself as a delicate health problem—Don't ask permission. . . . Be a bit mysterious—so he never knows exactly when you are going away or coming back—when you may walk into the house at home returning early from a trip . . . then he can't plan things around your absence. . . . Go places with him—fun places. . . . Go on foreign trips with him. . . . It will be hard for him to tell you you can't come. . . . Don't let him assume that you are Old Faithful. . . . Take vacations with your friends—not the family."

As she would summarily acknowledge in an oft-quoted remark, "Since Jack is such a violently independent person, and I, too, am so independent, this marriage will take a lot of working out."

Being married to a powerful politician would give her the larger life she craved. It would be a way of fulfilling the vague ambitions she'd had as a younger woman—to be "queen of the circus" and "Overall Art Director of the Twentieth Century." Like the women of the eighteenth-century French courts who intrigued her, she could change history, whether credited for it or not. She could become both participant in and observer of important turning points in the story of civilization, guiding the narrative without leaving a fingerprint. As she would later further explain in a letter to her sister-in-law Joan:

"You endure the bad things, but you enjoy the good. And what incredible opportunities—the historic figures you meet and come to know, the witness to history you become, the places you would never have been able to see that now you can. One could never have such a life if one wasn't married to someone like that.

"If the trade-off is too painful, then you just have to remove yourself, or you have to get out of it. But if you truly love someone, you recognize it as an emotional problem that isn't about you personally. In trying to accept and understand these men as they are, you will also grow as a person. Every day with them may be torture and yet every day with them is a chance to change the world in large and small ways. You can have the most influence over historic events if you're not seeking credit but that also gives you the ultimate golden opportunity of power without the responsibility they must carry."

AS THE WEDDING DATE approached, Jack Kennedy sought advice on how to be a husband, writing Red Fay with a droll but realistic air that marriage might mean "the end of a promising political career as it has been up to now almost completely based on the old sex appeal. . . . As I am both too young and too old for all this, I will need several long talks on how to conduct yourself during the first six months, based on your actual real-life experience."

Jackie seemed more interested in absorbing all she could from the multitasking Ambassador as he stage-managed the wedding. The buffet luncheon would consist of open-faced chicken potpie, sliced ham, mixed green salad, hot rolls, fruit cups, molded ice cream, and petits fours. Endless numbers of guests continued to be added to the list; Pat Kennedy's beau, the British actor Peter Lawford, submitted eighteen names of *his* guests. Jackie went to Fall River to order the wedding cake—during his campaign, Jack had promised a local baker, Azarius Plourde, that when the day came, he would ask him to make it.

Jackie hired a temporary secretary, Katherine Donovan, to help her with the phone calls, letters, telegrams, and boxes of gifts that began to inundate her. Mummy tried to help with responses but told the young woman, "My writing gets worse each day. Jackie had better write them herself."

Aileen Bowdoin later reflected that the period between the engagement and the wedding "was the turning point for her going from private life to public life. I think she got cast into public life and [was] finding [out] quickly that she was really not enjoying it that much. She probably knew so ahead of time, too, but she made up her mind that she was going to make her mark, and that she was going to carry it off, which she certainly did. She was a woman of great determination, and spirit. In politics, she would need it."

Later to become a political wife herself, Aileen recognized the reason Jackie would endure a lifestyle at odds with her natural inclinations: "Never forget one thing. She wanted to help make him president. I don't say this meanly, but she was very ambitious for the presidency and he had what it took to get there but she saw he needed guidance, to be challenged on ideas, try to make every one of his speeches stand out. She built his ego up as nobody did and was extremely defensive of him against anyone. He had the goods, but she shaped them, she really did." Mini Rhea further observed: "Just as Jackie had wanted a career that was purposeful, she wanted a husband whose career was purposeful also."

This tacit recognition among her friends of her ambition to have Jack elected president was widespread. "Well, if he'd just stayed senator, she would have had a rotten time with it," John White asserted. "But she knew what she was doing." And, in time, Jack would also acknowledge that had he been "unsuccessful in his courtship," he would have been unlikely to "have reached the White House."

Even in the days before the wedding, the strength of the couple's ambition was understood. Aileen, along with her sister Bow and Martha Bartlett, performed a song at a Newport party a day or two before the wedding, to the tune of "East Side, West Side." It was about the Democratic groom and the formerly Republican bride: "Donkeys and the elephants strolling down the aisle. To see the greatest union since Caesar barged the Nile . . . They will form a fusion party, to the heights they are bent, they'll win by great majority—Jack for President!" Reports of the song made the papers.

"Jack thinks continually in historic and literary terms," Gore Vidal noted, but he also possessed "the coarse energetic quality that wins battles." Jackie Bouvier was composed of the same elements.

Jackie's experience as a columnist would prove to be better training for politics than it initially seemed, not only because her spontaneous interaction with strangers was exactly what she'd be doing on the campaign trail, but also as a "field course in psychology," as Mini Rhea called it. With her "adroit questioning of people, she had really gotten to learn how people thought."

On the early morning of August 27, Senator Kennedy walked, "fit and tanned," through the PanAm terminal at Boston's Logan Airport, where, though "obviously anxious to get off to Newport to see his fiancée," he stopped to talk with *Boston Globe* reporter Charles Tarbi. He began by referencing his June 30 Senate speech on Vietnam:

"During debates in the Senate on financial aid to France, I introduced an amendment urging that as much independence as possible be granted by the French to the Indo-Chinese people. I went over on August 6 to find out how the French themselves, at governmental levels, felt about it. Indo-China is the key to southeast Asia." He found opinions sharply divided among the French, some calling for withdrawal, others wanting to redouble the fighting against the Communist forces, a few believing the issue should be turned over to the United Nations for debate and resolution.

The amount of factual information in Kennedy's June 30 speech had perhaps proved too overwhelming for not only most of his colleagues to take in but also the journalists who covered the Senate, none of whom mentioned the enormous detail he put into what was typically the kind of speech prepared by staff. Syndicated columnist Holmes Alexander, however, had been noticing how much depth Kennedy brought to the complex issues involving Vietnam, asserting that he "has done a commendable amount of fact-finding to reach his conclusions."

In Alexander's column, based on an interview with Jack, he wrote of the "reference file" Kennedy was building on Vietnam, drawn from interviews he conducted with French military officials during his fall 1951 fact-finding mission to Saigon; books like Philippe de Villier's history of Vietnam, which he purchased during his trip there, and even some novels; and current military and diplomatic analysis in the scholarly publications *Public Affairs* and *World Politics*. It was also in Alexander's column that there came the singular acknowledgment, however brief and vague, of Jackie's Vietnam report. "Kennedy doesn't read French very glibly," Alexander noted in a sentence buried down in his fifth paragraph, "but his fiancée extracts the salient passages from the book and writes them out in translation." It was printed, then forgotten. None of the engagement articles about her mentioned it: they focused on her wedding, her riding, and her debutante ball. Not until the 2014 release of her oral history interview (recorded in 1964), during which she mentioned her Vietnam project, was her essential contribution noticed.

After the engagement, Jackie began to appear more often in Jack's Senate office, but the work she did for him remained behind the scenes. Aide Ted Sorenson recalled her coming to look over his Senate suite and meet the individual members of his staff but said, "Whatever political work she did for him, they kept strictly between them."

There was one person in the Capitol Building, however, with a far clearer idea of just what was going on between Jackie and her fiancé. Fritz Carl "Duke" Zeller was only fourteen when he became a Senate page, but he ran messages all around the Capitol—to and from the senators, between their colleagues and staffs, to their fiancées and wives—and picked up more about the lives of the people in the building than most. He remembered Jackie well; she made a distinct impression:

"She used to come often to the Senate and listen to the speeches and floor action and votes. [She] would sit, more often than not, in the diplomatic gallery, rather than the wives' gallery or family gallery. She would sit right in the center, just dressed very casual, and virtually nobody knew who she was, except inside people, Senate people. The first time I ever remember seeing her, she had on these Capri pants, a sleeveless white blouse, and a scarf over her head. . . . But yet here she was going to Senate deliberations!"

He recalled that she frequently came to entice Jack to have a quick lunch with her outdoors, packing a picnic, which they ate on the Capitol steps or on the lawn. Sometimes she slipped into the Senate reception room, asking Duke to tell Kennedy she was there to speak with him. Soon, Jack would have Duke "take a note up to her in the diplomatic gallery . . . then it got to be, kind of, a usual thing." The page, of course, "didn't read the notes" but soon "waited to see if she had a message for him." Jackie was also there, "listening to the proceedings [when] Senator Kennedy had nothing to do with the debate."

When Kennedy was speaking, however, the Senate page noticed how he often quickly glanced up at her, as if to send a slight signal. "While he was speaking, she was scribbling very quickly, taking notes, then tearing strips of this long yellow office paper and folding it up and having me rush it down to him. I don't know what she wrote him, but I passed them to him immediately, whether he was speaking or not. What was she telling him? I really don't know but it would have to be about the speech he was giving. It was just between them."

On April 4, 1954, nine months after Jack's amendment was defeated in the Senate, his moment arrived to reintroduce the issue of Vietnam, and he did so with energy and impact. He delivered a forceful speech, even more strongly demanding U.S. policy that would accelerate that country's independence. It would garner him the first national press coverage that began depicting him as a potential presidential candidate—and it would draw again on Jackie's Vietnam report.

ON SEPTEMBER 12, 1953, Jackie Bouvier committed her life to Jack Kennedy's at the St. Mary's Church altar, but their partnership had already been cemented in the U.S. Senate chamber.

Black Jack was not invited to any parties before the wedding, thanks to Janet's machinations, but in the typed lists of church seating, he was assigned a pew with his twin sisters and their husbands, two rows behind Janet and Unk. The accepted narrative claims that he spent the entire wedding day confined to his Viking Hotel room too intoxicated to participate in the ceremony (Janet having instructed the hotel staff to provide a full bar in his suite). But this was contradicted in a news report appearing exclusively in the *Washington Times-Herald*: a detailed paragraph unambiguously stated that Black Jack gave his daughter away. (Since press were not allowed in the church, the source may have been John White or other former colleagues who were wedding guests.) Under the sub-headline

"Given Away by Father," it read: "As the bride and her train of attendants approached down the center aisle, she was escorted by her stepfather, Hugh Auchincloss. But when they reached the third pew, her own father, John V. Bouvier, III, stepped forth and it was her father who gave the bride away." The presence of Black Jack inside the church would be corroborated by usher Chuck Spalding—who was part of the wedding party along with siblings, close friends Tucky, Lem, the Bartletts, Red Fay, Torb, Aileen, and Bow. Also contrary to popular myth: Gramps Lee attended the festivities. A photo shows him cutting in on his old nemesis Joe Kennedy to dance with Janet.

All of Joe Kennedy's carefully laid media plans had succeeded. The wedding turned Jack and Jackie Kennedy into a national celebrity couple. Pictures of the bride were featured in newspapers across the country and made the front page of the *Boston American*.

CYNICS WOULD INSIST THEIR marriage was entirely transactional, that Jack needed her for publicity and Jackie needed him for his money and power. But their partnership deepened because they shared an intellectual bond and respect, and it was *that* betrothal that would anchor their own version of love.

Being "Mrs. Kennedy" was a hybrid proposition: public and private. Jackie's deliberate, inimitable patterns of speech and movement; her personal charm and flattering attentiveness; her withering wit and scorching irony; her style and impeccable taste—these cumulatively created her intended public persona. But behind the scenes, her husband relied on her analytical, linguistic, and communication skills as crucial factors in their mutual, ambitious pursuit of the presidency.

Jackie wanted to be in the Senate chamber as much as the church. In the formative four years that preceded her marriage, she was influenced and inspired but never led by others. She set her own course. She took her own advice to "figure it out as soon as you can." During this period, she had been defined by people in myriad ways, from Deb of the Year to Inquiring Camera Girl, but never compromised her most meaningful identity: individual. She had, in her own words, "become distinct." Jacqueline Bouvier was determined not to merely witness history. She would make it.

Acknowledgments

First, I want to thank writer Kate Betts, who generously introduced me to her literary representatives at Aevitas Creative Management. Agent David Kuhn and his colleague Nate Muscato, along with Francesca Capossela, fine-tuned my book proposal, overlooking no detail and offering refinements in a way that no agents have ever done with any other proposal of mine; they utterly committed themselves to creating the best possible version. They were judicious in all stages of the process.

This book is the result of equally tireless commitment to excellence provided from the moment I met my editor, Aimée Bell of Gallery Books at Simon & Schuster, and associate editor Max Meltzer. From the start, the entire Simon & Schuster team provided support, patience, and confidence in the project, and I would like to thank Jennifer Bergstrom, publisher; Jennifer Long, deputy publisher; Sally Marvin, director of publicity and marketing; Jennifer Robinson, executive publicist; Mackenzie Hickey, marketer; Jennifer Weidman and Edward Klaris, in legal; Nancy Tonik, production editor; Caroline Pallotta, managing editor; Geoff Shandler, editorial advisor; Scott Ferguson, copy editor; and Jonathan Karp, CEO.

I must especially thank my friends Jason Durtschi and Andrea Smith for helping me get through the extremely trying final weeks of this project. Ditto to Steven Barrow Barlow and Scott Hopkins. As always, Edward

Purcell was both materially and personally supportive of the project. Cory Martin transcribed data and provided observations that gave momentum to the story and was an encouraging confidante during the writing. Evan Carson helped transcribe data as well. Brent Stewart asked wise questions about the story, as did Diane Zelman.

My late father, a contemporary of Bouvier's and likewise raised in New York, answered many questions about the region as it was in the 1930s through the 1950s. My late mother was especially supportive during the six months it took to craft a detailed book proposal, always infusing optimism during what was a highly uncertain period.

Don Harold, like Jackie Bouvier an American student at the Sorbonne, translated a portion of the French textbook she used there. I am greatly appreciative of the time given me—whether over the phone or over dinner—by Claude de Renty du Granrut, Priscilla McMillan, Nina Auchincloss Straight, Mamie Moore, and Martha Bartlett. Claude even invited me to her birthday dinner in Paris, and Mrs. Bartlett hosted me at a wonderful luncheon and tour of her Americana. David Eisenhower and Julie Nixon took me to an autumn lunch in Philadelphia at the start of my research trip and provided a context of early 1950s Washington. Susan Eisenhower was, as always, a compelling dinner date. An individual whose name I failed to notate was working as the front desk guard at the old *Times-Herald* building in early November 2019 and was very helpful. Maya Auchincloss, the daughter of Yusha—without whose interviews and letter collection this book could never have been done—was a delightful conversationalist. I would also like to thank Caroline Kennedy and Lauren Lipani.

I want to thank several archivists, librarians, and historians who were kind in responding quickly to my inquiries: Abigail Malangone, archivist at the John F. Kennedy Presidential Library; Ilaria Della Monica, head archivist at the Harvard University Center for Italian Renaissance Studies; Jeffrey Schlossberg, archivist of the National Press Club; Stéphanie Koenig, documentation manager in the Louvre History Service's Research and Collections Directorate; Derek Gray, Washingtoniana archivist at the DC Public Library, Special Collections; Margaret Phalen, former Octagon House manager; Cynthia Cathcart, director of the Condé Nast Library; Craig G. Wright, supervisory archivist of the Herbert Hoover Presidential Library; Kopana Terry, archivist at the Nunn

Center for Oral History, University of Kentucky Libraries; Dan Hinchen, reference librarian at the Massachusetts Historical Society; Tim Rives, deputy director of the Eisenhower Presidential Library; Gerald Nestler, the Franz Bueb estate manager; Michael Baker, Leica Camera brand ambassador, Los Angeles Gallery; Leah Richardson, Special Collections librarian, George Washington University; and Dan Meader, researcher and curator, McGinnis Auctions. I would like to most especially thank Mary Rose Grossman, JFK Library audiovisual archivist, who went above and beyond in the effort to track down copyrights on many images, and who became a friend. A longtime friend, author Pamela Keogh provided help on the Vassar years.

Kent Bartram of Chicago, who is researching and writing the first full biography of Edith "Little Edie" Bouvier Beale, surpassed all generosity in sharing correspondence between the Beales and Black Jack Bouvier, as well as unknown aspects of Bouvier family history.

Thanks to friends who checked in with great enthusiasm and support: Tim Boyce, Rachel Gluck, Cayman Adams, Joe Guthrie, Claire Sanders Swift, Nancy Hackscaylo, Nathaniel Bradford, Bernd Kroeber, Kevin Brouillard, Jonnie Dokuchitz, James Burnham, Aja Morris-Smiley, James Sherrard, and Vincent Van Zwanenberg. The last three also lent me books and transcribed tapes. During the stretch of writing and research, I lost one of my dearest friends, Diane Monahan, a saintly soul especially supportive of the book. And while dogs comprehend appreciation differently, they express love as fully as we do. Thanking mine is unconventional, but I must mention Hooch, who remains with me, and Hudson, who sat loyally at my side while I wrote the first half of the book—until he was no longer here.

Through some personally difficult periods while writing this book, I relied heavily on the support of Robert Sandoval, Jon Georges, and Laura Mulligan. At the start of the process, both Greg Faktor and Justin Oberts made sacrifices to help things get underway. Other friends with an affinity for and a deep grasp of the subject contributed their findings and answered questions, including Jake Gariepy, Jane Wypniszyki, Stan Honeycutt, Charlotte Scholten, Kim Rivers, and Michelle Morrissette.

I would also like to thank a number of previous Jacqueline Bouvier Kennedy Onassis biographers: Jan Pottker, Alice Kaplan, Sarah Bradford, Barbara Leaming, Ed Klein, and the late Stephen Birmingham. Some of them did groundbreaking and intensive research into specific aspects of her life, and without their books my own would be sorely lacking. These biographers also managed to interview many individuals I was unable to reach not only for this book but also for my 1997 Onassis oral history biography, or they asked important questions of some of the same individuals I did interview that I failed to ask. Very few historical lives can be reconstructed without passionate diligence. While David Heymann and Kitty Kelley wrote biographies with interpretations that proved controversial, I found much of the basic data they were the first to record to be fact-based. Conducting their research in the 1970s, both were able to interview key figures in the story of Jacqueline Bouvier.

Notes

Abbreviations Used in the Notes:

CLB Caroline Lee Bouvier [Radziwill]
EBB1 Edith Bouvier Beale
EBB2 Edith "Little Edie" Bouvier Beale
ELP Evelyn Lincoln Papers
FCW Frank C. Waldrop
JFK John F. Kennedy
JLA Janet Lee Auchincloss
JLB Jacqueline Lee Bouvier
JLBK Jacqueline Lee Bouvier Kennedy
JLBKO Jacqueline Lee Bouvier Kennedy Onassis
JPK Joseph P. Kennedy
JVB John Vernou Bouvier
KLB Kirk Lemoyne "Lem" Billings
MVT Mary "Molly" Van Rensselaer Thayer
YDA Hugh D. "Yusha" Auchincloss II

AI Author Interview
AIAW Author Interview, *As We Remember Her*
AWRH *As We Remember Her*
BBC Bernard Berenson Collection
CNNLKL "Jack, Jackie Kennedy's Wedding 50 Years Ago Remembered by Friends, Family," CNN's *Larry King Live*, September 23, 2003
JB John H. Davis, *Jacqueline Bouvier*
JBK Mary Thayer, *Jacqueline Bouvier Kennedy*
JFKL John F. Kennedy Presidential Library
LC Library of Congress
McG McGinnis Auction Catalog
MVTP Mary Van Rensselaer Thayer Papers, Library of Congress
OHI Oral History Interview
TB John H. Davis, *The Bouviers*
TKDD John H. Davis, *The Kennedys: Dynasty and Disaster*

TVF The Vogue File, John F. Kennedy Presidential Library
WTH *Washington Times-Herald*
YDAM Yusha Auchincloss, "Life with Jackie," memoir, John F. Kennedy Presidential Library

NOTE TO READER: When quoting from source material, original spelling and punctuation have been kept. Additionally, multiple quotes clustered in the text share the same source(s), and these are included within the abbreviated first and last quotes of individual entries listed herein.

1. Getting Her Camera

May–August 1949

3 *"terrific camera":* YDA AIAW.
3 *"really proved . . . question on a test":* Ward L. Johnson to MVT, December 13, 1967, MVTP.
4 *"swamped with work . . . till exams are over":* JLB to YDA, May 17, 1949.
4 *"that camera store":* YDA AIAW.
4 *Peerless Camera:* Camera Store advertisement, *New York Daily News*, June 7, 1949.
4 *Leica IIc:* Michael Baker, Leica Camera brand ambassador, Leica Gallery, Los Angeles, to author, September 19, 2020.
4 *Had the Leica IIc price:* YDA AIAW.
4 *"liked her martini . . . down her dress":* MVT notes on Helen Spaulding interview, MVTP.
5 *"the most exciting":* Helen Spaulding AIAW.
5 *"lock . . . in a closet":* JLB to YDA, February 18, 1948.
5 *"finagled into":* MVT draft of 1960 profile on JLBK, p. 5, and MVT's JLA interview notes, MVTP.
6 *"Jackie's concern for the men . . . to be of service":* YDAM, pp. 9–13.
6 *"wondered how the Roosevelts":* Ibid.
6 *"I'd rather be":* JLB to YDA, October 9, 1943.
7 *"Anything you write":* Ibid., April 28, 1947.
7 *"If you could just stay":* YDA to JLB, January 8, 1943.
7 *Vivi Taylor:* Her mother, Margaret Fahnestock, was one of JLA's first Newport friends, and her first husband, Henry Stillman Taylor, was a navy friend of JFK's. "Countess Viviana Crespi, 1923–2014," *Malta Independent*, September 16, 2019; Vivi Crespi, findagrave.com entry; Crespi divorce, "Cholly Knickerbocker," *Pittsburgh Sun-Telegraph*, March 25, 1949; Taylor marriage to Crespi, *New York Daily News*, June 24, 1949.
7 *"First of all . . . 'Become distinct' ":* Vivi Crespi AIAW.

8 *"Can you think of anything worse":* JLB to R. Beverley Corbin, Jr., October 3, 1946, Christie's Auction Catalog, May 19, 2011.

8 *"don't want to be tied down":* JLB to "Woodleigh" (Puffin Gates), n.d. (circa 1942–46), Heritage Auctions Catalog, February 20–21, 2006.

8 *"think of getting married . . . still in college":* JLB to YDA, February 10, 1949.

8 *"Jackie skinny and underpaid . . . in Pittsfield, Mass":* JLB to Woodleigh, n.d. (circa spring 1949), Heritage Auctions Catalog, February 20–21, 2006.

9 *"tearing all over":* JLB to YDA, May 20, 1949.

9 *Janet could beam:* JLB photo album pages, McG.

9 *"I love nostalgia":* JLB to Woodleigh, n.d. (circa 1942–46), Heritage Auctions Catalog, February 20–21, 2006.

9 *"Mummy's being very extravagant":* JLB to YDA, n.d. (circa September–October 1944).

10 *"You can get the rest":* YDA AIAW.

10 *bridesmaid to Bow:* "Helen Bowdoin Wed in Capital," *New York Times*, June 30, 1949; party at Merrywood, "The Promenader by Go Peep," *Montgomery Advertiser*, June 26, 1949; Helen Bowdoin Spaulding AIAW; Charlie Bartlett OHI, JFKL, January 6, 1965, pp. 18–19.

10 *"I'm glad we walked . . . hither & yon":* JLB to YDA, n.d. (circa spring 1947).

10 *"I simply couldn't stand going":* Ibid., October 10, 1944.

10 *"You have to come up . . . receiving line with me":* Ibid., April 28, 1947.

10 *"I won't see you for a minute":* Ibid., May 17, 1949.

10 *"that she had a lot":* YDA, March 23, 1943, diary entry; see also March 26, 1943, diary entry, McG.

10 *"I don't love her as a brother":* YDA, January 7, 1946, diary entry, McG.

11 *"Will you look . . . lips of hers":* Davis, *JB*, p. 122.

11 *"Pet, I must admit you did look":* JVB to JLB, n.d., transcript, MVTP.

11 *using his Bloomingdale's . . . him on Easter Sunday:* Davis, *JB*, pp. 116, 124.

12 *Jackie's twentieth birthday party:* Ibid., pp. 128–30; EBB2 AIAW.

12 *Jackie took a bad fall:* Pottker, *Janet and Jackie*, p. 119.

12 *"that never happened":* Mimi Cecil AIAW.

12 *told his sister Maude:* Jack Davis AIAW.

13 *"heavenly dresses . . . let me keep them!":* JLB to Woodleigh, n.d. (circa 1942–46), Heritage Auctions Catalog, February 20–21, 2006.

13 *"When the allowance Mummy":* JLB to YDA, February 14, 1943; see also JLB hated being "stone broke," JLB to YDA, February 12, 1943.

13 *"that bitch . . . the drunk":* dentist, Jack Davis AIAW.

13 *their only known proximity:* Nancy Tuckerman AIAW.

13 *dentist:* Jack Davis AIAW.

13 *perched on the arm . . . "I'm so excited about France":* Davis, *JB*, pp. 128–30.

14 *"I envy you":* JLB to Woodleigh, Heritage Auctions Catalog, February 20–21, 2006.

14 *Beach Club costume party:* "Gardner Nuptials Bring Many Notables," *Philadelphia Inquirer*, August 28, 1949.

14 *Hedda Hopper . . . "La Vie en Rose":* Kaplan, *Dreaming in French*, pp. 1–3; Kashner and Schoenberger, *The Fabulous Bouvier Sisters*, p. 36.

14 *"bon voyage bonus":* YDA AIAW.

2. Daddy and Mummy
1929–1948

15 *"stork is hovering . . . a staid father":* "Saratoga Is the Topic of Social Week," *Chicago Tribune*, August 4, 1929.

15 *delayed her own birth:* Nancy Tuckerman AIAW. Born nine months before JLB to Roger and Betty Tuckerman, "Tucky" befriended her in kindergarten and remained her lifelong confidante to her death, living as her boarding school roommate, bridesmaid, travel agent, White House social secretary, Doubleday publishing colleague, and primary aide and spokesperson. When Tucky was so humiliated as a teenage debutante by the competitive social-climbing mother of a fellow deb that she suffered a traumatic reaction, both JLB and YDA were uncompromising in their protective defense of her, resorting to some minor acts of sabotage in the apartment of the offending woman. The mutual loyalty between Jackie and Tucky was ironclad and lifelong.

16 *"Janet had a little":* EBB2, July 28, 1929, diary entry, courtesy of Kent Bartram.

16 *departed on the* Augustus*:* Bouvier, *Black Jack Bouvier*, pp. 145–47.

16 *The first photograph: Brooklyn Daily Eagle*, December 29, 1929.

16 *second birthday:* "Jacqueline Bouvier Celebrates Second Birthday," *East Hampton Star*, July 31, 1931, and *Brooklyn Daily Eagle*, July 29, 1931.

16 *"one of the most attractive": East Hampton Star*, August 23, 1934.

16 *showed her seated:* "Winsome Miss," *New York Daily News*, September 9, 1937.

16 *"little Miss":* "Blue Ribbon Winner," *East Hampton Star*, August 19, 1937.

16 *"Daddy got us":* JLBKO response to MVT questions, MVTP.

17 *John Vernou Bouvier III:* Bouvier, p. 157; Davis, *TB*, p. 268; Davis, *JB*, pp. 144–45. MVT notes on JVB, MVTP.

17 *Jimmy Walker . . . Motor Parkway . . . Stinson Reliant:* Bouvier, pp. 90–94.

17 *Cole Porter:* Charles Schwartz, *Cole Porter: A Biography* (New York: Dial Press, 1977), p. 176; Heymann, *A Woman Named Jackie*, p. 38. JVB's nephew, family historian Jack Davis, gives subtle support to the suggestion that his uncle was bisexual, writing that JLA's "incessant quarrels" with JVB were not only "over other women" but also "other men." Davis, *TKDD*, p. 175.

17 *"little skip . . . ladies dressing room":* "The City's Jar," *New York Herald*, March 9, 1919; "Tells Why Mr. Bouvier Was Ejected from Hotel," *New York Tribune*, March 9, 1919.

18 Showboat*:* Bouvier, p. 128.

18 *Rhett Butler:* Ibid., p. 25.

18 *darkest possible tan:* JVB was so dark-skinned that he was compared to an Egyptian sheik, "so deeply tanned," transcription of unnamed newspaper gossip col-

umn clipping (circa 1931), "Additional Facts on JVB III," MVT personal notes on JVB, n.d., MVTP.

18 *Lillian B. Hyde:* "Golf Champion to Wed Nutley Man," *Newark Evening Star*, June 2, 1914.

18 *Eleanor Carroll Daingerfield:* "Bouvier 3d to Be Bridegroom," *New York Tribune*, April 8, 1920.

18 *Emma Stone:* Bouvier, pp. 67–70.

18 *"The bachelor may":* "The Bachelor at Three and Thirty," poem by Grampy Jack, Bouvier, pp. 109–10.

18 *Doris Duke . . . honeymoon voyage:* Bouvier, pp. 119–20.

18 *"lack of sexual guilt":* Vidal, *Palimpsest*, pp. 102–3.

18 *Virginia Kernochan:* Another image of JVB and JLA appears in the *New York Daily News*, August 12, 1933, on page 143. At the time of the Bouvier divorce, Kernochan suddenly married, a pregnancy announced three months later, "Virginia Kernochan Is Surprise Bride," *New York Daily News*, August 25, 1938; pregnancy, Society, *New York Daily News*, December 7, 1938; other social notes on her include "New York Flower Show," *Sioux-City Argus-Leader*, March 15, 1931, and *East Hampton Star*, July 18, 1930.

19 *"I'll never forget . . . So hopeful":* Anthony, *AWRH*, p. 27. CLB recalled the period when the family of four was "really happy" as being brief. Bradford, *America's Queen*, p. 1.

19 *"thrived on hot dogs":* JLBK response to MVT question, MVTP.

19 *"Both of our parents":* Ibid.

19 *"always tired . . . without their mother":* Davis, *TKDD*, p. 177. Transcript excerpts from the testimony of household staff members Bernice Anderson, Bertha Kimmerle, and Bertha Newey is from Davis, *TKDD*, pp. 177–86. It was sought by JVB, and provided by them as he assembled his case against his estranged wife but never used in court, as she sought and obtained a divorce in Reno, and he acquiesced to her demand for one in New York State. The transcripts were kept among family papers at Lasata, where they were rescued and preserved by Jack Davis. The current location of these and other family papers is unknown, there being no Davis descendants.

20 *eventually left her . . . perpetually begrudged:* Pottker, *Janet and Jackie*, pp. 81–82, 281.

20 *"a miser":* Bradford, p. 10.

20 *encouraging Jackie to excel:* Mimi Cecil AIAW.

20 *"beautiful teddy bear . . . I like it like that":* JLB to Jim Lee letters, n.d. (circa 1942–45), Bonham's Auction Catalog, December 6, 2017.

20 *She even tried to lure:* Ibid.

20 *"play the ponies":* Mimi Cecil AIAW. Grandmother Maggie Lee was also reported as having "attempted to slap Jacqueline in the face," Newey testimony, Davis, *TKDD*, p. 177.

21 *"I don't remember . . . I hated dolls":* JLB response to MVT questions, MVTP.

21 *"Sammy":* JLA to MVT, MVTP.
21 *"I loved books . . . developed from Daddy":* JLBK response to MVT questions, MVTP.
22 *"enough excitement . . . want to tear your hair":* JLB book report pamphlet, McG.
22 *"very clever . . . full of the devil":* Miss Platt interview with MVT, MVTP.
22 *"the most inquiring mind":* MVT notes on JLB education, MVTP.
22 *"Jacqueline was given a D":* report transcript, MVTP.
22 *"I was always being sent to":* JLBK in response to MVT questions, MVTP.
22 *Tucky remembered:* Nancy Tuckerman AIAW.
22 *"very strict":* JLBK in response to MVT questions, MVTP.
23 *"a standout":* JVB to JLB, Cassidy, *Jackie After O*, p. 30.
23 *"taken all the prizes":* Davis, *TB*, p. 268.
23 *"[Y]our hair looks":* Davis, *JB*, p. 144.
23 *"Doesn't Jackie look terrific?":* Davis, *TB*, p. 268.
23 *"an ideal father":* JLBK response to MVT questions about JVB, MVTP.
23 *"frequently yell[ing] . . . worse of the two":* Davis, *TKDD*, pp. 181–86.
24 *"emotional damage . . . warped values":* Martha Bartlett AI, November 1, 2019.
24 *"her life in the world":* Vidal, p. 384.
25 *"overly friendly" . . . Marjorie McKittrick Berrien . . . "unnamed woman":* "Society Broker Sued for Divorce," *New York Daily Mirror*, January 26,1940; "Sues Husband as Love Commuter," *New York Daily News*, January 26, 1940. Three years after being named by Janet in the divorce suit, Marjorie Berrien married an army lieutenant. Society, *Brooklyn Daily Eagle*, July 28, 1943. The press had even reported when the Bouviers returned to cohabitating after the initial trial separation, the *Harlingen Morning News* in Texas reporting in a December 19, 1937, gossip column that they were "plotting a renovation."
25 *"galloped across the Nevada desert":* JLB's first trip west, "Jacqueline Kennedy Onassis: Equestrian," *Equestrian Magazine*, summer 2016, p. 32.
25 *Perhaps to irritate:* "Golden Jubilee at Maidstone," *Brooklyn Daily Eagle*, July 13, 1941. Two months later, JVB got revenge, taking satisfaction in upsetting JLA by giving the girls a surprise gift of a large, untrained Bouvier des Flandres puppy that wrecked her apartment the first weekend his daughters were away from JLA and with him. Her niece recalled that JLA had to deal with the damage and excrement, Mimi Cecil AIAW.
26 *"Why did Mummy divorce Daddy?":* Bouvier, *One Special Summer* (unpaginated), 42nd printed page in 2005 edition.
26 *"Sweet, all you have to do":* JVB to JLA, September 1928, University Archives Auction Catalog, Lot 105, April 10, 2018.
26 *"all men are rats":* Nancy Tuckerman AIAW.
26 *modeling clothes at Macy's:* Mimi Cecil AIAW.
27 *Nina Gore Vidal Auchincloss:* Vidal, pp. 15–18.
27 *Esther Auchincloss:* Pottker, p. 88.
27 *Janet and Hugh:* Although Unk's paternal ancestry traced to Scotland in just four generations, with her sensitivity to not having genuine prestigious Anglo-Saxon

ancestry tracing to colonial America, she was pleased to discover that his ancestors had married into older families. Pottker, pp. 90–91.

27 *first tour of the White House:* JLBKO to author, December 8, 1989. When JLB recalled first visiting the White House, it was wartime and the mansion was closed to public tours. It seems likely that she recalled her tour of it during her first visit to Washington with JLA in the spring of 1938, *Washington Evening Star*, "By the Way," March 31, 1938.

28 *"labor overthrowing . . . working in coal mines":* JLB to YDA, February 12, 1943.

28 Little Rascals: EBB2 AIAW.

29 *"I was playing the Strip Polka . . . could see me now":* JLB to YDA, November 8, 1944.

29 *"Do you think in your wildest":* Ibid., November 9, 1944.

29 *"evil in the woods":* Ibid., February 14, 1943.

29 *"illegal food . . . give it up":* Ibid., April 8, 1943.

29 *"thought of some lovely":* Ibid., February 9, 1943.

29 *"praying that Main House . . . luxury and sin":* Ibid., February 14, 1943.

29 *"on bounds . . . Damn, damn, damn":* JLB to "Woodleigh" (Puffin Gates), n.d. (circa 1943–45), Letter 10, Heritage Auctions Catalog, February 20–21, 2006.

29 *"I stuck hot water":* JLB to YDA, December [n.d.] 1945.

29 *Uncle Lefty . . . French Enlightenment:* JLBKO to author, December 8, 1989.

29 *"hard taskmaster . . . helped me to write":* JLBK response to MVT questions about teachers, MVTP.

30 *"individualistic":* EBB2 AIAW.

30 *single unusual piece . . . full riding costume:* Davis, *JB*, p. 120.

30 *"I've a blazing . . . for the world":* JLB to YDA, May 17, 1943.

30 *"poodle cut":* Bouvier, pp. 214–15.

30 *Sally Butler:* Heymann, *A Woman Named Jackie*, p. 77.

30 *"I never wanted you to be a prig":* JVB to JLB, n.d. (circa late 1945–49), transcript, MVTP.

30 *"not giving in . . . lost respect":* Heymann, *A Woman Named Jackie*, p. 74.

31 *"the hardest girl":* YDA to JLB, January 25, 1945.

31 *"used to watch them . . . in the Bouvier cabana":* Davis, *JB*, p. 85; EBB2 claimed Anne Plugge and JVB were genuinely in love and would have married had she not been already married, transcript of C[lem] David Heymann phone interview with EBB2, April 24, 1986, Tape 1, Side B, State University of New York at Stony Brook archives, courtesy of Kent Bartram to author, November 14, 2020.

31 *"He carried on . . . the ground":* Martha Bartlett AI, November 1, 2019.

31 *"those old bags":* Davis, *TB*, p. 311.

31 *"ignorant and petty":* Kathy Bouvier AIAW.

31 *Serge Obolensky:* Davis, *JB*, p. 92.

31 *"in the day coach":* JLB to Woodleigh, n.d. (circa 1943–45), Letter 8, Heritage Auctions Catalog, February 20–21, 2006.

31 *Daddy's two-bedroom Upper East Side:* Davis, *JB*, p. 139; Edie Beale [EBB2]

AIAW; Bouvier, pp. 188, 196, 199–206; "The childhood home of Jackie Bouvier Kennedy Onassis at 125 East 74th Street, NY," www.mylusciouslife.com, July 22, 2014; "Apartment in Jackie O's Storied NYC Life Listed for $1.395M," by Laura Vecsey, April 21, 2016, streeteasy.com; building description by Christine Miller Martin, with apartment floorplans, streeteasy.com/building/125-east-74-street-new_york/floorplans.

32 *"horrible little dives . . . was really good":* JLB to Woodley, n.d. (circa 1943–45), Letter 8, Heritage Auctions Catalog, February 20–21, 2006.

32 *"just the right height":* JVB to JLB, n.d., transcript, MVTP.

32 *"Weekend at the Waldorf":* JLB to YDA, November 22, 1948.

32 *"Every cab driver . . . most important values":* Kathy Bouvier AIAW.

32 *"more common in Latin . . . expression of sexuality":* Davis, *TB*, pp. 243–44.

33 *"it sounds incestuous":* JLBK margin notation on MVT draft of JVB letter, MVTP.

33 *"Dearest":* JVB to JLA, July 8, 1945, transcription in MVTP.

33 *"Yours arrived and were divine":* JVB to JLB, n.d., MVTP.

33 *"absolutely worshipped":* Davis, *JB*, p. 120.

33 *Her most cherished image:* JLBK response to MVT on JVB, MVTP.

33 *"even the most vulnerable . . . I loved him":* Ibid.

3. A New Language

August–October 1949

35 *"The only thing that breaks":* JLB to YDA, April 8, 1943.

37 De Grasse: "French Line SS De Grasse Cabin Class List of Passengers 1949," Amazon.com listing, October 1, 2020; "French Line's SS De Grasse," by Michael von Grace, www.cruiselinehistory.com, April 1, 2015; Kaplan, *Dreaming in French*, pp. 1–3, 237; reported her departure date to YDA as August 23, 1949, JLB to YDA, May 17, 1949; the menu for JLB's crossing was entirely in French, "French Line 194 Ship Menu: SS De Grasse - Cie. Gle. Transatlantique," eBay item listing, October 2, 2020.

38 *Sorbonne's Reid Hall:* Kaplan, pp. 14–16, Columbia.edu.

38 *"dingy little alley . . . shabby":* MVT notes on JLBK letter excerpts, n.d. (circa 1949), MVTP; Claude de Renty du Granrut, AIAW.

38 *"a friendship that":* Claude de Renty du Granrut AIAW.

38 *"we were full of interest":* JLBKO recollections, *The Paris Review Sketchbook*, by George Plimpton and Norman Mailer, *The Paris Review*, Issue 79, Spring 1981.

38 *"way in back . . . speak French perfectly":* quoted JLB letter excerpt, Thayer, *Jacqueline Bouvier Kennedy*, p. 78.

39 *intensive language lessons:* Kaplan, pp. 15–16.

39 *"Last night I went . . . evenings are over":* JLB to JLA, n.d. (circa summer–fall 1949), University Archives Auction Catalog, Lot 128, January 23, 2019.

39 *"what are you . . . wild imagination":* YDA AIAW.

39 *"I just can't tell you what it is like":* quoted JLB letter excerpt, Thayer, p. 78.
40 *"The part I want to see":* Ibid.
40 *"most wonderful . . . 'Chattanooga Choo Choo'":* JLB to JLA, n.d. (circa summer–fall 1949), University Archives Auction Catalog, Lot 128, January 23, 2019.
41 *learn some Italian:* Helen Spaulding AIAW.
41 *using her French on Corsica:* Jack Davis AIAW, Vivi Crespi AIAW.
41 *"quite a rough place . . . than I do":* JVB to JLB, n.d. (circa September 1949), quoted in Davis, *JB*, pp. 130–32.
41 *"heaven on earth . . . Florence":* JLB to YDA, n.d. postcard (circa October 1949).
41 *Florence:* George Washington University TV videotape, 1994, courtesy of Muriel McClanahan.
42 *"I have to write Mummy . . . married to an Italian":* JLB to YDA, n.d. (November 1949), previously quoted in Thayer, pp. 78–79. JLA mistrusted Mediterranean men, CLB to Bernard Berenson, n.d. (circa 1952), BBC.
42 *"because they don't . . . I am ashamed of":* JLB to JLA, n.d. (circa summer–fall 1949), University Archives Auction Catalog, Lot 128, January 23, 2019.
42 *As later studies would suggest:* "How a Second Language Can Boost the Brain," by Ramin Skibba in *Knowable Magazine*, November 29, 2018.
42 *"It's so much more":* Thayer, p. 81.
42 *"much poorer . . . with beautiful manners":* JLB to JLA, n.d. (circa summer–fall 1949), University Archives Auction Catalog, Lot 128, January 23, 2019.
43 *In Alice Kaplan's account:* Kaplan, pp. 17, 22.

4. Paris

October–November 1949

44 *"dark pink walls . . . an ironing board":* MVT transcripts of previously unquoted letters or phrases in JLB to JLA and JLB to YDA, n.d., October–November 1949.
44 *"swaddled . . . and ear muffs":* JLBKO recollections, *The Paris Review Sketchbook*, by George Plimpton and Norman Mailer, *The Paris Review*, Issue 79, Spring 1981.
45 *"water sparkling like":* JLB to YDA, July 3, 1945.
45 *"always gray with a thick":* JLB to JLA, n.d. (circa October 1949), transcript, MVTP.
45 *"You just have to":* JLB to YDA, April 8, 1945.
45 *"I'll just splurge":* Ibid., October 10, 1944.
45 "Ecrives"*:* Ibid., November 13, 1947.
45 *"We never speak . . . gray rainy world":* Thayer, *Jacqueline Bouvier Kennedy*, p. 82.
45 *"I had every intention . . . ridiculously vague":* JLB to YDA, November 18, 1949.
45 *"terrified . . . so complicated":* MVT notes on JLB Paris letter excerpts to JLA, October–November 1949, MVTP.
45 *"psychoanalyst theorist":* Kaplan, p. 40.

46 *"I can almost tell":* JLB to YDA, November 18, 1949.

46 *"nude women":* Ibid., February 18, 1949.

46 *"my mother took . . . artists and intellectuals":* Claude de Renty du Granrut AIAW.

46 *her experiences during World War II:* Germaine de Renty's French Resistance work and Nazi imprisonment, "Engendering the Repatriation: The Return of Female Political Deportees to France Following the Second World War," by Debra Workman, University of St. Francis, *Journal of the Western Society for French History*, Vol. 35, 2007; "After Five Decades, a Spy Tells Her Tale," by David Ignatius, *Washington Post*, December 28, 1998; Germaine de Renty did not discuss her life in concentration camps with JLB, Heymann, *A Woman Named Jackie*, p. 81.

46 *Reid Hall . . . Jeanne Saleil:* Kaplan, *Dreaming in French*, pp. 38–41.

46 *"stands for so many things . . . courage":* MVT notes on JLB to JLA, n.d. (autumn 1949), letter excerpts, MVTP.

47 *"Jacqueline knew what":* Claude de Renty du Granrut AIAW; Germaine de Renty's French Resistance work and Nazi imprisonment, "Engendering the Repatriation," by Debra Workman; "After Five Decades, a Spy Tells Her Tale," by David Ignatius; Germaine de Renty did not discuss her life in concentration camps with JLB, Germaine de Renty interview, Heymann, *A Woman Named Jackie*, p. 81.

47 *"a Swiss boy . . . that's playing":* JLB to YDA, November 18, 1949; this letter has been partially quoted in Thayer, pp. 81–82.

47 *"We were meeting . . . with Jackie":* Claude du Granrut AIAW, and November 17, 2019, AI.

47 *"being swanky . . . a Frenchman":* JLB to YDA, November 18, 1949; this letter has been partially quoted in Thayer, pp. 81–82.

47 *the club scene:* Claude du Granrut AIAW and November 17, 2019, AI, unpublished manuscript on JLB; "Jazz Liberates Paris," by Leslie Gourse, *American Heritage*, April 2000.

47 *"pale, in a black . . . a strange bed":* JLBKO recollections, *The Paris Review Sketchbook*, by George Plimpton and Norman Mailer, *The Paris Review*, Issue 79, Spring 1981.

48 *fashion show:* Gloria Emerson AIAW.

48 *"so humiliated":* Ibid.

48 *"I'm starting to meet lots":* JLB to YDA, November 18, 1949.

48 *"lost her virginity . . . Paris's Left Bank":* Vidal, *Palimpsest*, p. 309.

48 *"when everything was beginning":* JLBKO recollections, *The Paris Review Sketchbook*, by George Plimpton and Norman Mailer, *The Paris Review*, Issue 79, Spring 1981.

48 *"Mostly the boys . . . romantic at all":* Anthony, *AWRH*, p. 40.

49 *"I tried to look . . . a big boy now!":* quoted in Leaming, *Jacqueline Bouvier Kennedy Onassis*, pp. 1–2.

49 *"As far as I can see":* YDA to JLB, October 12, 1945.

49 *"Just because I may write":* JLB to YDA, October 25, 1945.

49 *"I did love going to":* Carr, *Jacqueline Kennedy*, p. 18. JLB liked to lead conga line dances in Newport, Vivi Crespi AIAW.

49 *"I had a feeling":* "Jackie Onassis: Former First Lady, American Icon," by Mary McCarty, *Dayton Daily News*, May 20, 1994.

49 *"When I was about nineteen":* Anthony, *AWRH*, p. 70.

49 *a familiar presence at Social Register:* "Summer Colony," *East Hampton Star*, November 27, 1947, December 11, 1947, January 22, 1948, January 6, 1949; "Virginia Osborn and Mr. Earle to Wed Jan 14," *New York Daily News*, January 7, 1949; photo of JLB, "Debutantes Aid in Plans of Opera Benefit," *New York Times*, November 23, 1947.

50 *"I wanted terribly":* JLB to YDA, n.d. (circa 1948).

50 *"You shouldn't fall in love":* Ibid., January 24, 1945.

5. The "Terrific" Vacation
November 1949–January 1950

51 *Her father threatened to stop:* JVB threatens not to pay bills if JLB keeps riding, Davis, *JB*, p. 133.

52 *"about to run off":* YDA AIAW.

52 *"Mummy keeps asking me":* JLB to YDA, May 23, 1950.

52 *"Being away from home":* JLB autobiographical sketch, TVF.

52 *"Read, then think":* Vivi Crespi AIAW.

52 *"with Claude":* JLB to YDA, November 18, 1949.

52 *Deniau:* "Jean-François Deniau," by Richard Mayne, *The Guardian*, January 26, 2007.

52 *Claude remembered the dinner:* Claude de Renty du Granrut AI, November 2019.

52 *"All of a sudden . . . 'subversive deb!' ":* Gloria Emerson AIAW.

53 *"I was galled . . . literature or history":* JLBKO to author, December 3, 1987.

53 *Anne Plugge:* Despite JVB never denying parentage of the Plugge twins to JLB, Sarah Bradford assiduously researched and determined that they were conceived after JVB and Plugge parted, while he first underwent alcohol recovery at the Silver Hill sanitarium. JLB wrote that she spent Christmas in Paris, disputing accounts placing her in London on the holiday, Bradford, *America's Queen*, p. 41, Davis, pp. 133–34.

53 *"old soldiers . . . Germany go by":* JLB to YDA, December 26, 1949.

54 *"the Russian drivers . . . violence against women":* "After War, Patrolling Vienna," by Robert Farley as told to Abby Weingarten, *Sarasota Herald Tribune*, February 6, 2009.

54 *"[T]he Russians with tommy guns":* JLB to YDA, n.d. (circa January 1950).

55 *"the only time I have ever been scared":* JLBK to Robert McNamara, November 22, 1967, Sotheby's Auction Catalog, October 23, 2012; Robert McNamara AIAW; see also Bradford, p. 42, Mulvaney, *Diana and Jackie*, p. 57.

55 *"where Hitler lived":* JLB to YDA, n.d. (circa January 1950).

55 *town of Dachau:* Martha Rusk's recollections of her trip to Dachau with JLB, Kaplan, *Dreaming in French*, pp. 22–23.

55 *"She had wanted to see it":* Vivi Crespi AIAW.

55 *"appalled and outraged . . . touch his grave":* YDA AIAW, printed in Anthony, *AWRH*, p. 42.

56 *"the Germans are still Nazis":* JLB to YDA, n.d. (circa January 1950). There existed a plaster bust of a "Jacqueline Bouvier" sculpted by artist and architect Arno Breker, who designed works for the Third Reich, including one for the entrance to Albert Speer's chancellery building. It is unknown where it was made. In the postwar era, he successfully disclaimed Nazi association; it is unlikely JLB would have posed for him if he was identified as such. "Arno Breker made a bust of Jacqueline Bouvier in the late forties/early fifties . . . Arno Breker named the sculpture of Jackie Iris, a Greek goddess, a virgin who didn't want to marry," Charlotte Pitty Pepper to author, March 21, 2020. A digital image of the "Jacqueline Bouvier" bust, photographed from the catalog, closely resembles her. It could also, however, perhaps be a French actress by that name.

56 *struggled to maintain:* Robert McNamara AIAW.

56 *"the most terrific vacation":* JLB to YDA, n.d. (circa January 1950).

56 *"Stalin . . . as Mummy does":* YDA AIAW.

6. Autonomy

January–June 1950

57 *Pierre Renouvin:* Kaplan, *Dreaming in French*, pp. 40–41; JLB wrote JLA about her courses at the Sorbonne: "18th century literature, 19th century literature, 19th and 20th century history, correlating with literature of 1815 to 1914. Comparative literature—English, French, German, and the influence on each other. Political, Social, Religious movements," MVT notes on JLA dictation of a JLB letter to her, October–November 1949, MVTP; In *Les Origines Immédiates de la Guerre*, Renouvin provided irrefutable documentation that Germany instigated World War I, drawing him into heated debate with Harry Elmer Barnes, among the first Holocaust deniers. Renouvin was declared to be "scholarly and cautious" by Jay Winter and Antoine Prost in their book *The Great War in History: Debates and Controversies, 1914 to the Present* (New York: Cambridge University Press, 2005), p. 40.

57 *"dropped her pencil . . . be truly controlled":* YDA AIAW.

57 *"did not much care":* Heller, *Jacqueline Kennedy*, p. 76.

58 *"necessary part":* Renouvin, *The Far East Question, 1840–1940*, pp. 370–72.

58 *"three geniuses":* JLBKO to author, quoted in Anthony, *First Ladies*, Vol. 2, p. 27.

59 *"Yes, it would be better":* Vidal, *Palimpsest*, p. 369.

59 *"Isn't it awful about":* JLB to YDA, April 14, 1945.

59 *"would have given the world":* Ibid., April [n.d.] 1945.

59 *"I can't figure out":* MVT to JLBK, December 17, 1960, MVTP.

59 *"wonderful . . . very good for me":* JLB to YDA, September 24, 1947.

59 *"hardly anyone else":* Ibid., October 8, 1947.
60 *"troubled for a long . . . ever do that":* Ibid., September 24, 1947
60 *"prison . . . skip-rope tonight":* JLB to R. Beverley Corbin Jr., Christie's Auction Catalog, May 19, 2011.
60 *"You hear of people . . . go to church":* JLB to YDA, September 24, 1947.
60 *"could be a leader . . . expand her potential":* MVT notes on interview with JLBK Vassar teachers, MVTP.
60 *"schoolgirl among schoolgirls":* Davis, *JB*, p. 142.
60 *"suffocated . . . I need stimulation":* Vivi Crespi AIAW.
60 *a living as a print model:* Heymann, *A Woman Named Jackie*, pp. 76–77; Davis, *JB*, p. 124.
60 *"you don't waste":* JVB to JLB, n.d. (circa pre–January 10, 1950), quoted in Davis, *JB*, p. 124.
60 *"You may hate":* Ibid., January 10, 1950, quoted in Bradford, *America's Queen*, pp. 41–42.
61 *"dear mama . . . thrived on interfering":* Davis, *JB*, pp. 134–35, 138, 141.
61 *"taken aback":* Heymann, *A Woman Named Jackie*, p. 82.
61 *"muttered about . . . endorsement of the idea":* Spoto, *Jacqueline Bouvier Kennedy Onassis*, pp. 69–70.
61 *and work at his Wall Street office:* Jack Davis AIAW; Davis, *JB*, p. 141.
61 *A later Vassar dean:* Keogh, *Jackie Style*, pp. 82–83.
61 *"Jackie kicked out . . . was re-instated":* transcript of C[lem] David Heymann phone interview with EBB2, April 24, 1986, Tape 1, Side B, State University of New York at Stony Brook archives, courtesy of Kent Bartram to author, November 14, 2020.
62 *"purposely kept her . . . bastard":* Davis, *TKDD*, p. 197; see also Davis, *JB*, pp. 121–22.
62 *"biweekly letters":* JVB meeting with dean, Keogh, pp. 82–83.
62 *"I wish I had . . . my friends left":* JLBK response to MVT question about Vassar, MVTP.
62 *Mummy and Unk sailed home:* Exclusively Yours, by Betty Beale, *Washington Evening Star*, March 13, 1950.
62 *"persuaded him to accept":* Davis, *JB*, p. 142.
63 *"He always encouraged":* Mimi Cecil AIAW.
63 *"I honestly think . . . be a best-seller":* JVB to JLB, January 10, 1950, quoted in Bradford, pp. 41–42.
63 *"one of the most generous":* Davis, *JB*, p. 131.
63 *"[I]t caused him":* Ibid., p. 141.
63 *"a friend . . . around by myself":* JVB to JLB, quoted in Davis, *JB*, p. 135.
64 *"April in Paris":* MVT notes on JLBK to JLA excerpt, April [n.d.] 1950, MVTP.
64 *"incest":* transcript of *That Summer*, documentary (2017).
64 *"Every time I went . . . all those bookies":* transcript of C[lem] David Heymann phone interview with EBB2, April 24, 1986, Tape 1, Side B, State University of

New York at Stony Brook archives, courtesy of Kent Bartram to author, November 14, 2020.

64 *"I was madly":* transcript of *That Summer*, documentary (2017).

64 *"My father wasn't very nice":* Doris Francisco AIAW.

65 *"I went to Courance":* JLB to JLA, June 9, 1950, MVTP.

66 *"I haven't done any work":* JLB to YDA, May 23, 1950.

66 *"I've had three of my four":* JLB to JLA, June 9, 1950, MVTP.

66 *"wholly dependent . . . his bidding":* Davis, *TKDD*, p. 236.

67 *"You come visit me":* Ibid., p. 196.

67 *"Don't you ever intend . . . a rich husband":* JVB to JLB, January 10, 1950, quoted in Bradford, pp. 41–42.

67 *"I can't believe it":* JLB to YDA, May 23, 1950. JLB also urged YDA to call on Ambassador Perle Mesta in Luxembourg because she was hosting a late summer ball there, and JLB hoped she and YDA would be invited.

67 *"Don't tell Mummy":* JLB to YDA, May 23, 1950.

67 *"Whenever she was determined":* Davis, *JB*, pp. 123–24, 138.

67 *"a crumbling little . . . cocktails & dances":* JLB to JLA, May 7, 1950, University Archives Auction Catalog, Lot 128, January 23, 2019; see also MVT notes on JLB to JLA, July 1, 1950, MVTP.

68 *swap tickets:* JLB to JLA, May 7, 1950, University Archives Auction Catalog, Lot 128, January 23, 2019.

68 *"a bad idea . . . nothing could happen":* Ibid.

7. *Liberté*

June–September 1950

69 *The breathless, elaborate tale:* YDA AIAW.

69 *"retired soldiers":* Stéphanie Koenig, *Responsable de la Documentation*, Louvre Museum, to author, March 2, 2020.

70 *"She knew she was . . . making an exit":* YDA AIAW.

70 *"up the Eiffel Tower":* YDAM, pp. 2, 28–33.

70 *"What don't you see . . . were important too":* YDA AIAW.

70 Leica . . . *"the greys and silvers":* George Plimpton AIAW.

70 *"sense of the ridiculous":* Nancy Tuckerman AIAW.

71 *"capacity for concentration . . . real and imaginative":* YDAM, p. 2.

71 *a meandering road trip:* "A Summer Trip in France: Jacqueline Bouvier et Claude de Renty, July 15th–August 10th, 1950," unpublished manuscript, April 1996, by Claude du Granrut. They also made stops in Auvergne, La Rochelle, and Brittany.

71 *"the part of France":* JLB to JLA, August 15, 1950, MVTP.

71 *"decided to finish the job . . . behind the cedar trees":* "A Summer Trip in France."

72 *arrived in Dublin:* YDAM, pp., 30–31; YDA AIAW.

73 *"full of youthful . . . absolute heaven":* "Jackie Kennedy Correspondence with

Costello," by Michael Parsons, *Irish Times*, June 2, 2014; also see "Jackie Kennedy and the Costello Family," by Michael Parsons, *Irish Times*, June 2, 2014; "Jackie Kennedy Sought Copies of All Hallows Letters," by Michael Parsons, *Irish Times*, June 2, 2014; "Jackie Kennedy Almost Married an Irish Lawyer," by Shane O'Brien, *Irish Central*, April 25, 2020.

73 *"shake hands":* JLB to Father Leonard, reprinted in the *Boston Globe*, May 13, 2014, and the *Irish Times*, May 13, 2014; Leonard also brought JLB to visit Dublin's Restaurant Jammet, St. Michan's Church, "Jackie Kennedy Loved Ireland and Her Old Irish Priest," *Irish Central*, November 12, 2017.

73 *"would have been . . . The River Lee!":* YDA AIAW.

74 *"a religion that says":* JLB to YDA, January 27, 1945.

75 *Afghani students:* Ibid., November 8, 1944.

75 *"worship the Gods of Nature":* Ibid., late spring 1945.

75 *"shifty talent scout . . . dreary [train] trip":* Ibid., April 8, 1945.

75 *"by making a sound":* Ibid., September 24, 1947.

75 *"Her stay in France . . . everybody else's ideas":* Carr, *Jacqueline Kennedy*, p. 21.

75 *"making Yusha carry":* JLB to Father Leonard, reprinted in the *Boston Globe*, May 13, 2014, and the *Irish Times*, May 13, 2014.

75 *"tilted over . . . for good luck":* YDAM, pp. 30–31.

75 *"any ideas of what to . . . to share their gruel":* MVT notes on JLB letter to JLA, July 1, 1950, MVTP.

76 *"I loved it more":* JLB autobiographical sketch, TVF, JFKL.

76 *Korean War:* YDAM, p. 30.

76 *"ashamed . . . think there's any":* JLB to YDA, May 23, 1945.

76 *"I just know that . . . what's important?":* Ibid., March 8[?], 1943.

77 *"Once oppressed . . . be truly controlled":* YDA AIAW.

77 *"I don't want to":* Ibid.

77 *"Can't wait":* JVB to JLB telegram, Davis, *JB*, p. 139.

78 *"meet me . . . on arriving home":* JLB to JLA, May 7, 1950, University Archives Auction Catalog, Lot 128, January 28, 2019.

78 *"Mummy handed it":* JLB to Lucky Roosevelt letter (circa fall 1950), unused material *AWRH* first draft manuscript, author collection.

78 *"I'll send my trunks":* JLB to JLA, May 7, 1950, University Archives Auction Catalog, Lot 128, January 28, 2019.

8. East Hampton

September 1950

81 *the four-hour crawl . . . in East Hampton:* Carl Sferrazza, September 2, 2021; The 2008 Village of East Hampton's Report to Residents, Village of East Hampton Historic Preservation Program, by Robert Hefner, aaqeastend.com; "63 Years Ago: The Hamptons Was Very Different When I First Arrived Here," by Dan Rattiner, www.danspapers.com, January 18, 2018.

82 *"grey driftwood":* "Once in a Lifetime Hampton Beach House Auction," by Lynn Douglass, www.forbes.com, June 21, 2012.

82 *Bouvier family history:* "Mr. and Mrs. Wells, Jr., Entertain at Dinner," *Minneapolis Star*, June 1, 1934; horse show, "Al and Nick Can't Pick Dark Horse," *New York Daily News*, July 31, 1933; "Dog Shows at Village Fair," *East Hampton Star*, July 12, 1934; "Mrs. David B. Stone Shines," *East Hampton Star*, September 6, 1934; "Mugwumps to Play Bouvier Team in 'Cycle Polo," *East Hampton Star*, September 27, 1934; "Lost," *East Hampton Star*, October 17, 1930; St. Philomena's annual church fair, *Brooklyn Daily Eagle*, July 13, 1941, and "East Hampton's Yearly Fair Open," *Brooklyn Daily Eagle*, July 25, 1943; "Portrait Exhibition," *East Hampton Star*, July 22, 1943. A 1943 portrait of JLB by local artist Isabelle Magor was perhaps the earliest made of her. It was not to be confused with one done by artist Irwin Hoffman, who also had Cardinal Francis Spellman and Golda Meir as his subjects. "Rare Portrait of Young Jackie Bouvier for Sale," by T. E. Morrow, February 12, 2019, indyeastend.com; "Maidstone Celebration Duplicates 1892 Fete," *Brooklyn Daily Eagle*, August 16, 1942.

82 *"Lasata":* The Newport, Rhode Island, estate of M. C. Bouvier and his sister Mary, located on Central Street, was called Lasata, Society at Newport, *New York Herald*, July 9, 1922.

82 *Maude developed the landscaping:* Bouvier, *Black Jack Bouvier*, pp. 84–86.

82 *Democrat and a friend of New York Governor:* He initially supported FDR, but by 1936, after long-winded orations on the Declaration of Independence and the Constitution, he customarily railed against "the evils of New Deal legislation" for over an hour, campaigning as an anti-Roosevelt Democrat during the president's reelection. A year later, he used Lasata to stage a "Committee for Constitutional Conservation" meeting to further pontificate on his increasingly conservative politics. "Bacon Promises Republican Victory," *East Hampton Star*, October 8, 1936, "Rev. Gerald L. K. Smith to Give Address at Bouvier Home Sunday," *East Hampton Star*, August 19, 1937, and *East Hampton Star*, August 26, 1937.

82 *"Grampy" Jack Bouvier:* "John V. Bouvier, New York Lawyer, Last Rites Here," and "Courtly Gentleman," *East Hampton Star*, January 22, 1948; MVT notes on Bouvier family, MVTP.

83 *"Nothing is more . . . get it back":* EBB2 AIAW.

83 *The brothers' wealth:* "J. V. Bouvier's Exchange Seat Brought Record Price," *New York Herald*, January 14, 1920; "Bequest of $1,500,000 Listed in Bouvier Will," *Boston Globe*, September 4, 1935; "Oldest Members," *St. Louis Globe-Democrat*, July 30, 1935.

83 *proclivity for theatrical and scandalous:* "Mistrial Declared in Suit of Edith St. Clair," *Norwich Bulletin*, October 12, 1912; "Girl Seeking Balm Has Verne Lashed to Mast: Woolen Merchant's Attorney Says She Only Imagined Promise of Marriage," *Washington Times*, November 27, 1919; Bouvier also defended Melville Chapman against his wife, Lavinia, who was seeking a divorce on grounds that the millionaire Howard Gould had "lured" her husband away from her. "She Blames Gould," *Waterbury Evening Democrat*, November 2, 1907.

83 *"corrupting the morals":* EBB2 AIAW, May 21, 1995, June 21, 1995, and February 21, 1995.

83 *"It is a biological truth":* Davis, *TB*, pp. 160. Grampy even wrote a wittily philosophical poem about a hen crossing Main Street titled "Nature Faith," *East Hampton Star*, September 26, 1946.

83 *Mabel Ferguson:* Bradford, *America's Queen*, p. 13; Heymann, *A Woman Named Jackie*, p. 46; Davis, *TB*, p. 286; EBB2 AIAW.

83 *through his mother:* Grampy Jack Bouvier's mother, Caroline Maslin Ewing, was the daughter of Michael Miller Maslin (1788, Kent County, Maryland) and Elizabeth Sarah Maieler (1770, Hanover, York, Pennsylvania). The name Maieler is German, and Germans formed the majority population of York at that time. The first Maslin immigrant to the colonies was Thomas Maslin, born in England in 1690. He married Jane Britain (1695, Kent, Maryland). When their son Thomas married Mary Ann Lamb in 1735, they wed in the Quaker Cecil Meeting House of Kent, Maryland. Mary Ann Lamb's father was the son of Nottingham, England, immigrant Pearce Lamb (1630) and Mary Howe (1665). The antecedents of her mother, Rosamond Beck, are unknown, but were likely German Quakers. There was an entire Swedish branch, her Hanson ancestors. Johannes Sanderse Glen (1648), born in Schenectady, was the descendant of Scottish immigrants who migrated from Canada. He and his wife, Annatje Peeck (1651), born in New Amsterdam, had a son, Jacob Alexander Glen, who married Saertien Wendell in the Albany Dutch Reformed Church. Peeck's father, Jan, was born in the Netherlands, in 1615; her mother, Maria DuTrieux (1617), was born in Leiden, Holland, and immigrated to Canada before settling in New York: "worldconnect.rootsweb.com/trees/238661/P23363/-/ahnentafel; Name: vonlork—Centre Island, NY, updated 05-08-2019 06:05:68. Owner: Andrew." Accessed May 2, 2020.

83 *French Catholic:* Davis, *TB*, p. 276. During his youth, Grampy Bouvier recalled religious violence against Catholics in Philadelphia, such as hanging clergy in effigy and burning a Catholic church, and EBB2 speculated that while they kept the reason secret, this was a factor that prompted the Bouviers to leave Philadelphia. EBB2 AWAI, June 21, 1995; see "Defined by What We Are Not: The Role of Anti-Catholicism in the Formation of Early American Identity," a thesis submitted to the Faculty of the History Department in Candidacy for the Degree of Master of History, by Brandi H. Marchant, Lynchburg, Virginia, April 2012.

84 *"Catholics had no standing":* Claire Sanders to author, May 23, 2020, on her Maude Davis interview.

84 *"Black Jack . . . being different":* Ibid.

84 *"[t]he story one heard":* Charlie Whitehouse AIAW.

84 *"Why is that Negro":* Bouvier, p. 195. JVB's niece even thought he looked "Pakistani," Bouvier, p. 26.

84 *"not really 'in' anywhere . . . big sexy Negro":* Kuhn, *Reading Jackie*, p. 229.

84 *falsely claiming to have an ancestor who had spent most:* Davis, *TB*, p. 176; EBB2 AIAW, June 21, 1995.

84 *Van Salee:* "Jackie Kennedy's Lineage Was Not Royal, but She May Have Had Mixed Race Muslims in Her Family Tree," by Rose Heichelbech, www.dustyoldthing.com; "Was Jackie Kennedy the 1st Black First Lady?" New England Historical Society online; "The Van Salee Family," by Mario de Valdes y Cocom, https://www.pbs.org/wgbh/pages/frontline/shows/secret/famous/vansallees.html.

84 *"orchid . . . in a jungle":* MVT's Puffin Gates interview notes, MVTP.

84 *"rigidity of . . . even heard of":* Davis, *JB*, p. 120.

85 *"snapped his cane . . . time to kneel":* JLB essay on grandfather's funeral, TVF.

85 *"not very Catholic":* William Kuhn, *Jackie Stories: Eight Friends of Jacqueline Kennedy Onassis* (Montgomery Street Press: Boston, 2021), p. 22.

85 *"we both live and do very well":* Anthony, *AWRH*, p. 27.

85 *"Only those who . . . resembles the truth":* Davis, *TB*, p. 160.

85 *"fragrant Jacqueline . . . ever encountered":* Kelley, *Jackie Oh!*, p. 28.

85 *"He really adored . . . individuality she had":* Bradford, p. 3.

86 *"It was wise . . . before he reasons":* Grampy Bouvier to JLB, December 25, 1943, MVTP.

86 *"You really possess":* Ibid., May 20, 1942, MVTP.

86 *"a buoyant spirit . . . intent on developing":* Ibid., February 10, 1943, MVTP.

86 *"I discern in you":* Ibid., November 5, 1944, MVTP.

86 *"adequate preparation . . . male or female":* Ibid., March 2, 1943, MVTP.

87 *disinherit his son . . . to the will:* Davis, *TB*, pp. 283, 289.

87 *three years after her April 1940 death: East Hampton Star*, June 7, 1945; "Summer Colony," *East Hampton Star*, July 10, 1947.

87 *the real estate:* "Summer Rentals," *East Hampton Star*, March 6, 1947, May 6, 1948. As he had begun doing in the mid-1930s as his daughters matured, JVB separated them and himself from his parents and his married twin sisters and their families. Although the Bouviers held Wildmoor, Grampy sought to generate income by renting it each summer rather than offering it for free to his son and his family. JVB rented cottages that were either part of the Sea Spray Inn or on the large Baker estate, "Summer Rentals," *East Hampton Star*, May 17, 1951; JVB and daughters kept to themselves, Davis, *TB*, pp. 245–46; came to East Hampton for daughters, Bouvier, pp. 231–32.

87 *"old, large envelopes . . . items for destruction":* Davis, *TB*, p. 294.

87 *"damp, misty . . . papers and photographs":* Davis, *JB*, pp. 136, 139.

87 *"none of the letters":* Jack Davis AIAW, EBB2 AIAW, February 21, 1995. While JLB was in Paris, every last item in Lasata was sold, even the stove. "For Sale," *East Hampton Star*, April 20, 1950.

88 *"Zelda . . . an unreliable beauty":* YDA AIAW. An apt description of Zelda's interiors was recorded in the MVT interview with Nina Straight (circa late 1960), MVTP.

88 *"I snitched the station . . . But I didn't":* JLB to YDA, September [n.d.] 1944.

88 *"I plan to lure":* Gore Vidal quoted in "Jackie Kennedy's Secret Lovers," by Lauren Winter, *The Daily Mail*, May 28, 2014.

88 *continue to share Zelda:* Kathy Bouvier AIAW, YDA AIAW.
88 *"About the first . . . awhile besides yourself":* JVB to JLB, November 13 [n.y.] MVTP.
89 *"want of generosity . . . gold digger all her life":* Davis, *JB*, p. 123.
89 *"Mother said . . . pinch penny Mother":* EBB2 diary entry, circa September 1950, courtesy of Kent Bartram.
89 *"wrangling abuse":* JVB to EBB1, July 7, 1949, courtesy of Kent Bartram.
89 *"Where in God's name":* Ibid., January 16, 1950, courtesy of Kent Bartram.
89 *"Jack, you are using":* Bouvier, p. 236.
89 *using $7,000:* EBB2 AIAW, Jack Davis AIAW.
89 *"new Cuban mambo":* EBB2 AIAW.
89 *"worshipped . . . always longed for":* JLB to MVT, MVTP.
89 *collaborated:* Davis, *TB*, pp.162–63.
90 *"irresistible":* EBB2 to Janet Hosking, October 26, 1980; courtesy of Kent Bartram, September 4, 2020.
90 *"Oh, Doris":* Doris Francisco AIAW.
90 *"a thick stuffed envelope":* EBB2, May 21, 1995, AIAW.
90 *"would praise a poem":* JLB essay on Grampy Jack's wake, TVF.
90 *"nostalgia . . . a bit eccentric":* JLBKO to EBB1 and EBB2, January 25, 1972; reprinted in Beale, *Edith Bouvier Beale of Grey Gardens*, p. 186.
91 *"It amuses me":* JLB autobiographical essay, TVF.
91 *"I always live":* Nixon, *RN*, p. 503.

9. Newport

September–October 1950

92 *"I don't know what else . . . the Shanghai Lees":* YDA AIAW.
92 *Janet* was *Irish:* Pottker, *Janet and Jackie*, pp. 12, 16–17, 91; Mimi Cecil AIAW; "Jackie O Was More Irish than JFK but Was Ashamed of Her Family's Links to Ireland," by Patrick Counihan, irishcentral.com, June 23, 2013; Maria Curry Merritt entry in findagrave.com.
92 *Margaret Merritt . . . "Mum Maria":* Mimi Cecil AIAW; Davis, *TKDD*, pp. 169–71.
93 *assumed that, given her name:* Pottker, pp. 52–53.
93 *"I wish I'd had a Puritan":* JLB to YDA, February 9, 1943.
93 *"I don't know how Janet":* Vidal, *Palimpsest*, pp. 17, 372.
93 *"she was Jewish":* Charlie Whitehouse AIAW.
94 *English caricatures and drawings:* JLBK notes in response to MVT questions (circa late 1960), MVTP.
94 *By extending her stay:* In Social Circles, *Newport Mercury*, July 7, 1950, July 14, 1950, August 16, 1950; "New Awards Made at Flower Show," *Newport Mercury*, August 4, 1950; "Highlights of Opera Open Newport's Largely Attended Music Festival," *Newport Mercury*, September 22, 1950; "Portsmouth Farm Gets Breeder Prize at Newport County Guernsey Show," *Newport Mercury*, August

25, 1950. Other social activities of the Auchincloss family while JLB was in Europe, Local News Briefs, *Newport Daily News*, September 22, 1950; *Newport Mercury*, In Social Circles, September 22, 1950, September 25, 1950; In Social Circles, *Newport Daily News*, September 26, 1950. JLA also had Hammersmith host large civic meetings, "Proposed Bridge Location at Bay Entrance Opposed," *Newport Mercury*, August 11, 1950.

94 *"as much time outside . . . there were plenty":* Claiborne Pell AIAW.

94 *"sunny, drafty . . . tiny china animals":* Nina Straight interview notes, MVTP.

94 *Hammersmith Farm:* The entire massive shingled mansion built in 1888 by Unk's parents sat on a hill overlooking Narragansett Bay. During the war, with the nearby torpedo station so vulnerable, window shades were lined with blackout material. As a young naval officer in training at nearby Melville, JFK later recalled the view of the house and property from the bay as "one of the loveliest sights in the whole country." The twenty-eight rooms and thirteen fireplaces often seemed gloomy because Unk kept lights out to save money. In the main large "Deck Room," a stuffed pelican swung from the ceiling, and antlers and a moose head were mounted on the wall. In front of a brick fireplace were blue sofas with pink pillows, white upholstered armchairs, and linen-shaded floor lamps. A centerpiece was Unk's Victrola, on which he blared cha-cha records (he had poor hearing) while contentedly playing solitaire. JLB loved "lolling" here, listening to records, dancing with friends, and smoking when Mummy wasn't around. The rooms were defined by chintz seating and curtains, antique clocks, and china plates displayed on mantelpieces; the occasional family portrait hung on plain white walls. There were a number of large spaces, from a sunroom with white wicker furniture to a library with floor-to-ceiling French windows opening to a slate patio, which Unk used as his summer office. The dining room sat eight, each place set with silver serving bowls, salt-and-pepper shakers, and fine china with lace doilies beneath them, protecting the polished mahogany table. The staircase, with a white spindled arm rail topped by mahogany, had wide steps layered with a red runner rug. At the first landing was a tall grandfather clock, with chintz draperies over the windows looking out over the bay. Mummy and Unk shared a large room, where his portrait hung, and two beds were placed together. Janet kept her own private sitting room (a long hall, really), with a tall white-painted dresser, a wall of hundreds of family photographs pinned to a corkboard, and a vanity with a large oval mirror, all of it overlooking the bay, McG photos; Davis, *JB*, pp. 126–28; Nina Straight interview notes, MVTP; YDAM, pp. 5–6, 18–19.

94 *"explosive . . . threatened to use it":* Heymann, *A Woman Named Jackie*, p. 79.

94 *"[S]he was a small woman":* Vidal, pp. 19, 373.

94 *Uncle Lefty . . . their Farmington home:* "Wilmarth Sheldon Lewis (1895–1979)," by Herman W. Liebert, *Yale University Gazette*, vol. 54, no. 4 (April 1980), pp. 198–200; "A Treasure House in Farmington: The Lewis Walpole Library," book review by Peter Sabor, *Eighteenth-Century Studies:* Johns Hopkins University Press, vol. 33, no. 3 (Spring 2000), pp. 454–56.

95 *"Daddy will be":* JLB to YDA, n.d. (circa 1944–48).
95 *"I had heard . . . her away from him":* YDA AIAW.
95 *"did not sit well . . . preferred to remain passive":* YDAM, pp. 15–16.
95 *"that is if you care enough about":* JVB to JLB, quoted in Davis, *JB*, p. 87.
96 *"Anyway, it's one of . . . give her transfusions":* JLB to YDA, September 24, 1947.
96 *"How can I ever thank you":* JLB to JLA, May 7, 1950, University Archives Auction Catalog, Lot 128, January 28, 2019.
96 *"steadfast . . . common-sense intuition":* MVT interview notes with Nina Straight, MVTP.
96 *"[p]utting together . . . be looked at":* Straight, Suares, and Beck, *Uncommon Grace*, pp. 14–17.
97 *"havens of . . . and good manners":* "Janet Auchincloss, Jackie O's Mother, Dies," *Newport Daily News*, July 24, 1989; "Janet Auchincloss Morris, Mother of Jacqueline Onassis, Dies in Newport," *Journal-Bulletin*, July 24, 1989.
97 *"tough lady . . . of that house":* Bradford, *America's Queen*, p. 63.
97 *"She cared more about":* Martha Bartlett AI, November 3, 2019.
97 *"Janet would strike":* Bradford, p. 12.
97 *"Janet had black moods":* Kuhn, *Reading Jackie*, p. 230.
97 *"Jackie usually backed . . . for help either":* YDA AIAW. JLA told MVT that she had read about the *Vogue* contest in *Vogue*, clipping the announcement and sending it to JLB in Europe. This was patently false. JLA would not have been able to read the article, which hit newsstands on August 15, 1950, let alone send it to Europe by the time JLB was preparing to sail back to the U.S. Furthermore, JLB confirmed that she didn't know about the contest until she had returned to the U.S. (JLB to Mary Campbell, October 10, 1950.)

10. George Washington University
October–December 1950

101 *George Washington University:* Shelly Buring, Special Collections Reference Desk, GWU to author, October 11, 2019; *The Cherry Tree*, 1951, George Washington University yearbook; meeting with Dean Turner, unused material in *AWRH* manuscript, author collection; Kaplan, *Dreaming in French*, p. 75.
102 *"fall term marks":* JLB to "Woodley" (Puffin Gates), Heritage Auctions Catalog, February 20–21, 2006.
102 *"She was so striking . . . She always had that":* David Amram AIAW.
102 *"She was always very . . . other girls did then":* Heller, *Jacqueline Kennedy*, pp.135–38.
102 *"a lot of friends . . . imagination off-beat":* MVT's Jessie Leigh Hunt interview notes, MVTP.
102 *"[m]y life was not connected":* JLBK response to MVT questions about GWU, MVTP.
103 *"I returned from Europe . . . go ahead":* JLB to Mary Campbell, October 10, 1950, TVF. In the more formal "First Quiz" of November 3, 1950 (p. 2), she contra-

dicted herself to admit the truth that she "spent two years at Vassar" and spent a year at the Sorbonne.

103 *"ashamed to be asking . . . ahead of the deadline":* Ibid., October 31, 1950.

103 *"a common theory . . . chair hanging in space":* JLB essay one, November 1, 1950, TVF.

104 *"I do not have a sensational figure":* JLB autobiographical account, TVF.

104 *"good grooming . . . is waiting downstairs":* JLB, November 3, 1951, essay on grooming, TVF.

104 *"in the balcony of":* JLB autobiographical account, TVF.

104 *"nothing will be counted against you":* JLB, November 3, 1951, essay on grooming, TVF.

104 *"dark grey suit . . . you can cook too":* Ibid., essay on suggested outfits, TVF.

105 *"radio and cigarettes":* JLB to YDA, January 14, 1943.

105 *"always does something to me":* Ibid., August 6, 1945.

105 *"it still takes me ten minutes":* JLB to Mary Campbell, October 31, 1950, TVF.

105 *"the Nini, the Pinta":* Edward Purcell AI, November 17, 2021.

105 *"not much larger than a closet":* Vidal, *Palimpsest*, p. 16.

106 *"watched it grow dark . . . the dogwood trees":* JLB to YDA, n.d. (spring 1947).

106 *"I can remember a slight . . . but I found it somewhere":* JLB response to MVT questions, MVTP.

106 *"wonderful at spitting tobacco":* JLB to YDA, September 20, 1944.

106 *"the most peaceful feeling":* Ibid., April 8, 1945.

106 *"wet and fresh and beautiful":* Ibid., January 14, 1943. Other JLB references to Merrywood in letters to YDA include January 15, 1945, and May 25, 1948.

106 *"inner self . . . which is":* YDA to JLB, April 1946.

107 *"telling the elevator man . . . going out west":* JLB birthday poem for JLA transcript, MVTP.

107 *"jealous in his grave . . . in jail or on relief":* JLB poem after birth of her half sister, transcript, MVTP.

107 *"paint things that my mother":* JLB autobiographical essay, TVF.

107 *"a career on a magazine":* JLB to "Dear Sirs," October 10, 1950, TVF.

11. Last Semester
January–March 1951

108 *social columns:* In Social Circles, *Newport Mercury*, December 22, 1950; Society News, by Katherine M. Brooks, *Washington Evening Star*, December 5, 1950.

108 *"I slide down . . . freeze to death":* JLB to YDA, January 27, 1945.

109 *"my treasures . . . Shakespeare, etc.":* Ibid., October 26, 1950.

109 *"his novels":* Heller, *Jacqueline Kennedy*, p. 66.

109 *"thoughtlessness was crushing . . . abandoned and alone":* Davis, *TKDD*, p. 208.

109 *"criticized her love of books":* Leaming, *Mrs. Kennedy*, p. 7.

109 *"efface herself . . . did not sell":* JLB, January 15, 1951, essay on *Vogue* models, TVF.

109 *"new approach . . . variety and elegance":* Ibid., essay on men's fashions, TVF.

110 *"Famous Noses . . . diorama bottle":* Ibid., essay on perfume, TVF.

111 *heavy course load:* "Jackie, 'We Hardly Knew Ye': The University Remembers One of Its Most Celebrated Alumnae: Jacqueline Bouvier Kennedy Onassis, BA '51," by Karen Sibert, *GW Magazine*, fall 1994; *George Washington University Encyclopedia*, Jacqueline Bouvier entry.

111 *"I wanted to know":* JLBK to MVT, MVTP.

111 *"most incredible teacher . . . wasn't up to [it]":* Ibid.

111 *"always sat in the back . . . a simple activity":* Muriel McClanahan AIAW.

112 *"it would have been impossible":* Jane Lingo AIAW.

112 *"looked out . . . felt bad":* Martha Bartlett AI, November 1, 2019.

112 *"wonderful imagination":* Charlie Bartlett OHI JFKL.

113 *"already read his famous . . . Viet Minh":* YDA AIAW.

113 *"Well, you promised . . . you desperately":* JLB to YDA, November 8, 1944.

113 *"drag":* Ibid., January 18, 1947.

113 *"without ever having . . . have a home base":* JLBK to Mary Campbell, May 27, 1951.

113 *"The cook is out . . . I'm starving":* JLB to YDA, n.d. (circa September–October 1944).

113 *"messiest creative . . . go to heaven":* Ibid., September [n.d.] 1944.

114 *"I'm patiently waiting . . . 50 cents anyway":* Ibid., January 17, 1943.

114 *"keeping me in the home":* JLB to Mary Campbell, May 27, 1951, TVF.

114 *"[Y]ou seem to so emphatically":* YDA to JLB, October 20, 1945.

114 *Red Cross: East Hampton Star*, September 3, 1942.

115 *"mean":* YDA AIAW; JLB took her chicken obligation seriously, YDAM, p. 19.

115 *"watch the fathers":* JLB to YDA, July 24, 1945.

115 *"I waited on the tables":* Ibid., October 5, 1944. JLB also worked as a waitress while at Vassar. "Must go and wait on the stupid tables now," JLB to YDA, October 1, 1947.

115 *Vassar, she worked as a switchboard:* Ibid., October 20, 1948.

115 *"a woman on the make":* Heymann, *A Woman Named Jackie*, p. 77.

115 *"I couldn't be a ballet dancer":* JLBK to MVT, MVTP.

115 *"what I would like . . . through costumes":* Ibid.

115 *"the whole darn set":* JLB to YDA, March 4, 1943.

115 *"I am writing it":* Ibid., May 23, 1945.

115 *"what a strain . . . down my alley":* Ibid., October 17, 1944.

115 *"I think I'll be an actress":* JLB to Jim Lee, July 15, 1943, Bonham's Auction Catalog, December 6, 2017.

115 *"Do you think it's too late?":* Vidal, *Palimpsest*, pp. 284–85, 309–10.

115 *"I'd never be willing":* JLB to YDA, March 4, 1943.

115 *"Someday I'll send . . . swallow his braces":* Ibid., September 29, 1945.

116 *"yell scores":* Ibid., November 4, 1946.

116 *"I have always known":* JLB to Mary Campbell, May 27, 1951.

116 *"I have talked . . . a certain project":* Ibid.

117 *"went berserk . . . kinky hair":* YDA AIAW.
117 *"often my mother will run":* JLB autobiographical essay, TVF.
117 *"I know it's a revolting":* JLB to YDA, October 30, 1944.
117 *"having to wear glasses":* Ibid., April 18, 1945.
118 *"fake flattery":* YDAM, p. 2.
118 *"Even if they don't like her":* JLA to YDA, January 8, 1943.
118 *"dying to go to Europe":* JLB to Father Leonard, March 4, 1951, as reprinted in the *Boston Globe,* May 13, 2014, and the *Irish Times*, May 13, 2014.
118 *"mapped out . . . better guide":* Ibid.
118 *"[M]ystery always helps":* JLB to YDA, November 20, 1945.
118 *"to deport themselves":* Vidal, p. 32. Husted credited his aunt Helen Husted with formally introducing him to JLB at the Sulgrave Club dance, but first saw her while she played tennis with JVB in a Miss Porter's father-daughter tournament. Anderson, *Jackie Kennedy Onassis*, p. 91.
119 *"I was immediately attracted":* Kelley, *Jackie Oh!*, p. 14.

12. *Vogue*
April–June 1951

120 *"Nostalgia":* JLB's final *Vogue* essay, March 1, 1951, TVF.
122 *"Flat footed":* Mrs. Gleaves report, March 9, 1951, TVF.
122 *"Would definitely":* Miss Talmey report, March 16, 1951, TVF.
122 *"Wonderful possibility":* Miss Daves report, March 26, 1951, TVF.
122 *"A. Intelligent":* Miss Heal report, April 5, 1951, TVF.
122 *"AAAAAA . . . copy room team!!!":* Carol Phillips report, April 12, 1951, TVF.
123 *"very pleasing":* Virginia R. Kirkbride, GWU to Mary Campbell, April 27, 1951, TVF.
123 *"writes much better":* Muriel McClanahan quoted, ibid.
123 *"Nothing very much":* JLB to Father Leonard, March 4, 1951, as reprinted in the *Boston Globe*, May 13, 2014, and the *Irish Times*, May 13, 2014.
123 *"immature and boring":* Birmingham, *Jacqueline Bouvier Kennedy Onassis*, p. 68; Anderson, *Jackie Kennedy Onassis*, p. 25.
123 *"you are among . . . papers submitted":* Mary Campbell to JLB, April 24, 1951.
123 *"how alert everyone":* JLB to Mary Campbell, May 7, 1951.
123 *"about everything . . . to see him":* Ibid.
124 *"my arm is . . . dry out":* JVB to EBB1, March 29, 1951, courtesy of Kent Bartram; see also Klein, *All Too Human*, pp. 33–34.
124 *"secretly managed":* Lorraine Shevlin [Cooper] quoted in Kelley, *Jackie Oh!*, p. 29.
124 *"given . . . stole":* Kathy Bouvier AIAW.
124 *"running off so soon . . . satiated":* JLB to Mary Campbell, May 7, 1951, TVF.
125 *"I suddenly realized":* Ibid.
125 *"got to be quite a bore":* Anthony, *AWRH*, p. 52.
125 *"She was the odd . . . enjoyable evening":* Albert Gore OHI JFKL. Gore thought there were "eight or ten" guests, while Bartlett recalled "six," Charlie Bartlett

interview notes, MVTP; see also Charlie Bartlett OHI JFKL, and Bradford, *America's Queen*, pp. 54–56.

126 *"inquisitive mind . . . about the world"*: Logevall, *JFK Coming of Age in the American Century*, p. 254.

126 *"purposeful young man"*: JLA OHI JFKL.

126 *"My mother used to . . . he was different"*: Anthony, *AWRH*, p. 72.

126 *"When I met Jack Kennedy"*: JLBK response to MVT, MVTP.

127 *"muttering shyly"*: Charlie Bartlett OHI JFKL.

127 *"an awkward time"*: Ibid.

127 *"Delighted to announce"*: Edna Chase to JLB, May 15, 1951, TVF.

127 *"Can't believe I have won"*: JLB to Edna Chase, May 18, 1951, TVF.

128 *"In Janet's mind"*: Birmingham, p. 68.

128 *"the family . . . it was enough"*: Thayer, *Jacqueline Bouvier Kennedy*, p. 83; see also MVT draft of 1960 profile on JLBK, MVTP.

128 *"a foot in the door"*: JLB to Mary Campbell, May 21, 1951, TVF.

128 *"That, of course . . . at Jack's apartment"*: Davis, *JB*, p. 151.

128 *"Sciences, Math . . . books and photography"*: JLB Condé Nast application, May 1951, TVF.

129 *"I have been discussing . . . in the home"*: JLB to Mary Campbell, May 27, 1951.

129 *"It took a lot"*: Radziwill, *One Special Summer* (unpaginated, p. 2).

129 *"positive . . . Mummy realizes that!"*: JLB to Mary Campbell, May 27, 1951.

130 *"devastated, then enraged . . . angry she was"*: YDA AIAW.

130 *"Being mad comes"*: JLB to YDA, March 4, 1943.

130 *"Sometimes a day . . . becomes funny"*: Ibid., August 1, 1946.

130 *"enemies"*: Edward Purcell AI, September 9, 2020.

130 *"The whole* Vogue *thing"*: Vivi Crespi AIAW.

13. Lee

June–September 1951

131 *"quirks in the sex lives . . . Social Barriers"*: Radziwill, *One Special Summer* (unpaginated, pp. 7–8).

132 *"keen, active . . . Lee"*: JLB notations in *Book of Dogs*, McG.

132 *"When my mother . . . a motor boat"*: CLB[R], *T Magazine* 2013, Lee Radziwill interview, YouTube.

132 *"fat"*: "Lee Radziwill, Jackie Kennedy Onassis' Younger Sister, Dies at 85," by Bill Trott, *Reuters*, February 16, 2019.

132 *"Did you get"*: JLB to YDA, November 21, 1942.

132 *"new height of dieting . . . pathetic"*: Ibid., April 20, 1943.

132 *"epistle on . . . her first rattle"*: Ibid.

132 *"sad letter"*: Ibid., October 6, 1947.

133 *"like a starved"*: Ibid., February 18, 1949.

133 *"anorexic-looking"*: Dubois, *In Her Sister's Shadow*, p. 35.

133 *"[M]y father favored . . . exactly like him"*: CLB[R], *Happy Times*, p. 134.

133 *"He adored her . . . was born":* CLB[R] to MVT [November 1960], MVTP.
133 *"I often wonder":* Ibid.
133 *"I was constantly . . . quite a while":* Ibid.
133 *"You know Lee":* JLB to YDA, December 15, 1945.
134 *"Jackie said she was":* YDA, July 8, 1943, diary entry, McG.
134 *"my adored sister . . . similar tastes":* JLBK to MVT, MVTP.
134 *"to become so extremely":* CLB[R] to MVT [November 1960], MVTP.
134 "*We look like two*": "The Complicated Sisterhood of Jackie Kennedy and Lee Radziwill," by Sam Kashner, *Vanity Fair*, April 26, 2016.
134 *"our three-month odyssey":* JLB to Father Leonard, September 7, 1951, as reprinted in the *Boston Globe*, May 13, 2014, and the *Irish Times*, May 13, 2014.
134 *"never give anyone any compliments":* JLB to Bernard Berenson, Letter 10, p. 1, BBC.
134 *"how fascinated . . . heard is extraordinary":* CLB to MVT [November 1960], MVTP.
134 *"the greatest cello player":* Radziwill (unpaginated, p. 51).
135 *"size up":* Ibid. (unpaginated, p. 48).
135 *"minor riot . . . took sides":* JLB to Father Leonard, September 7, 1951, as reprinted in the *Boston Globe*, May 13, 2014, and the *Irish Times*, May 13, 2014.
135 *"dreary Switzerland . . . 2 sisters":* JLB to JLA, August 31, 1951, University Archives, Auction Catalog, Lot 119, May 8, 2018.
135 *"sitting here under":* Ibid.
135 *"I know you are":* Radziwill (unpaginated, p. 26).
135 *"kiss him on . . . with that city":* Ibid. (unpaginated, p. 20).
135 *"There is so much . . . in one summer":* JLB to Bernard Berenson, August 7, 1951, BBC.
135 *"capsized in . . . every day":* Ibid.
136 "a lover *named":* Radziwill (unpaginated, p. 34).
136 *"tried to do":* Benno Graziani AIAW.
136 *"A good photograph . . . to the spectator":* "Benno Graziani's Friendly Fire," by Rosemary Feitelberg, WWD.com, November 6, 2009.
136 *"His English":* Benno Graziani AIAW. No correspondence between JLBKO and Fellini seems extant, but they remained friendly over time. "The night she had him and his wife to dinner was a very big deal for her," Nancy Tuckerman later recalled. "She opened all the windows and she put fans out to blow the curtains and make it magical. All the guests were people in the arts but sort of unusual or eccentric like the characters in his movies." The party she referenced was hosted by JLBK at her apartment in November 1965 to mark the preview of his film *Juliet of the Spirits*, which opened in U.S. theaters in January 1966, Nancy Tuckerman AIAW.
136 "*the sleepy little . . . and waved goodbye":* Radziwill (unpaginated, pp. 43–44).
137 *"immediately talked to us":* Ibid. (unpaginated, p. 41).
137 *"intolerance trying to crush":* Anthony, *AWRH*, p. 58.

137 *"by using your eyes":* Ibid., p. 59.

137 *"humanism . . . most enduring legacy":* draft manuscript *AWRH*, author's collection.

137 *"life-diminishing . . . follow your senses":* Radziwill (unpaginated, p. 41).

137 *"constantly eavesdropping . . . in your house":* JLB to Bernard Berenson, August 7, 1951, BBC.

138 *"lived at the turn of the century":* Ibid., n.d. (circa 1951–53), letter 9, pages 5 and 6, BBC.

138 *"thoroughly disgusted . . . if I could see":* CLB to Bernard Berenson, August 7, 1951, and June 8, 1952, BBC.

138 *"aching . . . to a bank":* JLB to Father Leonard, September 7, 1951, as reprinted in the *Boston Globe*, May 13, 2014, and the *Irish Times*, May 13, 2014.

138 *"We split the fun . . . our adventures":* Radziwill (unpaginated, p. 3).

138 *"two or three days before":* CLB to JLA, n.d. (circa August 1951), postcard, McG.

138 *Jackie did not go:* In Social Circles, *Newport Daily News*, September 27, 1951, and October 13, 1951.

138 *"[I] thought I would . . . wonderful winter":* JLB to Father Leonard, September 7, 1951, as reprinted in the *Boston Globe*, May 13, 2014, and the *Irish Times*, May 13, 2014.

14. Office Clerk

September–December 1951

139 *staff at* Vogue*:* Edward Klein's book *All Too Human* (p. 75) suggests that JLB began work at *Vogue* on Monday, May 21, 1951, but this contradicts her May 27 letter to *Vogue*, along with the fact that she left for her trip to Europe in early June, which had been previously planned. The placement of it upon her immediate return, in September, as suggested by Sarah Bradford's *America's Queen*, seems more accurate, given that she had no school or travel schedule at that time. Bradford, p. 49.

139 *"confused and uncertain":* "*Vogue* Finds Essays by Jackie from a 1951 Contest," *Detroit Free Press*, August 2, 1994.

139 *"Go to Washington":* Ibid.

140 *her father had become more isolated:* Bouvier, *Black Jack Bouvier*, pp. 224–25; Davis, *JB*, pp. 144–45; Nancy Tuckerman AIAW, EBB2 AIAW.

140 *"but I know he":* Mimi Cecil AIAW.

140 *"She felt a great responsibility":* CLB to MVT [November] 1960, MVTP.

140 *"at first sight":* Heymann, *A Woman Named Jackie*, p. 92.

140 *"sensitivity . . . eternal surprise":* Bradford, p. 56.

140 *"What I hope for . . . boy next door":* JLB to Bev Corbin, undated letter (circa early 1952), quoted in Christie's Auction Catalog, May 19, 2011.

141 *thrown from her mount:* Davis, *JB*, pp. 157–58.

141 *"Uncle Toady":* Jack Davis AIAW.

141 *"only made her":* YDA AIAW.

141 *"some of her writing . . . in school too":* "Jackie Kennedy—Ex-Girl Reporter," Part II, by Dorothy McCardle, *Tampa Bay Times*, September 29, 1960.

141 *"Are you still hiring . . . can you do[?]":* MVT notes on FCW interview, MVTP.

141 *Waldrop:* "Frank Waldrop Dies," by Richard Pearson, *Washington Post*, December 23, 1997; FCW bio, FCW Papers, Herbert Hoover Presidential Library.

142 *"mumbled around . . . you're engaged":* "Jackie Kennedy—Ex-Girl Reporter," Part IV, by Dorothy McCardle, *Tampa Bay Times*, October 1, 1960; MVT notes on FCW interview, MVTP.

142 *congratulatory message:* Mary Campbell to JLB, October 15, 1951, TVF. Another clue as to JLB's first day as a clerical staff member of the *WTH* is her first-day registration signature as a client to dressmaker Mini Rhea on November 3, 1951, reflecting her ability to pay for her own work to be done, as she was now drawing a salary. Rhea, *I Was Jacqueline Kennedy's Dressmaker*, pp. 21–22.

142 *"gofer":* Martin, *A Hero for Our Time*, p. 70. FCW affirmed, "I had her doing the same thing that I had Kathleen [Kennedy] doing and a lot of girls—answer the phone and learning what the city room is like." FCW OHI, National Press Club, Part II, p. 72. JLB also ingratiated herself with FCW, once enigmatically advising her stepsister to "Kiss your boss," apparently meaning that one should treat a hiring superior with adoration. Edward Purcell AI, September 9, 2020. In later years, JLB implied that she was treated as an equal to reporters and hired to write for the paper without having to fight for it. "I don't go for all that," she said about equal pay for equal work and other gender equity issues in the workplace. Heymann, *The Georgetown Ladies Social Club*, p. 195.

142 *"I didn't care . . . handling it efficiently":* FCW AIAW.

143 *"I never imagined the daughter":* Alam, *Jackie Kennedy*, p. 63.

144 *"I know everyone . . . was that girl!":* Betty Beale AIAW.

144 *"I told her . . . I'm so sorry":* FCW AIAW.

144 *"Is Princess Elizabeth":* "Inquiring Photographer," *WTH*, November 2, 1951. *Washington Times-Herald* coverage on November 1, 1951, of Princess Elizabeth's visit includes "Elizabeth Is Visiting U.S. As Princess of Canada," "550,000 Line Parade Route, Guests Cheer," "Royal Program of Five Events Listed for Day," "Capital's '100' Attends Fete at Blair-Lee."

144 *"able to tell things":* FCW OHI, National Press Club, Part II, pp. 64–65. With the eccentric Cissy Patterson as its publisher, the *Washington Times-Herald* had hired a number of women columnists, including Mabelle Jennings (Along the Rialto); Krock's wife, Martha Blair (These Charming People); Inga Arvad (Did You Happen to See); Barbara Holmes (Advice to Brides, One Piece at a Time); Ruth Jones (Balls, Balls, Balls); and others like Edie Robert and Helen Essry. Waldrop, who edited them all, found that "every one of these women had the quality of being able to tell things in very concise short terms."

145 *"I knew I needed":* "Memories of Jackie the Journalist," by Chuck Conconi, *St. Louis Post-Dispatch*, August 22, 1994.

145 *"We used to joke . . . take the pictures":* Heymann, *A Woman Named Jackie*, pp. 93–94.
145 *"I'll tell you what . . . for this thing":* FCW OHI, National Press Club, Part II, p. 72.
145 *"Should a girl live at home":* "Inquiring Photographer," *WTH*, November 9, 1951.
146 *"adored mama . . . old-fashioned wife":* Vivi Crespi AIAW.
146 *"Is it possible":* "Inquiring Photographer," *WTH*, November 14, 1951.
146 *"What is the silliest . . . over deliberately":* "Inquiring Photographer," *WTH*, November 23, 1951.
146 *"devastating . . . sense of humor":* Anderson, *Jackie Kennedy Onassis*, p. 91.
147 *"had sort of . . . me your answer":* Ibid.
147 *"Should a girl pass up":* "Inquiring Photographer," *WTH*, December 6, 1951.
147 *"What was the closest . . . a weak moment":* Ibid., December 17, 1951.
147 *"come back after":* FCW OHI, National Press Club, Part II, p. 71.
147 *"If you are just marking":* "Jackie Kennedy—Ex-Girl Reporter," Part II, by Dorothy McCardle, *Tampa Bay Times*, September 29, 1960.
147 *"Being a journalist . . . of the world":* "Why Does This Woman Work?" Gloria Steinem interview with JLBKO, *Ms. Magazine*, May 1979.
148 *"She went silent . . . word:* 'Everything' *":* FCW AIAW.

15. Palm Beach

December 1951

149 *"breezed in . . . Yes":* Anderson, *Jackie Kennedy Onassis*, p. 91. Based on Husted's various recollections (Kelley, *Jackie Oh!*, pp. 14–15; Heymann, *A Woman Named Jackie*, p. 92; Bradford, *America's Queen*, p. 56, and those of FCW, and the dates of JLB's column questions, Florida trip, and return to work, it seems certain that she agreed to marry Husted on December 22, 1951.
149 *"Sure—but it will never work":* Kelley, pp. 14-15.
149 *"terribly much in love":* JLB to Father Leonard, n.d. (circa winter 1951–52), as reprinted in the *Boston Globe*, May 13, 2014, and the *Irish Times*, May 13, 2014.
150 *"extremely anxious":* Bradford, p. 57.
151 *"not a great deal of confidence":* "*Vogue* Finds Essays by Jackie from a 1951 Contest," *Detroit Free Press*, August 2, 1994.
151 *"I wish I could do":* Kuhn, *Reading Jackie*, p.18.
151 *"Jackie was engaged . . . of her hand":* Bartlett OHI JFKL, p. 21. His wife did not recall exactly how it was that the Bouvier sisters joined her and Charlie at the Kennedy house. Martha Bartlett AI, November 1, 2019.
152 *"shamelessly matchmaking":* Bill Adler, ed., *The Uncommon Wisdom of Jacqueline Kennedy Onassis: A Portrait in Her Own Words* (Citadel Press: New York, 1994), p. 14.
152 *"both well":* Eunice Shriver AIAW.
152 *"swimming pool, movies":* MVT notes on her Charlie Bartlett interview, MVTP. The 15,000-square-foot Mediterranean Revival mansion had been built in 1913

for Redman Wanamaker, a member of the family who owned the department stores of the same name. It was designed by the premier architect of Palm Beach, Addison Mizner, who gave the area its signature building style of white walls and red tile roofs. There were six bedrooms, and always more than enough people to quickly fill them and double up in them, especially in December. The current owner, who bought the two-acre property in 1933, had installed the tennis court, a swimming pool, a pool house, and an open-air "bullpen" where he could sit outside and conduct business by phone, as well as a garage that held the multiple cars of his children and their loyal circle of friends. One entered into a massive living room with a wood-beamed ceiling, a fireplace, worn chintz sofas and chairs, and dozens of silver-framed family photos. From the long dining room with a massive wood table that seated twenty, floor-to-ceiling windows looked out on a lush lawn, beyond which lay its two hundred feet of white-sand beachfront, which faced the crashing blue Atlantic Ocean. When the Wanamakers owned the property, they called it "La Guerida," which meant "bounty of war." Now it was sometimes called "the Ambassador's residence," or simply "the Kennedy house."; "The Kennedy Palm Beach Compound Reportedly Sold," by Guy Martin, *Forbes* magazine, June 24, 2020; "Kennedys Sell Family Home in Palm Beach," *New York Times*, May 24, 1995.

152 *Eunice and Jean had recently:* "Miss Eunice Kennedy," *Boston Post*, October 6, 1951.

153 *an intense public speaking schedule:* "Kennedy Sees Danger in Iran," *Lawrence Tribune*, October 11, 1951; "Tells of Liquat's Last Talk," *Boston Post*, October 19, 1951; "Rep. Kennedy Visits Nehru at Luncheon," *Boston Globe*, October 13, 1951; "Kennedy to Tell Rotary Club of Far East Tour," *News of Milford*, October 26, 1951; "Cong. John Kennedy Guest Speaker," *Hudson Sun*, November 15, 1951; "Prestige Lost," *Clinton Courant*, November 23, 1951; "Service Clubs to Hear Congressman," *Lawrence Eagle*, November 24, 1951; picture of JFK with his map during talk, *Boston Post*, November 25, 1951; "Cong. Kennedy to Speak at Westford," *Lowell Sunday Telegram*, November 25, 1951; "Congressman JFK Peers into the Future," Pastdaily.com, December 13, 2016; "Red Threat to Indo-China Is Underscored by Kennedy," *Berkshire Eagle*, February 2, 1952; "Kennedy Cites Dangers in Southeastern Asia," *Mattapan Tribune*, January 31, 1952.

153 *"tennis games and cocktail parties":* "Kennedy Raps U.S. Tennis and Cocktails Diplomats," *Boston Traveler*, November 19, 1951; "US Diplomats Criticized, Many Are Too Concerned with Social Life, Kennedy Says," *New York Times*, November 19, 1951.

154 *radio address:* Untitled Speech on Far East Trip, n.d., Speech File, 1946–1952, Pre-Presidential Papers: Box 96, JFKL; "Advance Copy Report on His Trip to the Far East by the Hon. John F. Kennedy, Rep. 11th District of Massachusetts over Mutual Broadcast Network from Station WOR, New York, New York," November 15, 1951, Boston Office speech files, 8/16/47–11/51, Pre-Presidential Papers: Box 95, JFKL.

154 *"French principalities . . . found anywhere":* JFK Mutual Broadcasting radio address, November 15, 1951.

154 *General MacArthur:* "Rep. Kennedy Calls on General MacArthur," *Berkshire Eagle*, June 1, 1951; "Timely Topics," *Dorchester Record*, June 1, 1951.

154 *President Truman:* "Bay State Group Visiting Truman," *Boston Traveler*, September 29, 1951.

154 *"In the field of . . . wide recognition":* "Kennedy of Massachusetts," *Brookfield Union*, June 1, 1951.

154 *becoming senator was a necessary:* "The Political Pot," by James D. Ryan, *South Boston Tribune*, December 20, 1951; "Seen and Heard," *East Boston Leader*, December 14, 1951; "Kennedy May Seek Senate Seat," *New York Times*, December 2, 1951; "Kennedy Admits His Interest in Running for Senate in '52," *Christian Science Monitor*, December 3, 1951.

155 *"He really wasn't . . . every day":* MVT notes on interview with Lem Billings, MVTP.

155 *"since it was so . . . talk about it":* Senator Edward Kennedy AIAW.

155 *"double-crossed . . . eternal enmity":* Kessler, *The Sins of the Father*, pp. 275–77.

155 *"Papa Kennedy . . . was great":* Charlie Bartlett interview, *CNNLKL*.

155 *"I am sick of . . . that man has":* JLBK to MVT, MVTP.

156 *"The first I ever . . . [W]ho is Jackie?":* Rose Kennedy, *Times to Remember*, pp. 346–47. JLBKO would later write that after their initial May 1951 meeting, she and JFK did "not see each other again for 7 months—January—when Congress opened." Yet seven months later was December 1951. It may have been a miscalculation of time or willful obfuscation to avoid admitting they met after she became engaged to John Husted but before it had been publicly announced, as if meeting with him publicly at the Shoreham after her engagement was formalized was more proper. This would fit into the larger effort she made to excise Husted from her biographical narrative. JLBK notation to MVT (circa November–December 1960), MVTP.

16. The Blue Room

January 1952

159 *"the first week . . . over Christmas":* FCW OHI, National Press Club, Part II, p. 72.

159 *"I've always liked . . . go to work":* Ibid., p. 71.

159 *"these bastards":* Ibid., p. 72.

160 *"I'm also a photographer . . . worried look":* "Memories of Jackie the Journalist," by Chuck Conconi, *St. Louis Post-Dispatch*, August 22, 1994.

160 *"She didn't know one end":* FCW OHI, National Press Club, Part II, p. 72.

160 *"pictures were awful":* FCW interview with MVT transcript, MVTP.

160 *"She was smart":* "Mrs. Kennedy—Photo-Reporter," by Dorothy McCardle, *St. Louis Post-Dispatch*, October 12, 1960.

160 *"exceptional skill": Picturing the Promise*, p. 205.

160 *"many amusing . . . best picture":* George Thames OHI, Senate Historical Society.

160 *"beautiful colored . . . very jealous":* JLBK to Janet Travell, July 2, 1957, Books and Manuscripts Auction #2256, Boston, November 21, 2004.

161 *female photographers:* "The surprising encounter between Berenice Abbott and Jackie Kennedy-Onassis," 2018, https://loeildelaphotographie.com/en/the-surprising-encounter-between-berenice-abbott-and-jackie-kennedy-onassis/; Museum of American Art, Lily Emmet Cushing Papers, Series 7: Photographs, 1940–1968, (Box 3–6 linear feet); Toni Frissell Papers, LC, and "Photographer Plucked from Oblivion," by Marjorie Kaufman, *New York Times*, August 28, 1994.

161 *"on a brief tour":* Thayer, *Jacqueline Bouvier Kennedy*, p. 86.

161 *"The column improved . . . people he met":* "Memories of Jackie the Journalist," by Chuck Conconi, *St. Louis Post-Dispatch*, August 22, 1994. For JLB's first days at the paper, see also "Jackie Kennedy—Ex-Girl Reporter," Part II, by Dorothy McCardle, *Tampa Bay Times*, September 29, 1960; "Inaugural Parade Was Her Beat," by Dorothy McCardle, *Tampa Bay Times*, September 29, 1960.

161 *"Everything turns":* FCW interview with MVT transcript, MVTP.

161 *"She didn't know":* FCW AIAW.

161 *"chilly":* Bradford, *America's Queen*, p. 57.

161 *aunt Helen:* Anderson, *Jackie Kennedy Onassis*, p. 91.

161 *"peaceful but dull":* Bradford, p. 57.

162 *"She immediately . . . blasé about it":* Heymann, *A Woman Named Jackie*, p. 93.

162 *"stay away":* FCW AIAW. In one of his National Press Club interviews, FCW further recalled telling her: "a whole generation ahead of you" had hoped to marry JFK, "Lucy Hearst and on down, I really honestly did. And I said, 'You behave yourself.' She said, 'Yes, sir.'" FCW OHI, NPC, Part II, p. 73. In his interview with Molly Thayer, FCW recalled explaining to JLB about JFK: "He don't want to get married. You behave yourself, don't get your hopes up. He's too old for you. She rolled her eyes." MVT interview with FCW transcript MVTP.

162 *"first time . . . to dance":* JLBK to MVT, MVTP.

162 *"Supper Dance . . . in the Blue Room":* Shoreham Hotel's Blue Room menu (circa late 1940s), eBay.

163 *same-day round trip . . . barnstorming the Bay State:* JFK seemed to have been in Washington from Tuesday to Thursday, January 29 to January 31, 1952, and away extensively before and after those dates, based on the following news sources: "Kennedy Gets K. of C. Honor," *Boston Herald*, January 16, 1852; "Women Democrats Annual Meeting," *Boston Globe*, January 13, 1952; "Congressman Greeted at Anniversary Fete," *New Bedford Standard Times*, January 21, 1952; "Cong. Kennedy Is Fiery Speaker at B'nai B'rith Fete," *Chelsea Record*, January 30, 1952; "Rep. John Kennedy, 35, Has Eye on Bigger Job," *Providence Journal*, January 27, 1952; "Government Employees Lay-Off System May Face Overhauling," *Pensacola News Journal*, January 13, 1952; "Probe of Foreign Aid," *Knoxville News-Sentinel*, January 26, 1952; "Panel Speakers to Be Honored at Reception," *Berkshire Eagle*, January 24, 1952; "Kennedy Silent on Politics at Shamrock Dinner," *Boston Globe*, March 18, 1952; "Rep. Kennedy Tells of More

Trouble Spots in Far East," *North Adams Transcript*, February 4, 1952; "Brother Citations Awarded Hynes, Kennedy," *Boston Globe*, February 25, 1952.

163 *"There wouldn't be . . . laughed about"*: Chuck Spaulding OHI JFKL, p. 11.

163 *"He had the wealth . . . anything else"*: Wilton Vaughn OHI JFKL, p. 25.

163 *"he was very much . . . honest intellectually"*: Olin Teague OHI JFKL, p. 3.

163 *Jean's jewelry:* "Gems Stolen from Daughter of Kennedy," *New Bedford Standard-Times*, January 28, 1952; "$34,000 Gems Stolen," *New York Times*, January 28, 1952; "Thieves Steal Jewels from Ex-Envoy's Daughter," *Newport Daily News*, January 28, 1952.

163 *"bigwigs . . . all the time"*: George Taylor OHI JFKL, pp. 8–9.

164 *"recognized talent"*: Terry Goldway interview in "The Real Story of JFK's Irish Inner Circle: Kennedy's Irish Mafia," by Timeline, YouTube.

164 *"intelligence and . . . be achieved"*: Dave Powers AI, July 29, 1987.

164 *"rather left out"*: JLBK to MVT, MVTP.

164 *"old society . . . insight"*: Dave Powers AI, July 29, 1987.

164 *"bland adroitness"*: "Bay State Senatorial Battle Is Being Waged on a High Plane," by Mary McGrory, *Washington Evening Star*, September 21, 1952.

164 *"Jackie is a perfectionist . . . and Lowell"*: Dave Powers AI, July 29, 1987.

164 *"I have never . . . girl I know"*: "Jack and Jackie in Love," *Life*, August 1995.

17. Out on the Street

February 1952

165 *"She concentrated . . . very serious"*: FCW AIAW.

165 *"pretty full . . . of the time"*: Heller, *Jacqueline Kennedy*, p. 136.

165 *"very efficient . . . street with"*: Bradford, *America's Queen*, p. 54.

165 *"become distinct"*: Vivi Crespi AIAW.

166 *"Like politics"*: "Mrs. Kennedy—Photo-Reporter," by Dorothy McCardle, *St. Louis Post-Dispatch*, October 12, 1960.

166 *"If something . . . they haunt me"*: FCW AIAW.

166 *"She loved the efficiency"*: Aileen Bowdoin AIAW.

166 *"precious books . . . putty to work with"*: JLB to Father Leonard, March 1953, as reprinted in the *Boston Globe*, May 13, 2014, and the *Irish Times*, May 13, 2014.

167 *"stomach drop"*: YDA AIAW.

167 *"too much long distance"*: Rhea, *I Was Jacqueline Kennedy's Dressmaker*, p. 31.

167 *"frivolous scholar"*: John White OHI JFKL, p. 14.

167 *"I had the distinct . . . went out occasionally"*: Heymann, *A Woman Named Jackie*, pp. 99–100.

168 *"undigested . . . afraid of it"*: Ibid., pp. 103–4.

168 *"We discussed . . . in her column"*: Ibid., p. 100.

168 *"throw your clothes around"*: "Inquiring Camera Girl," *WTH*, January 5, 1953. To disguise the fact that she made her stepsister Nina Auchincloss provide an answer for the column, JLB identified her as "Nina Gore, high school student," and listed her address as that of the Holton-Arms School on N Street.

168 *"I never said that":* Edward Purcell AI, April 16, 2021.
168 *"Bolivia . . . the country":* FCW AIAW.
168 *"dare to deviate":* Anthony, *AWRH*, p. 61.
169 *"You could make the column":* Ibid., p. 64.
170 *"gave better . . . at rehearsal":* JLBK response to MVT question, MVTP.
171 *music inspired by South American:* As a high school senior, JLB was known by her trademark quip, "Play another rhumba!" JLB entry, Miss Porter's 1947 yearbook.
171 *"something useful . . . limiting to me":* Rhea, p. 37.
171 *"represented the best":* Heymann, *A Woman Named Jackie*, p. 100.

18. Byline
March 1952

173 *"Leap Year Dance":* Exclusively Yours, by Betty Beale, *Washington Star*, March 3, 1952. Other social activities that winter included a bon voyage party she attended with John White and Congressman Frank Roosevelt, the son of the late president ("Bon Voyage for Mrs. Talman," *Washington Evening Star*, April 1, 1952), and serving as a model of knitted clothing made by British Home Industries at an American Red Cross Flood Relief Fund benefit fashion show ("Mrs. Woods' Guests Plan Style Benefit," *Washington Evening Star*, May 1, 1952).
173 *"Everything was done in groups":* Farris, *Inga*, p. 38.
173 *"I didn't know . . . most he dated":* KLB OHI JFKL, July 7, 1964, pp. 377–79.
174 *"Saw Jack occasionally":* JLBK to MVT, MVTP.
174 *"I never saw such passion":* John White OHI JFKL, p. 32.
174 *"said that the most . . . compassionate man":* Ibid., p. 14.
174 *"He had fallen in genuine love":* Farris, p. 88.
175 *"One of ex-ambassador . . . Kennedy no like":* "Man About New York," *Winchell on Broadway*, by Walter Winchell, January 12, 1942.
175 *"You take it too seriously":* YDA AIAW.
175 *"help her with . . . stupid questions":* Kelley, *Jackie Oh!*, p. 14.
176 *"figure it out":* YDA AIAW.
176 *"a distaster . . . good in tails' ":* Sohier commented during the oral history interview with KLB, KLB OHI JFKL, July 7, 1964, p. 388.
176 *"realized that the . . . broke the engagement":* JLBK to MVT, MVTP.
176 *"drivel . . . mean a thing":* Kelley, p. 15.
176 *"John Husted's name":* JLBK to MVT, MVTP.
176 *"decided they were . . . their engagement": Washington Evening Star*, March 23, 1952. News of the breakup "by mutual consent" seems to have first been printed in a *Newport Daily News* column, In Social Circles, on March 22, 1952. Most other papers announced the breakup the following week, on March 28. JLB remained friends with the Husteds, even inviting his sisters to use the Merrywood pool in the summer of 1952. Rhea, *I Was Jacqueline Kennedy's Dressmaker*, p. 59.
176 *"rather confused . . . very wrong":* "Nine Things You Might Not Know About the Kennedys," by Caroline Newman, *UVA Today*, March 27, 2018.

176 *"I am ashamed that we both"*: JLB to Father Leonard, March 1952, as reprinted in the *Boston Globe*, May 13, 2014, and the *Irish Times*, May 13, 2014.
177 *"made me so homesick"*: Ibid.
177 *"I have my name . . . but it's fun"*: Ibid.

19. Working Woman
April 1952

178 *"the line of my stockings"*: JLB autobiographical essay, TVF.
178 *"Jackie leaned over . . . speeding ticket"*: YDAM, p. 11.
179 *"Mrs. Rhea . . . with a cigarette"*: Rhea, *I Was Jacqueline Kennedy's Dressmaker*, pp. 33–34.
180 *"bold and positive strokes . . . with a zipper"*: Ibid., pp. 26, 36, 42, 61.
180 *"She hated to tell . . . opinion on others"*: Anthony, *AWRH*, p. 56.
180 *"that lesbian picture"*: JLBK to MVT, January 10, 1961, MVTP.
181 *"She didn't have any froufrou"*: FCW AIAW.
181 *"She never dressed fancy"*: Heller, *Jacqueline Kennedy*, p. 138. Mini Rhea provided a description of JLB's typical work wardrobe, Rhea, pp. 46–47.
181 *"She didn't dress as well"*: Heller, p. 138.
181 *"Love me, love my dog"*: Rhea, p. 58.
181 *"such rough . . . he expected"*: JLB to Father Leonard, March 1952, as reprinted in the *Boston Globe*, May 13, 2014, and the *Irish Times*, May 13, 2014.
181 *"staff tried to . . . get going"*: Reader comment, December 16, 2013, by Jack Schneider on presidentialpicturestories.com (site discontinued).
181 *"shy and aloof . . . friendly enough"*: Guthrie, *Jackie*, p. 52.
181 *"few felt they . . . friendly"*: Heller, p. 136.
181 *"untrained . . . out of focus"*: Heymann, *A Woman Named Jackie*, p. 94.
182 *"As a reporter . . . tea and crumpets"*: Ibid., p. 95.
182 *"a poor little . . . had money"*: Ibid., p. 96.
182 *"got her share"*: Heller, p. 136.
182 *"In the grim . . . up on her"*: Heymann, *A Woman Named Jackie*, pp. 95–96.
182 *"a fellow"*: FCW AIAW.
183 *"keen mind"*: Rhea, p. 58.
183 *"When I'm really . . . the* New Yorker*"*: JLB to Father Leonard, March 1952, as reprinted in the *Boston Globe*, May 13, 2014, and the *Irish Times*, May 13, 2014.
184 *"the great American novel"*: "Jackie Kennedy—Ex-Girl Reporter," Part II, by Dorothy McCardle, *Tampa Bay Times*, September 29, 1960.
184 *"beautiful piece of work"*: Heymann, *A Woman Named Jackie*, p. 100.
184 *"She was always . . . her own living"*: Anthony, *AWRH*, p. 60.
184 *"myth that I . . . and a half"*: Ibid., p. 61.
184 *"Do we own . . . was shifting"*: FCW AIAW.
185 *"extra man"*: Martha Bartlett AI, November 1, 2019.

20. A Second Dinner

May–June 1952

186 *"leaned across . . . that night":* Anthony, *AWRH*, p. 56.
186 *"trite story . . . for anecdotes":* Kennedy, *Historic Conversations*, p. 5.
186 *"the column . . . all the time":* Senator Edward Kennedy AIAW.
187 *"My courting . . . only private time":* JLBK to MVT, MVTP.
187 *"He came tramping . . . his driveway":* Ibid.
187 *"[N]ever once did":* Laura Berquist OHI JFKL.
187 *"Oh, there were . . . marry Jackie Bouvier":* Jean Mannix OHI JFKL.
188 *"with her camera":* Brien McMahon OHI Senate Historical Society.
188 *Worcester tea party:* "Kennedy to Run for U.S. Senate," *Worcester Daily Telegram*, April 7, 1952; "Kennedy Opens Drive, Hits U.S. Taxing Inequity," *Berkshire Eagle*, May 19, 1952; "400 Women Jam Worcester Hotel for Rep. Kennedy Tea," *Springfield News*, May 19, 1952.
188 *next six weeks:* "Local People on Reception Group for Cong. Kennedy," *Holyoke Transcript-Telegram*, May 24, 1952; "Hostesses Named for Tea on Sunday," *Springfield Union*, May 28, 1952; "At Kennedy Reception," *Milton-Mattapan News*, June 5, 1952; "Cong. Kennedy and Mother Feted at Tea," *East Pepperell Free Press*, June 5, 1952; "Brockton Reception for Kennedy Attended by Many District Women," *Holbrooke Times*, July 4, 1952; "Cong. Kennedy Is Detained; 1000 Women Meet Kin," *Brockton Enterprise and Times*, July 4, 1952.
188 *Ted Williams:* "Memories of Jackie the Journalist," Chuck Conconi, *St. Louis Post-Dispatch*, August 22, 1994.
189 *"Jacqueline seems . . . 5-3":* "Inquiring Photographer," *WTH*, May 10, 1952.
189 *"sheer agony":* Martin, *A Hero for Our Time*, p. 71.
189 *well-timed tactic:* FCW AIAW.
189 *trademark sunglasses:* Bradford, *America's Queen*, p. 54.
190 *"Arthur Krock talking":* "Gridiron Reception Wows 800 Guests," *Washington Evening Star*, May 12, 1952.
190 *"highly intelligent . . . estimation of people":* Heymann, *A Woman Named Jackie*, pp. 102–3.
190 *"around the corner":* Dinah Bridge OHI JFKL, p. 4.
191 *"tell me to go":* Spoto, *Jacqueline Bouvier Kennedy Onassis*, p. 94.
191 *"My father . . . impressed me":* Eunice Shriver OHI AIAW.
191 *"It's not what . . . think you are":* "Two Sons, One Destiny," by Cari Beauchamp, *Vanity Fair*, December 2004.

21. Hyannis Port

July 1952

195 *"Handsomest":* "Kennedy Wins Poll as Most Handsome of U.S. Congressmen," *Berkshire Eagle*, July 2, 1952; "Kennedy Voted Handsomest Member of Congress by 300 Newsfolks," *Washington Times-Herald*, July 2, 1952.

195 *"Attractive . . . to the altar":* "Leap Year Doesn't Bother Bachelors in Washington," by Jane Eads, *New Bedford Standard-Times*, February 24, 1952.

195 *"I had already . . . I adored him":* Rose Kennedy, *Times to Remember*, p. 347.

195 *Joe's tales:* Vidal, *Palimpsest*, p. 37.

195 *"They would talk about":* Bill Walton quoted in Martin, *A Hero for Our Time*, p. 84.

196 *"Joe soon became . . . conquering his son":* Lem Billings quoted in Heymann, *A Woman Named Jackie*, p. 116.

196 *"sense of fun":* Guthrie, *Jackie*, p. 69.

196 *"Meals were . . . the whole time":* Dinah Bridge OHI JFKL, p. 6.

196 *"There was a tremendous . . . insubordinate about it":* Chuck Spalding OHI JFKL, pp. 4–5.

196 *"while there was . . . him very much":* Arthur Krock OHI JFKL, p. 10.

196 *"So . . . Telephone Booth'":* Chuck Spalding quoted in Martin, p. 84.

197 *Boston baked beans:* Rose Kennedy, 1974 interview, Thames TV, YouTube.

197 *"It's incredible how . . . out of his mind":* Lem Billings OHI JFKL, July 7, 1964, pp. 321–28.

197 *"It was the first time":* Rose Kennedy, pp. 347–48.

197 *"morally, mentally . . . about his clothes":* Rose Kennedy, 1974 interview, Thames TV, YouTube.

198 *"so strong . . . read a book":* JLB to Father Leonard, July 1952, as reprinted in the *Boston Globe*, May 13, 2014, and the *Irish Times*, May 13, 2014.

198 *"had a shyness . . . in the limelight":* Polly Fitzgerald OHI JFKL, p. 43.

198 *"[H]e read that set":* JLBK to John Steinbeck, March 22, 1964, Heritage Auctions Catalog, October 27, 2019.

198 *"bragged":* Senator Edward Kennedy OHI AIAW.

198 *"a bully for . . . that Jack did":* JLBK to John Steinbeck, March 8, 1964, Heritage Auctions Catalog, October 27, 2019.

199 *"socialist-labor czars":* The editorial also appeared in the *East Boston Leader*, January 11, 1952.

199 *his right to his opinion:* "Rep. John Kennedy, 35, Has Eye on Bigger Job," *Providence Journal*, January 27, 1952; "Cong. Kennedy Is Fiery Speaker at B'nai B'rith Fete," *Chelsea Record*, January 30, 1952.

199 *complaints of Jack's:* "Absenteeism in Congress," *Haverhill Gazette*, June 9, 1952; "Kennedy Unable to Give Speeches," *Springfield Union*, June 30, 1952; Kennedy Sends Regrets to Area," *Greenfield Recorder-Gazette*, July 1, 1952.

199 *unspoken strategy . . . marital status:* Senator Edward Kennedy AIAW; Dave Powers AI, July 29, 1987.

199 *women voters:* "Kennedy Wants Women's Vote," *Springfield Union*, June 28, 1952.

200 *Hauptmann . . . Roosevelt:* Anthony, *AWRH*, p. 67.

200 *campaign buttons:* YDA AIAW.

200 *"the first political voice":* Anthony, *AWRH*, p. 67.

22. Summer in the City

August–September 1952

201 *"How do you keep cool?":* "Inquiring Photographer," *WTH*, July 10, 1952.

202 *"something of a grind . . . to another":* Heymann, *A Woman Named Jackie*, pp. 97–98.

202 *"your pool":* Ibid., p. 96.

202 *Octagon House:* script, JLB File, AIA archives.

203 *Stephen M. Walter:* Walter was a registered lobbyist for the National Association of Electric Companies, and he earned an annual income of contemporary equivalence to $630,000. A World War I veteran awarded the naval cross by President Wilson, he was proud of his nickname, "Hole-in-the-Head," bestowed on him after a bullet punctured his helmet. At the time he met JLB, he was beginning to work on inventing an "excavating tool combined with a firearm." In 1940, he avidly publicized Wendell Willkie as that year's Republican presidential candidate. He'd begun professional life as a reporter for the *Wichita Beacon*, then the *Lima Gazette* in Ohio, before moving to Washington, where he briefly continued in journalism and became an active member of the National Press Club. *Congressional Record*, May 20 to June 4, 1959, Vol. 105, Part 7; 1940 Washington, D.C., Census; "Washington Memo," *Minneapolis Star Tribune*, December 22, 1953; "Edison in Washington," *Selma Times-Journal*, May 22, 1947; "Press Club Gives Roosevelt Cake," *Washington Sunday Star*, March 3, 1935; "St. Joseph Boy Decorated," *St. Joseph News-Press*, December 29, 1920; "Washington Letter," *[Madison] Capitol Times*, September 5, 1948; "Washington Memo," *Minnesota Star-Tribune*, December 22, 1953; "Utility Lobbyist Boomed Willkie, PM," August 1, 1940; JLB to Stephen M. Walter, n.d. (circa 1952), William Hetzler to Nancy Hadley, American Institute of Architects, March 27, 2011, JLB File, AIA; Margaret Phalen, Octagon House manager to author, April 27, 2020.

203 *"kicked the bucket . . . last three years":* JVB to EBB1, October 2, 1952, courtesy of Kent Bartram.

203 *Newport Hospital:* Society, *Washington Evening Star*, August 4, 1952.

203 *"roam wild":* YDA AIAW. JLBK incorrectly recalled the year of the World Bank Conference as 1951—the event in Mexico City was held in 1952.

204 *"[I] loved Acapulco . . . honeymoon in":* JLBK response to MVT, MVTP.

204 *"interesting . . . attracted to her":* YDA AIAW.

205 *"He's already left town":* early draft manuscript *AWRH*, author's collection.

205 *"spasmodic . . . the following Wednesday":* Anthony, *AWRH*, p. 72.

205 *Schrafft's:* "Around Boston," *Boston Record*, July 7, 1952.

205 *"I don't want . . . had all four":* YDA interview, *CNNLKL*.

205 *"Jack cooked":* YDA, September 1952, diary entry, McG.

206 *"an amazing insight . . . I'm in love":* JLB to Father Leonard, July 1952, as reprinted in the *Boston Globe*, May 13, 2014, and the *Irish Times*, May 13, 2014.

23. Massachusetts

October–November 1952

207 *"Worked on the paper . . . much of Jack":* JLBK to MVT, MVTP.

207 *"only made suggestions":* Martha Walter interview, "Jacqueline Bouvier as Aspiring Writer," *Washington Post*, February 10, 1976.

208 *"Here it is":* JLB to Stephen Walter, JLB file, AIA archives. Earlier that year, on January 14, 1952, NBC had debuted a weekday morning program called the *Today* show, expanding the fifteen-minute news show format to include human interest and celebrity stories.

208 *"[p]olitics is no place":* Jack Davis AIAW.

209 *the Kennedy women:* Jean Smith and Margaret Truman, *Boston Globe*, October 17, 1952; "Joseph P. Kennedys Have First Grandson," *Boston Globe*, September 25, 1952; "Mrs. Kennedy Will Fly Here from Paris," *Berkshire Eagle*, August 19, 1952.

209 *Jackie turned up:* Martin, *A Hero for Our Time*, p. 78; "Adlai's Schedule," *Boston Globe*, October 26, 1952; "Adlai Warns of McCarthy," *Boston Globe*, October 27, 1952; "Quincy Crowd Swells to 500 to Hear Adlai," *Boston Globe*, October 27, 1952; "Adlai Attends Unitarian Church in Cambridge," *Boston Globe*, October 26, 1952; "Stevenson Sidelights," *Boston Globe*, October 26, 1952; "Dever, Kennedy Cheered," *Boston Globe*, October 26, 1952; Rose Kennedy, Charlie Bartlett interview with MVT, MVTP; anecdote of JLB shaking JFK's hand at event, Dave Powers AI, 1987.

210 *Jack's two-bedroom apartment:* Eunice Shriver AIAW, Senator Edward Kennedy AIAW.

210 *"frank play": Congressional Quarterly*, October 3, 1952.

210 *"the woman was":* Whalen, *Kennedy Versus Lodge*, p. 159.

210 *"Every unmarried woman":* Ibid., p. 85.

211 *"bought it":* Martha Walter interview, "Jacqueline Bouvier as Aspiring Writer."

211 *"to congratulate . . . deserve it":* YDA to JLB, December 18, 1952.

212 *"Jackie was especially . . . to go there":* Rhea, *I Was Jacqueline Kennedy's Dressmaker*, p. 79.

213 *"She had on a pink . . . joined in":* Mamie Moore AI, May 14, 2021.

215 *"I noticed how . . . Camera Girl":* Davis, *JB*, p. 162.

215 *"He hurt me . . . needs a wife":* JLB to Father Leonard, post-1952, as reprinted in the *Boston Globe*, May 13, 2014, and the *Irish Times*, May 13, 2014.

215 *"bushy and fluffy . . . President someday":* Davis, *JB*, p. 163.

24. Palm Beach, II

November–December 1952

216 *"became immediately":* Mamie Moore AI, May 14, 2021.

216 *"do something to make":* Anthony, *AWRH*, p. 66; see also "Jackie Kennedy—

Ex-Girl Reporter," Part IV, by Dorothy McCardle, *Tampa Bay Times*, October 1, 1960; "infuriated," *Carlsbad Current-Argus*, October 26, 1960.

216 *"stood there . . . probation":* FCW AIAW.

217 *"bad thing":* JLB to Bess Furman Armstrong, November 24, 1952, Furman Papers, LC.

217 *"told people . . . much publicity":* Rhea, *I Was Jacqueline Kennedy's Dressmaker*, p. 87.

218 *"[I]f I could only . . . ten years old":* JLB to Bess Furman Armstrong, November 24, 1952, Furman Papers, LC.

218 *"went off the air":* Martha Walter interview, "Jacqueline Bouvier as Aspiring Writer," *Washington Post*, February 10, 1976.

219 *"For my hopeful Jackie": The Estate of Jacqueline Kennedy Onassis*, April 23–26, Sotheby's: New York, 1996, p. 523, Lot 1029.

219 *"shopgirls . . . Merry Christmas!":* Rhea, p. 7.

220 *"She had real talent":* "Mrs. Kennedy—Photo-Reporter," by Dorothy McCardle, *St. Louis Post-Dispatch*, October 12, 1960.

220 *"terrific idea . . . Bouvier stole":* Rhea, pp. 88–92.

220 *"fundamentally more . . . merely smiled":* Ibid., pp. 61–62, 102–3.

221 *European trip:* "See in Europe Says Kennedy After Visit," *Boston Globe*, December 18, 1952.

221 *"Very pleased":* YDA to JLB, December 18, 1952.

221 *"woman's whole existence":* JLB to Father Leonard, post–November 1952, as reprinted in the *Boston Globe*, May 13, 2014, and the *Irish Times*, May 13, 2014; "Jacqueline Kennedy Letters Reveal Her Private Side," *The Daily Gazette*, by the Associated Press, May 14, 2014.

221 *"wondered about it":* Dave Powers OHI JFKL, p. 20.

222 *"they spoke of me":* Vidal, *Palimpsest*, p. 312.

222 *"I think Jack knew":* Charlie Bartlett interview, *CNNLKL*.

222 *"I think he was probably . . . always there":* Kennedy, *Historic Conversations*, p. 3.

223 *"mutual affection . . . and an admirer":* Martin, *A Hero for Our Time*, p. 77.

223 *"I'm more like":* Ibid.

223 *"the only one who really knew":* Frischauer, *Jackie*, p. 49.

223 *"told me that":* Martin, p. 74.

223 *"Nobody would have":* Lem Billings OHI JFKL, July 7, 1964, pp. 392–93.

223 *"Mr. Kennedy didn't":* Ibid., January 15, 1965, pp. 495–96.

223 *"Senator-Elect Jack Kennedy":* "The Gold Coast," by Aileen Mehle, *Miami Daily News*, December 21, 1952.

223 *"U.S. Senator-elect":* "Voice of Broadway," by Dorothy Kilgallen, *Scranton Times-Tribune*, December 23, 1952. In some cases, newspapers carried the column as just "Broadway."

224 *"he never was successful":* Lem Billings OHI JFKL, July 7, 1964, pp. 361–62.

224 *"swamped . . . seems to happen":* "JFK: In His Own Words," 1988 documentary, Kunhardt Productions, Inc., YouTube.

25. Inauguration
January 1953

226 *"I told her . . . better understand him":* Lem Billings OHI JFKL, July 7, 1964, pp. 389–91.

227 *"glittering gold drapes":* "Ike, Mamie Celebrate—Inaugural Ball Is Brilliant," by Relman Morin, and "Fancy Inaugural Affair," by George Shannon, both *Shreveport Journal*, January 21, 1953. See also "Inaugural Ball," *New York Times*, January 21, 1953; *Boston Globe*, January 21, 1953.

227 *"Looking a little":* "Inaugural Great on TV," *Boston Globe*, January 20, 1953.

227 *"He wins . . . other women":* The story was published under different titles in different papers, including "Morning After and One," by Inez Robb, *Hackensack Record*, January 21, 1953, and "Kennedy Rates Tops with Mothers of Marriageable," by Inez Robb, *Cedar Rapids Gazette*, January 21, 1953.

228 *"If I know one thing . . . talk to them":* Lincoln, *My Twelve Years with John F. Kennedy*, p. 15.

228 *Paul Healy:* January 26, 1953, entry, JFK appointment book, Evelyn Lincoln Papers [ELP], JFKL.

228 *Jefferson–Jackson Day Dinner:* "Democrats Want Senator Kennedy," *Wichita Beacon*, January 26, 1953; Senator Kennedy addressed the Women's National Democratic Club on February 12, 1953, see "Senator to Speak," *Washington Evening Star*, February 11, 1953.

228 *"went out constantly":* JLBK to MVT, MVTP.

228 *"He began taking":* Lem Billings OHI JFKL, July 7, 1964, pp. 379–80.

229 *romantic musical* Gigi*:* February 14, 1953, entry, JFK appointment book, ELP, JFKL.

229 *"Catherine Plummer . . . a job":* June 15, 1953, and July 10, 1953, entries, JFK appointment book, ELP, JFKL.

229 *"If he were in New York":* Lem Billings OHI JFKL, July 7, 1964, pp. 379–80.

229 *"Later . . . a challenge'":* Ibid., pp. 389–91.

230 *"He's like my father":* JLB to Father Leonard, July 1952, as reprinted in the *Boston Globe*, May 13, 2014, and the *Irish Times*, May 13, 2014.

26. Love and Sex
February 1953

233 *"They were very much alike":* Davis, *JB*, p. 166.

233 *"needing a haircut":* Bouvier, *Black Jack Bouvier*, p. 226.

233 *"young Mr. Kennedy":* Davis, *JB*, p. 166.

233 *"heartbreaking figure . . . in some way":* This epitaph was also later attributed to CLB[R], Davis, *JB*, p. 166.

234 *"in love":* Davis, *TKDD*, p. 156.

234 *"[w]e have two brain systems":* Helen Fisher quoted in "Romantic Jealousy and Romantic Envy: A Seven-Nation Study," by Ralph B. Hupka, Bram Buunk,

Gábor Falus et al., *Journal of Cross-Cultural Psychology* 16, no. 4 (December 1985): pp. 423–46.

235 *"crazy about girls . . . as friends":* Lem Billings OHI JFKL, July 7, 1964, pp. 381–83.

235 *"He was very attentive":* Anthony, *AWRH*, p. 88.

235 *"He wasn't by nature":* Chuck Spalding OHI JFKL, p. 21.

235 *"heightened perception . . . kind of detachment":* Ibid., pp. 104–5.

236 *first times that Miss Bouvier's:* February 10 and February 20, 1953, entries, JFK appointment book, ELP, JFKL.

27. Meeting of the Minds
March 1953

237 *"He was not the":* early draft manuscript *AWRH*, author's collection.

237 *"respect for each other's":* YDA interview, "Jack, Jackie Kennedy's Wedding 50 Years Ago Remembered by Friends, Family," *CNNLKL*.

237 *"He loved to pull":* Clement J. Zablocki OHI JFKL, p. 34.

237 *rowboat:* MVT interview with Charlie Bartlett notes, MVTP.

237 *St. Patrick's Day party:* "The Night Ethel Kennedy Met Jackie Bouvier," New England Historical Society online magazine, updated 2019 [no author listed], www.newenglandhistoricalsociety.com/night-ethel-kennedy-met-jackie-bouvier/.

238 *"George, you're thin-skinned":* George Taylor OHI JFKL, pp. 9–10.

238 *Never known to use:* Amanda Smith interview, C-SPAN Book TV, February 27, 2001.

238 *Florida postcard:* JFK postcard to Boston Senate staff member Grace Burke, March 7, 1955, RR Auctions Catalog, Lot 161, September 13, 2017.

238 *mildly caricatured:* JLB to YDA, April 8, 1945.

238 *stereotyped:* the lines of stereotyped dialect were: "But watch yo' step, honey / On that path of roses / There's more thorns beneath them / Then you now knowses." JLB to "Woodleigh" (Puffin Gates), n.d. (circa spring 1949), Heritage Auctions Catalog, February 20–21, 2006.

238 The Invisible Man*:* YDA AIAW.

238 *"effeminate":* JLB to JLA, May 7, 1950, University Archives Catalog, Lot 128, January 23, 2019.

239 *"I'm not that kind of boy":* Farris, *Inga*, p. 91.

239 *his many health problems:* "A New View of JFK's Addison's Disease," by Thomas H. Maugh II, *Los Angeles Times*, September 5, 2009; "All the President's Secrets: John F. Kennedy and Addison's Disease," by Lee R. Mandel, *Healio News*, July 12, 2019.

239 *"There were stretches . . . and he did":* Chuck Spalding OHI JFKL, pp. 7–8.

240 *"determined to snatch":* Leaming, *Jacqueline Bouvier Kennedy Onassis*, p. 38.

240 *"something that he . . . what he could":* Chuck Spalding OHI JFKL, pp. 13–14.

240 *"cabbage":* "A Seaman Remembers John F. Kennedy," by Larry Habermehl, *The Sea Breeze*, The Boston Seaman's Friend Society, July 1964.

240 *"a standing joke":* Chuck Spalding OHI JFKL, p. 14.

240 *"You haven't paid me":* "A Seaman Remembers John F. Kennedy."

240 *"became acquainted":* Olin Teague OHI JFKL, p. 4.
240 The Raven . . . Pilgrim's Way*:* Anthony, *AWRH*, pp. 72–73.
241 *"mad, bad and dangerous":* Bradford, *America's Queen*, p. 60.
241 *"He knew all the great":* JLBK to John Steinbeck, March 22, 1964, Heritage Auctions Catalog, October 27, 2019.
241 *"Jackie's mind was":* Letitia Baldrige OHI AIAW.
241 *"His whole mind could":* Lem Billings OHI JFKL, July 22, 1964, pp. 426–27.
241 *"Jack did not write . . . own private reading":* JLBK to John Steinbeck, March 8, 1964, Heritage Auctions Catalog, October 27, 2019.
242 *"bluestocking":* JLBK to MVT, MVTP.
242 *"full of love . . . love for me":* JLBK to John Steinbeck, March 22, 1964, Heritage Auctions Catalog, October 27, 2019.
242 *"We both have curious":* "Jackie Can't Campaign," by Mary Cremmen, *Tampa Tribune*, September 29, 1960.
242 *"interested in everything . . . think objectively":* Ibid.
242 *"I make ghastly":* JLB to YDA, October 20, 1948.
242 *"I don't think that Jack Kennedy":* Lem Billings OHI JFKL, July 7, 1964, p. 368.
242 *"the man who made me":* "Pat and Jackie: A Contrast," by Fran Lewine, *Washington Evening Star*, October 16, 1960.
242 *"When I studied French":* "Jackie Can't Campaign."
243 *ambassador from Vietnam:* February 18, 1953, entry, JFK appointment book, ELP, JFKL.
243 *Ed Gullion:* Priscilla Mullins phone AI, October 26, 2019.
243 *"One of my most . . . things at once":* JLB autobiographical essay, TVF JFKL.
244 *"happiness . . . one's scope":* "Why Does This Woman Work?" Gloria Steinem interview with JLBKO, *Ms. Magazine*, May 1979.
244 *"unsentimental realism . . . informed calculation":* Logevall, *JFK Coming of Age in the American Century*, p. 254.
244 *"had some firsthand . . . political events":* Chuck Spalding OHI JFKL, p. 21.
245 *"Once you can . . . about by words":* Caroline Kennedy, *The Best-Loved Poems of Jacqueline Kennedy Onassis* (New York: Hyperion, 2001), p. 168.

28. The Vietnam Report
March–April 1953

Unless otherwise noted, all quotations in this chapter are from JLB's "Vietnam Report," Senate Files, General Files, 1953–1960, Indo-China [Speech], April 20, 1953–January 8, 1955, and Undated, [IC (Indo-China) File] JFKL.

246 *comprehensive study:* JFK to Secretary of State John Foster Dulles, May 7, 1953, IC File, JFKL.
246 *"nerve-racking":* Exclusively Yours, by Betty Beale, *Washington Evening Star*, December 21, 1952.
247 *"he gave me all these French books":* Kennedy, *Historic Conversations*, pp. 64–65.

JLBK's memory that she worked on the Vietnam Report "the summer before we married" is incorrect, since JFK did not begin his service as U.S. senator until January 1953.

247 *"Yeah, he could read . . . facts and things":* Ibid., p. 65.

247 *"I couldn't tell . . . the pages":* Ibid., p. 64.

249 *danger to any public figure:* The "red-baiting" Senator Joseph McCarthy and his hearings on suspected communist sympathizers in the U.S. government posed an especial challenge for JFK. JPK was a friend to McCarthy; Eunice dated him; RFK worked for him until the summer of 1953. When, in the fall of 1954, McCarthy was censured and JFK was unable to vote, his brother Teddy later credited Jackie as being "one of those who urged him to release a public statement" condemning McCarthy's tactics, permitting JFK to at least be on the record as having opposed to them. Senator Edward Kennedy AIAW.

249 *Jackie had discussed Indochina:* YDA AIAW.

250 *"Palestinian problem . . . of self-defense":* YDA to JLB, December 18, 1952.

250 *"for success":* Replies to questions that accompanied the letter of May 7, 1953, U.S. State Department to JFK, p. 1, IC File, JFKL.

250 *"cover so many . . . the information":* Thruston B. Morton, assistant secretary of state to JFK, May 8, 1953, IC File, JFKL.

250 *"While I knew . . . earliest convenience":* JFK to Secretary of State John Foster Dulles, May 25, 1953, IC File, JFKL.

250 *"support of the legitimate":* "Far Eastern Trip, 1951," Pre-Presidential Papers, Box 011, Boston Office Files, Speech Files 46–52.

250 *"He has got to . . . for him":* Leaming, *Jacqueline Bouvier Kennedy Onassis*, p. 37. Leaming quotes from a conversation Dorothy Schiff had with JLBK. "I had to be married for my contribution to that," is how JLBK recalled it in slightly different language for her oral history. Kennedy, *Historic Conversations*, p. 64.

29. Dating

April–May 1953

251 *"Wish you were here":* Anthony, *AWRH*, p. 80.

251 *"involved . . . thing at a time":* MVT interview with Charlie Bartlett notes, MVTP.

251 *"No, he just never . . . connubial life":* Chuck Spalding OHI JFKL, p. 25.

252 *"I'm not the heavy romantic":* Anthony, *AWRH*, p. 184.

252 *"We said . . . send him the bill":* Lorraine Cooper OHI, John Sherman Cooper Papers, University of Kentucky.

252 *offered her insights:* JLBK heard on privately recorded conversation between journalists and Senator JFK, *NBC Nightly News*, October 13, 2008 (David Von Pein's JFK Channel, YouTube). She did not appreciate all the political strategy sessions she joined; see Davis, *TKDD*, p. 155.

252 *"Bouvier":* March 10, 1953, entry, JFK appointment book, ELP, JFKL.

252 *Norman Blitz:* Kennedy, *Historic Conversations*, p. 10; Anthony, *AWRH*, p. 116.

253 *Pell:* Claiborne Pell AIAW.
253 *Brandon:* Henry Brandon OHI JFKL.
253 *"could really think":* Joan Braden AIAW.
253 *"inquisitive . . . sort of comfort":* YDA interview, *CNNLKL.*
253 *"I knew right away . . . same whole":* Anthony, *AWRH*, p. 84.
253 *"always surer to last":* JLB to "Woodleigh" (Puffin Gates), n.d., Heritage Auctions Catalog, February 20–21, 2006.
254 *"nearly killed Mummy":* JLB to Father Leonard, July 1952, as reprinted in the *Boston Globe*, May 13, 2014, and the *Irish Times*, May 13, 2014.
254 *"She was going . . . permitted divorce":* YDA AIAW.
254 *"would learn that marriage":* Author screenshot of JLBKO Autograph Manuscript Unsigned [n.d.] Page "3," memo on yellow-lined paper (post-1963), likely provided to Rose Kennedy in preparation for her memoirs, at one time available for purchase online at "History for Sale," ID#285921, copy in author's collection.
254 *"has a tendency":* JFK letter to Red Fay, read by the latter during his September 23, 2003, interview, *CNNLKL.*
254 *"I kept him company":* CLB[R] to MVT, November 1960, MVTP.
255 *"ballerina-length":* MVT notes, interview with Nina Straight, MVTP.
255 *"How did you guess . . . get mad":* Ibid.
255 *"danced Janet around":* Kuhn, *Reading Jackie*, p. 229. Many presume JFK attended the Bouvier-Canfield wedding (one claim indicated that JFK watched JLB catching the bouquet "with a wry smile." Pottker, *Janet and Jackie*, pp. 125–26). JFK photos at a Merrywood reception are from the Auchincloss-Straight wedding, for which he was a groomsman. On the Bouvier-Canfield wedding day, JFK appeared live at 6:30 p.m. on the WEEI Boston television station's "Report from Washington," interviewed by Ron Cochran, "Radio-Television-FM," *Boston Globe*, April 18, 1953, but it was almost certainly pretaped. He was scheduled to appear the next day at a Lexington, Massachusetts, Patriot Day parade (*Boston Daily Globe*, April 20, 1953), a fact verified by his senate calendar, which included events starting at 11:30 a.m.
255 *"But Jackie":* Dubois, *In Her Sister's Shadow*, p. 71.
255 *"She insisted":* YDA AIAW.
256 *"I am going to quit . . . hard news":* Heymann, *A Woman Named Jackie*, pp. 97–98.
256 *"a whole generation":* FCW OHI, National Press Club, Part II, p. 73.
256 *"You behave . . . her assignment":* MVT interview with FCW notes, MVTP.
257 *"We were all young . . . a given":* "Jackie Onassis: Former First Lady, American Icon," by Mary McCarty, *Dayton Daily News*, May 20, 1994.
257 *"rolled her eyes":* FCW OHI, National Press Club, Part II, p. 73.
257 *"[t]he editor liked it . . . newspaper office":* JLB to Mrs. McCrea, n.d. (circa April 1953), RR Auction Catalog, Item 88, June 2010.
258 *"if I'll live":* Anthony, *AWRH*, p. 75.
258 *"having a tough time . . . know tomorrow":* Aileen Train AIAW.
258 *"I felt she really . . . felt about you":* JLA OHI JFKL.
259 *"[S]he had gone":* Aileen Train AIAW.

259 *"We had been trying . . . every day":* "Memories of Jackie the Journalist," by Chuck Conconi, *St. Louis Post-Dispatch*, August 22, 1994.
259 *"if they [the* Times-Herald*]":* JLA OHI JFKL.
259 *"Jackie insisted . . . every receipt":* Aileen Train AIAW.
259 *"[H]e wanted to get . . . the coronation":* Joan Braden AIAW.
259 *"[h]e had asked her":* Aileen Train AIAW.
259 *"Jackie, to my . . . that sure":* Lem Billings OHI JFKL, June 19, 1964, p. 70.
259 *"I couldn't visualize":* Peter Collier and David Horowitz, *The Kennedys: An American Drama* (New York: Warner Books, 1984), pp. 237–38. Billings granted an interview to the authors nearly twenty years after his series of oral history interviews for the JFKL.
259 *"It wasn't until":* Lem Billings OHI JFKL, June 19, 1964, p. 70.
260 *"She wanted the White House . . . of the land":* Letitia Baldrige remarks, "The President's Spouse" symposium, November 1, 1994, C-SPAN. John White asserted that, "More important to her than his morality was that he be at the center of events and that he acquit himself well and give her a decent role in the drama," Heymann, *A Woman Named Jackie*, p. 110.
260 *"Jackie had always known":* Vidal, *Palimpsest*, p. 511.
260 *"both very patriotic":* YDA interview, *CNNLKL.*
260 *"I wanted Jack to be":* JLBK to MVT, MVTP.
260 *"really part of the deal":* Charlie Bartlett interview, "Jack, Jackie Kennedy's Wedding 50 Years Ago Remembered by Friends, Family," *Larry King Live*, September 23, 2003.
260 *"Both of us knew":* Anthony, *AWRH*, p. 75.
260 *"[S]he expected to marry soon":* "Kennedy's Fiancée Sketched and Wrote About Coronation," *Boston Globe*, June 26, 1953.

30. Coronation
May–June 1953

Unless otherwise noted, all quotations in this chapter are from the author's 1995 interview with Aileen Bowdoin Train for *AWRH.*

261 SS *United States:* SS *United States* Conservancy website, ssusc.org, and the United States Lines, united-states-lines.org. The daily chronicle of onboard activities from Friday, May 22, 1953, to Wednesday, May 27, 1953, is under the latter's heading "The Passenger Experience," https://united-states-lines.org/the-passenger-experience/.
262 *"enjoy himself":* "Dogs Have Their Day on Coronation Cruise," by JLB, *WTH*, May 31, 1953.
262 *"I'll get a chance . . . camera overboard":* Rhea, *I Was Jacqueline Kennedy's Dressmaker*, pp. 114–15.
262 *"the more evolved":* Mimi Cecil AIAW.

264 *"theater boxes . . . jewel box"*: "Crowds of Americans Fill Bright and Pretty London," by JLB, *WTH*, June 2, 1953.
264 *third feature piece:* "The Mesta Fiesta—Second Only to the Coronation—Was the Show to See in London Last Week," by JLB, *WTH*, June 3, 1953.
264 *"very clever"*: JLA OHI JFKL.
264 *"I could see . . . as a writer"*: Rhea, p. 115.
264 *"Articles Excellent"*: Anthony, *AWRH*, p. 76.
265 *Eunice Kennedy's wedding:* "Miss Eunice Kennedy Becomes Bride of Robert Shriver, Jr.," *Palm Beach Post*, May 24, 1953.
265 *"Something was said"*: Jean Mannix OHI JFKL.
265 *"Oh, we do wish . . . mature intellectually"*: Margaret Coit OHI JFKL.
266 *"Look at my father!"*: Bradford, *America's Queen*, p. 66.
266 *"Read the newspapers"*: Vidal, *Palimpsest*, pp. 309–10.
266 *"with zebra cushions . . . hotel Bisson"*: MVT notes on Aileen Bowdoin Train interview, MVTP. While they were in their hotel, Aileen recalled, the restaurant manager brought glasses of champagne to them, then poured rose liqueur in her glass and violet liqueur in JLB's glass, declaring the drinks to be "L'Aileen" and "La Jacqueline." Aileen Train AIAW.
267 *"I don't think it was settled"*: Lem Billings OHI JFKL, July 7, 1964, pp. 380–81.
267 *"giving up her job"*: FCW AIAW.
267 *"I'm just about to fly"*: JLB to Glen Hearin postcard n.d. (June 1953), first-draft manuscript *AWRH*.
268 *"I'm going to meet her"*: JLA OHI JFKL.
268 *"I don't know how he"*: Lem Billings OHI JFKL, July 7, 1964, p. 387.
268 *"popped the question . . . like that"*: Rhea, p. 124.

31. Engagement

June 1953

269 *"At that point . . . married to him"*: Anthony, *AWRH*, p. 79.
270 *"to talk matters over"*: "Senator, Fiancée Jackie Enjoying Cape Weekend," by Joan McPartlin, *Boston Sunday Globe*, June 28, 1953.
270 *As suggested in remarks:* "Kennedy, Fiancée Plan 'Simple, Small Wedding,'" by Virginia Bohlin, *Boston Traveler*, June 25, 1953.
270 *"in their hats . . . Yes, Mother"*: Rose Kennedy, *Times to Remember*, p. 350.
271 *"sent his wife . . . difficult discussion"*: Jamie Auchincloss interview, *CNNLKL*.
271 *"Her mother was so sensitive . . . public figure"*: Anthony, *AWRH*, p. 80.
271 *"[M]y mother stood up to"*: Jamie Auchincloss interview, *CNNLKL*.
271 *"dominant figure"*: Red Fay interview, *CNNLKL*.
271 *"an alien force"*: Jamie Auchincloss interview, *CNNLKL*.
271 *"Oh, Mummy, you don't"*: Mulvaney, *Diana and Jackie*, p. 117.
271 *"a title that was"*: Jamie Auchincloss interview, *CNNLKL*.
271 *"Mrs. Auchincloss . . . hive of bees"*: YDA AIAW.

272 *"One of his . . . absolutely delighted":* Jamie Auchincloss interview, *CNNLKL.*

272 *"One hundred Irish":* "The Grotesque American Wedding," by Kevin D. Williamson, *National Review*, July 21, 2020.

273 *"heiress":* "To Wed Heiress: Most Eligible Bachelor in Washington Is Engaged," *Traverse City Record-Eagle*, June 25, 1953. The syndicated United Press story ran, for example, in the June 26, 1953, *Alliance [Nebraska] Times-Herald*, under the title "Washington Heiress, Senator John F. Kennedy to Marry."

273 *"storybook romance":* "Inquiring Camera Girl to Be Sen. Kennedy's Bride," *WTH*, June 25, 1953.

273 *"trim, dapper":* Kessler, *The Sins of the Father*, pp. 294–95. See also "John C. Dowd a Child Prodigy Who Delivered on His Promise," by Joseph F. Dineen, *Boston Globe*, February 16, 1951.

274 *"Do it quickly":* Kessler, pp. 294–95.

274 *"Mr. and Mrs Hugh D. . . . the* Washington Times-Herald*":* Wedding, 1953: Dowd Publicity Material: Engagement, Press Release, JPK Personal Papers, JFKL.

274 *forced to give up her job:* The fact that JLB was tired of writing the column and eager to marry JFK has often been conflated with the fact that she was manipulated into abandoning her writing aspirations. The first person she talked about it with was Virginia Bohlin on Wednesday evening. "They told me I could take the summer off and come back in the fall," she told her, adding apathetically, "I don't think I will now, though." At some point the next day, as the news spread of her engagement, JLB was in contact with the *Times-Herald*. Later that day, the *Boston Globe*'s John Harris spoke with her colleagues, reporting that she was a "star on the staff," "personally a real favorite of people working on the paper," and that Washingtonians were "going to miss the lively sketches and stories." Published on Friday, his statement confirmed that she "gave up her newspaper job yesterday." Two days later, however, Percy Williams reported her more hopeful declaration that although she gave up her "newspaper work," she would "continue writing." Jackie Bouvier would long associate marriage with being led to relinquish her work. "We were engaged," she explicitly stated to Molly Thayer, "when I gave up my job at the paper." "Newspaper Staff Will Miss Lively Jacky: Kennedy's Fiancée Sketched and Wrote About the Coronation," by John Harris, *Boston Daily Globe*, June 26, 1953; "Kennedy, Fiancée Want 'Quiet, Family Wedding,'" by Percy Williams, *Boston Sunday Herald*, June 28, 1953; JLB to MVT, MVTP.

274 *"You couldn't ask . . . to the story":* "Turnabout 'a Little Frightening' to Jackie," by Elizabeth Watts, *Boston Globe*, June 26, 1953.

275 *"not long after . . . stomach disorder":* "Senator Loses Bachelorhood to Camera Girl," by Ruth Montgomery, *New York Daily News*, June 25, 1953.

275 *"If I hadn't married":* "Why Does This Woman Work?" Gloria Steinem interview with JLBKO, *Ms. Magazine*, May 1979.

275 *"get rid of . . . family is enough":* Rhea, *I Was Jacqueline Kennedy's Dressmaker*, pp. 124, 129.

275 *"So Happy"*: JLB to Father Leonard, June 1953, as reprinted in the *Boston Globe*, May 13, 2014, and the *Irish Times*, May 13, 2014.

276 *"that occasion . . . welcome"*: YDAM, p. 16.

276 *"My mother had written"*: Bradford, *America's Queen*, p. 72.

277 *"in plenty of time . . . men must know"*: "Fiancée Almost Misses Cape Hop with Kennedy," *Boston Globe*, June 27, 1953.

278 *"They just shoved me"*: "The Real Story Behind Hy Peskin's Camelot," by Jason Serafino, *Mental Floss*, June 27, 2017.

278 *"obliged news . . . their love story"*: "Kennedy, Fiancée Together on Cape," *Boston Sunday Post*, June 28, 1953.

278 *"Jacqueline speaks French . . . to the movies"*: "Kennedy to Wed Post-Debutante, Miss Bouvier Bride-to-Be of Senator," by John Harris, *Boston Daily Globe*, June 25, 1953.

278 *"I guess I'm a Democrat now"*: "Bride to Turn Democratic for Kennedy," *Boston Evening American*, June 27, 1953.

278 *"We hardly ever talk politics"*: "The Senator Goes A-Courting," *Life*, July 20, 1953.

278 *"knew the state's problems"*: "Kennedy, Fiancée Want 'Quiet, Family Wedding,'" by Percy Williams, *Boston Sunday Herald*, June 28, 1953.

279 *"I'm quite sure that"*: "Senator, Fiancée Plan Fall Service," *Boston Herald*, June 25, 1953.

279 *"recently been seen"*: Ibid.

279 *"false reports"*: "Bride to Turn Democratic for Kennedy," *Boston Evening American*, June 25, 1953. The newspaper equated the senator's giving up the freedom of bachelorhood with the columnist's giving up her career, saying she was "ready to match his sacrifice with one of her own."

279 *Walter Winchell:* The Winchell item seems to have been first printed on June 15, 1953, in papers including the *Philadelphia Inquirier* and the *Camden Courier-Press*.

279 *"Actress K.K. Kensington"*: "Big Gamble: More Dough Not Enough in Las Vegas," by Dorothy Kilgallen, *Indianapolis News*, June 22, 1953.

279 *"off and on"*: "Kennedy, Fiancée Want 'Quiet, Family Wedding.'"

279 *"this was the only serious"*: Ibid.

279 *"When she came back"*: "Kennedy to Wed Post-Debutante, Miss Bouvier Bride-to-Be of Senator."

279 *"It was just understood"*: "Senator Kennedy's Fiancée Quits Job to Plan Their Fall Wedding," by Elizabeth Watts, *Boston Daily Globe*, June 25, 1953.

279 *"[t]he folks are all"*: Ibid.

279 *"bristled at the intrusion"*: "The Real Story Behind Hy Peskin's Camelot."

280 *"She's a very lovely girl"*: "Kennedy, Fiancée Together on Cape."

280 *"romance has intrigued"*: "Kennedys Fete Jack's Fiancée," by Jean Cole, *Boston Sunday Advertiser*, June 28, 1953.

280 *"We're still looking"*: Ibid.

280 *"old-fashioned"*: Mulvaney, p. 117.

280 *"the dress my mother"*: Ibid.

280 *"looked like a lampshade"*: "The Untold Story of Jackie Kennedy's Wedding Dress," by Kayla Keegan, *Good Housekeeping*, August 11, 2020.

280 *"It makes me uncomfortable"*: "Jackie Can't Campaign," by Mary Cremmen, *Tampa Tribune*, September 29, 1960.

280 *"reserved . . . first of the land"*: "Kennedy, Fiancée Together on Cape."

280 *"Smile . . . side of the camera"*: "No Time for Ring Yet . . . Senator, Fiancée Jackie Enjoying Cape Week-End," by Joan McPartlin, *Boston Globe*, June 28, 1953.

280 *"Everything has happened so fast"*: "Kennedy, Fiancée Want 'Quiet, Family Wedding.'"

281 *"a few pointers"*: "Kennedy, Fiancée Together on Cape."

32. Partner

July–September 1953

282 *"encourage the freedom . . . and treaties"*: June 30, 1953, Indochina Speech, Congressional Record, Senate 99, 6 (1953), pp. 7622–25. See also the debate, July 1, 1953, in ibid., pp. 7780–84.

283 *"The greatest peril to"*: "Four Pioneer Merchants in Hall of Fame," by Philip Hampson, *Chicago Tribune*, July 1, 1953.

283 *He told Jackie to meet him:* Lincoln, *My Twelve Years with John F. Kennedy*, pp. 29–30.

283 "*Met Senator Kennedy's*": Pat Nixon's July 8, 1953, diary entry; Eisenhower, p. 134.

284 *"I think she was still"*: Aileen Train AIAW.

284 *"war-related malady"*: "Senator Kennedy 'Much Better,'" *New York Times*, July 15, 1953.

284 *"recurring malarial"*: "Hospitalization for Malaria Attack," *Boston Herald*, July 16, 1953.

284 *"great French holiday"*: *Boston Herald*, July 15, 1953.

284 *Worcester on Sunday:* "$150,000 Check for Tornado-Torn College," *Burlington Free Press*, July 20, 1953.

284 *feted at a dinner:* Society News, "The Chief Justice . . . Senator Kennedy Here Briefly," by Catharine M. Brooks, *Washington Evening Star*, August 4, 1953.

285 "*personal interest in*": Ibid.

285 *"No man in love"*: Pottker, *Janet and Jackie*, pp. 136–37.

285 *"I told her"*: Betty Beale AIAW. As early as June 25, 1953, however, it was made clear that Senator Kennedy would be making the trip to Europe on official business. "Couple Will Week-End at Hyannisport: Senator Kennedy's Fiancée Quits Job to Plan Their Fall Wedding," by Elizabeth Watts, *Boston Daily Globe*, June 25, 1953.

285 *"[I]t is hard for me"*: JLBK to JFK, n.d. (circa 1958), RR Auction Catalog, Lot 2043, September 25, 2016.

285 *"You are an atypical"*: Ibid.

285 *"She told a friend . . . between them":* Anthony, *AWRH*, p. 73.
286 *"Don't explain apologetically":* JLBKO to Joan Kennedy, unsigned, undated, handwritten letter (circa 1979), Alexander Auctions Catalog, February 24, 2007.
286 *"Since Jack is such":* Guthrie, *Jackie*, p. 66.
287 *"You endure the bad . . . they must carry":* Joan Kennedy AIAW.
287 *"the end of a promising":* "Historical Notes: Sex & the Single Senator Friday," *Time*, July 1, 1966.
288 *"My writing gets":* JLA to Miss Donovan, November 11, 1953, JPK Personal Papers, Wedding, 1953, Gifts, Folder 1, JFKL.
288 *"was the turning . . . she really did":* Aileen Train AIAW.
288 *"Just as Jackie had wanted":* Rhea, *I Was Jacqueline Kennedy's Dressmaker*, p. 129.
288 *"Well, if he'd just stayed":* John White OHI JFKL, pp. 32–33.
288 *"unsuccessful in his courtship":* YDAM, p. 7.
289 *"Donkeys and the elephants":* Society News, *Washington Evening Star*, September 16, 1953.
289 *"Jack thinks continually":* Vidal, *Palimpsest*, pp. 367–68.
289 *"field course . . . people thought":* Rhea, p. 127.
289 *"fit and tanned . . . to southeast Asia":* "Finds Split Opinion on Indo-China: Kennedy Lands Here After Visit to France," by Charles Tarbi, *Boston Globe*, August 27, 1953.
289 *"has done a commendable . . . in translation":* "On the National Front," by Holmes Alexander, *Reno Gazette-Journal*, July 16, 1953.
290 *"Whatever political work":* Ted Sorenson AIAW.
290 *"She used to come . . . just between them":* Duke Zeller AIAW.
292 *"As the bride":* "Miss Bouvier Becomes Bride of Senator Kennedy: Given Away by Father," *Washington Times-Herald*, September 13, 1953. Chuck Spalding corroborated that JLB had conveyed the wish that JVB be brought into the church. "We got him into a pew but it was an interesting maneuver." Charles Spalding interview, "Secret Lives: Jackie Kennedy" documentary, YouTube.
292 *"figure it out":* YDA AIAW.
292 *"become distinct":* Vivi Crespi AIAW.

Bibliography

Primary Sources

Broadcasts

Senator-Elect John F. Kennedy, *Meet the Press*, December 2, 1951; journalist James M. Cannon tape-recording, "Listening In: JFK on Running for President," JFKL (YouTube); ThamesTV, Mavis Nicholson interview with Rose Kennedy, 1974 (YouTube); "The President's Spouse" Symposium, Tish Baldrige interview, November 1, 1994 (C-SPAN); Book TV interview with Amanda Smith on *Hostage to Fortune: The Letters of Joseph P. Kennedy*, February 27, 2001 (C-SPAN); *Larry King Live*, "Jack, Jackie Kennedy's Wedding 50 Years Ago Remembered by Friends, Family," September 23, 2003, CNN; Senator John F. Kennedy privately recorded conversation with journalists, *NBC Nightly News*, October 13, 2008 (David Von Pein's JFK Channel, YouTube): "In His Own Words," documentary, Kunhardt Productions, Inc. 1988 (YouTube); "History in Focus, 1950–1959," documentary (YouTube); "SS *United States*: Made in America" (YouTube); "A Crossing Aboard the SS *Liberté*" (YouTube); "French Line's - SS *De Grasse*" (YouTube); "The Real Story of JFK's Irish Inner Circle, Kennedy's Irish Mafia," by Timeline (YouTube); *That Summer*, documentary produced by Lee Radziwill (2018); *New York Times* "T Magazine," video interview with Lee Radziwill, 2013 (YouTube).

Manuscript Collections

American Institute of Architects Library, Washington, D.C.
Jacqueline Kennedy Onassis script file.

Carl Sferrazza Anthony Author Collection, Private, Los Angeles, California

As We Remember Her: Jacqueline Kennedy Onassis in the Words of Her Family and Friends: oral history interview notes and transcripts from conversations with Yusha Auchincloss, Betty Beale, Vivi Stokes Crespi, Nancy Tuckerman, Senator Edward M. Kennedy, Edith B. Beale, Charles Whitehouse, Claiborne Pell, Nuella Pell, Gloria Emerson, Eunice Kennedy Shriver, George Plimpton, John Davis, Mimi Cecil, Claude de Renty du Granrut, Joan Braden, Helen Bowdoin Spaulding, Aileen Bowdoin Train, Joan Kennedy, Letitia Baldrige, Lucky Roosevelt, Muriel McClanahan, Frank Waldrop, Duke Zeller, Arthur Schlesinger, Ted Sorenson, Doris Francisco.

Conversation notes: Dave Powers (1987), John Kennedy (1995, 1996), Betty Beale (1987, 1989, 1994–96), Gloria Emerson (1995), Yusha Auchincloss (1995, 1996, 1997, 1998), Claude de Renty du Granrut (2019, 2020), Martha Bartlett (2019, 2020), Vivi Stokes Crespi (1994–99), Nina Auchincloss Straight (2019), Edward Purcell (2019–22), Priscilla McMillan (2019, 2020), Mamie Moore (2021), Julie Nixon Eisenhower (2019). E-mail correspondence with Tricia Nixon Cox (2020).

Correspondence: Nancy Tuckerman (1987–96), Arthur Schlesinger, (1995, 1997), Edie Beale (1994–97).

Claude de Renty du Granrut Materials, Private, Paris, France

Pierre Renouvin Indochina textbook, 1950; "A Summer Trip in France: Jacqueline Bouvier et Claude de Renty, July 15th–August 10th, 1950," unpublished manuscript, April 1996, by Claude du Granrut; correspondence with Jacqueline Bouvier Kennedy Onassis (1953–93).

Condé Nast Library, New York, New York

Vogue, Prix de Paris announcement, August 1950; second and third round of questions, December 1950 and March 1950 issues; announcement of contest winners with photos and biographies, August 15, 1951, issue.

Herbert Hoover Presidential Library, West Branch, Iowa

Frank C. Waldrop Papers, biographical sketch.

John F. Kennedy Presidential Library, Boston, Massachusetts (JFKL)

Evelyn Lincoln Papers (ELP): Senator Kennedy's 1952, 1953 calendar books with daily schedule of appearances, meetings.

Hugh D. "Yusha" Auchincloss (YDA), III Papers: correspondence with Jacqueline Bouvier, 1942–94, "Growing Up with Jackie, My Memories 1941–1953" manuscript (YDAM). *It should be noted that many of the letters are undated or with dates unknown.*

John F. Kennedy Pre-Presidential Papers: "Far Eastern Trip, 1951," Box 011; untitled Speech on Far East Trip, n.d., Speech File, 1946–52, Pre-Presidential Papers: Box 96; "Advance Copy Report on His Trip to the Far East by the Hon. John F.

Kennedy, Rep. 11th District of Massachusetts over Mutual Broadcast Network from Station WOR, New York, New York," November 15, 1951, Boston Office speech files, 8/16/47–11/51, Box 95; Thurston B. Morton, Assistant Secretary of State to JFK, May, 8, 1953, JFK to Secretary of State John Foster Dulles, May 25, 1953, reply to questions that accompanied May 7, 1953, letter, Indochina Speech, JFK Senate Speech File; Boston Office Files, Speech Files 46–52; June 30, 1953, Indochina Speech, JFK Senate Speech File, JFKL.

John F. Kennedy Scrapbooks, 1951–53: newspaper clippings covering second congressional term, foreign trips, Indochina; Senate campaign; Massachusetts speeches and appearances.

Joseph P. Kennedy (JPK) Personal Papers: Wedding, 1953: Dowd Publicity Material: Engagement, Folders 1, 2, and 3, General, Folders 1, 2, 3, 4; Gift, Folders 1, 2; Guest Lists and Planning Wedding, 1953, Guest Lists and Planning, JPK Papers, JFKL.

Oral Histories: Janet Lee Auchincloss, Charles Bartlett, Lem Billings, Henry Brandon, Dinah Bridge, Margaret Coit, Mark Dalton, Polly Fitzgerald, Jean Mannix, Frank J. O'Connor, Chuck Spalding, George Taylor, Olin Teague, Arthur Krock, Dorothy Tubridy, Dave Powers, Tip O'Neill, Robert A. Wallace, John White, Clement J. Zablocki.

The *Vogue* File (TVF): Jacqueline Bouvier Prix de Paris entry application, essays, correspondence with *Vogue* editors.

John Sherman Cooper Papers, University of Kentucky

Lorraine Cooper Oral History.

Kent Bartram Materials, Private, Chicago, Illinois

Correspondence of John Vernou "Black Jack" Bouvier III, Edith "Big Edie" Bouvier Beale, Edith "Little Edie" Beale, 1947–53.

Library of Congress, Manuscript Division, Washington, D.C.

Bess Furman Papers: Bess Furman to JLB, November 1952; JLB to Bess Furman, November 1952.

Mary "Molly" Van Rensselaer Papers (MVTP): partial transcript of JLB to JLA letters 1949–50; JLBK responses to MVT interview questions for her *Ladies' Home Journal* biographical series and first published biography of her, *Jacqueline Bouvier Kennedy*, and the subsequent *Jacqueline Kennedy: The White House Years*. Telephone and written responses to MVT interview questions with JLA, CLB, YDA, Nini Auchincloss Straight, Puffin Gates, Frank Waldrop, Madame de Renty, Charlie Bartlett, Lem Billings, Ward Johnson. *It must be noted that the MVTP are in great disarray and it is difficult to date and distinctly attribute material.*

Martin Luther King Jr. Memorial Library, Washington, D.C.

Washingtonian Collection, *Washington Times-Herald* 1951–53, microfilm.

National Press Club Oral History Library, Washington, D.C.
Frank C. Waldrop oral history transcript (2).

State University of New York at Stony Brook Archives, Stony Brook, New York
C[lem] David Heymann Papers, interview tapes with Edie Beale.

United States Senate Historical Office, Washington, D.C.
Online Oral Histories: Roy L. Elson, administrative assistant to Senator Carl Hayden and candidate for the United States Senate, 1955–69; George Tames, Washington photographer for the *New York Times*; John D. Lane, administrative assistant to Senator Brien McMahon.

Villa I Tatti, The Harvard University Center for Italian Renaissance Studies, Berenson Collection, Florence, Italy
Jacqueline and Lee Bouvier correspondence with Bernard Berenson, 1951–57.

Online Autograph Auction Catalogs

JBK to Janet Travell, July 2, 1957, Books and Manuscripts Auction, Boston, November 21, 2004.

JLB to "Woodley" (Ellen "Puffin" Gates), letters (1942–51), Heritage Auctions Catalog, February 20–21, 2006.

JLBK to Joan Kennedy, n.d. (circa 1970s–80s), Alexander Auctions, February 24, 2007.

John F. Kennedy letters to Inga Arvad, Christie's Auction Catalog, June 18, 2007.

JLB to Mrs. McCrea, n.d. (circa spring 1953), RR Auction Catalog, June 2010.

JLB letter to Beverly Corbin (1940s), Christie's Auction Catalog, May 19, 2011.

JLB letter to "Woodley," RR Auction Catalog, April 2012.

JBK undated memo on JFK idea of marriage (circa post-1969), Heritage Auctions Catalog, November 23, 2013.

JLBK to JFK, n.d. (circa 1958), RR Auction Catalog, September 25, 2016.

JLB to JLA (circa 1949–51), JLB to Jim Lee (circa 1942–44), Christmas poem, Bonham's Auction Catalog, December 6, 2017.

JLB to JLA, five letters (circa 1949–51), RR Auction Catalog, March 7, 2018.

Margaret Lee to JLA, August 1929, University Archives Auction Catalog, April 10, 2018.

JLB to JLA, August 31, 1951, University Archives Auction Catalog, May 8, 2018.

JLB to JLA, letters (1949–51), University Archives Auction Catalog, Lot 128, January 23, 2019.

JLB letters and cartoons to Rosamund Lee (circa 1943), University Archives Auction Catalog, February 27, 2019.

JLB childhood drawings, books, photos, Auchincloss-family memorabilia, Yusha Auchincloss diaries (circa 1929–52), McGinnis Auction Catalog, October 13, 2019.

JBK letters to John Steinbeck (1964), Heritage Auctions Catalog, October 27, 2019.

Secondary Sources

Selected Articles

"Absenteeism in Congress." *Haverhill Gazette*, June 9, 1952.
"Adlai Attends Unitarian Church in Cambridge." *Boston Globe*, October 26, 1952.
"Adlai's Schedule." *Boston Globe*, October 26, 1952.
"Adlai Warns of McCarthy." *Boston Globe*, October 27, 1952.
Alexander, Holmes. "On the National Front." *Reno Gazette-Journal*, July 16, 1953.
"Alfred Valentine Leaman, Jr." *New York Times*, August 8, 1933.
"Around Boston." *Boston Record*, July 7, 1952.
Associated Press. "Jacqueline Kennedy Letters Reveal Her Private Side." *Dayton Daily News*, May 14, 2014.
"At Kennedy Reception." *Milton-Mattapan News*, June 5, 1952.
"Barkley, in Lynn, Stresses Purchase of Israel Bonds." *Boston Globe*, October 13, 1952.
"Bastille Day." *Boston Herald*, July 15, 1953.
"Bay State Voters to Nominate Senate Candidates Tuesday." *Washington Evening Star*, September 14, 1952.
Beale, Betty. Exclusively Yours. *Washington Evening Star*, March 13, 1950.
———. Exclusively Yours. *Washington Evening Star*, March 16, 1953.
———. "Husted Family." Exclusively Yours. *Washington Evening Star*, July 5, 1950.
———. "Leap Year Dance." Exclusively Yours. *Washington Star*, March 3, 1952.
Beck, Kent M. "The Kennedy Image: Politics, Camelot, and Vietnam." *The Wisconsin Magazine of History* 58, no. 1 (1974): 45–55.
Belair, Felix, Jr. "Senate Approves Foreign Aid Bill." *New York Times*, July 2, 1953.
"Benno Graziani." *Paris Match*, May 2013.
"Bequest of $1,500,000 Listed in Bouvier Will." *Boston Globe*, September 4, 1935.
"Blue Ribbon Winner." *East Hampton Star*, August 19, 1937.
Bohlin, Virginia. "Kennedy, Fiancée Plan 'Simple, Small Wedding.'" *Boston Traveler*, June 25, 1953.
"Bon Voyage for Mrs. Talman." *Washington Evening Star*, April 1, 1952.
Bostdorff, Denise M., and Steven R. Goldzwig. "Idealism and Pragmatism in American Foreign Policy: The Case of John F. Kennedy and Vietnam." *Presidential Studies Quarterly* 24, no. 3 (1994): 515–30.
"Bouvier-Canfield Wedding." *New York Times*, April 19, 1953.
"Bouvier 3d to Be Bridegroom." *New York Tribune*, April 8, 1920.
"Bride to Turn Democratic for Kennedy." *Boston Evening American*, June 27, 1953.
"Brockton Reception for Kennedy Attended by Many District Women." *Holbrooke Times*, July 4, 1952.
Brooks, Catharine M. Society News. "The Chief Justice . . . Senator Kennedy Here Briefly." *Washington Evening Star*, August 4, 1953.
"Brother Citations Awarded Hynes, Kennedy." *Boston Globe*, February 25, 1952.
By the Way. *Washington Evening Star*, March 31, 1938, November 7, 1941.
Callahan, William R. "Abp. to Perform Kennedy Nuptials." *Boston Globe*, August 6, 1953.

"Camera Girl Deb to Marry Rich Senator." *Los Angeles Mirror*, June 25, 1953.

"Chapin Nursery Charity." *East Hampton Star*, May 16, 1935.

"Charles L. Bartlett, Journalist and a Kennedy Matchmaker, Dies at 95." *New York Times*, February 19, 2017.

"Cherry Blossom Ball, Dignitaries to Attend Gala Affair." *Washington Evening Star*, April 1, 1952.

Cheshire, Maxime. "Jacqueline Bouvier as Aspiring Writer." *Washington Post*, February 10, 1976.

"The City's Jar." *New York Tribune*, March 9, 1919.

Cole, Jean. "Kennedys Fete Jack's Fiancée." *Boston Sunday Advertiser*, June 28, 1953.

Conconi, Chuck. "Memories of Jackie the Journalist." *St. Louis Post-Dispatch*, August 22, 1994.

"Cong. Kennedy and Mother Feted at Tea." *East Pepperell Free Press*, June 5, 1952.

"Cong. Kennedy Is Detained; 1000 Women Meet Kin." *Brockton Enterprise and Times*, July 4, 1952.

"Cong. Kennedy Is Fiery Speaker at B'nai B'rith Fete." *Chelsea Record*, January 30, 1952.

"Cong. Kennedy to Speak at Westford." *Lowell Sunday Telegram*, November 25, 1951.

Congressional Record, June 30, 1953.

"Congressman Greeted at Anniversary Fete." *New Bedford Standard-Times*, January 21, 1952.

"Congressman John Kennedy Guest Speaker." *Hudson Sun*, November 15, 1951.

Counihan, Patrick. "Jackie O Was More Irish than JFK but Was Ashamed of Her Family's Links to Ireland." *Irish Central*, June 23, 2013.

Cremmen, Mary. "Jackie Can't Campaign." *Tampa Tribune*, September 29, 1960.

"Debutantes Aid in Plans of Opera Benefit." *New York Times*, November 23, 1947.

del Bono, Laurent. "Jackie K.: Les Derniers Clichés D'une Femme Heureuse." *Gala*, November 12, 2008.

"Democrats Want Senator Kennedy." *Wichita Beacon*, January 26, 1953.

"Dever, Kennedy Cheered." *Boston Globe*, October 26, 1952.

Dineen, Joseph F. "John C. Dowd a Child Prodigy Who Delivered on His Promise." *Boston Globe*, February 16, 1951.

"Dinner Climaxes Centennial Fete of Dorchester Heights." *Boston Globe*, May 25, 1952.

"Dog Shows at Village Fair." *East Hampton Star*, July 12, 1934.

"Duchess Turns Model at Charity Ball." *Boston Globe*, January 6, 1953.

Dudley, Rosemary. "Jackie and Her Mother: She Loved My Sister More." *Movie TV Screens*, August 1965.

Eads, Jane. "Leap Year Doesn't Bother Bachelors in Washington." *New Bedford Standard-Times*, February 24, 1952.

"Edson in Washington." *Selma Times-Journal*, May 22, 1947.

"Elizabeth Is Visiting U.S. as Princess of Canada." *Washington Times-Herald*, November 1, 1951.

"False Reports." *Boston Daily Globe*, June 25, 1953.

Feitelberg, Rosemary. "Photographer Benno Graziani Shoots the Jet Set." *WWD*, November 6, 2009.

"550,000 Line Parade Route, Guests Cheer." *Washington Times-Herald*, November 1, 1951.

"For Sale." *East Hampton Star*, April 20, 1950.

"400 Women Jam Worcester Hotel for Rep. Kennedy Tea." *Springfield News*, May 19, 1952.

"Four Pioneers in Retail Field Chosen for Merchandising Hall of Fame." *New York Times*, July 1, 1953.

Fritchey, Clayton. "Jacqueline's View of JFK." *Boston Globe*, November 22, 1966.

"Golden Jubilee at Maidstone." *Brooklyn Daily Eagle*, July 13, 1941.

"Golf Champion to Wed Nutley Man." *Newark Evening Star*, June 2, 1914.

"Government Employees Lay-Off System May Face Overhauling." *Pensacola News Journal*, January 13, 1952.

"Grand Duke a Grand Guy." *New York Daily News*, November 22, 1931.

Gray, Christopher. "Jacqueline Kennedy Onassis's Grandfather; Quality Developer with a Legacy of Fine Buildings." *New York Times*, March 12, 1995.

Graziani, Benno. "Collection Privée, 1955–1975, Les Années d'or d'un Grand Reporter." *Relie*, November 6, 2008.

Great Britain Courts. *The Jurist, 1851*, vol. 15, part 2. London: S. Sweet, 1852.

"Gridiron Reception Wows 800 Guests." *Washington Evening Star*, May 12, 1952.

Habermehl, Larry. "A Seaman Remembers John F. Kennedy." *The Sea Breeze*, The Boston Seaman's Friend Society, July 1964.

Hampson, Philip. "Four Pioneer Merchants in Hall of Fame." *Chicago Tribune*, July 1, 1953.

Harris, John. "Kennedy Asks Freedom Tag on Indo-China Aid." *Boston Globe*, July 1, 1953.

———. "Newspaper Staff Will Miss Lively Jackie: Kennedy's Fiancée Sketched and Wrote about the Coronation." *Boston Daily Globe*, June 26, 1953.

Hatfield, Julie. "Jacqueline Bouvier's Forgotten Essay." *Boston Globe*, July 28, 1994.

Healy, Paul. "The Senate's Gay Young Bachelor." *Saturday Evening Post*, June 13, 1953.

"Highlights of Opera Open Newport's Largely Attended Music Festival." *Newport Mercury*, September 22, 1950.

"Hospitalization for Malaria Attack." *Boston Herald*, July 16, 1953.

"Hostesses Named for Tea on Sunday." *Springfield Union*, May 28, 1952.

Hupka, Ralph B., Bram Buunk, Gábor Falus, Ante Fulgosi, Elsa Ortega, Ronny Swain, and Nadia V. Tarabrina. "Romantic Jealousy and Romantic Envy: A Seven-Nation Study." *Journal of Cross-Cultural Psychology* 15, no. 4 (December 1985): 423–46.

In Social Circles. *Newport Daily News*, September 26, 1950, September 27, 1951, and October 13, 1951.

In Social Circles. *Newport Daily News*, March 22, 1952.

In Social Circles. *Newport Mercury*, July 7, 1950, July 14, 1950, August 16, 1950, September 22, 1950, September 25, 1950.

"Inaugural Ball." *New York Times*, January 21, 1953.
"Inaugural Great on TV." *Boston Globe*, January 20, 1953.
"Infuriated." *Carlsbad Current-Argus*, October 26, 1960.
"Inquiring Camera Girl to Be Sen. Kennedy's Bride." *Washington Times-Herald*, June 25, 1953.
Ireland, Corydon. "Bernard Berenson, Recalled." *Harvard Gazette*, February 14, 2014.
"Jackie Kennedy Loved Ireland and Her Old Irish Priest." *Irish Central*, November 12, 2017.
"Jackie Kennedy's Secret Letters to Dublin Priest . . ." *Irish Central*, May 13, 2014.
"Jacqueline Bouvier Celebrates Second Birthday," *East Hampton Star*, July 31, 1931.
"Jacqueline Bouvier to Wed John G. W. Husted." *East Hampton Star*, January 24, 1952.
"Jacqueline Kennedy Onassis: Equestrian." *Equestrian Magazine*, Summer 2016.
"Janet Auchincloss, Jackie O's Mother, Dies." *Newport Daily News*, July 24, 1989.
"John V. Bouvier, New York Lawyer, Last Rites Here" and "Courtly Gentleman." *East Hampton Star*, January 22, 1948.
Jones, Jerry. "Admired by Hitler, Dated by JFK, She Chose a Cowboy." *Burlington County Times*, March 29, 2009.
"J. V. Bouvier's Exchange Seat Brought Record Price." *New York Herald*, January 14, 1920.
Kaufman, Marjorie. "Photographer Plucked from Oblivion." *New York Times*, August 28, 1994.
"Kennedy Admits His Interest in Running for Senate in '52." *Christian Science Monitor*, December 3, 1951.
"Kennedy, Bride-to-Be Enjoy Cape Weekend." *Boston Daily Globe*, June 27, 1953.
"Kennedy Favors Ike's Trip." *Boston Globe*, November 6, 1952.
"Kennedy, Fiancée Join Kin on Cape." *Boston American*, June 26, 1953.
"Kennedy, Fiancée Together on Cape." *Boston Sunday Post*, June 28, 1953.
"Kennedy Gets K. of C. Honor." *Boston Herald*, January 16, 1852.
"Kennedy Has Spoken in 311 of 351 Cities, Towns." *Boston Globe*, July 29, 1952.
"Kennedy Headquarters Planned for City." *Worcester Telegram*, July 2, 1951.
"Kennedy May Seek Senate Seat." *New York Times*, December 2, 1951.
"Kennedy Opens Drive, Hits U.S. Taxing Inequity." *Berkshire Eagle*, May 19, 1952.
"Kennedy Raps U.S. Tennis and Cocktails Diplomats." *Boston Traveler*, November 19, 1951.
"Kennedy Sees Danger in Iran." *Lawrence Tribune*, October 11, 1951.
"Kennedy Sends Regrets to Area." *Greenfield Recorder*, July 1, 1952.
"Kennedy Silent on Politics at Shamrock Dinner." *Boston Globe*, March 18, 1952.
"Kennedys Sell Family Home in Palm Beach." *New York Times*, May 24, 1995.
"Kennedy to Run for U.S. Senate." *Worcester Daily Telegram*, April 7, 1952.
"Kennedy to Tell Rotary Club of Far East Tour." *News of Milford*, October 26, 1951.
"Kennedy to Wed Newport Girl." *Boston Herald*, June 25, 1953.
"Kennedy Unable to Give Speeches." *Springfield Union*, June 30, 1952.

"Kennedy Voted Handsomest Member of Congress by 300 Newsfolks." *Washington Times-Herald*, July 2, 1952.

"Kennedy Wants Women's Vote." *Springfield Union*, June 28, 1952.

Kilgallen, Dorothy. "Big Gamble: More Dough Not Enough in Las Vegas." *Indianapolis News*, June 22, 1953.

———. "Broadway." *Scranton Times-Tribune*, December 23, 1952.

Kristen, Mark P., Erick Janssen, and Robin R. Milhausen. "Infidelity in Heterosexual Couples: Demographic, Interpersonal, and Personality-Related Predictors of Extradyadic Sex." Received September 4, 2009, revised December 10, 2010, accepted February 12, 2011. *Archives of Sexual Behavior* 40 (2011): 971–82.

"Leamans." *London Gazette*, Part 3, September 2, 1851–December 30, 1851, London: T. Neuman, 1851

Leavitt, Martha. "Beauty Brevities." *Washington Evening Star*, May 5, 1935.

Levy, Claudia. "Eleni Epstein, Star Fashion Editor, Dies." *Washington Post*, January 29, 1991.

Lewine, Fran. "Pat and Jackie: A Contrast." *Washington Evening Star*, October 16, 1960.

Liebert, Herman W. "Wilmarth Sheldon Lewis (1895–1979)." *Yale University Library Gazette* 54, no. 4 (1980): 198–200. http://www.jstor.org/stable/40858736.

Local News Briefs. *Newport Daily News*, September 22, 1950.

"Local People on Reception Group for Cong. Kennedy." *Holyoke Transcript-Telegram*, May 24, 1952.

"Lorraine Cooper, Wife of Senator, Dies." *Los Angeles Times*, February 7, 1985.

"Lost." *East Hampton Star*, October 17, 1930.

Louviere, Vernon. "Jacqueline Met Husband on Routine Assignment." *Shreveport Times*, November 17, 1960.

"The Lyons Den." *Quad-City Times*, August 22, 1953.

"Maidstone Celebration Duplicates 1892 Fete." *Brooklyn Daily Eagle*, August 16, 1942.

"Mamie's Health Checked at Hospital Here." *Washington Times-Herald*, November 19, 1952.

Mandel, Lee R. "All the President's Secrets: John F. Kennedy and Addison's Disease." *Healio News*, July 12, 2019.

"Many Capital Residents at Newport." *Washington Evening Star*, July 26, 1952.

Marquard, Bryan. "Jackie Grants Her First Interview." *Boston Globe*, February 17, 2021.

Martin, Guy. "The Kennedy Palm Beach Compound Reportedly Sold." *Forbes*, June 24, 2020.

Maugh, Thomas H., II. "A New View of JFK's Addison's Disease." *Los Angeles Times*, September 5, 2009.

Mayberry, George. "Review of Ralph Ellison's *Invisible Man*." *New Republic*, September 25, 2013.

McAfee, Tierney. "Inside JFK's Forbidden Romance with Former Beauty Queen—and Suspected Nazi Spy—Inga Arvad." *People*, April 12, 2016.

McCardle, Dorothy. "Coronation Fell to Jackie's Quick Pencil." *Tampa Bay Times*, October 2, 1960.

———. "Inaugural Parade Was Her Beat in 1953." *Tampa Bay Times*, September 29, 1960.

———. "Jackie Kennedy—Ex-Girl Reporter, Part II." *Tampa Bay Times*, September 29, 1960.

———. "Jackie Kennedy—Ex-Girl Reporter, Part IV." *Tampa Bay Times*, October 1, 1960.

———. "Jacqueline Kennedy as Inquiring Camera Girl." *St. Louis Times-Dispatch*, September 29, 1960.

———. "Mrs. Kennedy—Photo-Reporter." *St. Louis Post-Dispatch*, October 12, 1960.

———. "Why Jacqueline Kennedy Took Newspaper Job." *St. Louis Post-Dispatch*, September 30, 1960.

McCarty, Mary. "Jackie Onassis: Former First Lady, American Icon." *Dayton Daily News*, May 20, 1994.

McGrory, Mary. "Bay State Senatorial Battle Is Being Waged on a High Plane." *Washington Evening Star*, September 21, 1952.

McPartlin, Joan. "Senator, Fiancée Jackie Enjoying Cape Weekend." *Boston Sunday Globe*, June 28, 1953.

McVicar, D. Morgan. "Janet Lee Auchincloss Morris, 81, Mother of Jacqueline Onassis, Dies in Newport." *[Providence] Journal-Bulletin*, July 24, 1989.

Milligan, Lauren. "Benno Graziani Interview." British *Vogue*, September 14, 2009.

"Mini Rhea Calder, 86, Obituary." *Washington Post*, October 2, 1998.

"Miss Bouvier Becomes Bride of Senator Kennedy." *Washington Times-Herald*, September 13, 1953.

"Miss Bouvier, Bride to Be of Senator." *Boston Daily Globe*, June 25, 1953.

"Miss Eunice Kennedy." *Boston Post*, October 6, 1951.

"Miss Eunice Kennedy Becomes Bride of Robert Shriver, Jr." *Palm Beach Post*, May 24, 1953.

Montgomery, Ruth. "Senator Loses Bachelorhood to Camera Girl." *New York Daily News*, June 25, 1953.

Morin, Relman. "Ike, Mamie Celebrate—Inaugural Ball Is Brilliant." *Shreveport Journal*, January 21, 1953.

"Mrs. John V. Bouvier Dies." *Brooklyn Daily Eagle*, April 3, 1940.

"Mrs. Woods' Guests Plan Style Benefit." *Washington Evening Star*, May 1, 1952.

"Mugwumps to Play Bouvier Team in 'Cycle Polo." *East Hampton Star*, September 27, 1934.

Newkirk, Walter. "Edie Beale Interview." *Daily Targum*, Rutgers University, April 22, 1976.

Newman, Caroline. "Nine Things You Might Not Know About the Kennedys." *UVA Today*, March 27, 2018.

"Newport Colonist, Sen. John Kennedy to Be Married Here in September." *Newport News*, June 25, 1953.

"Nix on Ike, I'll Just Vote for Daddy." *Minneapolis Star Tribune*, November 8, 1952.

"No Rash Moves for Me, Vows Jackie's Ex-Roommate." *Dayton Daily News*, February 24, 1963.

"Nutley." *Newark Star and Newark Advertiser*, October 18, 1909.

"Nutley" and "Receive Toys for Christmas Tree to Be Erected in Nutley." *Newark Evening Star and Newark Advertiser*, December 2, 1914.

O'Brien, Shane. "Jackie Kennedy Almost Married an Irish Lawyer." *Irish Central*, April 25, 2020.

"Oldest Members." *St. Louis Globe-Democrat*, July 30, 1935.

O'Leary, J. A. "Further Foreign Aid Cuts Indicated as Bill Goes to Conference." *Washington Evening Star*, July 2, 1953.

"$150,000 Check for Tornado-Torn College." *Burlington Free Press*, July 20, 1953.

"Palm Beach Notes." *Palm Beach Post*, December 21, 1952.

"Panel Speakers to Be Honored at Reception." *Berkshire Eagle*, January 24, 1952.

Parsons, Michael. "Jackie Kennedy and the Costello Family." *Irish Times*, June 2, 2014.

———. "Jackie Kennedy Correspondence with Costello." *Irish Times*, June 2, 2014.

———. "Jackie Kennedy Sought Copies of All Hallows Letters." *Irish Times*, June 2, 2014.

———. "Letters to Priest Provide Rare Insight into Life of Jackie Kennedy." *Irish Times*, May 13, 2014.

"Picture of What." *Indianapolis Times*, November 17, 1933.

"Press Club Gives Roosevelt Cake." *Washington Sunday Star*, March 3, 1935.

"Prestige Lost." *Clinton Courant*, November 23, 1951.

"Princetonians Will Set Rathskeller Rafters Ringing." *Washington Evening Star*, March 23, 1951.

"Probe of Foreign Aid." *Knoxville News-Sentinel*, January 26, 1952.

"Quincy Crowd Swells to 500 to Hear Adlai." *Boston Globe*, October 27, 1952.

"Red Cross." *East Hampton Star*, September 3, 1942.

"Red Threat to Indo-China Is Underscored by Kennedy." *Berkshire Eagle*, February 2, 1952.

"Rep. John Kennedy, 35, Has Eye on Bigger Job." *Providence Journal*, January 27, 1952.

"Rep. Kennedy Tells of More Trouble Spots in Far East." *North Adams Transcript*, February 4, 1952.

"Rep. Kennedy Visits Nehru at Luncheon." *Boston Globe*, October 13, 1951.

Rhea, Mini. "The Young Jacqueline Kennedy." *Ladies' Home Journal*, January 1962.

"Riding Pants Are Breeches of Etiquette." *Waterbury Democrat*, October 27, 1934.

Robb, Inez. "Kennedy Rates Tops with Mothers of Marriageable." *Cedar Rapids Gazette*, January 21, 1952.

———. "Morning After and One." *Hackensack Record*, January 21, 1952.

"Royal Program of Five Events Listed for Day." *Washington Times-Herald*, November 1, 1951.

Russo, Julia, and Molly Kaiser. "Beyond the Walls: Examining the History of Campus Building Names, Colonials Moniker." *GW Hatchet*, September 28, 2020.

Ryan, James D. "The Political Pot." *South Boston Tribune*, December 20, 1951.

Sabor, Peter. Review of *A Treasure House in Farmington: The Lewis Walpole Library,* in *Eighteenth-Century Studies* 33, no. 3 (Spring 2000): 454–46.

"Saratoga Is the Topic of Social Week." *Chicago Tribune*, August 4, 1929.

"See in Europe Says Kennedy After Visit." *Boston Globe*, December 18, 1952.

Seen and Heard. *East Boston Leader*, December 14, 1951.

"Sen. Kennedy's Fiancée Covers Inaugural Parade." *Boston Globe*, June 28, 1953.

"Senate Rejects Move to France on Indochina." *Tampa Morning Tribune*, July 2, 1953.

"Senator Kennedy Here." *Newport Daily News*, June 15, 1953.

"Senator Kennedy 'Much Better.'" *New York Times*, July 15, 1953.

"Senator Kennedy to Marry Heiress." *Delphos Daily Herald*, June 26, 1953.

"Senator to Speak." *Washington Evening Star*, February 11, 1953.

"Senator to Wed." *Montpelier Evening Argus*, June 27, 1953.

Serafino, Jay. "The Real Story Behind Hy Peskin's Camelot." *Mental Floss*, June 28, 2017.

"Service Clubs to Hear Congressman." *Lawrence Eagle*, November 24, 1951.

Shannon, George. "Fancy Inaugural Affair." *Shreveport Journal*, January 21, 1953.

Sheehy, Kate. "Jackie Kennedy's Letters to Priest Reveal Loneliness, Suspicion." *New York Post*, May 13, 2014.

Sheppard, V. J., E. S. Nelson, and V. Andreoli Mathie. "Dating Relationships and Infidelity: Attitudes and Behaviors." *Journal of Sex & Marital Therapy* 21, no. 3 (1995).

Sheridan, Daisy. Society News. *Washington Evening Star*, May 19, 1952.

Sibert, Karen. "Jackie, 'We Hardly Knew Ye': The University Remembers One of Its Most Celebrated Alumnae: Jacqueline Bouvier Kennedy Onassis, BA '51." *GW Magazine*, Fall 1994.

Smith, J. Y. "Lorraine Cooper, 79, Leader of Washington Society, Dies." *Washington Post*, February 6, 1985.

Social Notes. *East Hampton Star*, September 21, 1950.

Society. *New York Daily News*, December 7, 1938.

Society. *Washington Evening Star*, December 21, 1952.

"Society and Club News, Auchincloss Supper." *Washington Evening Star*, April 8, 1953.

Society at Newport. *New York Herald*, July 9, 1922.

"Society Broker Sued for Divorce." *New York Daily Mirror*, January 26,1940.

Society News. *Washington Evening Star*, May 19, 1952, August 4, 1952, September 16, 1953.

"St. Joseph Boy Decorated." *St. Joseph News-Press*, December 29, 1920.

Steinem, Gloria. "Why Does This Woman Work?" *Ms. Magazine*, May 1979.

"Stevenson Sidelights." *Boston Globe*, October 26, 1952.

"Sues Husband as Love Commuter; 'Other Women' Were Plural.'" *New York Daily News*, January 26, 1940.

Summer Colony. *East Hampton Star*, July 10, 1947, November 27, 1947, December 11, 1947, January 22, 1948, January 6, 1949.

Summer Rentals. *East Hampton Star*, March 6, 1947, May 6, 1948, May 17, 1951.

Suzy (Aileen Mehle). "The Gold Coast." *Miami Daily News*, December 21, 1952.

Swartz, Sally. "Permelia's Island: Son's Book Offers Look at Exclusive Jupiter Island." *Palm Beach Post*, February 19, 2011.

Tarbi, Charles. "Finds Split Opinion on Indo-China: Kennedy Lands Here After Visit to France." *Boston Globe*, August 27, 1953.

"Tells of Liquat's Last Talk." *Boston Post*, October 19, 1951.

"Tells Why Mr. Bouvier Was Ejected from Hotel." *New York Herald*, March 9, 1919.

"Tired Kennedy Elected as Lodge Concedes." *Boston Globe*, November 5, 1952.

"To Wed Heiress: Most Eligible Bachelor in Washington Is Engaged." *Traverse-City Record-Eagle*, June 25, 1953.

Trott, Bill. "Lee Radziwill, Jackie Kennedy Onassis' Younger Sister, Dies at 85." *Reuters News*, February 16, 2019.

"US Diplomats Criticized, Many Are Too Concerned with Social Life, Kennedy Says." *New York Times*, November 19, 1951.

"U.S. Sen. Kennedy, Mother Weekend Visitors with Mrs. H. D. Auchincloss." *Newport Daily News*, June 22, 1953.

"Utility Lobbyist Boomed Willkie." *PM*, August 1, 1940.

"Virginia Kernochan Is Surprise Bride." *New York Daily News*, August 25, 1938.

Viser, Matt. "New Letters Reveal More Intimate Side of Jackie Kennedy." *Boston Globe*, May 13, 2014.

Walton, Whitney. "Jacqueline Kennedy, Frenchness, and French-American Relations in the 1950s and Early 1960s." *French Politics, Culture & Society* 31, no. 2 (Summer 2013): 34–57.

"Washington Letter." *[Madison] Capitol Times*, September 5, 1948.

"Washington Memo." *Minneapolis Star-Tribune*, December 22, 1953.

Washington Social Events. *Baltimore Sun*, April 7, 1946.

Washington University Bulletin Calendar, 1950–1951.

Watts, Elizabeth. "Senator Kennedy's Fiancée Quits Job to Plan Their Fall Wedding." *Boston Evening Globe*, June 25, 1953.

———. "Turnabout 'a Little Frightening' to Jackie." *Boston Globe*, June 26, 1953.

White, Mark. "Apparent Perfection: The Image of John F. Kennedy." *History* 98, no. 2 (April 2013): 226–46.

Williams, Percy. "Kennedy, Fiancée Want 'Quiet, Family Wedding.'" *Boston Sunday Herald*, June 28, 1953.

Williamson, Kevin D. "The Grotesque American Wedding." *National Review*, July 21, 2020.

Wilson, Theo. "Object: Matrimony." *New York Daily News*, May 25, 1952.

"Winsome Miss." *New York Daily News*, September 9, 1937.

"Women Democrats Annual Meeting." *Boston Globe*, January 13, 1952.

Young, Patrick. "Jackie Kennedy Covered Inauguration 8 Years Ago." *Bristol Daily Courier*, December 24, 1960.

Selected Books

Adamthwaite, Anthony. *Grandeur and Misery: France's Bid for Power in Europe, 1914–1940.* London: Bloomsbury Academic, 1995.

Adler, Bill, ed. *The Eloquent Jacqueline Kennedy Onassis: A Portrait in Her Own Words.* New York: HarperCollins, 2009.

Alam, Mohammed Badrul. *Jackie Kennedy: Images and Reality.* New York: Nova History Publications, 2004.

Anderson, Catherine Corley. *Jackie Kennedy Onassis: Woman of Courage.* New York: Lerner, 1995.

Anthony, Carl Sferrazza. *As We Remember Her: Jacqueline Kennedy Onassis in the Words of Her Family and Friends.* New York: HarperCollins, 1997.

———. *First Ladies: The Saga of the Presidents' Wives and Their Power, 1789–1990.* Vols. 1 and 2. New York: William Morrow, 1990, 1991.

Baldrige, Letitia. *A Lady, First: My Life in the Kennedy White House and the American Embassies of Paris and Rome.* New York: Penguin Books, 2001.

Beale, Eva Marie. *Edith Bouvier Beale of Grey Gardens: A Life in Pictures.* Paris: Verlhac Editions, 2009.

Birmingham, Stephen. *Jacqueline Bouvier Kennedy Onassis.* New York: Grosset and Dunlap, 1978.

Bouvier, Kathleen. *Black Jack Bouvier: The Life and Times of Jackie O's Father.* Pinnacle Books: New York, 1979.

Bradford, Sarah. *America's Queen: The Life of Jacqueline Kennedy Onassis.* New York: Penguin Putnam, 2001.

Carpozi, George. *The Hidden Side of Jacqueline Kennedy.* New York: Pyramid Books, 1967.

Carr, William H. A. *Jacqueline Kennedy: Beauty in the White House.* New York: Magnum Publications, 1961.

Cassidy, Tina. *Jackie After O: One Remarkable Year When Jacqueline Kennedy Onassis Defied Expectations and Rediscovered Her Dreams.* New York: It Books, 2012.

Cassini, Oleg. *In My Own Fashion: An Autobiography.* New York: Simon & Schuster, 1987.

Collier, Peter, and David Horowitz. *The Kennedys: An American Drama.* New York: Warner Books, 1984.

Curtis, Charlotte. *First Lady.* New York: Pyramid Books, 1962.

Dareff, Hal. *Jacqueline Kennedy: A Portrait in Courage.* New York: Parents Magazine Press, 1966.

David, Lester. *Jacqueline Kennedy Onassis: A Portrait of Her Private Years.* New York: Birch Lane Press Books, 1994.

Davis, John H. *The Bouviers: Portrait of an American Family.* New York: Farrar, Straus and Giroux, 1969.

———. *Jacqueline Bouvier: An Intimate Memoir.* New York: John Wiley & Sons, 1996.

———. *The Kennedys: Dynasty and Disaster, 1848–1983.* New York: McGraw-Hill, 1984.

De Villiers, Philippe. *Histoire du Vietnam de 1940 à 1952.* Paris: Seuil, 1952.

Donohue, Kathleen G., ed. *Liberty and Justice for All? Rethinking Politics in Cold War America.* Amherst and Boston: University of Massachusetts Press, 2012.

Dubois, Diana. *In Her Sister's Shadow: An Intimate Biography of Lee Radziwill.* Boston: Little, Brown, 1995.

Eisenhower, Julie Nixon. *Pat Nixon: The Untold Story.* New York: Simon & Schuster, 1986.

Farris, Scott. *Inga: Kennedy's Great Love, Hitler's Perfect Beauty, and J. Edgar Hoover's Prime Suspect.* Guilford, CT: Lyons Press, 2019.

Frischauer, Willi. *Jackie.* London: Sphere Books, Ltd., 1977.

Gallagher, Mary Barelli. *My Life with Jacqueline Kennedy.* New York: David McKay, 1969.

Guthrie, Lee. *Jackie: The Price of the Pedestal.* New York: Drake Publishers, 1977.

Haag, Christina. *Come to the Edge.* New York: Spiegel & Grau, 2011.

Hall, Gordon Langley, and Ann Pinchot. *Jacqueline Kennedy: A Biography.* New York: Frederick Fell, 1964.

Hamilton, Nigel. *JFK: Reckless Youth.* New York: Random House, 1992.

Heller, Deane, and David Heller. *Jacqueline Kennedy.* Derby, CT: Monarch Books, 1961.

Heymann, David C. *The Georgetown Ladies' Social Club: Power, Passion, and Politics in the Nation's Capital.* New York: Atria Books, 2004.

———. *A Woman Named Jackie: An Intimate Biography of Jacqueline Bouvier Kennedy Onassis.* New York: Birch Lane Press, 1994.

Kaledin, Eugenia. *Mothers and More: American Women in the 1950s.* Boston: Twayne Publishers, 1984.

Kaplan, Alice. *Dreaming in French: The Paris Years of Jacqueline Bouvier Kennedy, Susan Sontag, and Angela Davis.* Chicago: University of Chicago Press, 2012.

Kashner, Sam, and Nancy Schoenberger. *The Fabulous Bouvier Sisters: The Tragic and Glamorous Lives of Jackie and Lee.* New York: HarperCollins, 2018.

Kelley, Kitty. *Jackie Oh!* Toronto: George J. McLeod Limited, 1978.

Kennedy, Jacqueline. *Historic Conversations on Life with John F. Kennedy.* Interview by Arthur M. Schlesinger Jr., 1964, annotated by Michael Beschloss. New York: Hyperion, 2011.

Kennedy, Rose Fitzgerald. *Times to Remember.* Garden City, New York: Doubleday, 1974.

Keogh, Pamela Clarke. *Jackie Style.* New York: HarperCollins, 2001.

Kessler, Ronald. *The Sins of the Father: Joseph P. Kennedy and the Dynasty He Founded.* New York: Time Warner Books, 1996.

Kinsey, Alfred C., Wardell B. Pomeroy, and Clyde E. Martin. *Sexual Behavior in the Human Male.* Philadelphia and London: W. B. Saunders, 1948.

Klein, Edward. *All Too Human: The Love Story of Jack and Jackie Kennedy.* New York: Pocket Books, 1996.

Koestenbaum, Wayne. *Jackie Under My Skin: Interpreting an Icon.* New York: Picador, 1995.

Krock, Arthur. *The Consent of the Governed and Other Deceits.* Boston: Little, Brown, 1971.

Kuhn, William. *Reading Jackie: Her Autobiography in Books.* New York: Nan A. Talese/Doubleday, 2010.

Lawrence, Greg. *Jackie as Editor: The Literary Life of Jacqueline Kennedy Onassis.* New York: St. Martin's Press, 2011.

Leamer, Laurence. *The Kennedy Women: The Saga of an American Family.* New York: Villard Books, 1994.

Leaming, Barbara. *Jacqueline Bouvier Kennedy Onassis: The Untold Story.* New York: St. Martin's Press, 2014.

———. *Mrs. Kennedy: The Missing History of the Kennedy Years.* New York: Free Press, 2001.

Lieberson, Goddard, ed. *John Fitzgerald Kennedy: As We Remember Him.* New York: Atheneum, 1965.

Lincoln, Evelyn. *My Twelve Years with John F. Kennedy.* New York: Bantam Books, 1965.

Logevall, Fredrik. *JFK: Coming of Age in the American Century, 1917–1956.* New York: Random House, 2020.

Malkus, Alida Sims. *The Story of Jacqueline Kennedy.* New York: Grosset & Dunlap, 1967.

Martin, Ralph G. *A Hero for Our Time: An Intimate Story of the Kennedy Years.* New York: Fawcett Crest Books, 1983.

Mulvaney, Jay. *Diana & Jackie: Maidens, Mothers, Myths.* New York: St. Martin's Press, 2002.

National Museum of African American History and Culture, eds. *The Scurlock Studio and Black Washington: Picturing the Promise.* Washington, D.C.: Smithsonian Books, 2009.

Nixon, Richard M. *RN: The Memoirs of Richard Nixon.* New York: Grosset & Dunlap, 1978.

100 Photographs: The Most Influential Images of All Time. The editors of *Time*. New York: Time Home Entertainment, 2016.

Peters, Marilyn, and Richard O'Connor. *Then & Now: Nutley.* Charleston, SC: Arcadia Publishing, 2002.

Peterson, Peter. *Jacqueline Kennedy: La Première Dame des États-Unis.* Paris: Centre Européen de Presse et d'Éditions, 1963.

Pollard, Eve. *Jackie.* London: Purnell & Sons, 1969.

Pottker, Jan. *Janet and Jackie: The Story of a Mother and Her Daughter, Jacqueline Kennedy Onassis.* New York: St. Martin's Press, 2001.

Radziwill, Lee Bouvier, and Jacqueline Kennedy Onassis. *One Special Summer.* New York: Delacorte Press, 1974.

Radziwill, Lee. *Happy Times.* New York: Assouline Publishing, 2000.

———. *Lee.* New York: Assouline Publishing, 2015.

Renouvin, Pierre. *The Far East Question, 1840–1940.* Paris: Librarie Hachette, 1946.

Rhea, Mini. *I Was Jacqueline Kennedy's Dressmaker.* New York: Fleet Publishing Corp., 1962.

Safran, Claire, ed. *Jacqueline Kennedy: Woman of Valor*. New York: Macfadden-Bartell, 1964.

Savage, Sean J. *The Senator from New England: The Rise of JFK.* Albany, NY: State University of New York Press, 2015.

Schlesinger, Arthur M., Jr. *A Thousand Days: John F. Kennedy in the White House.* Boston: Houghton Mifflin, 1965.

Shaw, John T. *JFK in the Senate: Pathway to the Presidency.* New York: Palgrave Macmillan, 2013.

Shaw, Mark. *The Reporter Who Knew Too Much.* New York: Simon & Schuster, 2016.

Smith, Sally Bedell. *Grace and Power: The Private World of the Kennedy White House.* New York: Random House, 2004.

Sorensen, Ted. *Kennedy: The Classic Biography*. New York: HarperCollins, 2009.

Sotheby's. *The Estate of Jacqueline Kennedy Onassis*. New York: Sotheby's, 1996.

———. *Property from Kennedy Family Homes.* New York: Sotheby's, 2005.

Spada, James. *Jackie: Her Life in Pictures.* New York: St. Martin's Griffin, 2000.

Spoto, Donald. *Jacqueline Bouvier Kennedy Onassis: A Life.* New York: St. Martin's Press, 2000.

Stevens, M. Meryl. *Jacqueline Bouvier Kennedy: First Lady of the United States.* New York: Lifetime Heritage, 1964.

Suarès, Jean-Claude, and J. Spencer Beck. *Uncommon Grace: Reminiscences and Photographs of Jacqueline Bouvier Kennedy Onassis.* Charlottesville, VA: Thomasson-Grant, 1994.

Taylor, Richard, and Sam Rubin. *Jackie: A Lasting Impression.* New York: Saint Martin's Press, 1990.

Thayer, Mary Van Rensselaer. *Jacqueline Bouvier Kennedy.* Garden City, NY: Doubleday, 1961.

Vidal, Gore. *Palimpsest: A Memoir.* New York: Random House, 1995.

von Post, Gunilla. *Love, Jack.* New York: Crown, 1997.

Whalen, Thomas J. *Kennedy Versus Lodge: The 1952 Massachusetts Senate Race.* Boston: Northeastern University Press, 2000.

Unpublished Papers

Marchant, Brandi H. "Defined by What We Are Not: The Role of Anti-Catholicism in the Formation of Early American Identity," a thesis submitted to the Faculty of the History Department in Candidacy for the Degree of Master of History. Lynchburg, Virginia, April 2012.

Pattullo, Claire L. "Coffee, Tea, and John F. Kennedy: Female Involvement in the 1952 Campaign of John Fitzgerald Kennedy," a study presented to the Faculty of Wheaton College. Norton, Massachusetts, May 8, 2013.

Websites

"Alfred C. Kinsey and the Politics of Sex Research," by John Bancroft. The Kinsey Institute for Research in Sex, Gender, and Reproduction, Indiana University. https://citeseerx.ist.psu.edu/viewdoc/download?doi=10.1.1.731.2332&rep=rep1&type=pdf.

Ancestral charts of Jacqueline Lee Bouvier Kennedy Onassis, Roots Web. worldconnect.rootsweb.com/trees/238661/P23363/-/ahnentafel.

"Anti-Colonialism." The Indochina War (1945–1956). Université du Québec à Montréal Bannière (UQAM), Faculty of Social Science and Humanities. http://indochine.uqam.ca/en/historical-dictionary/1615-anti-colonialism.html.

"Benno Graziani." The Eye of Photography. https://loeildelaphotographie.com/en/benno-graziani-at-that-time-life-was-dancing/.

"The Blurred Racial Lines of Famous Families: The van Salee Family." PBS, Frontline. Researched and written by Mario de Valdes y Cocom, a historian of the African diaspora. https://www.pbs.org/wgbh/pages/frontline/shows/secret/famous/vansallees.html.

"Congressman JFK Peers into the Future—1951." Pastdaily.com, December 13, 2016. https://pastdaily.com/2016/12/13/congressman-jfk-peers-future-1951/.

"The Desegregation of George Washington University and the District of Columbia in Transition, 1945–1954," by Andrew Novak. https://diversity.smhs.gwu.edu/sites/g/files/zaskib891/files/2021-11/Desegregation%20GWU%281%29.pdf.

"Edmund Gullion, JFK, and the Shaping of a Foreign Policy in Vietnam," by James Norwood. May 8, 2018. https://www.kennedysandking.com/john-f-kennedy-articles/edmund-gullion-jfk-and-the-shaping-of-a-foreign-policy-in-vietnam.

"Hy Peskin," essay by Preston Blaine Reynolds-Peskin, managing director of Hypeskin.com.

"Jackie Kennedy's Lineage Was Not Royal, But She May Have Had Mixed Race Muslims in Her Family Tree," by Rose Heichelbech, Dusty Old Thing. https://dustyoldthing.com/jackie-kennedy-muslim-heritage/.

"Jacqueline Kennedy Onassis," by Follers. January 14, 2018. https://ethnicelebs.com/jacqueline-kennedy-onassis.

"Jacquie and Lee Bouvier Meet Bernard Berenson in Florence in 1951," by Lauretta Dimmick. May 24, 2018. https://getbacklauretta.com/2018/05/24/jacquie-and-lee-bouvier-meet-bernard-berenson-in-florence/.

"JFK's Girlfriends." Daily JFK. https://dailyjfk.com/category/jfks-girlfriends/.

"Main Beach, East Hampton." The 2008 Village of East Hampton's Report to Residents, Village of East Hampton Historic Preservation Program, by Robert Hefner. https://aaqeastend.com/contents/portfolio/preservation-tours-portfolio/east-hampton-ocean-avenue-to-main-beach-tour/.

Maria Curry Merritt. https://www.findagrave.com/memorial/197416150/maria-merritt.

"The Night Ethel Kennedy Met Jackie Bouvier." New England Historical Society website (no author, updated 2022). https://www.newenglandhistoricalsociety.com/night-ethel-kennedy-met-jackie-bouvier/.

The Octagon House. https://ghosts.fandom.com/wiki/The_Octagon_House.

"Once in a Lifetime Hampton Beach House Auction," by Lynn Douglass. June 21, 2012. https://www.forbes.com/sites/lynndouglass/2012/06/21/once-in-a-lifetime-hampton-beach-house-auction/?sh=3d6132332a2e.

"Public Opinion, French." The Indochina War, 1945–1956. Université du Québec à Montréal Bannière (UQAM), Faculty of Social Science and Humanities. https://indochine.uqam.ca/en/historical-dictionary/1233-public-opinion-french.html.

Seventh Annual Meeting Begins at Del Prado Hotel in Mexico City, World Bank Group Archivists' Chronology, 1944–2013, produced by the World Bank Group Library and Archives. https://thedocs.worldbank.org/en/doc/1646a77bc4b2e1bad0d4c1ff17c07870-0240022014/original/PDF-World-Bank-Group-Archivist-s-Chronology-1944-2013.pdf.

"63 Years Ago: The Hamptons Was Very Different When I First Arrived Here," by Dan Rattiner. January 18, 2018. https://www.danspapers.com/2018/01/63-years-ago-hamptons-different-1955/.

SS *United States* Conservancy. www.ssusc.org.

"The Surprising Encounter Between Berenice Abbott and Jackie Kennedy-Onassis," by Anna Winand. The Eye of Photography. December 18, 2018. https://loeildelaphotographie.com/en/the-surprising-encounter-between-berenice-abbott-and-jackie-kennedy-onassis/.

"Was Jackie Kennedy the 1st Black First Lady?," New England Historical Society online. https://www.newenglandhistoricalsociety.com/jackie-kennedy-1st-black-first-lady/.

Index

Note: "JB" refers to Jacqueline Bouvier and "JFK" refers to John F. Kennedy.